JAZZ

SIXTH EDITION

PAUL O. W. TANNER
University of California, Los Angeles

MAURICE GEROW
University of California, Los Angeles

DAVID W. MEGILL
MiraCosta College

wcb
Wm. C. Brown Publishers
Dubuque, Iowa

Book Team

Developmental Editor *Carol Mills*
Designer *Julie E. Anderson*
Production Editor *Diane S. Clemens*
Photo Research Editor *Carol M. Smith*
Visuals Processor *Joyce E. Watters*
Product Manager *Kathy Law Laube*

wcb group

Chairman of the Board *Wm. C. Brown*
President and Chief Executive Officer *Mark C. Falb*

wcb

Wm. C. Brown Publishers, College Division

Executive Vice-President, General Manager *G. Franklin Lewis*
Editor in Chief *George Wm. Bergquist*
Executive Editor *John Woods*
Director of Production *Beverly Kolz*
National Sales Manager *Bob McLaughlin*
Marketing Research Manager *Craig S. Marty*
Manager of Design *Marilyn A. Phelps*
Production Editorial Manager *Julie A. Kennedy*
Photo Research Manager *Faye M. Schilling*

Cover design by Julie Anderson. Photography by Ken Smith, Design
Photography.

Library of Congress Catalog Card Number: 87–71921

ISBN 0–697–03663–4

Printed in the United States of America by Wm. C. Brown Publishers
2460 Kerper Boulevard, Dubuque, IA 52001

10 9 8 7 6 5 4 3 2 1

Contents

Recorded Examples

Demonstration 1 for written example 1A—Melody *without* jazz interpretation.

Demonstration 2 for written example 1B—Melody *with* jazz interpretation.

Demonstration 3 for written example 1C—Melody with *improvisation.*

Demonstration 4 for written example 6A—Bending a *minor* to a *major* third.

Demonstration 5 for written example 6B—Bending a *fifth* downward to a *flatted* fifth.

Demonstration 6 for written example 6C—Bending a tone *upward* to no specific pitch.

Demonstration 7 for written example 6D—Bending a tone downward to no specific pitch.

Demonstration 8 for written example 9A—A hymnlike melody used with the blues harmonic construction.

Demonstration 9 for written example 9B—The same melody given jazz interpretation.

Demonstration 10—Early New Orleans Dixieland.

Demonstration 11—Ragtime.

Demonstration 12—Chicago Style Dixieland.

Demonstration 13—Boogie-Woogie.

Demonstration 14—Swing.

Demonstration 15—Bop.

Demonstration 16—Cool.

Demonstration 17—Funky.

Demonstration 18—Free Form.

Demonstration 19—Crossover.

Demonstration 20—Synthesized drums.

Demonstration 21—Synthesized bass.

Demonstration 22—Synthesized brass.

Demonstration 23—Synthesized flute.

Demonstration 24—Crossover.

Photographs

Preface

Even though some of the eras of jazz music sound extremely different from others, it is our contention that jazz has evolved logically from one era to the next. This study attempts to show the logical musical derivatives and developments of jazz and at the same time to point out the important elements that comprise the individual styles of jazz as they evolved from era to era. *Jazz,* sixth edition, tries to define jazz and its developments as precisely as possible. The authors have strived for a comprehensive, complete, well-researched, and effectively organized textbook. Because video tapes are becoming more accessible and because several companies have made strong commitments to the production of jazz video tapes, we have added new in this edition a videography which lists many of the most recent available tapes on jazz.

Martin Williams has gathered a very impressive record collection for the Smithsonian Institution in Washington, D.C. This collection is superb and essential to the study and enjoyment of jazz. For the convenience of the teacher and student, we have utilized examples from the *Smithsonian Collection of Classic Jazz* at every specific point possible. To further emphasize this aid, we have placed a signal (S) after each record reference that is part of the Smithsonian Collection.

Another record resource which is easily available is found in an anthology called *New World Records* (Recorded Anthology of American Music, Inc.) which

is located at 3 East 54th St., New York City, NY 10022. As was accomplished in the Smithsonian collection, these researchers have obtained permissions to press what they consider to be the most important recordings in the history of American music. At this writing, there are exactly 100 albums available and more promised. It is impossible to detail the event of this collection here, but suffice to say, it travels through every type of music made in America, naturally, covering all phases of jazz. Any teacher or other serious student of this music must be encouraged to avail himself or herself of this memorable collection.

Once again, we have tried to simplify the difficult problem of logical jazz examples. Again we have examined the text and pointed out the many fine examples to be found in the *New World Records* collection; we have signaled these by placing (NW) after each one.

The authors also suggest the fine collection entitled *Folkways Jazz* which contains many excellent and pertinent examples. We have indicated certain recorded examples which can be found in this source with the signal (FJ) following the suggested record.

Therefore, the problem of available jazz examples has been simplified in this sixth edition. The faculty, school library, or students, may have one, or all three, of these truly fine collections. The signals are:

(S) for the *Smithsonian Collection of Classic Jazz*
(NW) for the collection by *New World Records*
(FJ) for the collection by *Folkways Jazz*

Additional Sources

Because we feel that certain inaccessible recordings may still be the best examples of some specific jazz styles described in the text, we offer some additional suggestions for those having difficulties locating these recordings. In the Spring of 1985, John Swenson wrote a useful book called *The Rolling Stone Jazz Record Guide*.[1] This publication specifies what Swenson considered available in retail sources at that time. Two of the better mail-order catalogues are Mosaic and Smithsonian. Mosaic can be contacted at:

Mosaic
197 Strawberry Hill Avenue
Stamford, Connecticut 06902

Suggestions on how to listen to jazz are expanded. References and lists for recommended reading are included as chapter resources. Of course, many features of the fifth edition have been retained, and, as in former editions, the written music in the text can be heard on the cassette accompanying the book. The record included with previous editions is now a cassette tape. There are also new demonstrations on this tape in order to bring the listener up to the present time.

New to this edition are over twenty examples of listening guides to visually aid the listener with a second by second account of what is being heard. These guides cover all the taped material plus many works found in the Smithsonian and New World collections.

There are new and intensely interesting jazz areas developed in this edition. Included are entire chapters devoted to such contemporary directions as Free Form—Avant Garde, Crossover—Fusion, including Third Stream and Jazz/Rock, The Big Band Legacy, Jazz and the New Technology, and a chapter on Jazz Esthetics and Criticism. Obviously, the authors have delved deeply into all of the newer electronic developments and have examined the works of the leaders in these fields.

This book can be used most effectively in a variety of situations, at either the secondary or college levels. At the high school level, it can be used to supplement and extend studies of southern folk songs, Stephen Foster's songs, black spirituals, blues, and work songs. At the college level, this book can be used as a text for a course entirely on jazz.

Much has been written about jazz, and, as a consequence, the references recommended for additional reading have been carefully selected for their accuracy, authenticity, and applicability to school and college use.

Acknowledgments

We wish to thank these reviewers for their assistance with the sixth edition of *Jazz:*

Ronald Pen
University of Kentucky, Lexington
Robert S. C. Myers
DePaul University
Robert G. Delwarte
California State University, Northridge
Craig Whittaker
University of North Carolina, Greensboro
Richard Lawn
University of Texas, Austin
Charles Blancq
University of New Orleans
Terry Steele
Slippery Rock University
Charlotte Mabrey
University of North Florida
Darhyl S. Ramsey
University of Texas, San Antonio

1. John Swenson, *The Rolling Stone Jazz Record Guide* (New York: Random House, 1985).

JAZZ

1
What Is Jazz?

For more than eighty years jazz has exerted an influence upon many composers of the twentieth century both in America and in Europe. Jazz audiences listen to their favorite music with the same intense interest as the most devoted symphonic or chamber music lovers. (It is interesting to note the popularity of jazz in the Far East. More American jazz records are sold in Japan than in any other country, including the United States.) Many modern jazz musicians are highly trained instrumentalists using the same complex harmonies and rhythms that classical composers use. All good musicians are painters with sound.

What is jazz? What are the unique characteristics distinguishing it from other types of musical composition and performance?

Throughout its chronology, jazz has been a melting pot, taking diverse cultural elements and forming them together into a music that has been accepted as American. It is both indigenous to this country and the most democratic music ever devised. Jazz is a way to shape musical material.

Some people consider all music that is not classical to be jazz, thereby putting jazz, country and western, rock, all levels of popular music, and other types of music into one all-inclusive category. Of course, much music that borrows from jazz is hardly jazz itself. Furthermore, academia must be encouraged to distinguish good jazz from bad just as it distinguishes good classical music from bad. Writer-teacher Leon

Dallin has this to say about the misunderstandings concerning jazz:

*In choosing between good and evil the acceptance of the one implies the rejection of the other. This is not true in choosing between the classics and jazz, though admittedly more often than not it works out that way. I prefer to think that the two aspects of musical art are perfectly compatible and that to appreciate both of them requires only an understanding of what each is—and is not. . . . There are some parallels, and music might be divided along similar lines into "music which costs" and "music which pays." Symphonies, string quartets and the like would constitute the former; Dixieland **combos,** swing bands and their successors, the latter.*

Symphony and chamber music players and composers would agree to this distinction. On the other hand, the very mention of the word "commercial" in jazz circles suggests Lombardo and Garber [and Welk]. Another argument against this distinction in music is that some of the more creative aspects of jazz have been the least successful financially and for a time, during the early days of the Depression, were pursued mainly, if not exclusively, for the sake of art.

Formerly the problem of pigeonholing music could be accomplished nicely by approaching the problem from the standpoint of use. There was dance

music and concert music. This distinction loses validity with the invasion of "dance" bands into Carnegie Hall and the prohibition of dancing in the "Storyville" and Basin Street Clubs, traditional haunts, for lack of a better term, of the jazz men. The issue is confused hopelessly by the mixture that streams out of radio and television sets, though there is no question where the emphasis lies.[1]

As far as considering jazz to be dance music and classical music to be concert music, it should be remembered that most jazz stopped being a music primarily for dancing in the 1940s. And it should be noted that two of the greatest composers of dance music were Wolfgang Mozart and Johann Strauss, and that in 1597 Thomas Morley published very precise instructions for writing actual dance music in *A Plaine and Easie Introduction to Praticall Musick*.

It is extremely doubtful that any amount of teaching can produce a jazz performer of the quality of Louis Armstrong or Charlie Parker—too much in jazz is concerned with personal experiences and feelings. But what can be taught are appreciation and discernment, at least to the capacity of each student. Incidentally, it must be emphasized that it is the capacity of the student, certainly not of the teacher, that sets the limit. In regard to the study and teaching of jazz, Charles Suber, editor of a leading jazz publication, *Down Beat*, has best expressed certain pertinent views:

To be a successful professional performing musician you need three basic things. First is a strong, outgoing ego—something inside of you that must speak out. Second is ambition—a strong, almost ruthless drive that makes everything besides music insignificant. The third, and the most elusive to define, is talent. Talent has many ingredients, such as mastery of instrument, thorough knowledge of the theory and literature of music, and the ability to communicate your music and personality to an audience. Talent is a quality that is usually regarded by others as a relative value—"He's the best (or worst)." To the top pro, talent is more of an absolute. He sets his own standard of excellence and consequently is his own best (and worst) critic and judge. You can be sure that Ellington or Parker or Heifetz set his own (seldom or never-to-be-achieved) standard and did not accept the criteria of others.

The same three things—ego, ambition, and talent—are needed to be a successful music educator; especially today, when there is a very thin line between professional teacher and professional performer. It is no longer true, if it ever was, that "only unsuccessful musicians teach." Being able to make it as a full-time working professional is denied to many musicians because of many other factors. (Remember that less than 5 percent of the 240,000 union musicians in the U.S.A. earn their full-time living from music.) It is fortunate that in today's education market there is a place for talented professional musicians to teach and perform in the jazz idiom. To be involved in school jazz as student or teacher is becoming a requirement for acceptance as a complete musician in all idioms.[2]

Along with many others, author-critic Henry Pleasants has tried to define jazz: "The influence of a variety of indigenous musical styles originating in the Negro communities of New Orleans and other American cities, in the Negro communities of the rural South, and in the Negro or mixed communities of the Caribbean islands and some areas of South America in the early decades of the twentieth century has been felt and reflected in the popular music of most of the civilized world."[3] Pleasants's formula, emphasizing the contribution of the American Negro and the geographical origins of jazz, is really no formula at all. He does, however, invalidate several of the misconceptions concerning jazz:

*Prevalent assumptions are: (1) that the distinguishing feature of jazz is **syncopation**; (2) that the distinguishing feature of jazz is **improvisation**; (3) that jazz cannot be played from notes; and (4) that jazz is a Negro music and can be played properly only by Negroes. All are easily disposed of: (1) If syncopation were the distinctive element in jazz, then much European [classical] music would be jazz. (2) Improvisation was common in European music well into the 19th century, and most church organists improvise to this day without producing anything that sounds like jazz. (3) The time has long passed when an astigmatic jazz musician could get by without spectacles. (4) While the Negro has certainly been the decisive contributor to jazz, there is no jazz in Africa that was not brought there by Americans or Europeans, white, black and mixed.[4]*

1.   Leon Dallin, "Classics and Jazz: An Eternal Conflict?" *Music Educators Journal* 45, no. 2 (November-December 1958):32.

2.   Charles Suber, "The First Chorus," *Down Beat* 35, no. 18 (September 1968):4.

3.   Henry Pleasants, *Serious Music and All That Jazz* (New York: Simon & Schuster, 1969), p. 51. Copyright © 1969 by Henry Pleasants. Reprinted by permission of Simon & Schuster, a Division of Gulf and Western Corporation.

4.   Pleasants, *Serious Music and All That Jazz*, p. 62. Copyright © 1969 by Henry Pleasants. Reprinted by permission of Simon & Schuster, a Division of Gulf and Western Corporation.

Many individuals who write about music state that improvisation is the *only* type of jazz or that jazz is strictly improvisation. Improvisation is the art of composing original music while performing the music, with or without the aid of written music. Most improvising musicians, however, make up their individual parts based on an overall plan that has been previously agreed upon by all the participating performers.

We contend that all jazz is *not* improvised, because if it were much of what is classified as jazz would not fall strictly into this category. To illustrate this point, look to the music performed by the smaller groups within the Benny Goodman orchestra. Very few would argue that the Benny Goodman trio, quartet, and other small ensembles are not playing jazz. In a particular composition or performance these smaller groups continuously alternate between music that is improvised and music that is notated or at least planned. The two- and three-part harmony strains played by the clarinet, piano, and vibraphone on "Avalon," for example, could not possibly be performed unless they had been previously contrived.[5] Hence, to those who hold the view that jazz consists exclusively of improvisation, the Goodman groups would seem to fluctuate continually between jazz and some other style of musical performance.

Writers often refer to the use of improvisation in dixieland music. Those who have never been involved in the actual performance of dixieland music seldom realize the musical techniques used by performers of this type of music. (These techniques are explained in chapter 5.) Regardless of the feeling of spontaneity perceived by the listener, there is actually very little improvisation in the ensemble portions of dixieland music. The better dixieland players have performed their repertoire for so long that during the ensemble sections they usually play established lines or at least planned patterns instead of improvisation.

Count Basie's orchestra is generally accepted as a jazz organization; yet this musical group plays written arrangements with parts left open for improvisation by solo instruments. It cannot be maintained that such small groups as those led by Charlie Parker and Dizzy Gillespie and the early Miles Davis groups play music containing a few bars of jazz followed by a few bars of something else. It is our opinion that everything these groups perform is jazz.

Therefore, it is clear that jazz can be both written (planned) and improvised and that jazz and improvisation are not synonymous.

It is also our opinion that certain elements are generally found in jazz that distinguish it from other music, and that all of these elements may not be equally present in any one jazz performance. These elements are jazz interpretation, improvisation, rhythm, syncopation, sounds associated with jazz, and particular musical forms. Only by understanding and identifying the elements that comprise jazz can the listener develop an appreciation and understanding of jazz itself.

Jazz Interpretation

The interpretation of music in the jazz style originally came about when Afro-Americans attempted to express themselves on European musical instruments. The natural way for these early instrumentalists to think of their musical lines was as the lines would be treated vocally. Eventually, the attitude developed that *what* was played was not as important as *how* it was played.

In jazz interpretation, the player restricts interpretative ideas to his or her conception of the melody, coloring it by the use of rhythmic effects, dynamics, and any other slight alterations that occur to him or her while performing. The player remains enough within such melodic restrictions as would allow a listener to easily recognize the melody regardless of the player's interpretation. Almost any kind of a melodic line can be performed with jazz interpretation. Most jazz musicians will agree that to write down an exact jazz interpretation is next to impossible, and all will agree that only a musician who has played jazz can even approximate the notation.

Another way of explaining jazz interpretation is to speak of the jazz "idiom." Classical music and jazz music differ primarily in idiom. A classical musician plays the notes, but the playing lacks the same idiomatic execution usually found in jazz. The European system of musical notation cannot represent this kind of expression. "The conventional symbols could, in other words, indicate in a general way *what* should be played, but could not indicate [precisely] *how* it should be played."[6] Idiomatic expression in jazz is the result of the black American musicians interjecting African music into European music. However, ". . . when jazz compromises its own characteristics of pulse, contour and cadence, to accommodate a more nearly European frame of expressive reference, calling upon strings, or employing its own European instruments in a European [classical] manner, it jeopardizes its idiomatic identity."[7]

5. Benny Goodman, "Avalon," *Benny Goodman Carnegie Concert*, Columbia Records, OSL–160.

6. Pleasants, *Serious Music and All That Jazz*, p. 32. Authors' brackets. Copyright © 1969 by Henry Pleasants. Reprinted by permission of Simon & Schuster, a Division of Gulf and Western Corporation.

7. Ibid., p. 44.

This technique is illustrated by examples 1A and 1B, the first without jazz interpretation and the second with suggested jazz interpretation. Listen to the differences in the performances on the cassette that accompanies this book.

Today, two completely diverse directions in jazz interpretation are very active. One kind of interpretation seems to be closer than ever to classical music. This trend started about 1950 and continues as more schooled musicians enter the jazz field. The other direction is toward **avant garde** jazz, in which some players disregard all earlier approaches to musical lines. These musicians maintain that instead of interpreting lines per se they are playing emotions such as rage or pain.

Improvisation

Improvisation is similar to interpretation, but without melodic restriction. When a jazz player improvises, the "standard" procedure is to use the original as a point of departure and to invent a new melodic line while still fairly well restricted by the harmonic structure of the original melody. However, as discussed in chapter 13, there is a contemporary style called "free form" or "free improvisation" in which the player's only restriction is to compose lines related to the musical sounds made by the other musicians in the group.

Improvisation did not come into being with jazz nor is the technique confined solely to jazz, as some authorities state. Jazz improvisation in principle is no different than the time honored improvisational techniques

Example 1A
Taped Demonstration 1

Example 1B
Taped Demonstration 2

Example 1C

Taped Demonstration 3

used in classical music. It is only the manner of using their individual idioms that distinguishes them from one another. The Greeks improvised two thousand years ago,[8] and at one time improvisation was extremely important in baroque and classical music. J. S. Bach, Mozart, Beethoven, Liszt, and many others were superb improvisers. Therefore, listeners who say they cannot understand jazz because of improvisation also cannot understand much of the great traditional classical music. Improvisation in classical music can be heard today performed by groups such as the Improvisation Chamber Ensemble.[9] Although jazz is not the only musical idiom that uses improvisation, it is certainly one that places improvisation in high regard. In contrast with interpretation, example 1C is an improvisation (written out) of the same melody used in example 1A. Listen to the cassette and compare examples 1A, 1B, and 1C.

Rhythm

An emphasis upon rhythm has always been an integral part of jazz. One reason is that for many years jazz was considered primarily music for dancing. While jazz players have found that a steady, unbroken beat is necessary for dancing, it also aids in developing the emotional pitch identified with jazz, even though in some cases the pulse is merely implied rather than obvious.

The jazz player does not always play exactly in rhythm with the pulse. He or she sometimes feels the need to be slightly ahead of (on top of) the beat, sometimes to lag a trifle behind the beat. This is more a feeling than something that can be measured accurately; it varies from one style to another and indeed from one individual to another. But throughout the development of most jazz, performers have felt the need

for this pulse in order to play what they consider jazz. However, recent experiments in jazz have not used a steady beat. (These experiments toward rhythm are discussed further in chapter 13.) For years it was thought that all jazz must be played in 2/4 or 4/4 **meter.** This attitude changed when 3/4, 5/4, 9/4, and other meters began to be used in performing well-accepted jazz works. Pianist Dave Brubeck first brought newer meters to public notice with an extremely popular 5/4 recording of Paul Desmond's "Take Five."[10] Most jazz is still in 4/4.

Syncopation

Jazz often shifts the melody so that it does not always align itself with the basic beat. This displacement of melodic and harmonic accents off the strong beats in a given meter is called syncopation. As a result of this shift, accents end up on weak beats in a measure, namely 2 and 4 in a 4/4 meter, or on the weak part of individual beats. The following two examples of the same melody illustrate this technique: example 2A has no syncopation; example 2B does.

Example 2B shows syncopated notes that have been shifted off the the beats so that many of the melodic notes begin between the four metric beats in each

8.   Leroy Ostransky, *The Anatomy of Jazz* (Seattle: University of Washington Press, 1960), p. 50.

9.   Improvisation Chamber Ensemble, *Studies in Improvisation,* RCA Victor Red Seal Records, LSC–2558.

10.   Dave Brubeck Quartet. *Time Out,* Columbia Records, CL–1397 and *Time Further Out,* Columbia Records, CS–8490; Don Ellis Orchestra, *Live at Monterey,* Pacific Jazz Records, PJ–19112, and *Live in 3⅔/4 Time,* Pacific Jazz Records, PJ–10123; Elvin Jones Quartet, "That Five-Four Bag," *The Definitive Jazz Scene,* vol. 3, Impulse Records, A–9101.

Example 2A

Example 2B

measure. The melodic move from the third to the fourth measure shows how the first beat of the fourth measure is anticipated with a syncopation. The weight of the normally strong first beat of a measure is then out of synchronization with the last note of the melodic line. These syncopated notes are often accentuated by the performer to heighten the syncopated feel. Certainly there is syncopation in all musics, but in jazz, syncopation is used often and becomes highly intricate. There is very little jazz that does not use syncopation. As a consequence, syncopation is more natural for the jazz musician and is more closely connected with jazz in the mind of the public. Of the many examples, we suggest something like Count Basie's "Jumpin' at the Woodside."[11]

Gunther Schuller has defined the syncopation of jazz as "no more than an idiomatic corruption, a flattened-out mutation of what was once the true polyrhythmic character of African music."[12]

Sounds Associated with Jazz

In classical music, each instrument has an "ideal" sound or tone, or at least there is a consensus as to what the ideal sound is. The jazz musician, though, finds that conformity is of little importance. As long as the sound communicates well with peers and listeners, the jazz musician appreciates the individuality of personal sounds. This situation, in which personal expression is more important than aesthetic conformity, often causes listeners not tuned to jazz to question the sounds that they hear. Frankly, the quality of much great classical music is lost in the search for authenticity instead of for beauty and emotion.

There are certain sounds peculiar to jazz that are a consequence of jazz having originated from oral tradition. Many of the sounds are the results of instrumentalists attempting to imitate vocal techniques.

Jazz singers and instrumentalists use all the tone qualities employed in other music and even increase the emotional range through the use of growls, bends, slurs, and varying shades of **vibrato,** employing any artifice available to assist their personal interpretation of the music. Jazz musicians have always had a great affinity with good singers, especially those whose interpretation closely resembles their own. Such singers include the early great blues singers (to be discussed later) and other talented performers such as Bing Crosby, Ella

11. Count Basie Orchestra, "Jumpin' at the Woodside," *The Best of Basie,* Roulette Records, RE118.

12. Gunther Schuller, *Early Jazz* (New York: Oxford University Press, 1968), p. 15.

Fitzgerald, Billie Holiday, Frank Sinatra, Sarah Vaughan, Billy Eckstine, and Betty Carter.

Distinctive jazz **instrumentation** produces unique sounds. A featured saxophone section or **rhythm section,** for example, is seldom found in other types of music. And while some authorities are mistaken when they claim that mutes are indigenous to jazz (mutes were used in the 1600s), it is true that a larger variety of mutes is used in jazz.

To many listeners the sounds of jazz are personified and identified through the musical interpretation of specific artists. Listeners who have not heard much jazz are often surprised that the well-initiated can recognize a soloist after hearing only a few notes—at least within the listener's preferred style. Talented jazz musicians seem to have their own personal vibrato, attack, type of melodic line, choice of notes in the **chord,** indeed, their own sound. Very few classical connoisseurs can say for sure who is conducting a standard work, let alone identify the individual soloists or section leaders.

Form

Form is the construction of the music; in classical music, for example, the **sonata allegro, fugue,** and **rondo** are typical forms, or constructions. Jazz is usually written in certain forms: the twelve-bar (**measure**) blues strains and the sixteen- and thirty-two-bar **choruses,** usually AABA or ABAB. Since the 1940s, some jazz players have combined the AABA and blues forms. The performer does this by playing the first strain (A), repeating it (A), following with a different strain of usually only eight measures (B), and ending with the original strain (A). The first, second, and fourth parts all have twelve measures.

Since the advent of the long-playing record, some modern jazz players have tended to adopt extended musical forms such as the **theme and variation,** fugue, and rondo.[13] The Modern Jazz Quartet offers several albums with examples of extended forms such as the excellent recording titled *Collaboration* in which they perform Bach's "Fugue in A Minor" with guitarist Laurindo Almeida.[14] In fact, jazz players have used the theme and variation form since the beginning of this art. The tune is established and then each repetition is given a variation, whether improvised or planned, in order to constantly create new interest as the work progresses. This form is often compared to the chaconne, in which a series of improvisations is played from a predetermined chord progression.

The authors have considered the possibility that the most important element in all jazz—that of emotion—is overlooked. There is no question that emotional force has been the strongest ally of jazz throughout its history. Jazz can make one dance with joy, weep with sadness, and contemplate deeply. However, since the authors are involved in the performance of music, we are totally convinced that emotion is too necessary an element of all types of music to be considered the exclusive element of any one kind of music—any music without emotion simply does not seem worth listening to.

Summary

In summary, a listener must decide whether a specific performance contains enough recognizable jazz elements to make it jazz. Identical melodies can be played or sung in a jazz or another musical style. A good example is "Empty Bed Blues" as sung on the Leonard Bernstein record *What Is Jazz?*[15] The melody is sung by both Sherry Ostrus and Bessie Smith. Miss Ostrus's interpretation lacks jazz elements, while Miss Smith uses the jazz elements we have discussed. There can be no question in any listener's mind which rendition is jazz.

In contemporary classical music, the composer remains the focal point. In general, a performer of classical music follows the conductor and what the conductor understands the composer to have intended. In a jazz performance, on the other hand, if the performer does not integrate something of his or her personality and background into the music, the audience (which is itself a part of the performance) rightfully feels cheated. In classical music, *how* a work is performed is rarely considered as important as the work itself. In jazz, the work itself is never really as important as the *way* in which it is played. Even more unusual is that in jazz the *way* a performer plays determines *what* he or she plays. That is, the strong as well as the weak aspects of an individual's abilities on an instrument cause stylistic directions to appear in the playing, which in turn dictate both *what* and *how* he or she plays, and *what* and *how* tend to merge. For example, what Charlie Parker played on "Parker's Mood" or "Bird Gets the Worm" or "Merry Go Round" *was* precisely how he

13.   Gunther Schuller, "Variants on a Theme of Thelonious Monk," *Jazz Abstractions,* Atlantic Records, 1365; "A Fugue for Music Inn," *The Modern Jazz Quartet at Music Inn,* Atlantic Records, 1247; "On Green Mountain" (chaconne form), *Modern Jazz Concert,* Columbia Records, WL127; Dave Brubeck Quartet. "Blue Rondo a la Turk," *Time Out,* Columbia Records, CL1397.

14.   Modern Jazz Quartet with Laurindo Almeida, "Fugue in A Minor," *Collaboration,* Atlantic Records, 1429.

15.   Leonard Bernstein, *What Is Jazz?* Columbia Records, 919.

played the saxophone;[16] (NW "Parker's Mood", 271, side 1, band 4) there is no way of separating style from content. This approach, this attitude, distinguishes jazz from most other music.

Perhaps Bryce Jordan has one of the clearest definitions of jazz:

Jazz, then, is not a composer's art. The particular melody and harmonies which formed the basis of a performance, improvised or arranged, are of secondary importance. Rather jazz is the art of the performer, the performing ensemble, the arranger. And the quality of the art is dependent upon their creative ideas.[17]

Suggested Classroom Activities

1. Name the six elements of jazz that distinguish it from other types of music.

2. Give a definition of syncopation.

3. Clap the following 4/4 rhythm:

While tapping the beat with your foot, clap an example using a syncopated pattern.

4. Sing or play the melody of the song "Swanee River." Sing or play this melody with a jazz interpretation. What did you alter or perform differently in order to change the style of your performance?

5. It is fun to improvise. With little musical knowledge, you can make up your own melody at the piano keyboard. Using only the black keys on the piano, start with the black key C sharp and play any series of tones with the rhythmic patterns found in the familiar song "Twinkle, Twinkle, Little Star." Repeat the same melody you made up and vary the rhythmic patterns.

6. Listen to "The Kid from Red Bank" from $E = MC^2$ (Roulette R-52003). In your own words, describe some of the improvisational techniques the pianist uses. For example, does the player use primarily melodic or harmonic configurations?

7. Classical composers have frequently used the theme and variations form in their compositions. Listening to a number of compositions that use this form will help a listener identify the various elements of jazz and how they can be altered or changed in jazz performances.

a. Ravel uses the theme and variations design in his composition *Bolero*. Listen to this piece and discover which musical element is used predominately in the eighteen variations— melody, rhythm, harmony, or tone color (instrumentation).

b. Rimski-Korsakov uses four variations in his composition *Spanish Caprice*. The theme is in a two-part form, each part being nine measures in length. How does Rimski-Korsakov treat the variations?

c. Listen to Lucien Cailliet's *Variations on the Theme 'Pop! Goes the Weasel.'* You will have to be somewhat of a musical detective in order to follow Cailliet's musical variations on this well-known melody. In which of the variations do you hear at least two of the jazz elements just described? Name the elements.

8. Jazz performers and composers often base their variations on themes of other composers. Compare the different ways that themes are treated in the following examples:

a. *The Great Benny Goodman*, "Let's Dance," Columbia Records, CL–820.

b. *Big Band Beat*, "Strike Up The Band," Richmond Records, B–20034.

c. *Four Freshmen and Five Trombones*, "You Stepped Out of a Dream," Capitol Records, T–683.

d. "Scheherajazz," Somerset Records, P–9700.

e. *Barney Kessel Plays 'Carmen,'* Contemporary Records, 3563.

f. *Dizzy in Greece*, "Anitra's Dance," Verve Records, MEV–8017 ("Anitra's Dance," Grieg, *Peer Gynt Suite*).

9. Listen to the Modern Jazz Quartet's rendition of the very familiar carol "God Rest Ye Merry Gentlemen" (*The Modern Jazz Quartet At Music Inn*, Atlantic Records, 1247). Describe as many of the jazz ingredients as you can, including specific instrumental sounds.

10. Benny Goodman Trio and Coleman Hawkins on saxophone use jazz interpretation and jazz improvisation in the same composition. Listen to "Body and Soul" (S, side 4 and band 3) and identify the places where there is interpretation and improvisation. Do the same with Coleman Hawkins (S, side 4 and band 4).

16. Charlie Parker, "Parker's Mood," "Bird Gets the Worm," "Merry Go Round," *Charlie Parker Memorial Album*, vol. 1, Savoy Records, MG–12000; "Parker's Mood", *Bebop*, New World Records, 271.

17. Homer Ulrich, *Music: A Design for Listening*, 2nd ed. (New York: Harcourt, Brace & World, Inc., 1962), p. 449.

2

How to Listen to Jazz

To appreciate music the listener must be actively involved. Research studies indicate that in full appreciation of music, understanding and enjoyment go hand in hand. Passive listening to music will not bring intelligent musical enjoyment. Rather, musical enjoyment is fostered through active participation that includes understanding, careful listening, and emotional response. The thrust of all musical learning should be to develop a sensitized awareness of those expressive elements of music that will foster a wide range of musical interests and activities and a variety of musical pleasures. One music educator has some remarks about jazz and musical enjoyment:

The concert hall providing Beethoven and Bach offers a convenient refuge for the American since little confrontation could possibly arise from accepting carte blanche, the accepted. The paradox of the whole situation is that the American does not operate in this manner in his other spheres of living. In this respect he can become highly divergent, challenging, adventurous and even egotistical, when choosing his own experiences; yet, when he moves into the area of the fine arts he can become docile and congenial, partaking in those artistic activities which offer the least amount of exploration.

As the American follows this artistic sense on one track, the educational system of America on another track adheres to a value system which rewards only one type of intelligence, one which can easily be assessed, tested and graded, thus only stroking lightly the "creative thinker." . . . Thus the divergent thinker is submerged in the competitive process of education and can only find solace in recognizing that the value system, which has inculcated millions of children and adults, has produced an artistic environment which can only cope with the tangible, the measured, and what in the final analysis is the most convenient.

The combination of the American in his competitive arena, the educational system in its stereotype value system, and the university consumed in perpetuating the traditional music of another continent, could only produce an American music educator and general educator who is thwarted intellectually when he approaches jazz as an art form and expressive language. It's not written; it's not tangible; it's too American; it's spontaneous, and if one can't play it or understand it, then the best thing to do is to disinherit it. Possibly even the music educator as well as the general educator, when it comes to the arts, has been endowed with a somewhat strict adherence to convenience, a most unfortunate dilemma for jazz.[1]

1. Harry Evans, "On Jazz—From an Educator," *NAJE Educator* (Official magazine of the National Association of Jazz Educators) 2, no. 4 (April–May 1971): 17.

Listening Techniques

When listening to a composition the primary aim is to focus one's attention on the various musical events as they unfold—not an easy task. Mental concentration of a high order is needed. We are so conditioned to hearing music as a background **accompaniment** to daily activities—in the dentist's office, at the supermarket—that it is difficult to devote full attention to listening to music.

In daily living we encounter many spatial relationships—high walls and low walls, houses and garages, sidewalks and streets, country and urban vistas—that are immediately visual and easily identified. In listening to music we must forget visual mindedness and learn to concentrate on nonvisual elements.

Another difference is that music moves in time, and time relationships are less obvious in daily living. A painting, for example, can be viewed at leisure, and its parts can be observed in relationship to the whole. Not so with a musical composition. Memory becomes an important factor in listening to music. The mind must remember at one point what has transpired so that one part of a piece of music can be compared or contrasted with another part.

Finally, if we are to learn more about the structure of music, it is important to develop the ability to separate juxtaposed musical sounds and focus attention on a single musical element. For example, when identifying the ostinato bass employed in boogie-woogie playing, we must be able to shut out the right-hand piano sounds if we are to recognize what the left hand is realizing at the keyboard.

What to Listen for in Jazz

Persons who can bring to the listening experience a fund of musical knowledge have an advantage in gaining insight into jazz. But *knowledge about* music and an *understanding of* music are not the same. Simply stated, the first deals primarily with information (vocabulary), while the second relates to direct musical experiences involving concepts and possession of the vocabulary to express understanding of the concepts. The term *concept* suggests a mental image or a complete thought that has been acquired through the senses—hearing, seeing, touching, tasting, and smelling.

As you listen to music, you will find that the concepts of melody, rhythm, harmony, texture, design, and tone color are common to all music. However, some concepts of rhythm, for example, are treated differently or at least are more prominent in jazz than in other types of music.

As a preparatory exercise for listening to jazz, you will find it helpful to list under each main musical element words and concepts that you identify with that musical element. For example, (1) under *melody:* high, low, smooth, jagged, **scale,** skips, **key, diatonic,** and **chromatic;** (2) under *texture:* thick, thin, few instruments, many instruments, **homophonic, polyphonic;** (3) under *form:* repetition, contrast, theme, variations, imitation, section, part, three parts, improvisation; (4) under *harmony:* tension, relaxation, rounds, and chords; (5) under *rhythm:* fast, slow, weak accents, strong accents, beat, **tempo,** pattern, and meter; (6) under *tone:* piano, soprano, contralto, bass, trumpet, sax, clarinet, and bass drum.

Jazz Ensembles

An initial consideration in listening to jazz ensembles is the size of the instrumental group. Does it sound like a large group of ten to twenty or thirty players or does it sound like a small combo of two to six or eight instrumentalists? If the group is a large band and there is a soloist, the listener has very few real clues to the size of the organization unless the soloist is supported by some other part of the band besides the rhythm section. An example is a saxophone solo backed up by a trombone section consisting of three or four trombones or by the entire brass section including trumpets and trombones. While the ensemble is playing, listen for the "bigness" or "thickness" of the overall sound. Sometimes the total sound may be so full that it is almost overwhelming, such as the ensemble portion of Kenton's "Commencement."[2] Listen for complete sections of instruments—saxophone, trumpet, and trombone sections. The sections are quite easy to determine on most albums by bands like Count Basie.[3] (S, side 5, band 7) Almost always, both large and small jazz groups have rhythm sections consisting of piano, bass, guitar, and drums. Some rhythm sections do not use all four, rather only piano with bass or bass and drums with piano.

Another problem with listening is that sometimes a small group or combo may confuse the ear by sounding larger than a full band if the playing and recording techniques are purposefully planned to give that illusion of sound. However, in a combo, listen for the

2. Stan Kenton, "Commencement," *The Jazz Study,* vol. 5, Capitol Records, W2141; Buddy Rich, "Westside Story," *Swingin' New Band,* Pacific Jazz Records, PJ-1013.

3. Count Basie, "Doggin' Around," "Taxi War Dance," Smithsonian Collection of Classic Jazz; Count Basie, *The Best of Basie,* Roulette Records, RE118; $E=MC^2$, Roulette Records, R52003.

individual instruments. Instead of the saxophone section, listen for the saxophone player; do this for other instrumentalists such as the trumpet or trombone player.[4] (S, side 7, bands 6 and 7; side 2, band 5)

Some Musical Concepts in Jazz

Melody

It is important that listeners of jazz music listen for the melodic inventiveness or improvisation on a given melody or the musical interpretation of a given melody. The emotional tone communicated by the jazz performer often reveals the temperament of the player and of society in general at the time of the playing. Usually music is quite accurate in mirroring the temperament of the times—war, peace, and so on.

Listen as the performers create. Is the emotional tone excitement? Is it calm? (Can calm music be exciting?[5]) Performing music is extremely personal to be sure, but so is listening. One person cannot listen for another. Sometimes big bands are very outgoing or hot, like Basie's "Jumpin' at the Woodside" or "Every Tub."[6] (S, side 5, band 7) (NW, 274, side 1, band 1) However, this is not an exclusive element of large groups. Combos can produce the same feeling—listen to such recordings as Kenny Clarke's "Be a Good Girl."[7] (S, side 7, bands 6 and 7; side 8, band 2) The same outgoing big band can sometimes produce an extremely calm, even introverted, feeling. Such an example can be heard in Basie's "Blue and Sentimental" and "Lil' Darlin' " and in Woody Herman's "Misty Morning."[8]

A person who has little technical knowledge of music and who cannot name individual pitches on the staff still may be able to hear the differences between two melodies by feeling ascending tones as they move in steps and descending tones as they skip in varied moves.

Texture

The term **texture** as it is used in music refers to the different ways melodies and harmonies interact. Some textures may give the impression of being open and airy while others seem quite dense. It not only includes the various ways of filling the octave and various ways of using the beat, but it includes the many possibilities of repeating the same melody at different pitch levels, of combining two or more different melodies, or of providing a single melody with accompanying chords or harmonies.

A single melody with neither an accompanying melodic part nor harmony is known as a **monophonic** construction. The field hollers of the slaves is a good example of a short melodic motive without any accompanying musical sounds.

Another way of treating a melody is to have two melodies start at the *same time* on *different pitch levels*. Another version starts two melodies at *different times* on the *same pitch level*. The combination of two voices singing or playing the same melody but entering at different times is called a **canon**. A canon repeated without a break is called a **round** (i.e., the melody chases itself around and around). The simultaneous sounding of one melody heard in imitation in another voice or instrument and the use of two or more different melodies of equal importance is known as **polyphonic** construction. Listening to polyphonic, or **"horizontal,"** texture in music is somewhat analogous to watching a three-ring circus. You realize something important is going on in each of the three rings, but it is difficult to concentrate on them simultaneously. However, it all adds to the excitement of the moment.

A third way of treating a melody is to have all of the voices or instruments move together with a single melody, usually in the highest voice part. Harmony in the form of chords in the lower voices acts as an accompaniment to the single melody. This is called **homophonic,** or **"vertical,"** construction. Hymns and spirituals are excellent examples of this type of melodic treatment.

4. Charlie Parker and Dizzy Gillespie, "Shaw 'Nuff," Smithsonian Collection of Classic Jazz; Charlie Parker, "KoKo," Smithsonian Collection of Classic Jazz; Louis Armstrong, "Struttin' with Some Barbecue," Smithsonian Collection of Classic Jazz; Charlie Parker, "Another Hair Do," *Charlie Parker Memorial Album*, vol. 1, Savoy Records, MG–12000; Louis Armstrong, "I Gotta Right to Sing the Blues," *The Essential Louis Armstrong*, Verve Records, V–8569; Cannonball Adderley, "I Can't Get Started With You," *The Jazz Story*, vol. 5, Capitol Records, W2141.

5. Count Basie, "Blue and Sentimental," *The Best of Basie*, Roulette Records, RE118; Gerry Mulligan and Ben Webster, "Chelsea Bridge," *The Greatest Names in Jazz*, Verve Records, PR 2-3.

6. Count Basie, "Doggin' Around," "Taxi War Dance," Smithsonian Collection of Classic Jazz; "Every Tub," *Jive at Five*, side 1, band 1, New World Records, 274; Count Basie, "Jumpin' at the Woodside," "Every Tub," *The Best of Basie*, and "The Kid from Redbank," *Basie E = MC²*.

7. Kenny Clarke, "Be a Good Girl," *The Jazz Story*, vol. 5; Dizzy Gillespie and Charlie Parker, "Wee," *Jazz at Massey Hall*, Fantasy Records, 6003; "Shaw 'Nuff," Smithsonian Collection of Classic Jazz; Charlie Parker, "KoKo," Smithsonian Collection of Classic Jazz; "Little Benny," Smithsonian Collection of Classic Jazz.

8. Count Basie, "Blue and Sentimental," *The Best of Basie*, and "Lil' Darlin'," *E = MC²*; Woody Herman, "Misty Morning," *The Jazz Story*, vol. 5.

Form

The word **form** in music denotes both shorter parts or sections (repetition, contrast, etc.) and specific overall schematic designs (binary, ternary, rondo, etc.). Perception and understanding of the elements of form present a greater challenge in listening to music than they do in consideration of visual art. In music, the various parts of a composition are presented in time, and a listener can compare them by memory only.

Repetition is the presentation of the same musical material in two or more parts of a composition. Contrast, on the other hand, is the introduction of different musical material. From earliest times, repetition of a melody has played a vital role in prolonging a game, a dance, or a story. A similar reason for repetition is found in the work songs where repetition of the melody depends on the amount of work. Soon contrasting musical ideas were introduced in two- and three-part forms. Here the repetitions tend not only to expand each part, but also to give a feeling of balance and symmetry to the melody as a whole. If you understand the principles of repetition and contrast, you can sharpen your listening focus by anticipating the parts that are repeated and those that are contrasted. Thus, you will have a much better idea of what to listen to and for, and consequently you will enjoy the music more as it unfolds.

The basic units of form in music are often compared to the basic units in written language. The individual musical note is comparable to the single alphabetical letter in written language. The musical motive or figure (two or more tones forming a distinctive rhythmic-melodic pattern) is the equivalent of a language syllable or word. The first appearance of a phrase (usually four measures in length) denotes a language phrase. The extension of the phrase into two **phrases** or **periods** (eight measures in length) denotes a language sentence. Sometimes language sentences are longer. In music, long phrases are called double periods, or phrase groups.

For easy identification, phrases and periods are designated by letters. The first phrase is called A, and as each new phrase appears, it is given a different letter (B, C, D, etc.).

The forms used extensively in jazz are the twelve-bar (measure) blues strain and the sixteen- and thirty-two-bar choruses that are usually designated ABAB or AABA.

The twelve-bar blues strain has two identical phrases of four measures each and a third phrase that is different. In the blues melody given in example 3, measures 1 through 4 are the first phrases, or A part.

Harmony

Closely akin to the need to recognize the melodic line is the necessity of response to the musical element of **harmony** in jazz. Harmony is the simultaneous sounding of two or more tones. Two tones sounding together make an interval. The effect produced by the interval depends upon the ratio between the vibrations created by the two tones. In general, simple ratios tend to be more harmonious and complex ratios more dissonant. For example, for most listeners the sound of three-tone chords with intervals of thirds seems pleasingly consonant and restful, whereas six- or seven-tone chords with intervals of thirds having more complex ratios seem to give listeners feelings of dissonance and tension.

A listener must decide whether the harmonies are too simple, have little variety, and hence are of little interest. In more academic terms, the harmonies or chord progressions should have a sense of forward motion. Sometimes a composition has a pleasing melodic line but is quite dull harmonically. The opposite situation occurs when the composer-arranger or piano soloist is so intent on playing interesting harmonies that the music sounds contrived. This seemed to be prevalent with some large bands in the 1940s and again in the 1960s. Rather than complex harmonies with very little melodic originality, a balance between the two is usually more acceptable.

Rhythm

Rhythm is the very heart of nature and of humanity. It is the pulse of life and is found in all kinds of physical activity. We unconsciously use rhythm—in walking, dancing, running, skipping, and so forth. However, **rhythm** is a generic term and has many meanings.

In music one basic element of rhythm is the repetition of sound, either felt or heard, called the beat or pulse of the music. To feel the beat or pulse of the music, listen and tap or clap the regular repetitions generated by the musical sound.

Although beat is a constant force in every composition, the speed of the beat varies greatly, and depends on the feeling, tone, and mood of the music. In some music the beat is fast; in others it is quite slow. The speed of the beat is called the **tempo.** Hence, when we say that the rhythm is slowing down, we mean that the beat is moving at a slower rate.

Occasions occur in which a great rhythmic pulse is felt but no melodic line is realized; the rhythm section merely sets a mood. These sections are usually called **vamps.** Some contemporary players play on melodic instruments but avoid the usual concept of melody. They say that they are playing a mood or an attitude. Listen to Joe Harriott's "Shadows."[9] (Mood and attitude are discussed more fully in chapter 13.) There are many situations in which there is a definite melody, but

9. Joe Harriott, "Shadows," *The Jazz Story,* vol. 5; Archie Shepp, "The Chased," *The Definitive Jazz Scene,* vol. 3, Impulse Records, A-99; "The Mac Man," *On This Night,* Impulse Records, A-97.

Example 3

Blues Melody

When the notes in the second line of a song look the same as in the first line or phrase they also sound the same. As you can tell, the second phrase of the song (measures 5 to 8) looks and sounds like the first phrase. This phrase may also be indicated by an "A":

The third phrase (measures 9 to 12) is obviously different. Therefore, it is indicated by the letter "B":

Next, examine carefully the AABA song (example 4). Look at the first period (measures 1 to 8). This is the A part. Now compare the second part (measures 9 to 16) with the A part. You will discover that the A part and the second part are identical. Thus far we have AA. Examine measures 17 to 24. You will discover that this part is different from the A part and is therefore called B. Look at the remainder of the song (measures 25 to 32). As you can see, this is the same as the A part, with a slight variation in the ending. This is the most commonly used form in jazz—the three-part form, or AABA thirty-two-bar chorus.

Example 4

AABA Song

it is subservient to the rhythmic sounds. It is primarily this rhythmic pulse or juxtaposition of patterns that expresses the emotion. The technique is quite common in many rock and jazz/rock recordings.[10]

One of the most important elements of rhythm is duration. The performing musician is concerned with translating the symbols on a page of music into sounds and silences (tone pauses, or rests). These sounds and silences may be of any duration. For this reason, clapping the rhythmic pattern does not accurately represent a melody, since the claps are all of equal duration.

Listen to the ticking of a clock. Do some of the ticks seem to be stronger than others? Try tapping on the table with your hand, imitating the regularity of

10. Blood, Sweat & Tears, "Spinning Wheel," *Blood, Sweat and Tears,* Columbia Records, CS9720.

16   Chapter 2

Example 5A

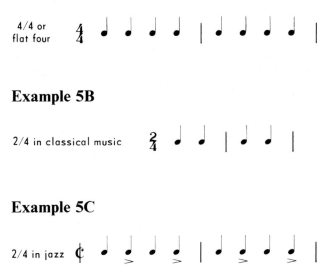

4/4 or flat four

Example 5B

2/4 in classical music

Example 5C

2/4 in jazz

the sound of a clock. Next, tap one beat louder than the following beat. Alternate between loud taps and soft taps. Try tapping one loud beat followed by two soft beats. You should find that in one case the beats occur in groupings of twos and in the other case in groupings of threes. The easiest approach to understanding accent, the basis of meter, is to study the grouping of louds and softs into twos, threes, fours, or more. Meter is the regular (or irregular) grouping of beats according to accent.

In musical notation the **time signature** located at the beginning of a composition tells a player that the music moves in groupings of threes, fours, or whatever. There are complete styles of jazz that stay primarily in one meter grouping, and the listener should be able to detect these groupings fairly easily. The feeling of 4/4, or flat-four, is used by players of Early New Orleans Dixieland, by most swing players, and by a great many bop and cool players.

When 2/4 meter is designated in jazz music, it denotes something different from 2/4 meter in classical music. In classical music, it means there are two beats to each measure and quarter notes receive one beat. In jazz, however, it means that there are four beats to the measure but that the second and fourth beats are accented. Hence, a jazz player never snaps his fingers or claps his hands on beats one and three but always on beats two and four as shown by the accents in examples 5A, 5B, and 5C. This is the only time when meter indication (time signature) in jazz is different than in other music.

The 2/4 beat in jazz is heard most prominently in ragtime and Chicago Style Dixieland music. When funky-style jazz music has four beats to the measure, the second and fourth beats are accented. Sometimes, however, funky is played in 3/4 meter. Rock drummers accent the second and fourth beats, feeling that it adds interest and momentum. Very good jazz, by both small combos and large orchestras, is performed in 3/4 meter.[11]

The style of jazz called boogie-woogie is performed in 8/8 meter, eight beats to each measure. (See chapter 8.) In fact, it is the identifying feature of this style, whether it is a piano solo or a large band.[12] (S, "Honky Tonk Train," side 4, band 2) (FJ) Rock players make excellent use of 8/8 meter without actually playing boogie-woogie. They seem to use 4/4 meter in a **double-time** fashion.[13]

Tone

Another important consideration in listening to music is **tone.** Some listeners prefer instrumental tones to have a soft, pretty sound, while other listeners consider this tone quality to lack intensity, sincerity, and even confidence. These listeners prefer to hear the type of tone made by a very strong trumpet player, for example. Which sound do you find more interesting: a smooth, pretty tone or a rough, aggressive sound? Listening is very personal, almost as personal as performing.

One of the most important points to be considered is the creativeness of individual players. Do their thoughts sound interesting and fresh or are they playing clichés that should be forgotten? Players have been known to improvise several consecutive choruses on just one tone. This kind of playing lacks all imagination. On the other hand, some players improvise lines so far

11. Clark Terry, "Hammer-head Waltz," *The Definitive Jazz Scene,* vol. 1, Impulse Records, A99; Les McCann, "A Little 3/4 for God and Company," *The Truth,* Pacific Jazz Records, PJ–2; Tommy Vig, "Sunrise Sunset," *The Sound of the Seventies,* Milestone Records, 9007.

12. Meade Lux Lewis, "Honky Tonk Train," Smithsonian Collection of Classic Jazz; "Honky Tonk Train," *Boogie-woogie,* Folkways Records, FJ2810; Will Bradley, "Beat Me Daddy, Eight to the Bar," Columbia Records, 35530; Count Basie, "Boogie-woogie," Columbia Records, 35959; Tommy Dorsey, "Boogie-woogie," Victor Records, 26054; Benny Goodman, "Roll 'Em," Victor Records, 25627.

13. Spirit, "Topanga Windows," *Spirit,* Ode 70 Records, Z18–4404.

ahead of their contemporaries that acceptance and acclaim come too late to be of much satisfaction.

The real judge, of course, is the listener who must hear the melodies, perceive the rhythm, detect the tone, and so on. Jazz observers are not particularly impressed by classical correctness. They hear enough excellent piano from Art Tatum to consider him a genius. They are not disturbed at all that Tatum's fingering was atrocious. Jazz listeners hear creativeness from Gillespie's trumpet and are not disturbed by the way he puffs out his cheeks. Present-day jazz observers actually appreciate the primitive approach to playing of many early jazz performers, most of whom had little or no musical schooling. Their lack of schooling, of knowing how to perform "correctly" by European standards, gave the early players a freedom that endears them to most jazz listeners.

One should be reminded that the "test of time" commonly used to judge music is not appropriate for jazz. It is true that there are jazz classics (Armstrong's "Savoy Blues," Hawkins's "Body and Soul," Parker's "Ornithology," and many others), but jazz players are much more concerned with immediate communication. In fact, many players do not like to compare their present playing style to works they have done in the past; they like to think that they have improved their style by fresher, more contemporary inventiveness and creativity.

Listening Suggestions

Techniques of perceptive listening improve as one develops an understanding of the musical vocabulary of jazz (and of other music). The jazz Listening Guide provided here (page 19) was developed to give you a systematic aid to use in identifying what to listen to and for. This identification leads to the development of effective listening habits.

A valuable aid in developing perceptive listening is to listen to a composition with other persons. After the first hearing, freely exchange ideas with the other listeners about what has been heard. After a brief discussion period, replay the record. This experience tends to improve one's ability to concentrate as well as to pick up previously missed nuances.

Read the Listening Guide before listening to be sure that you understand what the various items in the Guide mean. After the first hearing, quickly respond to the items you can identify easily. Do not labor over items about which you are unsure. After the second hearing, go back and fill in all the remaining items on the Guide. Obviously, some items may not apply to every listening experience. Effective listening takes practice by a listener as well as guidance by a teacher.

Passive listening will not aid in developing understanding and enjoyment of jazz. Listeners must train themselves to listen *to* and *for* the content of the music and to respond actively, not only emotionally but intellectually. The next step is for each listener to develop a specific set of references to use in deciding whether he or she enjoys and understands jazz.

Suggested Classroom Activities

1. If you were asked to describe why you prefer a particular type of music, what would you say?

2. In your own words, define the following: melody, harmony, rhythm, design, and timbre or tone color.

3. Skilled listeners should be able to focus attention on different musical elements as they listen. Listen several times to *Yancey Stomp* by Jimmy Yancey, pianist (Jazz vol. 10, Folkways Records, FJ 2810) and answer the following:
   a. Does the music have an introduction?
   b. Is the left hand at the piano (the bass part) realizing mostly harmony or a repeated melodic figure?
   c. Is the right hand realizing a distinguishable melodic line or short figures that seem almost harmonic in total effect?
   d. Is the meter in duple or triple feeling?

4. Listen to "Silver" from the album *The Modern Jazz Quartet with Laurindo Almeida* (Atlantic Records, 1429) and answer the following:
   a. Is the ensemble a large group or a small combo?
   b. See how many of the following instruments you can identify in the tune: violin, vibraphones, saxophone, oboe, piano, percussion (drums and others), string bass, and amplified guitar.

5. Listen to the three-part form of "Fish This Week" as played by Les McCann (*Les McCann Plays The Truth,* Pacific Jazz Records, PJ–2). Listen for the expanded improvised bridge part: A, A, B, bridge, A.

Listening Guide

Melody

Parts with jazz interpretation
Parts improvised
All parts improvised
Uses blue tones

Tempo

Slow
Moderate speed
Fast
Extremely fast

Meter

2/4
3/4
4/4 (flat-four)
Other (identify)

Rhythm

Syncopated patterns very fast

Harmony

Relaxed (not complex)
Uses IV to I
Tense (complex)
Chord progressions

Texture

Vertical (homophonic)
Horizontal (polyphonic)
Both

Tone color

Solo spots played by:
Banjo
Clarinet
Cornet (trumpet)
Guitar
Percussion
Piano
Saxophone
String bass
Trombone
Other (identify)

Form

Twelve-bar blues
AABA
ABAB
Other (identify)

Size of group

Small (2 to 8 players)
Large, with sections

Mood or feeling tone

Frantic, driving
Happy
Low key, understatement
Rough, aggressive
Soulful
Sweet, calm, smooth
Other (identify)

Era or style

Piano style

Left hand (bass part in 2/4 rhythm)
Left hand (walking bass)
Left hand (chordal)
Other (identify)

Other jazz influences

Classical
Contemporary large band
Electronic
Free form
Liturgical
Rock
Popular

3

Jazz Heritages

African and European

The beginnings of jazz came about through a blending of the musical cultures of Africa and Europe. From the merging of these heritages came American jazz. That the blending has never ceased is shown not only by the addition of more complex rhythms from Africa in the 1940s, but also by the innovation of present-day third stream music with its use of European musical forms. Too often, it has been stated that jazz is the music of the black person. This belief contains two quite erroneous implications: first, that only blacks can play jazz, thereby excluding such white musicians as Goodman, Teagarden, Beiderbecke, and Evans, and second, that blacks are successful in no other kind of music. There are far too many excellent musicians to begin to list the talented nonjazz black artists, both composers and performers. However, the point should be made clear that each new style (or era) in jazz was pioneered by an American black musician. Any talented player of any race can probably learn to play the different styles. Race has nothing to do with developing a style after its innovation, but the American black was and is the innovator.

Mrs. William Grant Still (Verna Arvey), the wife of an outstanding black classical composer, discussed this question as it related to her husband and George Gershwin:

It was with considerable surprise that I read in a recent book (Music in the Twentieth Century, *by William W. Austin, published by W. W. Norton and Company, 1966) by a Cornell University professor, the statement that "Gershwin's* Rhapsody *helped inspire William Grant Still to make use of Jazz and Negro folk song in his symphonies and operas." Surprise, because it seemed so unrealistic to assume that a Negro composer could have been motivated by a white composer who had made no secret of his own devotion to Negro musicians and their music.*

For Gershwin's indebtedness has been well documented over the years, and it does no disservice to his memory to acknowledge it, since he himself did just that during his lifetime. One of these acknowledgments came when on August 30, 1926 he autographed a copy of his Rhapsody in Blue *to W. C. Handy. "For Mr. Handy" he wrote respectfully (for at the time the beloved Father of the Blues was almost twice his age), "Whose early 'blue' songs are the forefathers of this work. With admiration and best wishes."*

Those people who lived—as did Gershwin—through the exciting Twenties in New York can attest to the presence of both Gershwins (George and Ira) at nearly every place where Negroes were performing, or even enjoying themselves at parties.[1]

1. Verna Arvey, "Afro-American Music Memo," *Music Journal* 27, no. 9 (November 1969):36.

Music from Africa

Music was by far the most vital and demonstrative form of expression in the life of the Africans. From morning until night, from the cradle to the grave, everything was done to the rhythm of their music. The art form was passed down by word of mouth from one generation to the next. It was a means of preserving tribal traditions, ambitions, and lore. Music performed a vital role in maintaining the unity of the social group. Singing the same songs in the same way at the same time bound individuals together and established a strong group feeling. Whether religious or secular, improvised or traditional, the music of the Africans was a powerful influence in their lives.

In Africa, music was for a whole community, and everyone from youngest to oldest participated. Music was so interwoven with work, play, and social and religious activities that to isolate one phase from its role in the total life of the people is difficult. The Africans themselves did not consider their music an art. Arts are seldom taken seriously in their birthplace. Innovators, Charlie Parker for example, have always suffered from this fact.

Many of the daily activities within a tribe were accompanied by the pulse and beating of a drum. It was a part of religious ceremonies and special occasions such as births, deaths, and weddings. Drums, ranging in size from very small hand drums to great tree drums, sometimes fifteen feet high, were used to frighten wild beasts and to bolster courage in times of emergency. The drum served as one fundamental means of coordinating the movements of the wonderful rhythmic native dances, aided hunting parties, and played an important part in sport and physical exhibitions.

It was this background, brought by African slaves to the United States and nurtured in the woe and hardship of slavery, that provided the seeds of jazz as we know it today. Obviously the slaves did not intentionally invent a new music at this point; the new music arose unconsciously out of the transplantation of the black culture and the blacks' struggle for survival.

African Rhythms

One common misconception about the origins of jazz is that jazz rhythms came from Africa. Actually, it is only the *emphasis* on rhythm that can truly be designated African, not the direct influence of any specific rhythmic pattern.[2] There are three important points to keep in mind concerning Africans and rhythmic sounds: (1) religion is very important in the cultures of Africans, a daily way of life, not just a Sunday activity;

(2) African religions are greatly oriented toward ritual—their sincerest form of expression; and (3) African rituals have always involved a great deal of dancing; hence, rhythmic sounds have always been very important in the lives of the Africans.

We do not imply that European music is not rhythmic. A very short excursion into Bach, for example, reveals that if his inventions are not played rhythmically they are not played well. At the time when the chief exponents of jazz were generically closest to their African ancestry, the rhythms used by these jazz performers were of a very simple nature, far removed from the complex pattern combinations actually used by the natives in Africa. The rhythm used by these early jazz players generally consisted of quarter notes evenly spaced in the measure of music without syncopation or accent. At this time the very complex African rhythms should have been most influential upon their performance!

However, emphasis on rhythm is such a natural element in African life that even African languages are very rhythm oriented. Because of their rhythmic cultures, Africans were interested in Spanish music. Some researchers even state that the main reason Spanish music is so rhythmical is because Spain was once conquered by the Moors from North Africa. Thus, it is conceivable that slaves in America heard something from their past in this particular branch of European music. In a pamphlet entitled *Afro-American Music* printed by the Music Educators National Conference, William Tallmadge writes of African penetration into Spain:

This penetration occurred during the Mohammedan conquest (758–1492), and accounts for much of the highly individualistic and non-European rhythmic character of Spanish music. Spanish fandangos, tangos, habaneras, etc., were derived from African antecedents. This Spanish music readily amalgamated with the music of the African slaves who were shipped to Latin American countries as early as 1510. Afro-Spanish music influenced the music in North America in two ways: through Spanish possessions in America and through the importation of slaves into America from Spanish colonies. Since New Orleans played such an important part in the early development of jazz, it should be mentioned that Spain controlled that city from 1763 to 1803.

It was soon discovered that slaves adjusted themselves to conditions in North America much better

2. "Royal Drums of the Abatusi," *History of Classic Jazz*, Riverside Records, SDP–11.

if they were first shipped to the West Indies and acclimatized there before being sent on. Latin American influences have, therefore, been a factor in Afro-American music from earliest times. "Jelly Roll" Morton, a jazz pioneer, once stated that Spanish rhythms were a part of jazz. In connection with that statement one might point out that the traditional bass pattern of [one strain of] the "St. Louis Blues" is a **tango.** *Latin American rhythms continue to exert an influence on the progress of jazz, as these rhythmic patterns are employed in many contemporary styles.[3]*

There is no doubt that the Moorish conquest considerably changed the music of Spain, Portugal, and Southern France. Therefore, European music brought to the United States had already been influenced by Africa. The Caribbean Islands were French or Spanish possessions before they became British. Many slaves brought to America were first kept on these islands for months and sometimes for years, and thus were heavily exposed to French or Spanish music before ever arriving in the United States.

Call and Response

The **call and response pattern** heard recurrently in jazz can be traced directly to African tribal traditions. In its original form, the call and response was a ritual in which a leader shouted a cry to which the group responded.[4] A common, present-day form is a congregation's response to a minister or other leader. One hears the influence of the call and response pattern constantly in jazz. One example is the musical instance called **"trading fours,"** when two improvising instrumentalists play solo parts on alternating four bars. In short, they are responding to each other's musical thoughts.[5] This interplay can be heard on many jazz recordings. Listen to Stanley Turrentine on tenor saxophone and Kenny Burrell on guitar as they use a minor blues tune to go as far as to alternate single measures of improvisation.[6] At one spot in "Casa Loma Stomp" the complete brass and saxophone sections alternate with one measure apiece.[7] (NW, 217, side 1, band 2) Another example is when a soloing instrument "calls" and is responded to by the background melodic and/ or percussive figures of the other members of the band or by a specific section of the band. Listen to the entire band responding to Count Basie's piano in "Queer Street."[8] On the swing part of the cassette with this book, the clarinet solo is answered by the trombone section; later, the saxophone section is answered by the brass section. In Manny Albam's "Blues Company,"

Oliver Nelson and Phil Woods on saxophones are answered by trombones.[9] In Benny Goodman's "King Porter Stomp," Goodman's clarinet has the brass section as a background, whereas the saxophone section is the background for Harry James's trumpet solo. Later in the same selection, the brass and saxes alternate measures.[10]

European Influences

The melodic feature of jazz is inherited directly from European music. The diatonic and chromatic scales used in jazz are the same as those used for centuries by European composers, whereas Africans used a **pentatonic** scale.

The harmonic sonorities also derive from European sources: polkas, quadrilles, hymns, and marches. This does not dispute the fact that Africans had varying pitches in their drums, reeds, and logs; but the sense of harmony absorbed by jazz is strictly that of the European school.

The Afro-Americans who first sang gospel music, work songs, and the like, satisfied the desire to imitate rich European melody and harmony. On the other hand, nothing in European music could compare with their oral sonority and the vitality of their music, so blessed with rhythmic tradition.

The musical forms of Europe became standard in jazz works. The twelve-bar strains such as those found in the blues are directly traceable to very early European music. A great majority of jazz is constructed in a theme and variations form. The Africans were not concerned with symmetry of form. In fact, if their music resulted in a symmetrical construction, they considered it crude and unimaginative.

3. William Tallmadge, "Afro-American Music," Music Educators National Conference, Washington, D.C., 1957. Authors' brackets.

4. Ethnic Folkways Library, 01482B, vol. 1, Secular.

5. Santos Brothers, "Beat the Devil," *Jazz for Two Trumpets,* Metro Jazz Records, E1015.

6. Kenny Burrell, "Chittlins Con Carne," *Three Decades of Jazz,* vol. 1 (1959–1969), Blue Note Records, BST89904.

7. Glen Gray, "Casa Loma Stomp," *The Jazz Story,* vol. 4, Capitol Records, W2140; Casa Loma, "Casa Loma Stomp," *Jammin' for the Jackpot,* New World Records, 217.

8. Count Basie, "Queer Street," Columbia Records, 36889.

9. Manny Albam, "Blues Company," *The Definitive Jazz Scene,* vol. 2, Impulse Records, A–100.

10. Benny Goodman, "King Porter Stomp," *The Great Benny Goodman,* Columbia Records, CL820.

Jazz to Rock

its origins

~~Jazz Heritage~~

Music from Africa -

1. Oral Cultures - How they ~~passed~~ carried their traditions + Songs from generation to generation

2. Go to Library find books on Slaves and their music

3. Stephen Foster

4. Spirituals

5. African Instr.

6. Suling
   Blues
   Be Bop
   Blacks in Early Colonies
   Congo Square
   Creole Music

Amer. Composer influenced by Black music

Jazz

Grass Roots — Spiritual

Beginnings of American music
Slavery to the present time —

He talk about forms of communication
in oral culture —

Blacks in the Early Colonies

The evolution of African music in the colonies greatly depended on the particular colony to which the slaves were brought. In the Latin Catholic colonies, their musical life was allowed more latitude. Latin planters were not too concerned with the activities of the slaves as long as the work was done. Thus, the slaves were allowed to play their drums and sing and dance when not working. The British Protestants, on the other hand, tried to convert the slaves to Christianity. The slaves in these colonies were required to conceal their pagan musical inheritance. (It is interesting to speculate about how the resulting music would have sounded if the slaves from Africa had been taken to some part of Asia. If African and Japanese music, for example, had influenced each other centuries ago, what would be the result? Would it resemble any music we know today?)

Congo Square

The name **Congo Square** is frequently mentioned in many accounts of jazz. Congo Square was a large field in New Orleans (called Beauregard Square today) where slaves were allowed to gather on Sunday to sing, dance, and play their drums in their traditional native manner. The principal significance of Congo Square to the history of jazz is that it gave this original African music a place to be heard where it "could influence and be influenced by European music."[11] When the famous dances of Congo Square began around 1817, the background of the participants produced a music that was often a cross between French and Spanish, with African rhythms.

Creole Music

About ten years after the Civil War, a segregation movement began. The **Creoles** were ostracized from white society and joined the ranks of the blacks. Prior to segregation, the Creoles had the rights and privileges of whites, which included conservatory training for musicians. The amalgamation of the musical talents of conservatory-trained Creoles and the spontaneous oral tradition of blacks resulted in an interchange of musical expression. The music that evolved from this early assimilation was one of the beginnings of jazz. The unfavorable aspects of this segregation movement are still apparent today, as pointed out by Charles Suber:

There is a sociological reason why more black student musicians are not involved in jazz. That reason lies in the images retained by many black educators, school administrators, and community leaders. Jazz means slavery, sporting houses, "natural rhythm" and sin and damnation. Jazz stands for those unpleasant things that could "reduce endowments" or "debase our cultural standards."[12]

An interesting point is that so much of the music teaching in the United States propagates the theory that the music that stems from European culture typifies what is good in the arts; yet the Europeans accepted jazz as an art form long before the Americans. It is often felt that jazz players are unregimented individualists who play together cohesively with a mutual feeling; these opposing concepts (individuality and unity) represent the freedom of America.

Most jazz historians leave a considerable gap between the activities at Congo Square and the first known jazz band led by Buddy Bolden at the turn of the century. In actuality, there was no gap because this period was filled by the Creole music in New Orleans. It was natural that this music was mainly French and Spanish and much more advanced (at least by European standards) than the music of the first jazz bands. Henry Pleasants points to the similarities of jazz and early European music:

What I want to stress, however, is not the differences separating the two idioms, but the similarities. The differences are, indeed, startling and disturbing to those who think of the traditional European criteria as immutable, so startling and disturbing that they have tended to overshadow and obscure the similarities. But it is in the similarities that I see a fertile area for the reconciliation of long standing incompatibility and for a fruitful give-and-take in music education.

This reconciliation is easier the further back we go in European musical history. The most common form of jazz has always been theme and variations, advanced and refined in bebop to something closer to chaconne or passacaglia. The jazz band arrangement or original composition bears an unmistakable resemblance to the concerto grosso of the eighteenth century. Without its distinctive rhythmic and phrasing characteristics, the jazz combo is indistinguishable from the Baroque chamber group.

Let me be precise about this. If I were a teacher today, trying to give my students an insight into seventeenth- and eighteenth-century musical conventions,

11. Marshall Stearns, *The Story of Jazz* (London: Oxford University Press, 1958), p. 38.

12. Charles Suber, "The First Chorus," *Down Beat* 36, no. 9 (May 1969):4.

I would suggest that they study sympathetically the conventions of jazz. How to fill in a bass line in continuo playing, for example; how to improvise from a figured bass. Every jazz pianist and every jazz bass player does it, and the best of them do it superbly. Or how to apply ornaments and embellishments. Every jazz musician does it, and the best of them do it every bit as well as it was done in the seventeenth and eighteenth centuries, and probably better. And the embellishments, I hasten to add, are essentially the same.

*If I were a singing teacher trying to assist my pupils to a mastery of seventeenth- and eighteenth-century practices, I would have them listen to Frank Sinatra, Sarah Vaughan, Ella Fitzgerald, and Peggy Lee. If you want to know what **appoggiatura** and **rubato** are all about, listen to Sinatra. No one has ever used them better than he. If you want to study the **mordent**, listen to Bing Crosby. If you want to know about the portamento and slurs and melodic deviation, listen to Sarah Vaughan. None of these singers, I may assume, think in those terms. They may not use those terms, but they do use those devices. And what makes their use of them so instructive is the spontaneity. They use tempo rubato, appoggiatura, mordent, slur, portamento, and so on not because they are told that someone else used them two or three hundred years ago, but because they feel they are appropriate or even essential to the articulation of text and melodic line, which is precisely why they came into use in the first place.*[13]

Field Hollers (Cries)

In West Africa there was no art music, by European standards, only functional music used for work, love, war, ceremonies, or merely communication. Slaves were often not allowed to talk to one another in the fields while working, but garbled singing was permitted. They established communication between themselves by field hollers, or cries, that whites could not understand. The outstanding element of the field cry that is constantly used in jazz is the bending of a tone.[14] This is simply the over-exaggerated use of a slide or slur. A tone is bent (slurred) upward to a different tone or pitch, downward to another pitch, upward to no specific tone, or downward to no specific tone. Examples of the four typical ways of employing this feature in jazz are as follows:

1. Example 6A demonstrates the bending of a minor third up to a major third.

Example 6A
Taped Demonstration 4

Example 6B
Taped Demonstration 5

Example 6C
Taped Demonstration 6

Example 6D
Taped Demonstration 7

2. Example 6B uses a blues cliché to show the bending of a fifth downward to a **flatted fifth.**

3. Example 6C illustrates the bending of a tone upward to no specific pitch.

4. Example 6D illustrates the bending of a tone downward to no specific tone. As it is demonstrated here it is a "fall off." Every jazz fan has heard ensemble endings with this type of bending.

The adaptation of these effects allowed the musician a freedom of embellishment not available in European music.

13. Henry Pleasants, "Afro-American Epoch—Emergence of a New Idiom," *Music Educators Journal* 57, no. 1 (September 1970): 35–36.

14. "Field Cries or Hollers," Album 8, Library of Congress Recording.

Example 7

GRUNT   GRUNT

Work Songs

Rex Harris has described work songs as "tribal songs which started life in West Africa."[15] In addition he stated that they were used "to ease the monotony of a regular task and to synchronize a word or exclamation with a regularly repeated action."[16] An example of this type of work song is the "Song of the Volga Boatman," probably the best known of all work songs. In example 7, the grunt indicates the exact time when concerted action is to take place—in this case, pulling on the oars. (Circus workers standing in a circle hammering huge tent stakes are another example of accomplishing a difficult task through rhythmic coordination.)

A good work-song leader was essential in coordinating the workers. He not only caused the work to be more efficient, but also helped to make time pass. Huddie Ledbetter (Leadbelly) is reputed to have been one of the best "leadmen" ever, and there are recordings available to prove it.[17]

Though work songs varied according to their use, the main contribution of the work song to jazz was the emphasis on rhythm and meter.

Religious Music

"The impact of Christianity on the Afro-Americans was, of course, the origin of the spiritual; owing to the fact that practically all of the missionary work was done by nonconformist ministers, their evangelical **hymns** set the style and flavour of the spiritual as we know it today."[18] Around 1800 a religious mass movement in this country known as The Great Awakening occurred. **Spirituals** and revival hymns with a great amount of emotion were sung at camp meetings. Spirituals, often called hymns with a beat, were the first original songs created by Protestant black slaves on American soil. Spirituals are an excellent example of the blend of African and European cultures and can be easily traced back to 1780. Most seem to have originated between 1790 and 1883. The slaves added their own rhythmic emphasis to any music taught to them, liturgical or other kind. The better-known spirituals of today are the type that were generally heard in large concert halls.

Examples are the familiar "Swing Low, Sweet Chariot" and "Nobody Knows the Trouble I've Seen." The European influence of more emphasis on melody and harmony than on rhythm is obvious in these songs. The greatest number of spirituals performed in the 1800s employed a call and response pattern,[19] in which there was great emphasis on rhythm, with hand clapping and foot stomping—an example of the West African influence on European liturgy. The clapping and stomping was in a set pattern of emphasis on the second and fourth beats; as Borneman states, "the accent was shifted from the strong to the weak beat."[20] Piano players executed this rhythmic accentuation with their left hand and brought it to ragtime music.

There are many similarities between popular songs and rhythms and religious music in black church services today. Methodist John Wesley once defended such similarities: "Why should the devil be the only one to make pleasing music?"[21]

The fervent participation in their 'syncopated hymns' is something very remote from the Western conception of reverent quietude as an expression of worship, but hymns without beat are to the Negro religion without God. It is as natural, and no more naive, for them to sing hymns in this style as it was for Renaissance painters to portray Christ in Italian dress and environment.[22]

15. Rex Harris, *Jazz* (Baltimore, Md.: Penguin Books, 1956), p. 34.

16. Ibid., p. 30.

17. *Leadbelly,* Columbia Records, C–30035.

18. Harris, *Jazz,* p. 47.

19. Stearns, *Story of Jazz,* p. 93.

20. Ernest Borneman, "The Roots of Jazz," in *Jazz,* eds. Nat Hentoff and Albert J. McCarthy (New York: Holt, Rinehart & Winston, 1959), p. 17.

21. Andre Francis, *Jazz* (New York: Grove Press, 1960), p. 20.

22. Avril Dankworth, *Jazz, An Introduction to Its Musical Basis* (London: Oxford University Press, 1968), p. 49.

Early black church music can be divided into three categories: (1) Many of the selections were improvised, made up at the moment by the preacher and his congregation; they would be remembered and eventually notated. Many of these were based on the blues chord progression because of its simplicity and the fact that this progression seemed natural and flowing. (2) Some black congregations would adopt European church music and add not only their own rhythmic concepts, but also their own variations. (3) In many cases, African ritual music was altered so that it could be used in these services on this continent.

"There are **gospel songs** with hillbilly and cowboy, mambo, waltz, and boogie-woogie rhythms. But most of all, the gospel songs have a strong, full beat."[23] Also it must be remembered that spirituals and gospel songs are not necessarily musical works of yesterday; their thoughts and their very lyrics are often contemporary. In fact, there is a fine set of recordings (four sides) that includes a collection of gospel songs recorded between 1926 and 1968.[24]

Spirituals sometimes contained symbolic references to the railways or rivers that led to freedom or to heaven, and sometimes the songs gave directions for escaping from slavery. Most spirituals and gospel songs refer to biblical characters such as Daniel, Moses, Joshua, Gabriel, and so forth. Many are not only well-known choral and nonjazz instrumental melodies ("Nobody Knows the Trouble I've Seen," "Swing Low, Sweet Chariot," etc.), but also standard dixieland and other jazz pieces ("When the Saints Go Marching In," "A Closer Walk with Thee," etc.).

Gospel songs and spirituals are often considered to be religious forms of the blues. Blues singer T-Bone Walker agreed:

Of course, the blues comes a lot from the church, too. The first time I ever heard a boogie-woogie piano was the first time I went to church. That was the Holy Ghost Church in Dallas, Texas. That boogie-woogie was a kind of blues, I guess. Then the preacher used to preach in a bluesy tone sometimes. . . . Lots of people think I'm going to be a preacher when I quit this business because of the way I sing the blues. They say that it sounds like a sermon.

The visitor to a church in Harlem, or on Chicago's South Side, will not find a great contrast to the ecstatic atmosphere that might be found at a jazz concert or in a jazz club. He will find the identical rhythms, the same beat, and the same swing in the music. Frequently, he will find jazz instruments— saxophones, trombones, drums; he will hear boogie-woogie bass lines and blues structures and see enraptured people who beat time with their hands and sometimes even begin to dance.[25]

In the early Catholic churches, participation in the services by even the most faithful worshippers was limited. In the Latin Catholic colonies, slaves often worshipped a combination of Catholic saints and voodoo deities:

On the English and Protestant side, the question is as diverse as are the numerous sects of the reformed churches. The Protestant churches are less rigid than the Catholic church; one listens to the sermon and then freely sings hymns. It is this freedom which allows one to celebrate God according to one's own conscience which was to encourage a host of Negroes into the Protestant religions. Furthermore, God, among the Protestants, is praised in everyday language and not in the dead language, Latin. This permitted the Negroes to sing to God according to their hearts and according to some of their own traditions. The ancestral rhythm was reborn, transfiguring a religion.[26]

Methodist hymns were the most emotional, but even these were too somber for the slaves, and therefore improvisation gradually began to creep into hymn singing. "The hymn book of the day stressed part-singing which harmonized only by accident."[27] This accidental vocal harmonization indicates that the voice lines were invented independently of each other. In music this is known as **polyphonic** (horizontal) construction. This approach to the creation of musical line was carried over into dixieland music and was also later employed

23. From the *Jazz Book: From New Orleans to Rock and Free Jazz* by Joachim Berendt, translated by Dan Morgenstern, copyright 1975 Lawrence Hill & Co., Westport, Connecticut.

24. *The Gospel Sound*, Columbia Records, KG 31086/KG 31595.

25. From the *Jazz Book: From New Orleans to Rock and Free Jazz* by Joachim Berendt, translated by Dan Morgenstern, copyright 1975 Lawrence Hill & Co., Westport, Connecticut.

26. Francis, *Jazz*, p. 20.

27. Stearns, *Story of Jazz*, p. 63.

in more contemporary jazz styles. Examples 8A and 8B demonstrate the difference between polyphonic and **homophonic** (vertical) harmonization. Example 8A is polyphonically constructed and shows the independence of the harmonic line. Example 8B is homophonically constructed and demonstrates the extreme dependency of the harmony part upon the melody.

There appears to be some confusion about the difference between spirituals and gospel songs. Often the two words are used interchangeably. However, gospel songs are usually considered religious songs that recount passages from the scriptures, and spirituals are considered hymns.[28]

In 1867, a choral group from Fisk University in Nashville, Tennessee, left school to do a series of concerts to raise money for their college. This group, called the Fisk Jubilee Singers (*jubilee* is another name for a very spirited, joyful hymn), traveled all over the United States, England, and Europe, carrying spirituals, gospel songs, and work songs to an international audience. Examples of this type of singing today are heard in the records of Mahalia Jackson.[29] Generally speaking, most gospel music is very simple in melody and harmony. The excitement comes from the jazz type of rhythmic pulse.

Mahalia Jackson and the Black Church

Gospel music as an art form was all but ignored until the recognition, or rather the great triumphs, of Mahalia Jackson. Miss Jackson never performed in a jazz situation and sang only songs that she believed served her religious feelings. She believed so profoundly in her religious convictions that she felt entirely free to expose her emotions as sincerely as any singer had ever done.

Francis Ward, writing about Miss Jackson in the *Los Angeles Times,* said, "the earliest important musical influence in her life was blues singer Bessie Smith whose recording of 'Careless Love' was a favorite of Miss Jackson's and from which she learned much about the phrasing of black folk music. Despite Bessie Smith's influence, Miss Jackson never sang blues or any kind of jazz, only gospel."[30]

For many years Mahalia Jackson's singing was not accepted in middle-class black churches. Her music was a reminder of a life-style that parishioners seemed to want to forget. But record sales grew, and she primed the world for the many gospel singers who eventually followed. Mahalia Jackson went on to become one of the most stirring, most sought-after singers in the world. Miss Jackson died from heart disease in Chicago on January 27, 1972.

When a Gospel group gets up on stage before an audience, two things become important to them. They

28. Francis, *Jazz,* p. 20.

29. Mahalia Jackson, "If We Ever Needed the Lord Before," *Come On Children, Let's Sing,* Columbia Records, CS8225; *Mahalia Jackson,* Columbia Records, CL 644.

30. Francis Ward, "Mahalia Jackson, Renowned Gospel Singer, Dies at 60," *Los Angeles Times,* 28 January 1972.

Example 8A

Example 8B

Mahalia Jackson with Louis Armstrong. *Courtesy of Les McCann.*

want to sing well and to express some religious convictions so that they can reach the souls of the listeners. When the soul of an audience is reached, you will very often see the people shouting, crying, screaming, clapping as a genuine response to the music.

Although many Gospel groups write some of their own material, most of the songs making up the repertoires of these singers are old spirituals and religious songs that date back to slavery.

These songs have been passed down from generation to generation and the people have sung them in church since early childhood. There are about fifteen or twenty "Gospel standards" that are sung by hundreds of choirs, quartets and groups throughout the country.

It is therefore important for a group or singer to create his own sound.[31]

The world-wide penchant for spiritual music has not dampened since the early tours by the Fisk Jubilee Singers. This fact is aptly demonstrated by Albert McNeil's Jubilee Singers who have given concerts to standing ovations in twenty-five countries.

Some black churches today still believe that association with jazz is wicked, and this attitude may account for the lack of black jazz critics. However, because of the sacred works of Ellington and many other fine jazz composers, this attitude has moderated considerably.[32] In an interview with Leonard Feather, singer Vi Redd explains:

The church was people's only hope in the midst of all the discrimination and oppression, so their ties to it

31. Charles Hobson, "Gospel," *Sounds and Fury* 1, no. 4 (February 1966):30.

32. Dave Brubeck, *The Light in the Wilderness*, Decca Records, DX3A–7202; Duke Ellington, *Concert of Sacred Music*, RCA Victor Records, LSP–3582; Duke Ellington, *Third Sacred Concert*, RCA Victor Records, APL 1–0785; Lalo Schifrin and Paul Horn, *Jazz Suite on the Mass Texts*, RCA Victor Records, LSP–3414.

remained very close and they felt obliged to go along with whatever precepts it dictated.

I was brought up in this environment, but not as strictly as some of the other children, perhaps because my father was a musician. Some of the kids I associated with were not even allowed to have a record player in the house. They used to come over to my place to listen to King Cole Trio records. That was their only opportunity to listen to jazz.

Her music [Mahalia Jackson's] has the same harmonic structure, the same feeling, in many of those gospel songs. By the same token, Milt Jackson is a product of the sanctified church. Sarah Vaughan, Dinah Washington and a lot of the greatest jazz artists came directly out of a church background; yet the people in the church, in all sincerity, still refuse to accept it when it's known as jazz.[33]

Milt Jackson, a leading jazz vibraphonist, has been asked many times about the origin of his "funky" style. His answer is always that it came from the church. When asked about "soul" in jazz, he replies "What is soul in jazz? It's what comes from inside."[34] Good contemporary jazz players often record music that is clearly church music, such as Stanley Turrentine's recording of "I Told Jesus."[35] Even the most casual listening to Ray Charles will reveal the obvious relationship between jazz and black church music:[36]

Ray Charles

The man who gave R and B [rhythm and blues] its fresh thrust was a blind, Georgia-born bard named Ray Charles, one of the most hauntingly effective and versatile Negro singers in the history of pop music.

Negroes have always rigorously maintained a distinction between gospel and blues—the sacred and profane—despite the affinity of their sounds. But Charles boldly brought them together, blending foot-stamping orgiastic jubilation shouts with the abrasive, existentialist irony of "devil songs." He even carried over the original gospel tunes and changed the words to fit the emotion. "Lord" became "you," or "baby," and it didn't matter if the bulk of the prayerful text remained the same. Thus Clara Ward's rousing old gospel song, "This Little Light of Mine," became Charles's "This Little Girl of Mine." (A wonderful identification!) Old timers who had once been forced to choose between the two genres were offended. "I know that's wrong," said Bluesman and former Preacher Big Bill Broonzy. "He should be singing in a church."

But Charles's innovation brought waves of gospel talent into the blues field, and at the same time offered blues performers a chance to employ the climactic cadences and mythic ritual of black evangelism. . . . Most important, once Charles broke the barrier between gospel and blues, the way was open for a whole cluster of ingredients to converge around an R and B core and form the potent musical mix now known as soul.[37]

Sam Cooke, who became a top rock singer, was a leading gospel attraction for years.

A more recent trend in jazz is labeled gospel jazz. Although this style encompasses eighty years of development in the art, it is directly traceable to the early religious roots.

The Pentecostal Church was perhaps the first to pave the way for gospel singing, but the individual who affected the acceptance so definitely was a jazz piano player named Georgia Tom before he was "saved," then he became Thomas A. Dorsey. His compositions are favorites today of proponents of this style of music.

Liturgical Jazz

Modern **liturgical** jazz must also be included in the discussion of religious music. Music of this type has been performed in the United States as well as other countries. These services have taken place in churches of various denominations. All types of contemporary music are being performed in celebration of various religious services. These works can now be added to the important repertoire of religious works of past centuries. In 1971, Leonard Bernstein's **"Mass"** premiered at the opening of the John F. Kennedy Center for the Performing Arts in Washington, D.C. Press coverage was most favorable. Critic David E. Anderson of United Press International called it a "powerful experience." Paul Hume of the *Washington Post* stated that the

33. Leonard Feather, "End of the Brainwash Era," *Down Beat* 36, no. 16 (August 1969):71.

34. From the *Jazz Book: From New Orleans to Rock and Free Jazz* by Joachim Berendt, translated by Dan Morgenstern, copyright 1975 Lawrence Hill & Co., Westport, Connecticut.

35. Stanley Turrentine, "I Told Jesus," *Salt Song,* CTI Recordings, 6010.

36. Ray Charles, "America," *A Message From the People,* ABC Records, ABCX 755/TRC.

37. James Baldwin, "No Music Like That Music," from *The Fire Next Time.* Reprinted by permission from *Time* The Weekly News Magazine; © Time Inc., 1968.

central message of "Mass" and its crucial challenge is the place and function of religion in a world of violence. Anderson agreed that Bernstein's message was "one of hope."[38]

Mary Lou Williams used her great compositional talents toward the writing of lengthy religious scores; examples are "St. Martin de Porres" and "Mary Lou's Mass."[39]

Currently, there are many recorded compositions that use the jazz elements in strict conformity to the mass.[40] Other performances are based on the historic liturgy of John Wesley and the Methodist Church and underscored by original contemporary music. These performances usually consist of jazz played in all portions of the service except during the actual sermon. These worship hours are not attended by curiosity seekers. This jazz is given serious thought and is well written and performed for these specific services, which are well-received by congregations and considered appropriate and in good taste. Sometimes they are called liturgical jazz services, sometimes jazz masses, sometimes jazz-rock masses.

Though Ellington's 1965 concert at Grace Cathedral in San Francisco seemed to include jazz and ecclesiastical elements, it consisted mostly of "Ellingtonia."

Of the many significant works, one that stands out is the "Jazz Suite on a Mass Text" by Lalo Schifrin and Paul Horn. The freest portion of this work is the "Credo," with a most unusual use of voices and Horn improvising on the alto saxophone. Actually, one of the problems in the acceptance of this music is its "free" quality; it seems in opposition to the inhibited, controlled performance of most church music. The beginnings of jazz and present-day liturgical jazz services prove that the supposed antithesis between jazz and liturgy is not valid. In 1970, Gerald Gipson of the University of Missouri wrote this about the controversy:

Can a musical language that is so charged with emotions and extra-musical connotations be admitted as a part of the church service?

To pass judgment on this question is difficult; there are as many arguments for as there are against. It must be remembered that jazz is a form of music alien to the church. Churchgoers are used to hymns and unison readings that have been so much a part of worship for years. They hesitate to make changes, partly out of fear and partly out of custom of thought. At times their attitude seems almost lackadaisical. There is fear of being embarrassed by the demonstrativeness of jazz by the person accustomed to the disciplined routine church service. Still jazz has a

religious origin. The spirituals of the Negro slaves of yesterday show the authentically religious roots of jazz. . . . Is this so-called embarrassment real on the part of the puritanical when we remember the emotion-packed sermons of the revivals, the public confession of sin, and the public adoration of Christ? . . . Services keyed to the thinking and problems of modern man should be offered as should music geared to the thinking of a modern world. . . . When jazz first made the crossover between the sacred and the secular, it was more of a folk cult than a commercial empire. The unnamed and unhonored jazz musicians of the earliest days never dreamed that jazz would become the idol that it is now. An example of the new thinking in modern music is Duke Ellington, who has performed in numerous jazz liturgies and written a great deal of music for this purpose. Dave Brubeck (The Light in the Wilderness) has also been fundamental in the organization of good jazz liturgical music.

There seems to be a need for an awakening. It is necessary to utilize the wants and desires of a modern people so that our churches will grow stronger instead of weaker.[41]

Reverend Norman J. O'Connor, director of the New York Paulist Fathers' office for radio and television, says of the Schifrin-Horn *Jazz Suite:* "At a moment in our lives when music is finding a new life in the church, this work turns our eyes from the past—where they have lingered too long—to the present and to the future. How could it be that (until now) liturgical music could fail to grow and incorporate the values of our world?"[42]

Charles Weisenberg has also commented on the place of jazz in modern church services:

Jazz has roots in the religious service through its association with the Negro spiritual. The contemporary use of jazz in church is thus not a new adventure. It is important to note that J. S. Bach, whose music is used in many church services, composed in a contemporary style. There is certainly no reason why 20th

38. "Bernstein's 'Mass' Wins Music Critics Acclaim," *Los Angeles Times,* 9 September 1971.

39. *Mary Lou's Mass,* Mary Records, 102.

40. Geoffrey Beaumont, *20th Century Folk Mass,* Fiesta Recordings, FLP–25000; Joe Masters, *The Jazz Mass,* Columbia Records, CS9398.

41. Gerald L. Gipson, "The Church and Jazz," *Music Journal* 28, no. 4 (1970):38.

42. Dan L. Thrapp, *Los Angeles Times,* 24 April 1966.

Duke Ellington and His Orchestra at the Fifth Avenue Presbyterian Church in New York City on December 26, 1965. *Photo from United Press International.*

Marching band in New Orleans. *Courtesy of Ray Avery.*

century contemporary music, whether or not it is jazz, cannot be suitably prepared for church use.[43]

The union of church and jazz should surprise no one. (There is an anonymous saying: "Each Sunday Buddy Bolden went to church and that's where he got his idea of jazz music.") Since the beginnings of jazz were in the church, it is only natural that modern concepts should also be acceptable. The authors of this book have personally been involved in such services and feel that jazz can express solemnity, peacefulness, dedication, vitality, rejoicing, and any other sentiment embraced by the church. One thing that must be remembered is that in order for this type of service to be successful the jazz must enhance the service; it must

reinforce the emotions, but not become the main attraction. It is true that it is next to impossible for a person to leave a jazz service untouched as surely happens in many standard services.

Marching Bands

At first, black music in this country was vocal, accompanied by a rhythm of clapping, stomping, and beating on virtually anything available. Then gradually, after the Civil War, the blacks were able to make some instruments and to buy pawned and war surplus instruments. Marching bands began to influence black music.

43. Charles M. Weisenberg, "On Brubeck and Others," *Frontier* 2, no. 9 (July 1960):24.

Military bands, important in all French settlements, also influenced the beginnings of jazz. There were many bands in the New Orleans area. Every secret society or fraternity, for example, had its own band, and there were bands for hire who were not attached to any organization. Most of the early jazz players started their careers in such bands, playing marches, polkas, **quadrilles,** and so on.[44] (NW, "Castle Walk," #269, side 1, band 2; NW, "Castle House Rag," #269, side 1, band 1; NW, "Memphis Blues," #269, side 1, band 3)

At the turn of the century the most publicized use of the marching bands was for funerals. Bands were used not only in New Orleans, but over the Southeast and as far west as Oklahoma. Such bands, usually composed of five or six players, should be considered a separate type of musical aggregation, in contrast to large modern bands. These small marching bands played an important part in the early development of jazz.

For a funeral procession, the black band would drone a traditional funeral march on the way to the cemetery. After the burial ceremony, the band would march two or three blocks from the cemetery with only a conservative drum beat. Then the band would break into a jazz type of march, such as "Didn't He Ramble" or "When the Saints Go Marching In." The reasoning behind this established plan of the music played at funerals was that the traditional funeral music depicted mourning, while the later use of the more rhythmic music signified the fact that the departed was going to a happier place, which was a cause for rejoicing.

When the band began to play a livelier version of the march, its followers would gradually respond more and more to the music. Their responses were often in the form of clapping, stomping, or any physical rhythmic movement leading toward dancing. In those early days a band often marched directly from the street into a hall and there the music was used for dancing instead of marching, even though the music was the same.[45]

The most common instrumentation used by these bands consisted of cornet, trombone, clarinet, tuba, banjo, and drums. According to research, the first leader of a jazz marching band was Buddy Bolden. Consequently, he is usually credited with establishing the set instrumentation for these bands. Bolden combined brass-band music with ragtime, quadrilles, and blues in the first stages of jazz. Its small size made the group adaptable for various functions such as advertising campaigns, weddings, serenades, and the like. A group often performed in a horse-drawn wagon. One of the authors played on such wagons while living in the South and discovered the reason for the name "**tailgate trombone**" when he sat at the end of the wagon in order to have sufficient room for his trombone slide.

Because this music lent itself so well to dancing, much of the early jazz repertoire developed from marches.

The transformation of straightforward marches into jazz may be compared with the process which took place when hymns were changed into spirituals. . . . This jazzing of marches was achieved partly by the trick of shifting the accent from the strong to the weak beat and partly by allowing solo players to "decorate" the melody they were playing—solo improvisation; or several players to indulge in their extemporization simultaneously—collective improvisation.[46]

The regularity of march music could have easily influenced early jazz; today people often "swing" as they march. The integration of the playing of the conservatory-trained Creoles with the self-taught blacks produced well-played marches with the freedom of an oral tradition.

Most important to jazz are the emphasis on rhythm taken from the African music, the harmonies taken from European music, and the melodies added by the improvisations from the American culture. All of these elements fuse to make jazz an American music, rather than the music of a specific ethnic group. However, we emphasize again that the pioneers and innovators of jazz were and are American black musicians.

Additional Reading Resources

Roberts, John Storm. *Black Music of Two Worlds.*

Roach, Hildred. *Black American Music Past and Present.*

Note: Complete information including name of publisher and date of publication is provided in the Bibliography.

44. "Castle Walk," "Castle House Rag," "Memphis Blues," *Steppin' on the Gas—Rags to Jazz 1913–1927,* New World Records, 269.

45. Olympia Brass Band of New Orleans, *New Orleans Street Parade,* BASF Recordings, 20678.

46. Harris, *Jazz,* p. 57.

Suggested Classroom Activities

1. American jazz came about through the blend of the musical cultures of Africa and Europe. Discuss those influences upon early jazz made by Africans and those made by Europeans.

2. Explain why it is incorrect to say that jazz rhythms came from Africa.

3. Explain the importance of Congo Square and other similar places in the South to the beginnings of jazz.

4. Compare and contrast spiritual songs with gospel songs and with modern liturgical jazz.

5. Describe the following and discuss their contribution to early jazz:
   a. Field hollers
   b. Work songs
   c. Spirituals
   d. Marching bands

6. Give the instrumentation most commonly used in the early marching bands.

7. What is the difference between the construction of homophonic (vertical) harmony and polyphonic (horizontal) harmony?

8. Pretend that you are pounding railroad spikes as you sing the work song "I Got To Roll." Notice the places in the music where the singers give a half-shout or grunt. This song is found on page 544 of Alan Lomax's *The Folk Songs of North America* (Doubleday & Company). This book is a splendid resource for background material on spirituals, work songs, ballads, and blues.

4

The Blues

Prior to any discussion of the blues, listen to the recording of the hymnlike melody on taped demonstration 8 (example 9A), which uses the blues harmonic construction.

Now listen to this same hymnlike melody (taped demonstration 9, example 9B) as it is given a jazz interpretation. We will analyze the blues construction.

The blues is neither an era in the chronological development of jazz, nor is it actually a particular style of playing or singing jazz. Because of the great variety of individual styles used by different singers who are referred to as "blues" singers, we contend that there is no single or set manner of interpreting this type of jazz that should be labeled a blues style. General research has pictured the blues as something sung by "old" people accompanied by guitar; yet in the middle 1920s and 1930s, young, energetic singers in Kansas City were accompanied by complete jazz bands.

In the development of jazz, the blues has been played and sung in every era and can be performed with many interpretations. Any recorded anthology of jazz in general or of blues in particular shows this great variety of styles.[1] Blues can be slow and sad like a dirge, or happy and rollicking. Blues is as important today in jazz as it ever was. Many modern jazz selections still use the basic blues progression with expanded harmonies. Charlie Parker's "Another Hair Do" is a good example of blues in bop; Milt Jackson's "Bags' Groove" is played in both cool and funky styles, showing minor blues to be apropos in a contemporary setting.[2] It is interesting to note that the cassette that accompanies this book is a blues number that progresses through demonstrations of each era. In fact, the exact same blues tune is used in each case, showing the flexibility of this form. Note that no matter how frantic sounding the music may become (the bop, for example) the same blues is very apropos.

1. *Many Faces of the Blues,* Savoy Records, MG12125; Bessie Smith, *Empty Bed Blues,* Columbia Records, G39450; *The Story of the Blues,* Columbia Records, G30008; *Jazz Odyssey,* vol. 1, *The Sound of New Orleans (1917–1947),* Columbia Records, C3L 30; *Jazz Odyssey,* vol. 2, *The Sound of Chicago (1923–1940),* Columbia Records, C3L 32; *Jazz Odyssey,* vol. 3, *The Sound of Harlem,* Columbia Records, C3L 33; Port of Harlem Jazzmen, "Port of Harlem Blues," Albert Ammons, "Boogie Woogie Stomp," Meade Lux Lewis, "Honky Tonky Train Blues," Ed Hall, "Profoundly Blue," Josh White, "Milk Cow Blues," Sidney de Paris, "The Call of the Blues," and Sidney Bechet, "Blue Horizon," *Three Decades of Jazz (1939–1949).* Blue Note Records, BST 89902.

2. Charlie Parker, "Another Hair Do" *Charlie Parker Memorial,* Savoy Records, MG 12000; Milt Jackson, "Bags' Groove," and Horace Silver, "Senor Blues," and Lou Donaldson, "Blues Walk," *Three Decades of Jazz (1949–1959),* Blue Note Records, BST 89903; Jimmy Smith, "Back at the Chicken Shack," Kenny Burrell, "Chittlins Con Carne," Lee Morgan, "The Sidewinder," and Stanley Turrentine, "River's Invitation," *Three Decades of Jazz (1959–1969),* Blue Note Records, BST 89904; McCoy Tyner, "Flapstick Blues," *The Definitive Jazz Scene,* vol. 1, Impulse Records, A–99.

Example 9A

Taped Demonstration 8

Example 9B

Taped Demonstration 9

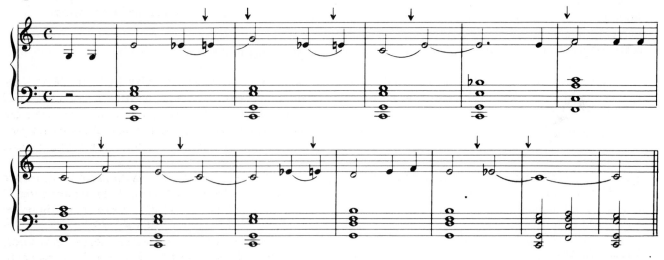

The Origin

When African and European music first began to merge, the slaves sang very sad songs concerning their extreme suffering. At this time, the name "blues" was not in popular use. The singing was in unison and no chords were determined and no specific form designated. After the Civil War, however, blacks could perform their music more openly, and, as it united with European music, eight-bar, twelve-bar, and sixteen-bar blues forms all developed. By World War I, the twelve-bar construction had become an accepted form.[3]

The blues, like all music, has built chords from the scale tones. If a chord starts on the first note of the scale and then uses every other note (scale tones 1, 3, and 5), the numeral I is used to define it. A chord built up from the fourth note would be given the numeral IV and so on. These harmonic symbols can be used to describe the harmonic construction of various musical forms.

Most blues researchers claim that the very early blues were patterned after English ballads and often

3. Gunther Schuller, *Early Jazz* (London: Oxford University Press, 1968), p. 37.

had eight, ten, or sixteen bars.[4] An example of eight-bar blues is "Trouble in Mind," sometimes called "Troubled in Mind," with the following chord progression: I, V₇, I₇, IV, I, V₇, I, I. Another eight-bar blues is "How Long Blues," using a different chord progression: I, I₇, IV, IV, I, V₇, I, I. Among the sixteen-bar blues one can find long lists of songs such as "Careless Love" (I, V₇, I, I—I, I, V₇, V₇,—I, I₇, IV, IV,—I, V₇, I, I), "Basin Street Blues" (I, III₇, VI₇, VI₇,—II₇, V₇, I, V₇,—I, III₇, VI₇, VI₇,—II₇, V₇, I, I), and sixteen-bar blues tunes that have the standard twelve-bar progression plus a four-bar tag (I, I, I, I₇,—IV, IV, I, I,—V₇, V₇, I, I,—and then the **tag**—II₇, V₇, I, I). Few researchers attempt to notate these early blues, perhaps because there are so many different structures.

The Accepted Chord Progression

Today, the blues is a particular harmonic sequence, a definite musical form in much the same manner that the sonnet is a poetic form. The blues now contains a definite set progression of harmonies and consists of twelve measures. The harmonic progression is as follows: I, I, I, I₇, IV, IV, I, I, V₇, V₇, I, I. Each roman numeral indicates a chord built on a specific tone in the scale. Since about 1960, due to the influence of rock 'n'

roll artists, the tenth chord in the progression of harmonies has been changed to IV₇. This alteration is now considered standard.

Each roman numeral as specified in the foregoing harmonic progression designates a chord to be played for one measure, resulting in a **twelve-measure strain.** Examples 10A, 10B, and 10C are in the key of C.

Slight variations and embellishments may be used to alter this pattern. If, however, the chord progression is not used as the basic construction, the music being played is *not in the blues* format. Therefore many melodies that have the word "blues" in the title, and which are often spoken of as being the blues, are not the blues because these melodies lack the blues harmonic construction. The well-known "Bye, Bye Blues," "Limehouse Blues," and "Wabash Blues" are examples. The chord progression for "Bye, Bye Blues" begins with the following harmonies: I, I, ♭VI, ♭VI, I, I, VI, VI. Regardless of the title and the fact that it is often placed in the blues category, its harmonic progressions are not constructed in the blues pattern. One of the most famous melodies with a blues title is "The St. Louis Blues." But of the three strains found in this music, only two are constructed in the blues pattern.

Blue Notes

Another characteristic associated with the blues is the **blue tonalities.** In our opinion these tonalities resulted from the West Africans' search for comparative tones not included in their pentatonic scale.[5] The easiest way to explain blue tonalities without the use of a piano is to use a diagram such as example 11.

All the tones indicated on the piano keyboard are included in Western diatonic and chromatic music. If the tonal center (C) is arbitrarily used as the basis for discussion, the tones marked with an X are included in the pentatonic scale of the West Africans. As is noted, the West African scale has neither the third or seventh tone nor the flat third or flat seventh. Because of this,

4. LeRoi Jones, *Blues People* (New York: William Morrow & Co., 1963), p. 62.

5. Marshall Stearns, *The Story of Jazz* (New York: New American Library, Mentor Books, 1958), p. 15.

Example 10A

C diatonic scale:

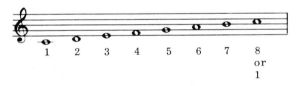

Example 10B

I and IV and V₇ chords spelled out in the key of C:

Example 10C

The *basic* chords that are used in the blues in the key of C:

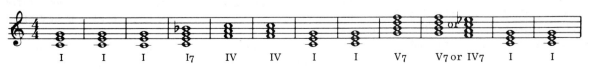

Example 11

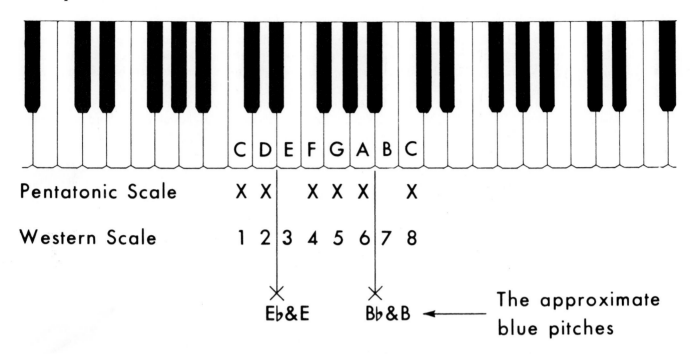

Pentatonic Scale

Western Scale

Eb&E   Bb&B ← The approximate blue pitches

in the attempt to imitate either of these tones the pitch was sounded approximately midway between the tone E flat and E natural, and B flat and B natural, causing what is called a blue tonality. Since there are no keys on the piano corresponding to these blue tonalities (or blue notes), pianists must obtain the blues effect by striking these two piano keys at the same time.

"Blues notes" or "blue areas" cannot be designated as concretely as stated in this explanation. Jazz players have always had a tendency to bend and twist notes as an additional means of self-expression. Long ago, lowering of the fifth became a standard device comparable to other blue notes. Therefore, the preceding explanation shows only the consensus of how these blue notes originated. One possible reason why a blues tune does not feel as melancholy when performed at a faster tempo is because there is less time to bend the blue notes around in a dramatic fashion. Some theorists designate a "blues scale" as the **Dorian mode** (such as the white keys of the piano from D to D) or the **Mixolydian mode** (the white keys of the piano from G to G). The false logic in this theory is that the blue areas cannot be pinpointed. The Dorian implies a lowered third and lowered seventh; the Mixolydian implies a natural third and a lowered seventh. These blue tonalities are not on definite notes. The problems of analysis result from the rigidity of the **well-tempered scale** and the fluctuations of the blue tonalities themselves.

Before the field cry, with its bending of notes, it had not occurred to musicians to explore the area of the blue tonalities on instruments. Blue tonalities and bending of notes can be heard on many records by early jazz brass bands.[6] (FJ, "Didn't He Ramble," Vol. 3) In fact, blue notes are heard in work songs, in spirituals, and in all styles of jazz. Tin Pan Alley (the popular music publishing industry) has used this element excessively. One can also find the use of blue notes in the works of many 20th century classical composers.

Wind and string instruments both offered an opportunity to use blue notes. The string player could pull on the string with the left hand to make a note slightly higher in pitch while the wind player could move the pitch slightly by making changes in the **embouchure** (mouth position). These slight adjustments would create a pitch that falls in the crack between two notes on the piano. This out-of-tuneness helped create that blue note feeling.

6. Bunk Johnson, "Didn't He Ramble," *Jazz,* vol. 3, *New Orleans,* Folkways Records, 2804.

Example 12A

The usual format showing fill-in areas:

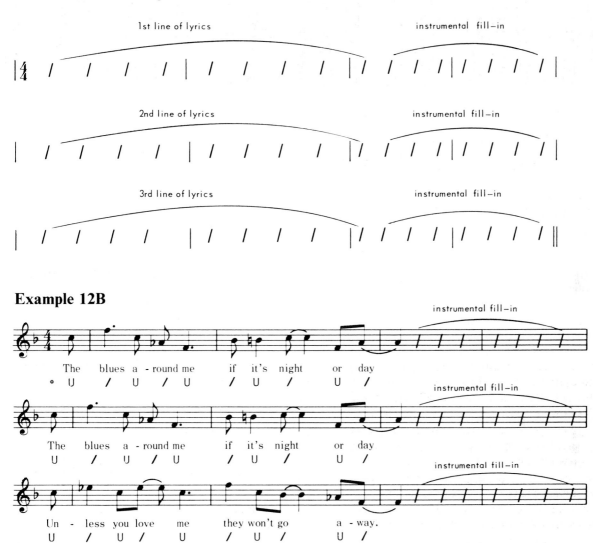

Example 12B

*Iambic pentameter markings.

Blues Lyrics

The meter of the blues lyrics is generally written in **iambic pentameter.**[7] For example: "I hate to see the ev'nin' sun go down." The first line is generally repeated (a throwback to the African call and response) and followed by an original third line. The repetition of the first line gives the singer the necessary time to improvise a third line. Very often the lyrics of the blues do not seem to fit the music, but good blues singers "would stress certain syllables and almost eliminate others so that everything falls into place neatly and

surely."[8] Each line of the lyrics consists of four measures of music. Because the lyrics seldom use the four measures completely, the remainder of each four-measure segment of the strain is completed by an instrumentalist. These specific areas within the strain are known as **fill-ins** (see examples 12A and 12B). Listen to the saxophone fill-ins for Billie Holiday on "Fine and

7.   Leonard Bernstein, "The World of Jazz," in *The Joy of Music* (New York: Simon & Schuster, 1959), p. 109.

8.   Rex Harris, *Jazz* (Baltimore: Penguin Books, 1956), p. 39.

Mellow" and the trombone performing the same function for Bessie Smith on "Empty Bed Blues," and Louis Armstrong playing the fill-ins on Bessie Smith's "Saint Louis Blues" and "Lost Your Head Blues."[9] (S, side 1, bands 4 and 5)

Fill-ins were the first means that some jazz instrumentalists had to be heard on records. It was in this way that some of the more talented players like Louis Armstrong began to build a broader reputation. (Armstrong can be heard playing fill-ins on some Bessie Smith recordings.) The fill-ins gradually developed in importance and interest to the point where they were called **breaks.** Often their importance was emphasized by the fact that the entire musical organization stopped playing in order to feature the solo instrument filling in the break.

The blues as they are sung use lyrics that are usually concerned with unhappy situations: out of work, hungry, broke, away from home, lonely, or broken-hearted because of an unfaithful lover. Consequently, their melancholy lyrics usually describe the blues emotion: "I'm laughin' to keep from cryin'," "Nobody knows you when you're down and out," "I've got the blues so bad, it's hard to keep from cryin'," and so forth. "By their very etymology the blues are songs of abandon, despair, or lyric sadness. However, content soon goes beyond form, and in the same mold all kinds of sentiments have been cast. Today, given blues are gay, ironic, sarcastic, vengeful. They were slow; they may now be fast (as in boogie-woogie) and even, in modern jazz, very fast."[10] The majority of the public recognizes the blues only by melancholy lyrics, and, as a consequence, many jazz listeners are not aware of the fact that the blues can also be happy swinging tunes. There is such a variety in this one form that some entertainers base their entire repertoire on blues.

Interpretation of the blues by instrumentalists and singers varied all over the United States as early as the latter part of the nineteenth century,[11] a fact that helps to support those who contend that jazz did not originate in any one area of the country.

Blue has been associated with melancholia as far back as Elizabethan times. Washington Irving is credited with first using the term "the blues" in 1807. By 1910, the word *blues* was in fairly wide use. Some writers state the first written-down blues was "Dallas Blues" by Hart Wand, a white violinist from Oklahoma City.[12] (NW, #217) It was published in 1912. But it is unclear which blues tune was "first." For example, W. C. Handy's "The Memphis Blues" was written in 1909 as a political campaign song. No individual city or state can claim the origin of the blues. W. C. Handy, who was called The Father of the Blues,

came from Alabama. His two most famous songs with blues in the titles are "The Memphis Blues" and "St. Louis Blues." W. C. Handy proved that money could be made from writing down and publishing blues tunes. Around 1917 blues began to be popular as ragtime began to fade. The first blues recording was Mamie Smith's "Crazy Blues" in 1920; it sold seventy-five thousand copies in the first month and a million copies in the first six months.

A common misconception is that the blues originated with work songs. Actually, work songs were functional, whereas blues were usually quite emotional and had no specific function. The consensus among authorities who write about jazz is that the blues was important to the beginnings of jazz. It is very apparent that this musical form has never lost its importance and is heard as frequently today as in all the previous eras of jazz. Blues performances in general are filled with subtleties. Recent adaptations, such as rhythm and blues in 1945 and rock 'n' roll in 1955, seem fairly devoid of subtleties, but the durability of the form is proved as it continues to survive through all adaptations.

Blues Performers

The history of the blues and the story of blues singers are complete studies in themselves, deserving of the fine volumes written about them. Students of the blues and blues singers will be aided greatly by the historically very important Library of Congress recordings. The aim of this book, however, is to point out a very few singers important in this field. The authors believe that all types of blues, from the beginnings to present-day forms, have greatly influenced how jazz players perform, but that certain singers have, of course, been heard more than others and, as a consequence, have had more influence. "The great blues singers of the twenties and the early thirties bred the jazz men, but they also bred a line of itinerant musicians who sang and played only the

9. Billie Holiday, "Fine and Mellow," *Billie Holiday,* Mainstream Records, S/6000; Bessie Smith, "Empty Bed Blues," *Empty Bed Blues,* Columbia Records, G39450; "Saint Louis Blues" and "Lost Your Head Blues," Smithsonian Collection of Classic Jazz.

10. Andre Francis, *Jazz* (New York: Grove Press, 1960), p. 17.

11. Marshall Stearns, "Sonny Terry and His Blues," in *The Art of Jazz,* ed. Martin T. Williams (London: Oxford University Press, 1959), p. 9.

12. Andy Kirk Orchestra, "Dallas Blues," *Jammin' for the Jackpot,* New World Records, 217.

Huddie Ledbetter. *Courtesy of Orrin Keepnews.*

blues."[13] Today, in retrospect, it is impossible to separate blues from jazz, as performed in the past or in contemporary settings.

After World War I there was a great migration of the black population to large northern cities. The black population wanted the type of entertainment it was accustomed to, and hence there was a demand for blues singers. Because records of blacks were bought and heard only by blacks, a collection of what were called "race records" developed. When whites eventually began to hear these records, fragile 78 rpm records became collector's items—sometimes selling for over one hundred dollars each.

There are essentially two periods of blues, the first from the latter part of the nineteenth century to approximately 1930, and the second from about 1930 to

13. Ralph J. Gleason, "Records," *Rolling Stones* (May 1971): 45.

the present. The early period is usually divided between performers who sang "country," or "rural," blues and those who sang "city," or "urban," blues. The best known early male blues singers were Big Bill Broonzy, Robert Johnson, Josh White, Blind Lemon Jefferson, Huddie Ledbetter, Son House, and Lightnin' Hopkins,[14] (NW, #261) and they were followed by Albert King, T-Bone Walker, B. B. King, and others. The early urban or city blues singers were mostly women—Ma Rainey, Chippie Hill, Mamie Smith, Trixie Smith, and, most famous of all, Bessie Smith.

The period from 1930 onward is divided primarily between singers and instrumentalists. The singers include such talented artists as Joe Turner, Jimmy Rushing, Joe Williams, and Jimmy Witherspoon. The problem with listing the best blues instrumentalists is that they were also singers—Louis Armstrong, Jack Teagarden, and Ray Charles, for example. It is an oddity that in the beginnings of jazz, instrumentalists copied vocal techniques, but that later some of the best jazz singers imitated instrumental jazz. Consequently, some of the best jazz singers were also instrumentalists.

City blues seems to be more rhythmic, more crisp than country blues. Most country blues singers accompanied themselves on guitar, whereas urban blues performers often used fairly elaborate accompaniment including jazz musicians like Louis Armstrong.

Huddie Ledbetter, known as Leadbelly, was discovered on a prison farm in Louisiana by John and Alan Lomax. He has been quoted as stating that he was born in 1885 in Louisiana and raised in Texas. He became a guide for Blind Lemon Jefferson and learned twelve-string guitar technique from him. Ledbetter spent a considerable amount of time in prison and became known as a valuable lead man for work songs. There are 144 songs in the Library of Congress recorded by Ledbetter between 1933 and 1940 under the supervision of the Lomaxes. Some recordings can be heard today on Folkways records and some on Columbia records. Ledbetter seldom played softly; he felt that blues tunes were meant to be danced to or worked to. His blues and folksongs gained him much popularity and led to many tours and concerts. Huddie Ledbetter died in 1949 in New York. His "Good Night, Irene" became extremely popular even among people who knew nothing about Leadbelly.

Big Bill Broonzy's recordings span a thirty-one year period. Broonzy directly influenced Josh White and many others. He composed about three hundred songs. One of the most famous of his records is "Troubled in Mind" (Folkways Records), which has lyrics in the

Ma Rainey. *Courtesy of Orrin Keepnews.*

eight-bar blues construction that have inspired many downtrodden persons to have hope:

Troubled in mind, I'm blue.
But I won't be blue always.
The sun's gonna shine
In my back do' someday.[15]

Ma Rainey, Bessie Smith, and other singers were trained on the minstrel circuits. Sadly, many black minstrels were copies of white minstrels. They were

14. Lightnin' Hopkins, "Hello Central," *Straighten Up and Fly Right—Rhythm and Blues,* New World Records, 261.

15. "Trouble in Mind," Words and music by Richard M. Jones. © Copyright 1926, 1937 by MCA Music, a Division of MCA, Inc. © Copyright renewed 1953 and assigned to MCA Music, a division of MCA, Inc. © Copyright 1971 by MCA Music, a Division of MCA, Inc., 445 Park Ave., N.Y., N.Y. 10022. Used by permission. All rights reserved.

truly imitations of imitations, and their performances were often not as artistic as they were capable of performing. As Ma Rainey was called The Mother of the Blues, her pupil Bessie Smith was called The Empress of the Blues. Even though Ma Rainey was born in 1886, recordings of her work are still available on Riverside and Folkways records. Reissues of Bessie Smith's work are now available on Columbia records. Technical mastery on these records is very good, and the records are quite important for historical documentation. They are also fine recordings for mere listening pleasure. (More on Bessie Smith in chapter 17.)

B. B. King considers the blues to be a contemporary experience, a living music rather than a folk art. He plays electric guitar, as did T-Bone Walker.[16] (NW, #261) King's album *Live and Well* on ABC Records shows the great freedom that was typical of early bluesmen.[17] Many rock superstars have acknowledged their debt to King's lyrical guitar virtuosity.

Since it is not the aim of this book to discuss, or even to mention, all of the talented blues personalities, the following resources are suggested. An important two-record set of early music in the United States is Arhoolie's *The Roots of American Music*.[18] Not only are both city and country blues represented, but also examples of Cajun (Clifton Chenier), gospel, and other types of music. Folkways and Riverside record companies have made truly remarkable efforts to preserve the sounds of important pioneers in music. Few researchers have delved more deeply into blues than Samuel B. Charters. His book *The Country Blues* is a standard among jazz musicologists.[19] Three other books of merit must be suggested: *Urban Blues* by Charles Keil, *The Meaning of the Blues* by Paul Oliver, and *Blues People* by LeRoi Jones.[20]

Additional Reading Resources

Balliett, Whitney. "Miss Holiday." In *Dinosaurs in the Morning*, pp. 74–80.

Bernstein, Leonard. *The Joy of Music*, pp. 95–111.

Charters, Samuel B. *The Country Blues*.

Harris, Rex. *Jazz*, pp. 34–42.

Hentoff, Nat, and McCarthy, Albert. *Jazz: New Perspectives in the History of Jazz*.

Jones, LeRoi. *Blues People*.

Keil, Charles. *Urban Blues*.

Oliver, Paul. *Bessie Smith* (King of Jazz Series).

———. *The Meaning of the Blues*.

Stearns, Marshall. *The Story of Jazz*, pp. 14, 75–81, 196–98.

Ulanov, Barry. *Handbook of Jazz*, chap. 1.

Note: Complete information including name of publisher and date of publication is provided in the Bibliography.

Additional Record Resources

The Blues. Folkways Records, FJ 2802.

The Blues, History of Classic Jazz, vol. 3. Riverside Records, SDP–11.

Roots of the Blues. New World Records, 252.

Suggested Classroom Activities

1. Play the hymn "Lord Jesus Christ, With Us Abide"* or any other hymn that contains the harmonic construction of the blues. Listen carefully and identify the blues chord progressions.

2. Select a blues melody such as the first twelve measures of "St. Louis Blues" and adapt a sonnet or original poem to this melody.

3. Select a sonnet and write a blues melody to the words. See example on page 45 ("When To The Sessions of Sweet Silent Thought," text by William Shakespeare).

4. Sing the C-major scale and note the location of the half steps. Next sing only the tones C, D, F, G, and A. You have just sung a pentatonic scale. Explain the difference between a major diatonic scale and a pentatonic scale.

5. Sing the spiritual "Swing Low, Sweet Chariot" in the key of F-major. What scale does this melody use? Explain your answer.

6. Sing the spiritual "Lord, Lord, Lord," shown on page 45. What melodic characteristics in this spiritual suggest a blues melody?

16. T-Bone Walker, "Call It Stormy Monday," *Straighten Up and Fly Right—Rhythm and Blues*, New World Records, 261.

17. B. B. King, *Live and Well*, ABC Records, S–6031; *Best of B. B. King*, ABC Recordings, 767.

18. *The Roots of American Music*, Arhoolie Records, 2001/2002.

19. Samuel Charters, *The Country Blues* (New York: Doubleday & Co., 1958).

20. Charles Keil, *Urban Blues* (Chicago: University of Chicago Press, 1966); Paul Oliver, *The Meaning of the Blues* (New York: Collier Books, 1960); LeRoi Jones, *Blues People* (New York: William Morrow & Co., 1965).

*Melody from Dresden Hymn Book, 1954, arranged by Johann Sebastian Bach, *Anniversary Collection of Bach Chorales*, ed. Walter E. Buszin (Chicago: Hall & McCreary, 1935), p. 6.

7. Give some titles of blues melodies that do not follow the usual harmonic construction but have the word *blues* in their titles.

8. In your own words, describe the "blue tonality." How does a pianist obtain the effect of blue tonality at the keyboard?

9. Listen to "In the House Blues" as sung by Bessie Smith (*The Story of the Blues,* Columbia, G30008) and answer the following:
   a. Is there an introduction?
   b. Do the lyrics follow the iambic pentameter plan, i.e., the first line repeats, while the third line is original?
   c. How many times does she sing the blues song?
   d. What instrument accompanies her? What instruments play the fill-ins?
   e. Finally, when you hear the melody sung, do you hear the singer interpolate the blue notes?

10. The twelve bar blues became standard with instrumental ensemble musicians during the 1920s. No further instruction was necessary once an experienced jazz musician was told "Blues in B flat." This structure with its set harmonic pattern became the norm. Listen to "Dippermouth Blues." (S, Side 1, band 6) After the four measure introduction, identify the following: How many ensemble improvised choruses (12 measures each) are there? How many choruses did the clarinet and cornet play? Do you hear the "stop-time" device used by the ensemble?

Listening Guide

From Smithsonian Collection
(side 1, band 4)

Bessie Smith

"St. Louis Blues"

:00 Chord on reed organ and muted trumpet
:03 1st strain—vocal (Bessie Smith) accompanied by fill-ins on the muted trumpet (Louis Armstrong); listen for the standard blues chord sequence
:48 2nd strain—vocal with trumpet fill-ins
1:31 3rd strain—vocal with trumpet fill-ins; leaves the standard blues chord sequence
2:26 4th strain—same as above; back to the blues chords
3:07 End

When To The Sessions of Sweet Silent Thought

Text by William Shakespeare

That life is on-ly life for ev - er - more _____ That

I (C) Chord   I - C   I - C   I7 - C7

life is on-ly life for ev - er - more _____ To -

IV - F   IV - F   I - C   I - C

geth - er wing to wing and oar _____ to oar _____

V7 - G7   V7 - G7   I - C   I - C

Lord, Lord, Lord

Refrain   *Spiritual*

Lord, Lord, Lord, you've sure been good to me. Lord, Lord, Lord, you've sure been good to me _____

Lord, Lord, Lord, you've sure been good to me; For you've done what the world could not do.

5

Early New Orleans Dixieland
(1900–1920)

The life span of a musical masterpiece [or style] may encompass a number of generations, but music, being a reflection of society, is subject, like any other art, to social obsolescence. It may endure, metaphorically speaking, in libraries, on records and in the occasional archeological revival, but it will not satisfy a changing society's changing musical requirements.[1]

Each new era in jazz came into being as a reaction against the jazz of the preceding era, much as in the development of classical music. We have chosen to designate each era of jazz by its most commonly used name, and the dates given for each era are approximate since no style of jazz started or stopped at a given date. For an introduction to Early New Orleans Dixieland jazz listen to the cassette, demonstration 10, supplied with this book.

Too often, both musicians and lay listeners tend to identify their tastes with specific eras in jazz and to ignore all other styles as being unworthy of concern. Generally speaking, it is only the jazz *fans* who want *their* style to remain as the one authentic way to play jazz; the musicians seldom want this themselves. Such clichés as *I don't know much about it but I know what I like* are used to defend this attitude, but most humanities teachers agree that people *like* what they *know*. A deeper understanding of the unfamiliar areas of this art form will develop better discernment and more enjoyment. The intolerant attitude of some musicians who state that the only true jazz is the style in

which they and their favorite performers are involved shows an extremely narrow outlook usually based on a minimum of "outside" listening.

At this point, the authors would like to apologize for the "accepted" labels that are used throughout this book. Most musicians do not restrict themselves to one era or style of jazz; their style may even vary within a given improvised chorus. However, the various styles do have certain characteristics that differentiate them, and only by the use of labels can these differences be discussed. Labels are used only to further communication. On the other hand, one of the most exciting aspects of contemporary jazz is its lack of established explanation, hence, lack of labels.

New Orleans

The era of jazz discussed in this chapter is called Early New Orleans Dixieland jazz not because New Orleans was the only geographical origin of this type of music, but because at the beginning of the twentieth century New Orleans bred more jazz and more notable jazz musicians than any other area. However, when considering New Orleans as the birthplace of jazz, we must keep two facts in mind: (1) Slaves were brought first to Virginia in 1619, and they brought with them their

---

1. Henry Pleasants, *Serious Music and All That Jazz*, p. 47. Copyright © 1969 by Henry Pleasants. Reprinted by permission of Simon & Schuster, a Division of Gulf and Western Corporation.

musical traditions, thereby producing, through the merging of their music with European music, the first faint beginning of jazz; (2) The first instrumental jazz was recorded in New York City about three hundred years later (1917).

The deeper the research probes, the more difficult it becomes to claim one city as the origin of this art form. W. C. Handy said that music that was later called jazz was played in Memphis around 1905, but that the performers did not know until about 1917 that New Orleans had the same kind of music.[2] However, jazz critic Dan Morgenstern writes: "Jazz: one of the great and wonderful mysteries of our age. New Orleans: the cradle of this mystery. You don't agree? Have you a better myth? Have you Louis Armstrong?"[3] The word *early* is included to differentiate between the dixieland music played from approximately 1890 to 1920 from the jazz developed in Chicago after 1920. The dixieland music performed in New Orleans today, however, often includes elements of all the jazz eras since 1920.

The historical background of New Orleans, an exciting city that keeps alive many of its early customs and traditions, provided a receptive environment for jazz to develop and grow. For the first forty-six years, New Orleans was a French possession. It was then ceded to Spain in 1764 and remained a Spanish possession for the next thirty-six years when it once again came under French rule. In 1803 it came to the United States as part of the Louisiana Purchase. This heterogeneous atmosphere was tolerant of all races and was a natural setting for the music of West Africa and Europe to meet and to merge. New Orleans was and is an exciting city with great activity of all sorts, both business and pleasure.

Oddly enough, recognition of jazz players in New Orleans by the New Orleans press has always been quite poor ever since the art form took shape at the turn of the century. The New Orleans musicians "testify that it is easier to get national and international recognition of their talents than it is to get the attention of the *Times-Picayune* and the *States & Items* . . . when their talents are adequately fossilized, their instruments museum pieces, and the musical forms they are creating safely a part of jazz history, they probably will show up on the cover of the *Picayune* Sunday supplement."[4]

The Oral Tradition

It has been stated previously that early jazz combined the techniques of formally trained Creole musicians with the techniques of blacks whose playing was based on oral tradition. There is no better example of playing based on the oral tradition than that heard on any Louis Armstrong record when he sings first and then plays the melody. His phrasing in each instance is identical. This is an example of how the instrument is used as an extension of the voice.

Charles "Buddy" Bolden, who led one of the earliest marching bands, is usually credited with establishing the fixed instrumental combination used in this era.[5] The first jazz instrumentation was logical since the same instruments were also used in the marching bands and in the music halls. In its beginnings, this music was generally a creation of blacks, with the exception of a few whites like the drummer Jack "Papa" Laine who led a band as early as 1891. But soon the music was being created by both blacks and whites. It should be noted, however, that the black musicians did much more to foster these beginnings and to continue its development. Bolden was eighteen years old when the African type of dancing in Congo Square every Sunday came to an end. He was a cornet player in his brass band and was a member of a "shouting congregation" in his church. Obviously, he was heir to many of the early influences leading toward jazz. His band played ragtime melodies, marches, quadrilles, and a great amount of the blues. Bolden stopped playing entirely in 1907, a fact that points out the diversity of this music at an early date. Unfortunately there are no recordings of Bolden.

Small bands playing dixieland music developed concurrently with ragtime. Dixieland and ragtime influenced each other and were influenced a great deal by the same sources. The same players were often involved in both, and ultimately the two styles merged. In their beginnings, however, early dixieland music used no piano, while early ragtime was primarily piano music. Eventually, though, there were ragtime bands. All Early New Orleans Dixieland bands did not sound the same. In New Orleans there were at least thirty quite well known bands in just the first decade of the twentieth century. It was only natural that the bands varied according to the personnel of the outfit, just as jazz groups do today.

2.   From the *Jazz Book: From New Orleans to Rock and Free Jazz,* by Joachim Berendt, translated by Dan Morgenstern, copyright 1975 Lawrence Hill & Co., Westport, Connecticut.

3.   Dan Morgenstern, "The Meaning of New Orleans," *Down Beat 36,* no. 12 (June 1969): 13.

4.   Charles Suhor, "Jazz and the New Orleans Press," *Down Beat 36,* no. 12 (June 1969): 19.

5.   Barry Ulanov, *Handbook of Jazz* (New York: Viking Press, 1959), p. 8.

Another important point is that a given jazz band altered its style according to each job. The music played in some black clubs was considered far too "rough" for the white dances, where the musicians would have to adjust to a more "sweet" style.

In any discussion of New Orleans at about the turn of the century, the name *Storyville* figures prominently. In 1896 a New Orleans alderman, Sidney Story, sponsored a civic ordinance confining the red-light district to a thirty-eight-block section adjoining Canal Street. Undoubtedly Mr. Story was humiliated when the area came to be called Storyville. Some of the larger night spots in this section hired small bands, but mainly solo piano players were employed. However, there was much activity for street bands. Before the Navy closed Storyville in 1917, the district made important contributions to the beginnings of jazz. Contrary to what some writers claim, Storyville was not as important to the origins of jazz as were the religious services.

Instrumental Obligations

There is a certain amount of solo work in dixieland music, but from its very beginnings each of the **frontline** players (cornet, clarinet, and trombone) had a definite obligation to fulfill in ensemble playing.

Since by usual standards it is the loudest instrument in the orchestra, the cornet (or trumpet) played the melody. The cornet player was allowed to "decorate" the melody according to individual interpretation. The melody was usually not altered to the point where it became unrecognizable to the layman.

The clarinet player had a dual role: to play a harmony part, a countermelody above the melodic line carried by the trumpet (a natural task for the clarinet because it can be played at a higher pitch than the trumpet) and to create momentum because the clarinet can be played with more agility than can the two other melodic instruments.

The role delegated to the trombone was to play the most important note in the chord change. One example is in the tune "Indiana." The first chord is composed of the notes F, A, C, D; the second chord moves to F-sharp, A, C, D. The natural resolution for the trombone player is from F to F-sharp, pointing out to the other players that the chord has changed and that this is the change that has occurred.

The banjo, tuba, and drums played straight rhythm parts as they had in the marching bands. No piano was used in these first dixieland groups because they were often the same group that played in the street

marches, where a piano could not be used. For this same reason the tuba rather than the string bass was used.

In example 13, twelve measures are scored in Early New Orleans Dixieland style to point out musically the role assigned to each instrument.

Another identifying feature of the music of this era was that the rhythm section played in a flat four, that is, with no accents, four even beats to a measure (or bar).[6] This is contrary to the belief of many dixieland advocates who believe that all dixieland music uses a 2/4 rhythm with accented afterbeats. One need only to listen to recordings of the King Oliver band (typical of this era) for confirmation that these rhythm sections played with no regularly accented beats.[7] (S, "Dippermouth Blues," side 1, band 6)

Some people believe that Latin rhythm was an element added to jazz in the 1940s by the orchestras of Dizzy Gillespie, Stan Kenton, and others, or in the 1960s when the bossa nova became popular. Actually, the addition of Latin rhythm can be traced to the beginnings of jazz. One example of Latin rhythm in early jazz is the tango section of "St. Louis Blues" written by W. C. Handy in 1914.

Another important aspect was that the frontline players conceived their parts polyphonically (horizontally), as explained in example 8A. It should be noted that the direct roots of the counterpoint in modern jazz are from the music of the dixieland bands and very early classical music since both used the polyphonic approach in construction.

The customary structure of a dixieland format consists of an ensemble chorus, the solo choruses, and a return to the ensemble.

The case is often stated that all dixieland music is composed of improvisational playing. But it can be pointed out that while improvising during ensemble playing, patterns were often established in which a player repeated the same part on the last chorus of the arrangement that was played on the opening chorus. Thus these choruses were played from memory rather than by strict improvisation. In spite of this, this type of music has a feeling of spontaneity.

One of the most interesting aspects of dixieland music is the rhythmic complexity caused by "collective improvisation." Example 14 illustrates the involved

6. Larry Gushee, "King Oliver's Creole Jazz Band," *The Art of Jazz,* ed. Martin Williams (London: Oxford University Press, 1959), p. 45.

7. King Oliver's Creole Jazz Band, "Dippermouth Blues," Smithsonian Collection of Classic Jazz; King Oliver's Savannah Syncopaters, "Snag It," *Introduction to Jazz,* ed. the Reverend A. L. Kershaw, Decca Records, DL8244.

Example 13

syncopation that causes the accents to shift constantly among the three lines being played by the trumpet, clarinet, and trombone.

The King

In this phase of jazz, one musician was designated by his peers to be the "king." He was always a trumpet player. Freddie Keppard succeeded Bolden as king.[8] (NW, "Stock Yard Strut," #269, side 1, band 6) The last trumpeter to be called king was Joe "King" Oliver.

Keppard left New Orleans in 1912, played in Los Angeles in 1914, Coney Island, New York, in 1915, and Philadelphia in 1918. These facts surely dispute the "up-the-river" legend, perpetuated by many jazz writers, that has it that jazz came up the river by steamboat directly to Chicago from New Orleans. Other famous New Orleans players, trombonist Kid Ory, for example, went to Los Angeles before going to Chicago.

8. Freddie Keppard's Jazz Cardinals, "Stock Yard Strut," *Steppin' on the Gas—Rags to Jazz 1913–1927*, New World Records, 269.

Early New Orleans Dixieland (1900–1920)   49

Example 14

The type of jazz played by Joe "King" Oliver exemplifies that performed before and during World War I. It is extremely difficult, however, to obtain recordings that have the exact instrumentation and approach to performance that was popular before 1920 because no instrumental jazz was recorded before 1917. By the time Oliver went into recording studios, his style had been somewhat influenced by the activity in Chicago. He was using two trumpets (Louis Armstrong on a second trumpet) and a piano (Lil' Hardin Armstrong). Nevertheless, his recording output around 1923

(thirty-seven numbers in all) is considered a cornerstone in traditional jazz.

The Early New Orleans Dixieland bands relied more on ensemble than on solo improvisation, certainly less improvisation than Chicago Style Dixieland. Still, every member of a band like Oliver's was a star and capable of good solo improvisation. Yet everyone's solos were considerably shorter than those by Oliver himself. Oliver was the leader and hence the featured attraction. Proof of the esteem in which present-day musicians hold Oliver is that whenever the tune "Dippermouth Blues" is played, the trumpet player must

Joe ("King") Oliver and His Orchestra. Left to right, Baby Dodds, Honore Dutrey, Oliver, Louis Armstrong, Bill Johnson, Johnny Dodds, and Lil' Armstrong. *Courtesy of Orrin Keepnews.*

always play Oliver's choruses note for note or he is not considered to be even playing the right number. Yet Oliver was actually improvising when he recorded the tune.[9] (S, "Dippermouth Blues," side 1, band 6) (FJ, Vol. 2)

Dixieland Jazz Spreads Out

Jazz seemed to become more permanent as it became less localized. Oliver moved to Chicago as did many other well-known bands. The Original Dixieland Jazz Band went to Chicago in 1916, then on to New York in 1917. In fact, The Original Dixieland Jazz Band was the first band to record instrumental jazz instead of merely play background for blues singers; this was in

1917. They were also the first group to go into New York City where they opened at Reisenweber's Cafe (near Columbus Circle) in 1917, and they were the first jazz band to go to Europe (1919). This band consisted of a group of young white musicians who listened very intently to and absorbed what the black bands in the

9. King Oliver's Creole Jazz Band, "Dippermouth Blues," Smithsonian Collection of Classic Jazz; King Oliver, *King Oliver*, Epic Records, LA16003; "Jazzin' Babies Blues," *Jazz Odyssey*, vol. 1; "New Orleans Stomp," and "Where Did You Stay Last Night," *Jazz Odyssey*, vol. 2; King Oliver, "Working Man's Blues," *Folkways Jazz*, vol. 2; "Snake Dance," and "Dippermouth Blues," and "High Society," *Folkways Jazz*, vol. 3; "Sugarfoot Stomp," *Folkways Jazz*, vol. 5; "Sweet Lovin' Man," *Folkways Jazz*, vol. 6; "Froggie Moore," *History of Classic Jazz*, Riverside Records, SDP–11.

Original Dixieland Jazz Band. Left to right, Tony Spargo, Eddie Edwards, Harry Barth, Larry Shields, Nick La Rocca, and Russell Robinson. *Courtesy of Leo Walker.*

New Orleans area were playing. They copied these bands until their own style began to develop.[10] Some jazz critics imply that their music and that of The New Orleans Rhythm Kings was more toward barnyard sounds and clowning. It should be kept in mind, however, that the imitation of barnyard animals was as much "in" at that time as electronic distortion became in years later. The Original Dixieland Jazz Band even recorded a piece called "Barnyard Blues."[11] No matter what may be a listener's stylistic preferences, it would be impossible to deny the great energy and exuberance of The Original Dixieland Jazz Band.

Summary

Although jazz has undergone many changes since its origin, some bands today play jazz almost as it was played at the turn of the century. The Early New Orleans Dixieland style had a great revival in the early 1940s. Prominent in this movement was Lu Watters and his Yerba Buena Jazz Band (based in Oakland, California). This band, like others in the movement, did everything possible to recreate King Oliver's style.

10. Original Dixieland Jazz Band, "At the Darktown Strutters' Ball," *Jazz Odyssey*, vol. 1; *The Original Dixieland Jazz Band*, RCA Victor Records, LPV–547.

11. The Original Dixieland Jazz Band, "Barnyard Blues," *Jazz Odyssey*, vol. 1.

The advocates of this style of jazz refer to their music as the "real" or "pure" jazz. This "purist" jazz school is fairly intolerant, as are other jazz schools. But how, and at what point, with all the borrowings that transpire in jazz and other musical styles, could there be purity? While traveling in England during the summer of 1961, one of the authors found a tremendous emphasis on the "Trad" (traditional) bands in which the musicians imitated the Early New Orleans Dixieland style by using both the instrumentation and interpretation of that time.

Even though the type of jazz known as dixieland started nearly 100 years ago mainly in New Orleans, it is still with us. As a "played-by-ear" combination of European melodies, African rhythms, and European brass marching band sounds, it was, and is, colorful, exciting, and carefree. Dixieland is still being played and listened to with all its standard tunes. Dixieland players portray their music as if the music itself is fun. Maybe that is why it is still so popular.

Additional Reading Resources

Berendt, Joachim. *The New Jazz Book,* pp. 4–12, 32–35.

Buerkle, Jack V., and Barker, Danny. *Bourbon Street Black.*

Dexter, Dave. *The Jazz Story,* pp. 6–19.

Feather, Leonard. *The Book of Jazz,* pp. 30–38.

Francis, André. *Jazz,* pp. 27–34.

Harris, Rex. *Jazz,* pp. 77–93.

Hentoff, Nat, and McCarthy, Albert. *Jazz: New Perspectives on the History of Jazz,* pp. 21–43.

Schuller, Gunther. *Early Jazz: Its Roots and Musical Development,* pp. 63–88.

Stearns, Marshall. *The Story of Jazz,* pp. 33–60.

Note: Complete information including name of publisher and date of publication is provided in the Bibliography.

Additional Record Resources

Bechet, Sidney, *Master Musician.* Bluebird Records, 2 AXM–5516.

Encyclopedia of Jazz on Records, vol. 1. Decca Records, DXSF–7140.

Jazz at Preservation Hall, vol. 2. Atlantic Recordings, S–1409.

King Oliver's Jazz Band. Smithsonian Collection, R–001.

The Original Dixieland Jazz Band. RCA Victor Records, LPU–547.

Suggested Classroom Activities

1. Discuss why New Orleans was important in the development of jazz at the beginning of the twentieth century.

2. At first, early dixieland music used no piano. What was the instrumentation of these bands?

3. Discuss the influence of Storyville upon jazz.

4. Discuss the role each instrument assumed in the overall sound of Early New Orleans Dixieland ensembles.

5. What was the overall plan or design of the music?

6. Listen to the recorded example of the original melody played in Early New Orleans Dixieland style (taped demonstration 10) and answer the following:

   a. Do you hear the steady pulse of the flat four rhythm? Which instruments realize this musical characteristic?

   b. In this dixieland arrangement which instrument is realizing the solo chorus part?

   c. In the return section which instrument is playing the melody?

Listening Guide

From Tape Demonstration 10

Early New Orleans Dixieland

:00 Ensemble chorus (trumpet, clarinet, trombone) (tuba, banjo, and drums keep 4/4 rhythm)
:22 Clarinet solo (one chorus, low register)
:47 Ensemble chorus (same as first chorus)
1:13 End

**From Smithsonian Collection
(side 1, band 5)**

King Oliver's Creole Jazz Band

"Dippermouth Blues" also called "Sugarfoot Stomp"

:00 Introduction—ensemble
:04 Two ensemble choruses—2 cornets, clarinet, trombone; rhythm played by piano, bass, banjo, and drums—4/4 rhythm. True collective improvisation with Oliver on lead cornet. Trombone slides into each chorus.
:33 Two choruses of clarinet solo (Johnny Dodds). The entire rest of the band plays what is called "stop time"; it seems to make the solo more predominant.
1:03 Ensemble chorus, same pattern as first chorus.
1:17 Three choruses of cornet solo by Oliver; note his use of the plunger as a mute for his instrument. The clarinet and trombone also play as in an ensemble chorus, except now they are very soft.
1:58 Vocal break ("Oh play that thing!")
2:00 Ensemble chorus similar to the first chorus but a short tag is added on the end.
2:16 End

6

Ragtime
(1900–1917)

Ragtime music has been considered by some to be outside the jazz tradition because it is completely composed before being performed. But as was pointed out in chapter 1, if jazz has to be improvised to be jazz, then most of the music generally conceded to be jazz would have to be classified as some other style of music. Even without being improvised, ragtime has the "improvisatory feel" that seems so essential to jazz. On the other hand, there are those who consider ragtime to be another name for early jazz.[1] (For an introduction to ragtime, listen to the cassette, demonstration 11, included with this book.)

Ragtime is often said to have originated in Sedalia, Missouri, because of the large number of such players who performed there, even though a great deal of ragtime was played before these performers migrated to Sedalia. When reform government came to Sedalia in 1901, all ragtime activity there ceased. Ragtime, then, predated jazz if Buddy Bolden is considered to be the one who brought the elements of jazz, or at least of dixieland jazz, together.

Ragtime had a direct impact on the development of jazz, but because of its juxtaposition chronologically to Early New Orleans Dixieland, ragtime was really a piano style that developed as a result of special conditions.

Because pianists were not used in the first dixieland bands (evolved from marching bands), the pianists developed a solo style of playing. A piano player was hired in place of a six- or seven-piece band, a circumstance that forced the player to develop a technique that provided a full sound. The left hand had to play both the bass notes and the chords, leaving the right hand free for highly syncopated melodic lines. This playing was much more difficult than merely accompanying a vocalist or instrumentalist in which a pianist was responsible only for the bass notes with the left hand and the chords with the right. The extreme difficulty of the technique, in fact, caused many academic piano players to completely oppose the "unusual" style of ragtime. Examples 15A and 15B point up the difficulty of ragtime interpretation.

In example 15A the accompaniment consists of the bass part confined to the first and third beats and the chords played on the second and fourth beats or **offbeats.** Because of the physical action of the left hand, it became the practice for pianists to accent these offbeats, a technique that led to the new rhythmic style of the following era.

The intricate syncopation demonstrated by these two examples could well have been the reason why this music was called ragtime, meaning "ragged time." This is only one of many versions of the origin of the name **ragtime.** As in the case of the name **jazz,** it is impossible to say which explanation is correct.

1. Guy Waterman, "Ragtime," in *Jazz,* eds. Nat Hentoff and Albert J. McCarthy (New York: Holt, Rinehart, & Winston, 1959), p. 107.

Example 15A

Example 15B

Ragtime was a refreshing change from the usual songs with often commonplace melodies and predictable rhythmic feeling. Unlike many of the blues tunes and some of the spirituals, the mood of ragtime is happy. The country welcomed this happy music because it had just experienced the long depression of the 1890s. The general public first became aware of ragtime during a series of World's Fairs held in Chicago, Omaha, Buffalo, St. Louis, and other cities where peripatetic piano players from the Midwest and the South found employment along the midways. Ragtime flourished for over twenty years. When the music publishing industry (called **Tin Pan Alley**) began to sell "rags," the music was too difficult for uninitiated pianists to play, and had to be considerably simplified in order to sell. Ragtime players frequently earned substantial income teaching ragtime style.

The ragtime players began to migrate to Sedalia, Missouri. As noted earlier, many critics state that ragtime was born in Sedalia, but actually these players merely drifted into the town because of employment opportunities. One player, Tom "Million" Turpin, owned a series of clubs in Sedalia, and he sponsored many other ragtime players. Turpin's "Harlem Rag" (1897) is reputed to be the first rag ever published (some say William Krell's "Mississippi Rag," also published in 1897, was first). When reform came to Sedalia in 1901, many ragtime players moved to St. Louis, which then became the ragtime center of the world.

There is a great deal of controversy about who composed what rag. Possibly, some rags were a compilation of ideas "borrowed" from many players, and the player who had the knowledge to notate the rag on music manuscript received credit for the composition.

An interesting aspect of typical ragtime selections is that they were composed to a definite format, which showed a European influence with its concern for balance and form. Each selection included four themes (or melodies), and each theme had equal stress, equal importance, within the composition. Examples are "Tiger Rag" and "Maple Leaf Rag." This fairly rigid form was probably borrowed from the construction of marches. Ragtime players, both black and white, were expected to be good readers, and sheet music was one of the principal means of disseminating ragtime music.

The most prolific composer of ragtime music was Scott Joplin. Joplin published approximately fifty rags (some say he composed about six hundred). The most famous was "Maple Leaf Rag" (1899), which sold hundreds of thousands of copies in the first ten years of publication.[2] (S, side 1, band 2) Joplin was a schooled musician. Many jazz critics are not aware that he wrote a symphony and two operas. One opera, *Treemonisha,* is still performed today.

A monument in honor of Joplin has been erected in Sedalia, at the site of the old Maple Leaf Club. Some of the citizens of Sedalia expressed concern about the popularity of ragtime since the movie *The Sting.* They seem worried that Joplin's tunes will be associated only with the film and that the composer and the city itself

2. Scott Joplin, "Maple Leaf Rag," Smithsonian Collection of Classic Jazz.

will be lost to obscurity. One hindsight suggestion is that more recognition could have been given Joplin and his music when he was living there instead of sixty years later. Two other very fine ragtime composers are certainly deserving of mention: James Scott and Joseph Lamb.

The best known ragtime piano player was Jelly Roll Morton (Ferdinand de Menthe). In his Library of Congress recordings and on his calling card, Jelly Roll claims that he originated jazz in 1902, and also ragtime, swing, and just about everything else in this area of music. He may not have been that important, but he was surely at the top of the ragtime players. Morton had no peer as a soloist.[3] (S, "Maple Leaf Rag," side 1, band 2), and he also performed successfully with a variety of bands.[4] (S, "Grandpa's Spells," side 1, band 7; "Dead Man's Blues," side 1, band 8)

As soon as their finances permitted, some ragtime pianists formed their own orchestras (Jelly Roll Morton and His Red Hot Peppers, Jelly Roll Morton's Stomp Kings, Jelly Roll Morton's Jazz Band), and some already established jazz bands added piano players (Lil' Hardin, later to be Lil' Armstrong, joined King Oliver's orchestra). As the ragtime bands had to have piano players as leaders, this trend carried over to bands not so involved with ragtime. This was especially true in the Southwest (as examples, Bennie Moten, Count Basie, Jay McShann, and many other piano players were leaders). Morton was an ideal ragtime band leader. He was an excellent piano player, a creative and knowledgeable **arranger,** a fair singer, and had an extremely attractive and outgoing personality. In fact, Morton was the first jazz musician who reputedly planned very precisely what each musician was to play on his recordings, and thus opened the way for recorded arrangements of jazz. The recordings on which he plays piano and talks with folklorist Alan Lomax are important in the history of jazz to the 1930s.[5] "In Jelly Roll Morton, we recognize for the first time in jazz that the personality of the performing musician is more important than the material contributed by the composer."[6] Since ragtime players were becoming bandleaders, the need for more musical schooling for players became obvious.

When the piano players began to play with other instrumentalists, the two music styles, dixieland and ragtime, began to merge. There are many recorded examples of bands playing rag tunes that were primarily meant to be played on a piano. Listen, for example, to Paul Mares's recording of "Maple Leaf Rag," The New Orleans Rhythm Kings' recording of "Tiger Rag," and others.[7] (FJ, Vols. 6 and 3)

Jelly Roll Morton. *Courtesy of Ray Avery.*

Two important changes resulted from the merging of dixieland and ragtime: (1) the basic melodic concept of the rags was changed, and (2) the

3.   Jelly Roll Morton, "Maple Leaf Rag," Smithsonian Collection of Classic Jazz; *Jelly Roll Morton,* Mainstream Records, S/6020.

4.   Jelly Roll Morton, "Grandpa's Spells" and "Dead Man's Blues," Smithsonian Collection of Classic Jazz; "Black Bottom Stomp," Smithsonian Collection of Classic Jazz; Jelly Roll Morton, *The King of New Orleans Jazz,* RCA Victor Records, LPM–1649.

5.   Jelly Roll Morton, *The Saga of Jelly Roll Morton,* Riverside Records, 9001–9012; Smithsonian Collection of Classic Jazz, Columbia Special Products, F6 11891.

6.   From the *Jazz Book: From New Orleans to Rock and Free Jazz* by Joachim Berendt, translated by Dan Morgenstern, copyright 1975 Lawrence Hill & Co., Westport, Connecticut.

7.   Paul Mares, "Maple Leaf Rag," *Folkways Jazz,* vol. 6; New Orleans Rhythm Kings, "Tiger Rag," *Folkways Jazz,* vol. 3; Joe King Oliver, "Snake Rag," *Folkways Jazz,* vol. 3; New Orleans Feetwarmers, "Maple Leaf Rag," *Folkways Jazz,* vol. 11; Papa Celestin, "Original Tuxedo Rag," *Jazz Odyssey,* vol. 1.

rhythmic accentuation indigenous to the rags was carried over into dixieland jazz. As a consequence, a new repertoire was added to the music of the jazz bands, who began to play the rags but altered the form. The first melody became a **verse,** the second and third melodies were omitted completely, and the fourth became a repeated chorus and the basis for improvisation.[8]

The rhythm of the bands changed from a flat-four (four equal pulsations in each measure) to a two-four (2/4) rhythm (four beats to a measure with accents on beats two and four). These measured offbeats correspond to the action of the left hand of the ragtime pianists.

Stride Piano

As we have explained, jazz bands ignored the original construction of the rags. Piano players were no longer compelled to play alone; consequently the piano was considered a part of the jazz band instrumentation. Another factor is that, as tempos were increased, the relaxed feeling of the early ragtime gave way to virtuoso displays. In addition, improvisation, not present in early ragtime, began to gain importance in piano music. The culmination of these developments resulted in what is known as "**stride**" piano, an extension of ragtime. There are three basic differences between stride piano playing and ragtime:

1. Stride players were not at all concerned with ragtime form. They played popular tunes of the day and any other kind of music that appealed to them.

2. Original ragtime was a composed music, whereas stride players were often very proficient improvisers and used this element in their performance.

3. The feeling of stride music was intense because, in general, stride pianists played faster and with much more drive than the more relaxed players of ragtime.

James P. Johnson, composer of the famous tune "Charleston" (among many others), is considered to be the father of stride piano. There are many fine recorded examples of his performances.[9] (S, "Carolina Shout," side 2, band 4) (FJ, "Snowy Morning Blues," Vol. 9) Closely akin to Johnson and usually discussed in superlatives is Willie "The Lion" Smith. We believe, however, that the most entertaining and exciting stride piano player was Thomas "Fats" Waller, a student of Johnson. Waller mugged and clowned incessantly, and

if a purist found this disturbing he merely had to concentrate on the piano playing to hear true artistry and a most energetic rhythmic pulse.[10] (S, "I Ain't Got Nobody," side 4, band 1) (FJ, "Handful of Keys," Vol. 9, "Squeeze Me," Vol. 11) Waller began to accompany blues singers on recordings in 1922. He was Bessie Smith's accompanist on tour and worked for a short time in Fletcher Henderson's orchestra. In 1927 he formed a solo act. His records sold well, and he even performed in motion pictures.

Art Tatum was possibly the best, surely the most versatile, piano player in the history of jazz. It is impossible (thankfully) to put Tatum in a stylistic category, but stride was certainly one of his favorites. His recordings include some of the best stride piano on record.[11] (S, "Willow Weep for Me," side 5, band 1) Some musicians never have the opportunity to record their achievements for posterity. This cannot be said of Tatum. He was hired by Norman Granz for two days of recording in December 1953, and for two days in April 1954. The result was a set of thirteen long-playing records (twenty-six sides). They were released to the public in 1974 (Pablo Records) and are truly an historic event for Tatum followers in particular and for jazz fans in general.[12] Another collection of previously unreleased recordings of Tatum received a Grammy Award from the National Academy of Recording Arts and Sciences as the best solo album of 1973.[13] The collection was recorded on a portable home-recording device by a young friend of Tatum. Some songs were recorded in an apartment and others in various afterhours clubs. The title of the album *God Is in the House*

8. Waterman, "Ragtime," *Jazz,* p. 7.

9. James P. Johnson, "Harlem Strut," *History of Classic Jazz,* vol. 8; "Snowy Morning Blues," *Folkways Jazz,* vol. 9; "Keep off the Grass," *Jazz Odyssey,* vol. 3; "Black Bottom Dance" and "Mr. Freddie Blues," *Piano Roll Hall of Fame,* Sounds Records, LP 1202; "Carolina Shout," Smithsonian Collection of Classic Jazz.

10. Fats Waller, *Ain't Misbehavin',* RCA Victor Records, LPM–1246; "Mama's Got the Blues," *History of Classic Jazz,* vol. 8; "Handful of Keys," *Folkways Jazz,* vol. 9; "Squeeze Me," *Folkways Jazz,* vol. 11; "Draggin' My Poor Heart Around," *Jazz Odyssey,* vol. 11; "Do It Mr. So-and-So," and "If I Could Be With You," *Piano Roll Hall of Fame,* Sounds Records, LP 1202; "The Flat Foot Floogie," *Jazz Story,* vol. 3; Fats Waller, *The Complete Fats Waller,* Bluebird Records, 2AXM–5511; "I Ain't Got Nobody," Smithsonian Collection of Classic Jazz.

11. Art Tatum, *The Art of Tatum,* Decca Records, DL 8715; *Piano Discoveries,* vols. 1 and 2; 20th Fox Records, Fox 3032/3; Art Tatum, "Willow Weep for Me," "Too Marvelous for Words," Smithsonian Collection of Classic Jazz.

12. *The Tatum Solo Masterpieces,* Pablo Recordings, 2625 703.

13. Art Tatum, *God Is in the House,* Onyx Recordings, ORI 205.

Fats Waller. *Courtesy of Orrin Keepnews.*

was taken from a remark made by Fats Waller when Tatum entered a club where Waller was playing. The remark reveals a respect for Tatum that is quite general among musicians. Oscar Peterson, though also difficult to label stylistically, often ventures into some of the best stride piano on record. He is a most talented and versatile musician.

Both Basie and Ellington often went into very authentic stride piano during improvisation. Stride can also be heard in a most interesting manner in the 5/4 excursions of Johnny Guarnieri.[14]

Ragtime Lives On

Ragtime, then, was a style of playing piano solo that coexisted with Early New Orleans Dixieland jazz. It influenced the interpretation of jazz by shifting the rhythm from a flat 4/4 to 2/4 interpretation and by additions to the jazz repertoire, such as "Maple Leaf Rag" and "Tiger Rag."

Ragtime is still played today, and recordings are available from several sources. One source is the recordings of ragtime played today on a **"tack" piano.** A tack piano is a piano altered to sound much older than it is, so that the ragtime sounds more authentic. This is accomplished in various ways. One way is to put thumb tacks in all the felts of the piano hammers. Other ways include laying a light chain across the strings or putting newspaper, aluminum foil, or something similar over the strings.[15] Most such adjustments are quite harmful to the piano felts.

14.   Johnny Guarnieri, *Breakthrough in 5/4,* Bet Records, BLPS–1000.

15.   Phil Moody, *Razz-Ma-Tazz,* Urania Records, UR 9009; Joshua Rifkin, *Scott Joplin Ragtime,* Nonesuch Records, H–71248.

Art Tatum. *Courtesy of Ray Avery.*

Another good ragtime source is the re-pressing of old master recordings by such players as Morton, Joplin, and others.[16] (S, "Grandpa's Spells," side 1, band 8; "Dead Man's Blues," side 1, band 8; "Black Bottom Stomp," side 2, band 1) (FJ, Vols. 5, 9, 11) Many good ragtime and stride players made piano rolls that can be purchased, and recordings made from rolls are quite satisfactory.[17] (S, "Maple Leaf Rag," side 1, band 2)

Another important source is the recordings of old-timers, such as the two-record set called *The Eighty-Six Years of Eubie Blake,* played by Eubie Blake.[18] Eubie Blake, 98 years old in 1981, received the Medal of Freedom from President Reagan in October 1981. After charming the nation as a composer and performer for over seventy-five years, James Hubert Blake died on February 12, 1983 at the age of one hundred.

Interest in authentic ragtime began to wane because some players played the style so fast and aggressively that the original relaxed feeling dissipated, and as a result stride playing became more popular.

Also, the dixieland players had destroyed the important ragtime form. Since 1920, however, revivals of this style continue to bring talented composers and players to public notice.

16. Jelly Roll Morton, "Grandpa's Spells," *Piano Roll Hall of Fame,* Sounds Records, LP1202; "Perfect Rag," *History of Classic Jazz,* vol. 2; "Big Fat Ham," and "Black Bottom Stomp," *Folkways Jazz,* vol. 5; "Tom Cat Blues" and "Wolverine Blues," *Folkways Jazz,* vol. 9; "Kansas City Stomps," *Folkways Jazz,* vol. 11; "London Blues," *Jazz Odyssey,* vol. 1; "Someday Sweetheart," *Jazz Odyssey,* vol. 2; "Grandpa's Spells," "Dead Man's Blues," "Black Bottom Stomp," Smithsonian Collection of Classic Jazz; Scott Joplin, "The Cascades," *History of Classic Jazz,* vol. 2; "Original Rags," *Folkways Jazz,* vol. 11; *History of Classic Jazz,* vol. 2; *The Jazz Story,* vol. 2; *Reunion in Ragtime,* Stereoddities Records, S/1900.

17. *Piano Roll Hall of Fame, Piano Roll Ragtime,* Sounds Records, 1201; Jelly Roll Morton, *Rare Piano Rolls,* Biograph Records, 1004Q; Fats Waller, *Rare Piano Rolls,* vols. 1 and 2, Biograph Records, 1002Q, 1005Q; "Maple Leaf Rag," Smithsonian Collection of Classic Jazz.

18. Eubie Blake, *The Eighty-Six Years of Eubie Blake,* Columbia Records, C2S–847.

The public was more aware of ragtime in 1973 than during any time since 1920 due to a very popular motion picture called *The Sting*. Throughout the movie Scott Joplin's rags established the mood for the period in which the movie was set, and the composer's name once again became a household word. Marvin Hamlisch, the musician who adapted the Joplin rags for the movie, received an "Oscar" award for the best movie score of the year. As he accepted the award, Hamlisch acknowledged his absolute indebtedness and gratitude to Scott Joplin and his genius. Joplin was given screen credits as well. It is sad to know that Joplin died frustrated and penniless.

It is interesting to note that while *The Sting* was set in 1936, ragtime had not been popular since 1920, and that though ragtime had not been played at all in 1936, the music was still most apropos for the movie. It is also interesting to note that a quiet revival of ragtime had preceded the movie. It was common during 1971 and 1972 to hear students in college practice rooms working on the intricacies of "Maple Leaf Rag." After the release of the film, students turned their efforts to "The Entertainer," a piece used extensively in the movie. The authors feel that the revival preceded the movie and that the makers of the movie used the music because of the revival. The important thing, however, is that ragtime is once again popular, to the delight of its present-day practitioners.

At the beginning of this chapter we mentioned that some authorities do not consider ragtime to be jazz. To illustrate this point, in 1974 the Academy of Recording Arts and Sciences gave an award to a ragtime record without placing it in any of their specific award categories. The ragtime record "The Red Back Book" won a "Grammy" for being the best **chamber music** record of 1973. Its competition included string quartets, classical piano duos, and woodwind trios.

The musical example on demonstration 11 of the cassette accompanying this book (see example 2A) is the basis of an interpretation showing ragtime style.

Additional Reading Resources

Blesh, Rudi. *Classic Piano Rags.*

Blesh, Rudi, and Janis, Harriet. *They All Played Ragtime.*

Gammond, Peter. *Scott Joplin and the Ragtime Era.*

Harris, Rex. *Jazz*, pp. 60–72.

Hentoff, Nat, and McCarthy, Albert. *Jazz.*

Hodeir, Andre. *Jazz: Its Evolution and Essence.*

Kimball, Bob, and Bolcum, Bill. *Reminiscing with Sissle and Blake.* Viking Press, 1973.

Rose, Al. *Eubie Blake.* Shermer, 1979.

Shapiro, Nat, and Hentoff, Nat, eds. *The Jazz Makers*, pp. 3–17.

Stearns, Marshall. *The Story of Jazz.*

Ulanov, Barry. *Handbook of Jazz.*

Note: Complete information including name of publisher and date of publication is provided in the Bibliography.

Additional Record Resources

Classical Jazz Piano Styles. RCA Victor Records, LPV–543.

Johnson, James P. *Father of Stride Piano.* Columbia Records, CL 1780.

———. *1917–1921, Rare Piano Rolls,* vol. 1. Biograph Records, 1003Q.

Joplin, Scott. *Joplin.* Biograph Records, 1013/4Q.

Kansas City Piano. Decca Records, DL–9226.

Maple Leaf Rag (Ragtime in Rural America). New World Records, 235.

Morton, Jelly Roll. *The Immortal Jelly Roll Morton.* Milestone Records, MLP 2003.

———. *New Orleans Memories.* Atlantic Records, 2–308.

———. *Stomps and Joys.* RCA Victor Records, LPV–508.

New England Conservatory Ragtime Ensemble. "The Red Back Book," by Gunther Schuller and The New England Conservatory Ragtime Ensemble (playing Scott Joplin music). Angel Records, S–36060.

Waller, Fats. *African Ripples.* RCA Victor Records, LPV–562.

———. *1934–1935.* RCA Victor Records, LPV–516.

Suggested Classroom Activities

1. Compare the musical role of a ragtime pianist with that of a pianist in an instrumental ensemble.

2. How did the techniques of the pianist's left-hand playing alternately bass parts and chords influence the flat-four rhythm played in early dixieland music?

3. Listen to "Grandpa's Spells" as played by Jelly Roll Morton (S, side 1, band 7) and discover the offbeat accents in the left hand. Is this left-hand technique continuous or does it change at times? If there are changes, what are they?

4. Now listen to "Kansas City Stomp" by Jelly Roll Morton (*The King of New Orleans Jazz,* Dixieland Jazz, RCA Victor, LPM–1649) and compare the ragtime rhythm Morton used in his piano playing with that used in his instrumental rendition of "Kansas City Stomp."

5. Usually, how many different themes or melodies are there in ragtime compositions?

6. As a result of the merging of rags and dixieland, what happened to dixieland's rhythm and rag's melodic design?

7. What is stride piano?

8. Listen to "Carolina Shout" (S, side 2, band 4). Is the tempo of the music like a stately march or is it faster? Listen to the left hand. Is it the oompah of the earlier ragtime pianists or is it broken up with irregular and shifting beat patterns?

Listening Guide

**From Taped
Demonstration #11**

Ragtime

:00 to :28—2 choruses of piano solo (tuba, banjo, and drums play 2/4 rhythm)

*From Smithsonian Collection
(side 1, band 2)*

Jelly Roll Morton

"Maple Leaf Rag"

:00 Introduction—driving very hard, influencing a future era to come (Swing)

:11 The A strain—shows Morton to be a master of syncopation

:27 Introduction re-enters, helps to hold framework together

:33 B strain as a relief from A, usually called a bridge.

:52 The A strain again but with noticeable additions in both hands

1:13 Interestingly contrasting section—C

1:34 Repeat of the C section with new variations

1:53 New strain—D—vacillates between a tango and a swing feeling

2:12 Repeat of the D strain, this time in most acceptable stride style

2:32 End

7

Chicago Style Dixieland

(the 1920s)

The closing of Storyville in 1917, a district in New Orleans where a great number of musicians were employed, shifted the heart of the jazz scene to Chicago. By 1918 many musicians had left New Orleans, and when Congress passed the Volstead Act in 1919, prohibiting alcoholic beverages, employment for jazz musicians in New Orleans came to a real halt. Quite a few jazz players drifted to Chicago.

The Roaring Twenties

There was a demand for jazz in Chicago during the Roaring Twenties. Chicago was a prosperous city with many opportunities for employment because of the railroads, stockyards, and mills. Many workers in Chicago had migrated from the South and wanted the type of entertainment they had left behind. King Oliver came to Chicago in 1918 and went to work immediately at the Royal Gardens with Johnson's Creoles from 8 P.M. to 1 A.M., and then every night went to the Dreamland Cafe and worked until 6 A.M..

As an introduction to Chicago Style Dixieland, listen to the cassette demonstration 12 included with this book.

In 1920, the leading national entertainer was Al Jolson, while Bessie Smith was a big success in the Atlanta, Georgia, area. In September of that year, the first radio broadcast took place. Radio soon became a part of many households and did much to popularize jazz in general and some jazz artists in particular.

In the 1920s, recordings were as important as they are today. Although jazz could be heard in several cities, most of the recording was done in New York (blues singers) or on the outskirts of Chicago.

In Los Angeles in 1921, New Orleans trombonist Kid Ory recorded what most historians feel were the first instrumental jazz records by a black band. In 1923, Ory scored another first with his radio broadcasts. Kid Ory trombone solos may sound very rough and dated today, but in his time his playing was so modern that he is credited with freeing the trombone from playing glorified tuba parts and allowing the instrument such choices as long flowing lines and even improvisation with the aid of a plunger mute.[1] (NW, "Ory's Creole Trombone," "Society Blues," 269, side 1, bands 7 and 8) Kid Ory was also a recognized jazz composer. His most famous work became a dixieland standard, "Muskrat Ramble."

In New York around 1924, Fletcher Henderson was organizing recording sessions and accompanying blues singers. Chicago Style Dixieland seeped into New York, too. Trumpeter Red Nichols, trombonist Miff

---

1. Kid Ory, "Ory's Creole Trombone," "Society Blues," *Steppin' on the Gas,* New World Records, 269; "Weary Blues," *History of Classic Jazz,* vol. 10.

Mole, and saxophone-clarinet player Jimmy Dorsey each recorded records that have become jazz classics.[2] (FJ, "Original Dixieland One Step," Vol. 7)

In Detroit around 1927, a band named McKinney's Cotton Pickers featured a fine young saxophonist-arranger, Don Redman. Jean Goldkette had a fairly commercial type of orchestra in spite of the fact that his personnel included such jazz greats as Bix Beiderbecke, Frankie Trumbauer, and Pee Wee Russell.

And in Los Angeles, a former New Orleans Rhythm Kings drummer, Ben Pollack, organized a Chicago Style Dixieland band. Pollack used mainly Chicago musicians like Benny Goodman plus a Texas clique like the Teagardens.

The jazz activity in Kansas City in the twenties is discussed in chapter 9 because it was more truly swing jazz.

To appreciate Chicago Style Dixieland, one must picture the times. It was the Roaring Twenties, what F. Scott Fitzgerald called "the Jazz Age." There were straw hats and arm bands, both Model T and Model A Fords as well as Stutz Bearcats, raccoon coats, and **speakeasies.** Gangsters ruled Chicago during this period, and with the musicians playing in the saloons, there is no question that these same racketeers had a great deal to say about the careers of the musicians.

In spite of the fact that Chicago was almost entirely in the hands of gangsters, these were happy times for the general public. Everything seemed to be based on having fun. In fact, musicians today call dixieland music "happy music." World War I was over, and the big stock market crash of 1929 was not even envisaged. Life seemed to be a party. New dances such as the Charleston and Black Bottom were invented to suit the new energetic music.

Chicago of the gangster period, the Golden Era, saw the first Vitaphone "talkie" movie, Al Jolson's The Jazz Singer, *from Warner Brothers opening in November 1926. Thirteen months later, the Negro weekly the* Chicago Defender *commented on a new-fangled "Amplivox" in a South Side restaurant. It was a machine that reproduced Louis Armstrong's scatting vocal of "Heebie Jeebies." Few musicians recognized the potential popularity of the primitive juke box. And even fewer anticipated the eventual sale of $600 million in records annually, and the millions in fees and royalties payable to the musicians and singers for their services on records.[3]*

The Two Dixieland Styles

There are several technical differences which distinguish Chicago Style Dixieland, developed in the 1920s, from New Orleans Dixieland.

1. A saxophone (usually a tenor saxophone) was added.
2. The guitar replaced the banjo.
3. Fairly elaborate (by comparison) introductions and endings were common.
4. Ease and relaxation in playing style gave way to tension and drive.
5. Individual solos became more important.
6. Rhythm changed from 4/4 to 2/4.

Listen to the cassette to hear these items and compare the two different ways of performing dixieland jazz.

Both dixieland styles used cornet, trombone, clarinet, and drums. The piano was now used in both styles, and the **string bass** had replaced the tuba. The last two changes occurred because the bands that played for dancing no longer played for marching.

The players of the Chicago era preferred the guitar to the banjo. Banjo players made the shift to guitar quite easily, mainly because the type of guitars first played in bands were four-stringed instruments and tuned like banjos. The addition of the tenor saxophone gave more body to ensemble playing and added additional solo color. When one more player is added to an ensemble of twenty or so, the change could go unnoticed. But in early dixieland the front line was only three players; to add another musician to these three made a decided difference.

The Original Dixieland Jazz Band added a baritone saxophone and an alto sax in 1920. The role of the saxophone in ensemble playing was comparable to that of the clarinet, except that its harmony line (or countermelody) was directly under the melodic line of the cornet.

As mentioned before, the rhythmic feel in Chicago Style Dixieland changed from the four even beats in each measure of Early New Orleans Dixieland to measures with accents on the second and fourth beats

2. Red Nichols, "Ida," *The Jazz Story,* vol. 2; Miff Mole, "Original Dixieland One Step," *Folkways Jazz,* vol. 7.

3. Dave Dexter, *The Jazz Story: From the Nineties to the Sixties,* © 1964. By permission of Prentice-Hall, Inc., Englewood Cliffs, N.J.

Example 16

*Early New Orleans Dixieland (no
accents—flat four or 4/4)*

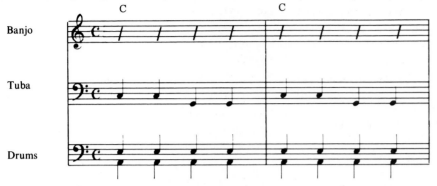

Example 17

*Chicago Style Dixieland (accented 2nd and
4th beats—2/4)*

(or the offbeats) and was called 2/4 rhythm in jazz. The reason for the change was that the bands, no longer used for marching, could hire piano players, and these piano players had been playing ragtime with its accented offbeats. The jazz drummer was now influenced by the addition of the piano, and he began to accent the second and fourth beats. Listen to young drummer Gene Krupa toward the end of the Chicagoans' record of "Nobody's Sweetheart." Krupa, playing in the Chicago style at that time, plays **rim shots** on the second and fourth beats; this is as loudly as he can accent these beats without putting a hole in his drum.[4] (FJ, "Nobody's Sweetheart," Vol. 6) The bass player followed the left hand of the piano and played only on beats one and three. The guitar player played on two and four or, at least, accented two and four to adjust to the piano. Examples 16 and 17 demonstrate the difference between the approaches of the rhythm sections of both styles.

4. Chicagoans, "Nobody's Sweetheart," *Folkways Jazz,* vol. 6.

Earl Hines. *Courtesy of Bob Asen, Metronome Magazine.*

These examples show why jazz-oriented people always clap their hands or snap their fingers on beats two and four instead of on one and three.

Chicago

During the 1920s Louis Armstrong and Earl "Fatha" Hines began a long association, a fact that proves that Armstrong influenced not only all wind players but also piano players.[5] (S, "Weather Bird," side 3, band 1)

Hines developed a way of playing called "trumpet-style" piano because he played with the melodic style so natural to his friend Armstrong instead of that of ragtime or boogie-woogie.

Armstrong was considerably involved in Chicago jazz during the 1920s, and his recordings with the Hot

5. *Louis Armstrong and Earl Hines,* Columbia Records, CL 853; "Weather Bird," Smithsonian Collection of Classic Jazz; *The Father Jumps.* (Hines, Earl) Bluebird Records, AXM 2–5508.

Five and Hot Seven are truly jazz classics.[6] (S, "Sweethearts on Parade," side 3, band 2; "I Gotta Right to Sing the Blues," side 3, band 3; "Potato Head Blues," side 2, band 7; "S.O.L. Blues," side 2, band 6; "West End Blues," side 2, band 9; "Struttin' with Some Barbecue," side 2, band 5) But Armstrong is a good example of a musician who cannot and should not be categorized so narrowly. He had been a member of King Oliver's band earlier, and then later had a famous swing band. His last band was a dixieland group, one of the most enjoyable in the history of jazz.[7]

The period of the 1920s brought many professionally trained instrumentalists into jazz. Until this time, jazz had been a predominantly black art form. The only formally trained black musicians, with the exception of a few piano players, were the Creole performers. With the advent of Chicago Style Dixieland, large numbers of white players with formal musical training entered the jazz field.

As is the case with every new style of jazz, Chicago Style Dixieland brought into jazz many youngsters who were avid fans of the jazz groups who had moved into Chicago. There was a high school clique called the "Austin High Gang." The group formed an important nucleus in the development of this style. Among these young players were Pee Wee Russell, Dave Tough, Bud Freeman, Gene Krupa, Eddie Condon, Mezz Mezzrow, and their friends Benny Goodman, Bix Beiderbecke, Muggsy Spanier, and Bunny Berigan—a group of talented young players for the jazz roster. A jazz historian could never find more enthusiasm than these young Chicago players had for their brand of music. However, by comparison with other styles of jazz, the recordings of these musicians simply do not exemplify either their energetic feeling or musicianly technique.

As Benny Goodman grew up in the hurried pace of Chicago in the twenties, he patterned his early efforts after Jimmy Noone of New Orleans and Frank Teschemacher of Chicago's Austin High Gang, but he soon surpassed his models and went on to become the "King" of the Swing Era.

One of the best and most popular groups in the Chicago era was named the New Orleans Rhythm Kings, even though they never played in New Orleans.[8] (FJ) This group influenced and inspired many young musicians in the vicinity of Chicago. It should be noted that combos such as this one and the personnel from Austin High School played in downtown Chicago, while Armstrong and Oliver reigned on the south side of town. Whereas the Original Dixieland Jazz Band denied (falsely) being influenced by black musicians, the New Orleans Rhythm Kings stated that they did whatever they could to sound like Oliver and others. It also appears that the New Orleans Rhythm Kings were a link between the New Orleans players and the roster of players entering jazz in the Chicago days. They were actually more important as an influence than as individual players; in other words, those players they influenced often surpassed them.[9]

Bix Beiderbecke

Until Beiderbecke came to Chicago, the best white trumpet player was Francis Spanier, a youngster who followed Armstrong every hour possible. Armstrong nicknamed him "Muggsy." His recordings are some of the best examples of the way these young players attempted to play. The music has great vitality and creativeness, and yet it was meant to be and truly is "fun" listening.[10]

Leon "Bix" Beiderbecke was born in 1903 and lived for only twenty-eight years; his name on a record makes it a collector's item. It is said that his style was fairly well formed from listening to records of The Original Dixieland Jazz Band and others before he had heard Armstrong. In Chicago, he listened to Oliver, Armstrong, and The New Orleans Rhythm Kings. Some historians state that Beiderbecke developed his style from listening to Emmet Hardy. Hardy played on the riverboats that stopped at Davenport, Iowa, Beiderbecke's hometown. Beiderbecke's first employment was with a group called The Wolverines, whose first recordings were made in 1924.[11] (FJ, "Jazz Me Blues," Vol. 6)

6. *Louis Armstrong and His Hot Five,* Columbia Records, CL 851, Louis Armstrong, "Struttin' with Some Barbecue," "S.O.L. Blues," "Potato Head Blues," "West End Blues," "Sweethearts on Parade," "I Gotta Right to Sing the Blues," Smithsonian Collection of Classic Jazz.

7. *Louis Armstrong Plays W. C. Handy,* Columbia Records, CL 591.

8. New Orleans Rhythm Kings, "Sweet Lovin' Man," *Folkways Jazz,* vol. 6; "Livery Stable Blues," *History of Classic Jazz,* vol. 4; Dave Dexter, *The Jazz Story,* p. 34.

9. New Orleans Rhythm Kings, "Tin Roof Blues," *Introduction to Jazz,* Della Records, DL 8244.

10. Muggsy Spanier, "Muskrat Ramble," *History of Classic Jazz,* vol. 9.

11. Wolverine Orchestra, "Jazz Me Blues," *Folkways Jazz,* vol. 6; The Wolverines, "Royal Garden Blues," *History of Classic Jazz,* vol. 7; *Bix Beiderbecke and the Wolverines,* Riverside Records, RLP 12–133.

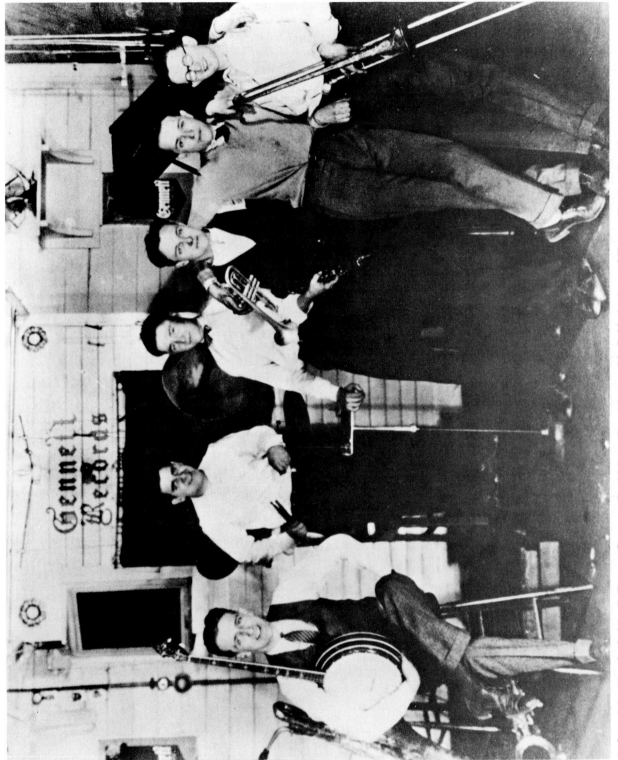

Left to right, Howdy Quicksell, Tommy Gargano, Paul Mertz, Don Murray, Bix Beiderbecke, and Tommy Dorsey. *Courtesy of Leo Walker.*

Beiderbecke worked for a while with his close friend saxophonist Frankie "Tram" Trumbauer. Trumbauer soon became dedicated to looking after Beiderbecke's welfare, guiding him to the big bands of Jean Goldkette and Paul Whiteman where top salaries were to be had. Some of Beiderbecke's best records were done with small combos "outside" his regular job with Whiteman. Especially notable are those with Trumbauer.[12] Beiderbecke's piano compositions show Debussy's influence, the best known of which is "In a Mist." On the cornet, Beiderbecke never seemed to let his style become as dramatic or sensual as Armstrong's. Instead, his cornet music is usually described as poetic, fluid, moving, and sensitive—if words can ever truly describe music.[13] (FJ, "Somebody Stole My Gal," "Margie," Vol. 6)

Many writers refer to Beiderbecke as the first "cool" artist. It is true that even though he could move an ensemble almost by himself, he usually did not play with the frenzy of most of the Chicago Style trumpets. This situation could be compared to that of Miles Davis during the Bop Era when Dizzy Gillespie's virtuosic style was in vogue.

Summary

To this day Chicago Style Dixieland music has not lost its appeal, due primarily to its rhythmic concept. When dixieland is played today, it is almost always Chicago Style. Many musicians are not even aware of the fact that there is more than one style of dixieland. There are clubs and societies dedicated to the preservation of dixieland music. However, this music is seldom played exactly as it was in the 1920s. The musicians have lived through other jazz eras, all of which have become part of their musical personalities. Of course, jazz musicians have always been more concerned about playing with good expression than about playing "authentically." Many seventeen- and eighteen-year-old musicians accept this style as the best way to express themselves and play Chicago Style Dixieland very well.[14] Today, this tradition is carried on most admirably by such groups as The World's Greatest Jazz Band and The Dukes of Dixieland and by individuals like Bobby Hackett.[15]

The style was perpetuated by large orchestras such as the Dorsey Brothers' orchestra and Bob Crosby's orchestra. Bob Crosby built a reputation on a big-band version of this small-band style.[16] In larger orchestras, complete sections play written parts based on lines originally invented for one instrument. This is an example of one style of jazz influencing the styles that followed.

Recording companies have not reproduced Chicago Style Dixieland records with nearly the same enthusiasm that they have Early New Orleans Dixieland, blues singers, and swing bands. Of the records that are available, there is more to be said for the soloists than for the ensemble passages.[17] This seems incongruous when one hears the excellence of ensembles on exceptional records like those of Muggsy Spanier.

Some writers feel that the "jazz age" ended about 1927. Although jazz did continue, the large bands began to absorb the better jazz players (for example, Beiderbecke joined the famous Paul Whiteman Orchestra). By the end of the 1920s, the heart of the jazz scene had again moved, this time from Chicago to New York.

Additional Reading Resources

Berton, Ralph. *Remembering Bix: A Memoir of the Jazz Age.*

Dexter, Dave. *The Jazz Story,* pp. 30–55.

Harris, Rex. *Jazz,* pp. 189–96.

Henthoff, Nat, and McCarthy, Albert, eds. *Jazz,* pp. 139–69.

Schuller, Gunther. *Early Jazz: Its Roots and Musical Development,* pp. 175–94.

Sudhalter, Richard M., and Evans, Philip R. *Bix: Man and Legend.*

Williams, Martin T., ed. *The Art of Jazz,* pp. 59–73.

Note: Complete information including name of publisher and date of publication is provided in the Bibliography.

12. *The Bix Beiderbecke Story,* vols. 1 to 3, Columbia Records, CL 844–6.

13. Bix Beiderbecke, "Somebody Stole My Gal" and "Margie," *Folkways Jazz,* vol. 6.

14. The Windjammers, *Jammin' with the Windjammers,* Argo Records, LP-4047.

15. *The World's Greatest Jazz Band,* Atlantic Records, 1570; *The Dukes of Dixieland,* Audio Fidelity Records, 5962, 5976; Harmony Music Records, 11149; Bobby Hackett, "Struttin' with Some Barbecue," *The Jazz Story,* vol. 2.

16. Bob Crosby, *Stomp It Off, Let's Go,* Mono Records, AH 29; *Greatest Hits,* Decca Records, 74856; "Maryland My Maryland," *The Jazz Story,* vol. 4; *Mardi Gras Parade,* Monmouth-Evergreen Records, 7026.

17. *The Best of Dixieland,* RCA Victor Records, LSP-2982.

See Appendix A for complete arrangement.

Additional Record Resources

Louis Armstrong. RCA Victor Records, VPM–6044.

Bix Beiderbecke and the Chicago Cornets (4 sides). Milestone Records, M–47019.

The Bix Beiderbecke Legend. RCA Victor Records, LPM–2323.

Chicagoans (1928–1930). Decca Records, 79231.

Chicago Ramblers. *Jazz of the 20's.* Merry Makers Records, 103.

Crosby, Bob. *Stomp Off, Let's Go.* Ace of Hearts Records, AH–29.

Dukes of Dixieland. *At the Jazz Band Ball.* RCA Victor Records, LSP–2097.

Encyclopedia of Jazz on Records, vols. 1 and 2.

Folkways Jazz, vols. 5, 6, and 7. Folkways Records, FJ 2805, 6, 7.

Hackett, Bobby. *The Hackett Horn.* Epic Records, EE 22004.

History of Classic Jazz, vols. 4, 6, 7, and 9.

Jazz Odyssey, vol. 2.

Jazz Story, vols. 1 and 2.

Ruedebusch, Dick. *Mister Trumpet.* Jubilee Records, 5015.

————. *Meet Mr. Trumpet.* Jubilee Records, 5008.

Suggested Classroom Activities

1. Who recorded the first instrumental jazz records by a black band?

2. Describe Chicago during the Roaring Twenties.

3. Musically, in what ways did the Chicago Style Dixieland music differ from the Early New Orleans Dixieland style?

4. In what way did ragtime piano playing influence the rhythm of Chicago Style Dixieland music?

5. In this era, what instruments were added to and what instruments replaced other instruments used in Early New Orleans Dixieland ensembles? Why did these changes take place?

6. Gradually, short solo spots crept into jazz ensembles. Listen to "Maple Leaf Rag" by Paul Mares and his Friars' Society Orchestra (Folkways Records, FJ 2806, vol. 6, Chicago no. 2). Identify the instruments that you hear in brief solo spots. Does the piano have an opportunity to play solo? Is there a string bass?

7. Listen to Bix Beiderbecke and His Gang play "Margie" (Folkways Records, FJ 2806, vol. 6, Chicago no. 2). In the opening statement of the melody, which instrument is featured? Is this a good example of the 2/4 rag rhythm? Notice that a bass sax is used in place of a tenor sax.

Listening Guide

From Taped Demonstration 12

Chicago Style Dixieland

:00 Introduction (trombone glissando leading into following chorus)

:05 Ensemble chorus (trumpet, clarinet, trombone, tenor sax) (string bass, guitar, piano, and drums keep 2/4 rhythm)

:19 Trumpet solo (one chorus)

:34 Trombone solo (one chorus)

:48 Ensemble chorus (same as first chorus)

1:03 End

From Smithsonian Collection
(side 2, band 9)

Louis Armstrong

"West End Blues"

:00 Armstrong on solo trumpet cadenza as introduction

:13 Ensemble chorus. Trumpet plays melody, clarinet and trombone mainly play sustained notes as harmony. Rhythm plays 4/4 with piano, banjo, bass, and drums

:49 Trombone solo. Rhythm section plays 4/4 except drummer who attains special effects by hitting blocks and other various items

1:21 Voice (Armstrong) and low register clarinet alternate measures, rhythm in 4/4

1:55 Earl Hines plays a piano solo

2:07 Hines (on piano) goes into his recognizable style of octaves in the right hand, mainly double-time

2:28 Ensemble chorus—trumpet, clarinet, trombone all play long sustained notes, 4/4 rhythm

2:40 Trumpet goes into more of a solo while others continue their sustained notes

2:52 Hines plays a short solo piano interlude

3:00 Trumpet, then other ensemble instruments join in

3:10 End

8

Boogie-Woogie
(the 1920s and 1930s)

Boogie-woogie is another stage in the evolution of jazz, and like ragtime it is a piano style important in the development of jazz. The term *boogie-woogie* itself is very descriptive. Although historically, the term is used by Rousas Rushdoony in reference to ancient rites in Morocco[1], the musical association is the feeling created by playing eight beats to the bar. This style of piano playing came into prominence during an economic crisis—the Great Depression of the early 1930s. Jazz again faced a situation in which a full style of piano playing was needed as a substitute for hiring a band. For an introduction to boogie-woogie, listen to the cassette (demonstration 13) included with this book.

Ostinato Bass

The most identifying feature of boogie-woogie is the eight beats to a measure that are played as an **ostinato.** *Ostinato* (an Italian word) is the technical term for a melodic figure that recurs throughout the music. The *ostinato* is a structural device that works as a stylistic coherence for the composition.

In boogie-woogie piano playing, this *ostinato phrase* is always in the bass. It is very possible, however, to hear boogie-woogie played by a big band when the *ostinato* is not present; there will still be eight beats to the bar. Distinguished from jazz played in the even 4/4 rhythm of Early New Orleans Dixieland or the 2/4 rhythm of ragtime and Chicago Style Dixieland, boogie-woogie employs eight beats to the bar in the *ostinato.*

There are two distinct methods of boogie-woogie playing. In both, the right hand is kept free for melodic interpretation or improvisation. The difference between the two methods occurs in the use of the left hand. In one, the left hand plays full, moving chords; in the other, a **"walking" bass** line outlines the chords in a melodic fashion. Examples 18A and 18B demonstrate the use of full chords. There are various means of outlining the chords with a melodic bass line. Examples 18C, 18D, and 18E illustrate three of the most common.

Although the right hand can play an interesting melodic line, the main feature of this style is rhythmic virtuosity. The left hand and the right hand operate so independently that boogie-woogie often sounds like it is being performed by two pianists instead of by one. The style is extremely taxing physically, since it is usually played loudly with tensed muscles—a most tiring means of performing. The **riff** emphasis, typical of Kansas City (to be discussed in chapter 9) is often heard in the right hand of the boogie-woogie player as the left hand busies itself with the *ostinato.* Boogie-woogie is generally, but not always, played in the blues form.

---

1. Rousas J. Rushdoony, *The Politics of Pornography* (Sandtron City, Sandtron, South Africa: Valiant Publishers, 1975) p. 98.

The Players

Boogie-woogie was usually played by untrained pianists. Ragtime had incorporated European influences, but it appears as though boogie-woogie piano players worked out their style without any thought of European concert tradition. Many could not read music; they simply listened and developed this full style of playing. Most of the time boogie-woogie players were comfortable playing only this one style of jazz. However, Pete Johnson, who was surely the number one boogie-woogie

pianist in Kansas City, was also a fine stride player. He really showed his versatility when he accompanied blues singer Joe Turner hour after hour.[2]

While it is true that boogie-woogie reached its peak of popularity during the depression of the early 1930s, the style surely was not invented then. The first time that the word *boogie* appears to have been used on a record was in 1928 by Chicago's Pine Top Smith as he recorded "Pine Top's Boogie."[3] (NW, side 1, band 4, 259) Huddie Ledbetter claimed that he first heard this type of playing in 1899; Bunk Johnson (an early New Orleans trumpeter) said 1904; Jelly Roll Morton said 1904; W. C. Handy said 1909. This music has also been called "Western rolling," "fast Western," and "Texas style," indicating that its origin was in the western part of the country, although Florida has also been named as a birthplace. Boogie-woogie has also been called "8 over 4." Example 19A shows the logic of this label in printed music where the meter signature is indicated correctly as 4/4. The boogie-woogie pianist super-imposes eight beats in the same 4/4 measure because he feels the individual eighth notes as single beats. It would be most correct to say that the pianist plays and feels the music as 8 beats to the bar or written with 8/8 meter as shown in 19B.

There were three fairly defined generations of boogie-woogie players. The earlier pianists were active primarily in the 1920s: Jimmy Yancey, Cow Cow Davenport, and Pine Top Smith.[4] (NW, Jimmy Yancey,

2. Joe Turner and Pete Johnson, "Roll 'Em Pete," Columbia Records 35959; "Johnson and Turner Blues," *Jazz of Two Decades,* EmArcy Records, DEM–2.

3. Pine Top Smith, "Pine Top's Boogie," *Encyclopedia of Jazz on Records,* vol. 1; side 1, band 4, *Cuttin' the Boogie,* New World Records, 259.

4. Jimmy Yancey, "The Fives," *History of Classic Jazz,* vol. 5; "Yancey Stomp," *Folkways Jazz,* vol. 10; "The Mellow Blues," "Tell 'Em About Me," side 2, bands 3 and 4, New World Records, 259.

Example 18A

Example 18B

Example 18C

Example 18D

Example 18E

Example 19A

Example 19B

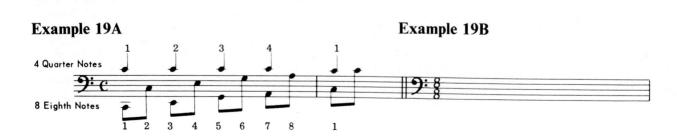

4 Quarter Notes

8 Eighth Notes

Meade Lux Lewis. *Courtesy of Bob Asen, Metronome Magazine.*

"The Mellow Blues," "Tell 'Em About Me," side 2, bands 3 and 4, 259) (FJ, "Yancey Stomp," Vol. 10) The middle group was popular during the early 1930s: Meade Lux Lewis, Albert Ammons, Joe Sullivan, Clarence Lofton, and Pete Johnson.[5] (S, "Honky Tonk Train," side 4, band 2) (NW, 259, side 1, band 6) (FJ, Vols. 9 and 10) The last group included such players as Freddie Slack, Cleo Brown, and Bob Zurke.

5. Meade Lux Lewis, "Honky Tonk Train," Smithsonian Collection of Classic Jazz; "Honky Tonk Train," *Cuttin' the Boogie*, New World Records, 259; "Special No. 1," *Folkways Jazz*, vol. 9; "Honky Tonk Train," *Folkways Jazz*, vol. 10; "Far Ago Blues," *History of Classic Jazz*, vol. 5; Albert Ammons, "St. Louis Blues," *Folkways Jazz*, vol. 10; Joe Sullivan, "Little Rock Getaway," *Folkways Jazz*, vol. 9; Clarence Lofton, "Brown Skin Gal," *Folkways Jazz*, vol. 10; "Blue Boogie," *History of Classic Jazz*, vol. 5; Pete Johnson, "Let 'Em Jump," *Folkways Jazz*, vol. 10; "Lone Star Blues," *History of Classic Jazz*, vol. 5.

Origin

Max Harrison states that this style of piano playing developed from a guitar technique used in mining, logging, and turpentine camps.[6] When three guitar players performed together, one picked out an improvised melody, the second played rhythmic chords, and the third played a bass line. In order to imitate three guitars at one time, piano players had to develop a very full style by having the right hand play the melodic improvisation and the left hand substitute for the other two guitars. In examples 18A and 18B, the bass line originally played by the third guitar is omitted; however, this is not apparent because the moving chords cause the music to sound very full and complete. In examples 18C, 18D, and 18E, the left hand plays the bass line while actually outlining the chords. The notes in example 20A are outlined in 20B.

Although boogie-woogie is considered a definite piano style, it has been successfully adapted by large bands such as Will Bradley's, Lionel Hampton's, Tommy Dorsey's, Count Basie's, Harry James's, Glenn Miller's, and others.[7] The eight beats to the bar created by the *ostinato* bass is considered its most important feature. This rhythmic component exemplifies the fact that jazz players are always searching for new means of expression. However, having been created within a fairly limited set of circumstances (the guitar origin), regardless of the rhythmic interest, the range of expression of this style is not very wide. Boogie-woogie has never really disappeared, though it is not prominent today. One major revival occurred as late as 1938.

Example 20A

Example 20B

Example 21

Summary

This music has not evolved further. If it were to change rhythmically, it would no longer be considered boogie-woogie. It could progress harmonically, but because of the very mechanics of performing this style, most players are only comfortable with quite simple harmonies. In fact, since the beginnings of this style, the standard chord sequence has been the blues chord progression; this is still true today.

The boogie-woogie revival around 1938 was so popular that almost all performing groups had at least one number in their repertoire. Some boogie-woogie pianists toured and even played in such notable concert halls as Carnegie Hall. Pete Johnson, Meade Lux Lewis, and Albert Ammons perform a boogie-woogie trio on the *Spirituals to Swing* album, which was recorded live at Carnegie Hall.[8] It seems that when three of these stylistic players perform at the same time, they almost try to outshout each other. In their exuberance they even lose the eight-to-the-bar feeling. The revival was a boon to these players and certainly raises a pertinent question: why, whenever a style or a group of artists *enjoy and benefit* from great popularity, do so many critics and unrealistic students of jazz claim "exploitation"?

The theme (example 2A) is now used as a basis for improvisation in the boogie-woogie style. Example 21 shows the bass pattern used by the pianist on taped demonstration 13.

6.   Max Harrison, "Boogie Woogie," in *Jazz,* eds. Nat Hentoff and Albert McCarthy (New York: Holt Rinehart & Winston, 1959), p. 107.

7.   Will Bradley, "Beat Me Daddy, Eight to the Bar," Columbia Records, 35530; Lionel Hampton, "Hamp's Boogie Woogie," Decca Records, 71828; Tommy Dorsey, "Boogie Woogie," RCA Victor Records, 26054; Count Basie, "Boogie Woogie," *The Best of Basie,* Roulette Records, R52081; Harry James, "Boo Woo," Columbia Records, 35958; Glenn Miller, "Bugle Woogie," *The Glenn Miller Chesterfield Shows,* RCA Victor Records, LSP–3981 (e).

8.   Pete Johnson, Albert Ammons, and Meade Lux Lewis, "Cavalcade of Boogie," *Spirituals to Swing,* Vanguard Records, VRS-8523/4.

Additional Reading Resources

Hentoff, Nat, and McCarthy, Albert, eds. *Jazz,* pp. 107–35.

Williams, Martin T. ed. *The Art of Jazz,* pp. 95–108.

Note: Complete information including name of publisher and date of publication is included in the Bibliography.

Additional Record Resources

Boogie Woogie. Folkways Records, FJ 2810.

Boogie Woogie, History of Classic Jazz, vol. 5. Riverside Records, SDP–11.

Boogie Woogie Piano: Original Recordings 1938–40. Columbia Records, KC–32708.

Boogie Woogie Rarities. Milestone Records, MLP–2009.

Cuttin' the Boogie. New World Records, 259.

Pitchin' Boogie. Milestone Records, MLP–2018.

Suggested Classroom Activities

1. Define the term *boogie-woogie* as applied to piano technique.

2. In this style of piano technique, how many beats are in each measure?

3. Describe two methods of boogie-woogie playing in the bass part or left-hand piano part.

4. Listen to "Yancey Stomp" by pianist Jimmy Yancey (*Jazz,* vol. 10, Folkways Records, Album no. FJ 2810).

5. Listen to "Honky Tonk Train" (S, side 4, band 2) and decide whether the left hand ostinato bass is in the "walking bass" style of boogie or in the "choral bass" style.

Listening Guide

From Taped Demonstration 13

Boogie-Woogie

:00 to :36 2 choruses on solo piano (note the left hand is playing 8 beats to the bar while utilizing what is known as the "Wagon Wheels" pattern) (drums play 8/8 rhythm)

From Smithsonian Collection (side 4, band 2)

Meade Lux Lewis

"Honky Tonk Train"

:00 Piano solo throughout. Trill for short introduction

:02 Chorus #1—left hand playing "full moving chords" pattern, right hand playing melodically and very independently

:19 Chorus #2—Lewis shows his control by playing six beats with the right hand while playing eight beats with the left. This occurs often on this record

:36 Chorus #3

:53 Chorus #4—Picks up last small idea from previous chorus and expands on it

1:10 Chorus #5—Uses trills and shows extreme independence of hands

1:27 Chorus #6—Shows a small thought then develops a technical display

1:44 Chorus #7—Many full chords and use of the "6 against 8" as in chorus #2

2:02 Chorus #8—Similar to chorus #7

2:19 Chorus #9

2:36 Chorus #10—Getting softer, seems to be tapering down, preparing to stop

2:57 End

9
Swing
(1932–1942)

Swing is the name given to the era following boogie-woogie in the development of jazz. In general, *swing* refers to large dance bands that played written arrangements, occasionally using improvised solos. Some jazz terms can become quite confusing; *swing* is one of them. Most noteworthy jazz has a rhythmic drive called swing. Still, the era of jazz in the thirties and early forties is called the Swing Era.

The confusion comes from the fact that some of the most popular swing music did not swing, but involved jazz players doing a jazz interpretation of pretty **ballads.** One of the unusual aspects of swing jazz is that though most people remember the **up-tempo** tunes, the swing bands actually played more ballads than anything else. But it should be remembered that those ballads were played by players who were very jazz-oriented. Listen, for example, to Benny Goodman, the King of Swing, play his theme, a very pretty ballad called "Good-bye"; jazz trumpeter Harry James plays an **obligato** in the background.[1]

Some listeners today feel that all of the swing bands sound alike. During the Swing Era, there were literally hundreds of name attractions, and so one of the biggest concerns for the leaders was identification. They wanted the fans to be able to distinguish their band from all other bands after hearing just a few measures of music. Therefore, most bands attempted to have an identifying trademark. For example, Tommy Dorsey probably played with a more beautiful tone and control on the trombone than anyone else; so he played solos

on just about every arrangement and the fans recognized his sound.[2] Glenn Miller used a clarinet playing lead over his saxophone section, a most identifying feature.[3] (As an introduction to swing, listen to demonstration 14 on the cassette included with this book.)

Beginnings of the Swing Era

Fletcher Henderson proved most influential in the Swing Era, and he is credited with having created, along with Don Redman, the pattern for swing arrangements.[4] That this pattern was successful is demonstrated by the fact that it was copied by almost every popular dance band of the era. Henderson is said to have established the independent use of the trumpet section, trombone section, saxophone section, rhythm section, together with the use of soloists. This exact same format is used today by most of the thousands of college and high school jazz bands around the country. The attitude (also fostered by music publishers) seems to be that this is the only avenue possible for today's jazz.

1. Benny Goodman, "Good-bye," *The Great Band Era,* RCA Victor Records, RD4–25 (RRIS–5473).

2. Tommy Dorsey, "I'm Gettin' Sentimental Over You," *The Great Band Era.*

3. Glenn Miller, "Moonlight Serenade," *The Great Band Era.*

4. Nat Shapiro and Nat Hentoff, eds., *The Jazz Makers* (New York: Grove Press, 1957), p. 118.

Fletcher Henderson and His Orchestra. Henderson is on the extreme right. *Courtesy of Ray Avery.*

In New York in 1924, Fletcher Henderson had Louis Armstrong, Coleman Hawkins, and Don Redman among his very exclusive personnel. In 1924 in Kansas City, Benny Moten put together his first saxophone section as such; the idea was simply to create more sonority. Moten added more brass as early as 1931, using three trumpets and two trombones. Henderson had done the same thing in 1929. Some say that the first jazz orchestra to play written arrangements in New York City was the Billy Paige Band with Don Redman as arranger and lead alto sax, in 1922. Redman then joined Fletcher Henderson, stayed with him until 1927, joined McKinney's Cotton Pickers in 1931, and eventually organized his own band. Henderson, Redman, and others took the parts that were generally conceived to be for one trumpet, for example, and harmonized them to be played by three trumpets (see examples 22A and 22B).

Jazz Arrangements

The general procedure in the creation of a swing jazz arrangement is to write a score (see example 23) in which specific notes are planned for each instrument to play in every measure. In jazz, the music arranger indicates measures for solo improvisation. After the arranger has decided what musical notations will result in the desired sounds, he gives the score to a music copyist who extracts from the score the individual parts for the various instruments. This then becomes a blueprint for each instrumentalist, and it shows him exactly what he is to play while the other instrumentalists play their parts.

Example 22A

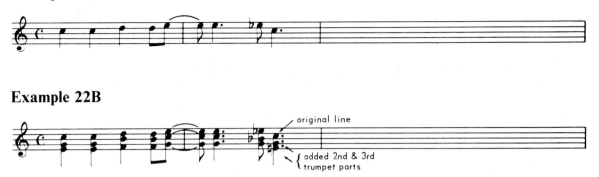

Example 22B

Short repeated refrains or phrases are quite typical in African music. In jazz, the phrases are called **riffs.** Sometimes riffs are used in an *ostinato* fashion as catalysts that hold the music together. Repeated riffs, which cause great momentum and impetus, were used extensively by Kansas City musicians such as Benny Moten (later Count Basie's band) in the 1920s and by New York musicians such as Fletcher Henderson who was scoring arrangements behind blues singers Bessie Smith, Ma Rainey, and others. The use of riffs became standard in the more jazz-oriented large bands. Sometimes they were used to back up a soloist; sometimes entire selections were made up of riffs. Listen to the swing excerpt on the cassette demonstration 14 supplied with the text in which the brass section plays the riff shown in example 24A behind the saxophones. The trombones play the riff shown in example 24B under the clarinet solo.

Fletcher Henderson

Fletcher Henderson, a schooled piano player from Georgia, came to New York City in 1920 originally to do postgraduate study at Columbia University as a chemistry major. Duke Ellington, from Washington, D.C., had a scholarship to the Pratt Institute of Art. Both Ellington and Henderson became so involved in music that their other goals were forsaken. Henderson was a pianist, but his most important talent was his arranging. He wrote most of the library of music that launched the career of the Benny Goodman orchestra. The personnel of Henderson's own orchestra was most impressive. At one time or another almost all of the important black musicians of the day played in his band: Louis Armstrong, Roy Eldridge, Don Redman, Coleman Hawkins, and Lester Young. Many members from the Henderson band went on either to have bands of their own or to become featured solo attractions.[5]

There always seem to be many (too many) controversies concerning jazz. Fletcher Henderson became deeply involved in one of the great controversies: the split between the advocates of small dixieland bands and those favoring the larger bands heading in the direction of swing. Many thought that the rise of the big bands meant the fall of jazz completely. The small band advocates considered these large ensembles "top-heavy" because of the unusually large number of horn players. Not only was the rhythm section now outnumbered, but as the ensembles grew in size, the arrangements tended to become more detailed to provide a tighter ensemble sound. With the larger number of musicians, the dixieland texture, which granted each player a great deal of individual expression, was no longer possible. The solo areas in a swing band composition offered chances for individual expression but they were only a small part of the whole composition. (See chapter 19 on criticism.)

At first, Henderson toyed with sort of an enlarged dixieland group. But with the addition of Don Redman, who had studied at the Boston and Detroit Music Conservatories, tighter harmonic control became a major interest. Henderson thought that too much improvisation was almost dreary, unless the improvisers were really exceptional. He also thought that the polyphony established in the dixieland styles was too risky, that there should be more control.

New York

During the 1920s when Chicago Style Dixieland was the most popular jazz expression, New York and Kansas City were the most important geographic areas for developments leading toward the swing style of jazz. In

5. Fletcher Henderson, *A Study in Frustration,* Columbia Records, C4L–19; *Fletcher Henderson,* vols. 1 and 2, Decca Records, 79227–8; Fletcher Henderson, *Developing an American Orchestra, 1927–1947,* Smithsonian Collection R–006.

Example 23

Example 24A

Example 24B

the mid-1920s, Ellington was becoming a name attraction, King Oliver was playing in the Savoy Ballroom in New York's Harlem, and Fletcher Henderson
was at the Roseland Ballroom in Times Square. In New
York were located network radio programs, booking offices, and recording studios, so that musicians began to
migrate to that city from all over the country. One of
the most swinging bands to invade New York was William McKinney's Cotton Pickers. This band, with many
ex-Henderson personnel, recorded more than fifty tunes
between 1928 and 1933.[6] (FJ, "Four or Five Times,"
Vol. 8) The band of Chick Webb was one of the fresh
new bands that kept appearing in New York around
1929 or 1930.[7] (NW, "Heebie Jeebies," #217) However, Fletcher Henderson and Duke Ellington were the
best-known performers developing toward swing in New
York City in the 1920s.[8] (S, "The Stampede," side 3,
band 6; "Wrappin' It Up," side 3, band 7; "East St.
Louis Toodle-oo," side 6, band 4; "New East St. Louis
Toodle-oo," side 6, band 5; "Creole Rhapsody," side 6,
band 6; "Harlem Air Shaft," side 6, band 7; "Concerto
for Cootie," side 6, band 8; "In a Mellow Tone," side
7, band 1; "Ko-Ko," side 7, band 2; "Blue Serge," side
7, band 3) (FJ, "Copenhagen," "Money Blues,"
"Jackass Blues," "Down South Camp Meeting," Vol.
8)

Generally, the New York bands had heavily
structured arrangements. But there was really no New
York school as there had been a New Orleans school,
a Chicago school, and a Kansas City school. There were
many important performers in New York in the 1920s,
but their styles did not seem to coincide. However, the
direction of most was at least toward swing.

Kansas City

There was great activity in Kansas City from the early
1920s to about 1938. A political organization known
as the Pendergast Machine did much more than encourage the nightclub atmosphere, and so there was an
abundance of employment opportunities for jazz musicians. The influx showed that Kansas City had become a jazz mecca: there was Bill Basie from Red Bank,
New Jersey; Ben Webster from Tulsa; Lester Young
from Mississippi; and Andy Kirk from Dallas.

The Benny Moten band was considered to be the
top band in the Kansas City area from about 1926 to
1935,[9] (S, "Moten Swing," side 3, band 8) (NW,

6. William McKinney, "Four or Five Times," *Folkways Jazz*, vol. 8.

7. Chick Webb, "Let's Get Together," *Jazz Odyssey*, vol. 3; *King of Savoy*, Decca Records, DL 9223; Chick Webb Orchestra, "Heebie Jeebies," *Jammin' for the Jackpot*, New World Records, 217.

8. Fletcher Henderson, "Copenhagen," and "Money Blues," and "Jackass Blues," and "Down South Camp Meetin'," *Folkways Jazz*, vol. 8; "The Stampede," "Wrappin' It Up," Smithsonian Collection of Classic Jazz; "Nagasaki," and "It's the Talk of the Town," *Jazz Story*, vol. 3; "Hop Off," *History of Classic Jazz*, vol. 8; Duke Ellington, *The Ellington Era*, Columbia Records, C3L 25; *Histori- cally Speaking—The Duke*, Bethlehem Records, BCP 60; "Hot and Bothered," *Folkways Jazz*, vol. 8; "Sophisticated Lady," *Jazz Story*, vol. 3; "Happy-Go-Lucky Local," *Jazz Story*, vol. 4; "Rainy Night," *History of Classic Jazz*, vol. 8; "East St. Louis Toodle-oo," "New East St. Louis Toodle-oo," "Creole Rhapsody," "Harlem Air Shaft," "Concerto for Cootie," "In a Mellow Tone," "Ko-ko," "Blue Serge," Smithsonian Collection of Classic Jazz.

9. Benny Moten's Kansas City Orchestra, "Moten Swing," Smith- sonian Collection of Classic Jazz; Benny Moten, "Kansas City Breakdown," and "Moten's Swing," *Folkways Jazz*, vol. 8; Benny Moten Orchestra, "Toby," *Jammin' for the Jackpot*, New World Records, 217.

Count Basie and His Rhythm Section: Walter Page, bass; Freddy Green, guitar; Jo Jones, drums. *Courtesy of Bob Asen, Metronome Magazine.*

"Toby," #217, side 2, band 1) (FJ, "Kansas City Breakdown," "Moten's Swing," Vol. 8) but the competition was extremely keen from the bands of Andy Kirk (piano and arrangements by Mary Lou Williams), Walter Page, Alphonso Trent, and others. The Kansas City bands were looser in musical setting and relied heavily on blues-based riffs.

One of the greatest performers to come out of the Kansas City area was undoubtedly the multi-talented Mary Lou Williams. She was the first woman in jazz history to compose and arrange for a large jazz band, and she dominated the performances of the great Andy Kirk band by her skillful piano playing.[10] Her compositions were in the libraries of a dozen leading swing bands. The last years of her life (she died in 1981) were filled with many honors. There is even a street in Kansas City named after her. Mary Lou Williams was always new, a perennial innovator.[11]

Count Basie was in New York in the early 1920s when he joined a road show that became stranded in Kansas City. Basie then joined the Benny Moten band and eventually became the leader after Moten died. However, Basie had started his own band before Moten's death, and most of Moten's better players had gone with Basie. It is therefore natural that some historians state that Basie took over Moten's band—especially since all of these events happened around the time of Moten's death. When Moten died and Basie became the leading figure in the Kansas City style of swing, Basie's players used to good advantage all of the musical advancements developed in the Kansas City territory. For example, Basie anticipated bop by freeing the piano from merely keeping time, and his drummer,

10. Andy Kirk, *Instrumentally Speaking,* MCA Records, 1308.

11. Andy Kirk, *My Mama Pinned A Rose,* Pablo Records, 2310819.

Jo Jones, added interesting accents to his very moving style. Count Basie died in June, 1984; however, the Basie organization still swings as hard as any band today, and is being led by the talented woodwind player Frank Foster.[12] (S)

Swing Becomes Accepted

The depression came in 1929. A few musicians like Armstrong and Ellington left for Europe. Some hotel-type bands like Lombardo's survived. Many of the better jazz players like Benny Goodman were able to find employment in staff radio jobs. But in general, the entire business suddenly failed. Music was a luxury that most of the public simply had to do without.

Many jazz authorities state that the Swing Era was launched in 1934 when Benny Goodman left the radio studios and formed his own band, using arrangements scored mainly by Fletcher Henderson. However, swing was certainly well on its way before 1934. In 1932, Glen Gray and his Casa Loma Orchestra was playing weekly radio shows for Camel cigarettes. This was a large band featuring precise arrangements laden with riffs often played with a call and response format between brass and saxes. There were reputable jazz players in the band. But before 1932, as stated earlier, the Fletcher Henderson band was already well established as was Duke Ellington's, and there were good swinging large bands in the Kansas City area. The fact that large jazz bands developed in two such diverse areas as New York City and Kansas City is another of the phenomena, such as the diverse origins of the music itself, that surround jazz.

The public was trying to forget the stock market crash and the ensuing depression, and one logical manifestation was the great upsurge in dancing. It was at this time that the jazz players of the Swing Era were so well accepted and performed their music for dancing. The speakeasies of the twenties were fairly small and could not house large bands. But with the repeal of the Volstead Act in 1933, social life so changed that large ballrooms were needed for the thousands who wanted to dance every night. Large bands seemed to be the answer to the dance halls. The country was covered with large ballrooms. Bands often played in towns so small that there would be only one house with an indoor bathroom. Yet there would be a ballroom large enough to hold the six or seven thousand people who would come from miles around to hear their favorite swing bands.

The bands of the Swing Era produced a fuller sound than that of the dixieland bands mainly because they used two or three times as many players. Because of the number of instrumentalists, the music was organized in a homophonic construction, as in example 23, making the musical sounds more organized in their effect. At times the music of the large bands even sounded less complex than the polyphonically conceived dixieland music. The big **blocks of chords** used by the swing bands are the obvious clues to the homophonic construction of this type of jazz. Most of the orchestras of the Swing Era returned to the use of a flat-four rhythm to give their music a rhythm distinct from that which immediately preceded it. During the 1920s, the widely imitated Chicago Style Dixieland was played in 2/4, but the Kansas City musicians at this same time played mainly in 4/4; swing jazz was usually in 4/4.

Paul Whiteman

The Original Dixieland Jazz Band had played in New York in 1917, but even more of the public was made aware of the possibilities of jazz elements when Paul Whiteman introduced George Gershwin's "Rhapsody in Blue" in Aeolian Hall in 1924. This work can hardly be considered jazz as it is defined in this text, but it pointed out some of the idioms of this music to the public and helped focus attention in the general direction of jazz. "Rhapsody in Blue" could conceivably be construed as the first third stream music effort. (This direction is discussed in chapter 14.)

Obviously Paul Whiteman's title, The King of Jazz, was a misnomer and merely a publicity name, but Whiteman was a very influential man and a great supporter of jazz players. He hired many name jazz musicians and paid the top salary of the day. Jazz players and critics are too quick to degrade Whiteman's position when they fail to consider that the jazz players joined Whiteman's orchestra of their own free will, often when they were not busy enough to keep financially stable.

Whiteman had great admiration for these players. Consider, for example, that Beiderbecke was away from the orchestra for nearly a year trying to recover from alcoholism and related problems. During that time, Whiteman retained him on full salary and, it is also reported, paid Beiderbecke's medical bills. During some

12. Count Basie, "Doggin' Around," "Taxi War Dance," Smithsonian Collection of Classic Jazz; Count Basie's Kansas City Seven, "Lester Leaps In," Smithsonian Collection of Classic Jazz; Count Basie, *The Best of Basie,* Columbia Records, C3L–33; E=MC², *Basie,* Roulette Records, ST 52003; Count Basie, *The Best of Count Basie,* MCA Records, 4050.

of the time, Beiderbecke played individual one-night engagements with competing orchestras.

A look at some of the personnel from the Whiteman roster establishes his regard for and financial support of the jazz players of the day: Bix Beiderbecke, Frankie Trumbauer, Red Norvo, Tommy and Jimmy Dorsey, Jack and Charlie Teagarden, Eddie Lang, and Joe Venuti. Most of the recordings of the Whiteman orchestra show very little influence of jazz as it is considered in this text. However, there are certainly noteworthy recordings of jazz players while members of Whiteman's band. For example, Whiteman established a group within his larger organization called The Swing Wing. Jack Teagarden and others were featured in this "band within a band."[13] Among jazz trombonists Jack Teagarden is *the* outstanding performer. He died in 1964, having recorded about 1,000 sides during his lifetime. His long musical lines, flexible technique, and beautiful tone will probably never be repeated.

The Recording Industry

The influence of the recording companies began to be felt during the Swing Era. The sale of records was a determining factor in the success of a musical organization. The arrangements and improvised solos were confined to fewer measures in order to adjust to the length of three-minute records. This restriction reduced individual solo expression to a minimum. This does not mean that one improviser is necessarily better than another. The limitations involved in making records that were only three minutes in length greatly affected the choice of material played by jazz bands as well as how they handled it. When technology improved to the point to where more music could be put on ten-inch records, the powerful jukebox operators still insisted on three minutes only. Not until 1948 when 33⅓ rpm records began to be produced did this situation change, opening the door for much broader musical expositions, much more freedom of expression.

There were great technical problems in the early days of the recording industry. The musicians had to play into a large horn and, as a consequence, were placed around the room according to how hard or easy it was to pick up their sound on recording. For example, softer reed instruments were placed close to the horn, and open brass instruments were placed quite a distance away. In fact, brass players were asked to play muted as much as possible. Often no bass drum was allowed. Musicians generally not only played more cautiously than they would have in a ballroom or night club, but also usually stood in places in relation to each other that were unfamiliar and uncomfortable to them. It is remarkable that they were able to produce records at all, let alone the important documentations that we have on discs.

Seriously researched discographies have become the most authoritative sources for hard evidence regarding which musician played where. Even more important, this documentation makes it easier to assess a musician's playing by supplying evidence from the records he made. These sources are more reliable than the opinions of old friends or avid fans.

To show how the depression affected the recording industry (which in turn affected the entire music industry), Ross Russell gave the following statistics:

From an all-time high of 104 million units reached in 1927, the sale of phonograph records fell to the astonishing low of 6 million when the returns were in for 1932, a ratio of about 17 to 1. Figures for the same year show that the sale of phonographs, the backbone of the Victor Talking Machines Company's business, dropped from 987,000 units to 40,000, a ratio of 21 to 1.[14]

It seems apropos at this point to make a few statistical observations regarding the record industry as it stands in the early 1980s. While some record companies release over a hundred new albums a year, the company that showed the most profit released only ten albums. This brings up the question of quality versus quantity. In 1978, 102 albums "went platinum" (meaning that each sold over a million *units;* an album that has "gone gold" has sold a million *dollars* worth of units); five years earlier that figure was 37; five years before that the number was so small that the designation had not even been coined. A word of caution concerning statistics about record sales: the figure noted is often the number of records shipped *on consignment;* no mention is ever made of the amount of records returned to the company unsold.

The recording industry realizes more money from the public than do either movies or spectator sports. The market potential was clearly demonstrated by the disco phenomenon in the early 1980s. The sudden rise

13.   Jack Teagarden (Paul Whiteman's Orchestra), "Aunt Hagar's Blues," Decca Records, 2145; Jack Teagarden, "Giants of Jazz," Time-Life Records, STL—J08.

14.   Ross Russell, *Jazz Style in Kansas City and the Southwest* (Berkeley, Calif.: University of California Press, 1971), p. 109. Reprinted by permission of The Regents of the University of California.

(and fall) of new musical styles is now greatly accelerated because of the industry's expansive media networks. Rock is probably the fastest changing music today. Performers find themselves skyrocketed to fame overnight. Their music, however, may only be popular for a short time because of the constant introduction of new material and the high speed marketing typical of the recording industry in that area.

The recording industry is no doubt a strong catalyst for the fusion of the many musical styles that emerge year after year. One of the most active fusion areas today occurs in the jazz/rock arena. Groups like Spyro Gyra, Return to Forever, and Weather Report are just a few who demonstrate the success possible at this intersection.

A few years ago, the biggest percentage of records was purchased by thirteen-year-old girls; now, 37 percent of all records and tapes are purchased by persons aged twenty-five to forty-four. Analyses have proven that, as far as 1985, this situation held fast.

There appears to be less profit from each album. On the average, a company invests $250,000 to place an album on the market. The royalty rates to various artists have at least doubled since their original contracts, averaging 5–15 percent. An album by a top-selling artist can easily cost a company over $1 million dollars including promotion. More than two-thirds of all records made today are absolute financial failures; in order to keep from losing money, the company must sell between 200,000 and 300,000 copies. Six major companies now control 85 percent of the market. In 1978, however, a little known company named Polygram became the first record company to gross over $1 billion in a single year.

One more important consideration is that of distribution. Small record companies are at such a disadvantage in comparison to the giants of the industry in this respect that many small manufacturers have arranged to have a large company handle their distribution. An example of this would be the fact that, at this writing, CBS distributes sixteen labels other than its own.

In contrast to the approximately 2,800 record companies at this writing, in 1933 there were only 3: The American Record Company, which owned Columbia, Brunswick, and Vocalion; Victor Records and its subsidiary, Bluebird; and Decca Records. There was a need for jazz recordings, and therefore Commodore and Blue Note were started in 1938 and 1939, respectively.

The Swing Bands

By the late 1930s prosperity was returning, and records and radio were extremely instrumental in publicizing jazz. As a consequence, for the first time a segment of jazz was the most-listened-to music in the world, and more excellent musicians were working in this field than during any previous period. During 1937, 18,000 musicians were on the road, and the number continued to increase. Rather suddenly, after having been frequently considered to be a fairly tawdry occupation, with the rise of swing, jazz became a respectable, remunerative profession. The jazz concerts given for the first time in Carnegie Hall in 1938 were milestones in the acceptance of jazz.[15]

The first jazz concert was in 1936 at New York's Onyx Club. It was called a "Swing Music Concert." The next year, 1937, found "Hollywood's Second Swing Concert" at the famous Palomar Ballroom. It featured Benny Goodman, Louis Prima, Les Hite, Ben Pollack, and a fine all-female big band under the direction of Peggy Gilbert. Today, Peggy Gilbert is the leader of a female dixieland band called the Dixie Belles; the band swings well in this traditional mode.

Benny Goodman was considered the King of Swing. It was understood that if a clarinet player did not play the instrument in the Goodman manner he was not playing clarinet correctly. This put great pressure on good clarinet players who wanted to play in their own style instead of copying Goodman.

By the time Goodman became a success, large black orchestras had already established the format for this size of organization. These were the orchestras of Moten, Kirk, and Trent from the Midwest and those of Henderson, Ellington, McKinney, and Jimmy Lunceford from the East. Goodman's success was not assured at all until he opened at the Palomar Ballroom in Los Angeles in 1935 after a very discouraging tour across the country. But from that moment on, there was no doubt that this next style of jazz was extremely well received by the public.[16] Dave Dexter wrote glowingly of Goodman:

Goodman often did generous things, and his courage in mixing Negroes with what was essentially an all-white orchestra and touring the Southern states can

15. *From Spirituals to Swing,* Vanguard Records, VRS–8523/4.

16. Benny Goodman, *The Great Benny Goodman,* Columbia Records, CL820; *Carnegie Hall Jazz Concert,* Columbia Records, OSL–160; *The Great Band Era,* RCA Victor Records, RD4–25 (RRIS–5473).

Benny Goodman and His Orchestra. Trumpets (left to right): Harry James, Ziggy Elman, Chris Griffin, Johnny Davis; trombones: Murray McEachern, Red Ballard; saxophones: Vido Musso, Hymie Schertzer, Art Rollini, George Koenig; piano: Jess Stacy; bass: Harry Goodman; guitar: Allan Reuss; drums: Gene Krupa. *Courtesy of Leo Walker.*

never be underestimated. He achieved as much in smashing segregation in the arts as anybody in history.

Through the years, Goodman's clarinet remained the model for all beginners. Shaw could play "prettier" notes at times, Barney Bigard added an elusive coloring to Ellington's ensemble and big Irving Prestopnik [Fazola] wove glorious improvisations above the Dixieland blowings of the Bob Crosbyites, but Goodman had a sound all his own, a technique no other could top and a swinging, rhythmic approach that was irresistible.[17]

The Dorsey Brothers started with a large band version of dixieland.[18] The male singer was Bob Crosby. When Bob Crosby developed his own band with the help of ex-Pollack saxophonist Gil Rodin, it was only natural that Crosby's band would be dixieland oriented because that was the style that Crosby had been weaned on in the early Dorsey Brothers' Orchestra.

17. Dave Dexter, *The Jazz Story: From the Nineties to the Sixties* © 1964. Reprinted by permission of Prentice-Hall, Inc., Englewood Cliffs, N.J., pp. 114–15.

18. Dorsey Brothers, *The Fabulous Dorseys Play Dixieland Jazz,* Decca Records, DL8631.

Occasionally there were cooperative bands in which all of the members shared in the profits and woes. Glen Gray and the Casa Loma Orchestra operated in this manner.[19] (NW, "Casa Loma Stomp," #217) In the beginning the Woody Herman Herds were cooperative, but later the band ended this means of operating. Herman's band went through several distinct changes. At first it was a mixture of an overgrown dixieland band and a Kansas City blues type of swing band. Later it progressed more toward the Goodman approach to swing. Later still, his band became "progressive" (described in chapter 10). Herman still heads one of the most exciting big bands.[20]

The public decided that the most popular of all the swing bands was the Glenn Miller band. Miller had been involved with jazz in its truest sense since childhood. He had worked with Red Nichols, Ben Pollack, and others in earlier styles. He had organized and worked with the Dorsey Brothers, Ray Noble, and others heading toward swing. Miller was a brilliant arranger, an outstanding businessman, and a fine trombone player. When he started his band, he went deeply in debt; but within two years, he was a millionaire. One of the authors found him to be an exemplary employer. The band worked only the best jobs in the country, had a commercial radio program three nights a week, recorded often, and even made motion pictures. It was an ideal job for a young sideman. Today there are Glenn Miller Societies all over the world, and at this writing Miller albums record extremely high sales.[21]

It was only natural that new bands continually developed, fronted by musicians who had been featured as solo artists in someone else's band. For example, from the Benny Goodman Band came Harry James, Gene Krupa, Lionel Hampton, Teddy Wilson, and others who became leaders in their own right.

Very often, the first recording of a new band would sound very similar to the band that the new leader had just left. This was because the new leader would hire friends from the band from which he had resigned to be on his first records. The musician's union had an established minimum salary that had to be paid to the musicians for recordings, so the new leader was wise to pay this to the experienced players rather than to those of lesser talents whom he was capable of hiring in his new band when first launching this new career.

A word should be mentioned at this time about pianist Stan Kenton's varied career. He organized and wrote arrangements in 1940 for a band to compete with the stylings of other swing bands. In his second stage, from 1945 to 1949, was a series of "Artistry" motifs.

This was a large band that used harmonic and melodic advancements of the bop era, labeled "progressive." Pete Rugolo was the chief arranger. Next Kenton had a very large orchestra that included classical woodwinds, horns, and a full string section. Kenton called this phase "Innovations in Modern Music." His next band, in 1954, was a more normal-size swing jazz band, but he featured the very modern writing of Bill Holman, Shorty Rogers, Gerry Mulligan, and others. The 1960s saw Kenton in front of what he called his "Neophonic Orchestra," a most interesting experiment involving many talented contemporary arranger-composers. For several more years Kenton remained one of the most energetic, exciting personalities in jazz with an exceptional band that toured the world. He died at the age of 67 on August 25, 1979.[22]

As the Swing Era emerged, the composer-arranger became important. Such excellent style-setting musicians as Fletcher and Horace Henderson, Don Redman, Duke Ellington, and too many others to list shifted the timbre of jazz from the early Paul Whiteman sounds to the sophisticated, swinging music of the large bands. Today fine textbooks by Bill Russo, Henry Mancini, George Russell, Russ Garcia, Van Alexander, and others deal with this art.

One of the oddities of big-band jazz was that soloists gained in importance also. Critic Joachim Berendt wrote of this situation:

Thus, the thirties also became the era of great soloists: the tenor saxists Coleman Hawkins and Chu Berry; the clarinetist Benny Goodman; the drummers Gene Krupa, Cozy Cole, and Sid Catlett; the pianists Fats Waller and Teddy Wilson; the alto saxists Benny Carter and Johnny Hodges; the trumpeters Roy Eldridge, Bunny Berigan, and Rex Stewart.

Often these two tendencies—the orchestral and the soloistic—merged. Benny Goodman's clarinet seemed all the more glamorous against the backdrop of his big band, Louis Armstrong's trumpet stood out

19. The Casa Loma Band, "Casa Loma Stomp," *Jazz Story,* vol. 4; Casa Loma Orchestra, "Casa Loma Stomp," *Jammin' for the Jackpot,* New World Records, 217.

20. Woody Herman, *The Thundering Herds,* Columbia Records, C3L 25; "Misty Morning," *Jazz Story,* vol. 5.

21. *Glenn Miller—A Memorial,* RCA Victor Records, VPM 6019; *The Great Band Era.*

22. Stan Kenton, *The Kenton Era,* The Creative World of Stan Kenton, ST 1030.

Glenn Miller and His Orchestra. Trombones (left to right): Paul Tanner, Jimmy Priddy, Frank D'Anolfo, Miller; trumpets: John Best, Steve Lipkin, Dal McMickle, Billy May; saxophones: Will Schwartz, Al Klink, Skip Martin, Ernie Caceres, Tex Beneke; drums: Moe Purtill; guitar: Bobby Hackett; bass: Doc Goldberg; piano: Chummy MacGregor; singers: Bill Conway, Hal Dickinson, Marion Hutton, Ray Eberle, Chuck Goldstein, Ralph Brewster.

in bold relief when accompanied by Louis Russell's orchestra, and the voluminous tone of Coleman Hawkins' or Chu Berry's tenor seemed to gain from the contrast to the "hard" sound of Fletcher Henderson's band.[23]

The epitome of swing tenor saxophonists was Coleman Hawkins with his large full tone, flowing lines, and heavy vibrato.[24] (S, "The Man I Love," side 4, band 5) A reassuring example of Hawkins' impeccable taste as an improviser is his recording of "Body and Soul."[25] (S, side 4, band 4) (NW, #274, side 1, band 8)

In comparing the early learning environment of two famous tenor saxophone players, Coleman Hawkins with Fletcher Henderson, and Lester Young with Count Basie,[26] Don Heckman has said:

Hawkins predated Young as an active participant in the jazz scene. As a member of the Fletcher Henderson Orchestra for ten years (1923–33), he was intimately involved with what was probably the most famous jazz ensemble of the time. Henderson's orchestra typified the Eastern approach.

The Henderson, Duke Ellington, and Charles Johnson orchestras all played for a variety of musical events before audiences that frequently were all white. Although they were considered (with the exception of Ellington at the Cotton Club), to be primarily dance bands, the type of dance music they played was considerably more diverse than the bands further west.

The Henderson group might be expected on any given night to play popular hits, tangos, Irish waltzes, and original jazz tunes. The music was usually written in complex arrangements, and the bands were carefully rehearsed. With some groups, in fact, well-drilled performances became more important than either improvisation or solos. Fortunately, this never happened with Henderson, who realized the importance of good soloists when Louis Armstrong joined the band in 1924. It was only logical that Hawkins' artistic growth would have been affected by such a musical environment.

. . . Young came into prominence in a completely different milieu. The Count Basie Band was the pinnacle of Kansas City and Southwestern jazz. Its music was blues-oriented, filled with riffing backgrounds, and frequently based on spontaneous head

23. From the *Jazz Book: From New Orleans to Rock and Free Jazz* by Joachim Berendt, translated by Dan Morgenstern, copyright 1975 Lawrence Hill & Co., Westport, Connecticut.

24. Coleman Hawkins, "The Man I Love," Smithsonian Collection of Classic Jazz; Coleman Hawkins, *The Hawk and the Hunter,* Mira Records, LPS–3003; *Coleman Hawkins,* Everest Records, FS–252; Coleman Hawkins, *Bean and the Boys,* Prestige Records, S–7824; Coleman Hawkins, "The Real Thing," Prestige Records, 24083.

25. Coleman Hawkins, "Body and Soul," Smithsonian Collection of Classic Jazz; Coleman Hawkins, "Body and Soul," *The Greatest Names in Jazz,* Verve Records, PR 2–3; Coleman Hawkins, "Body and Soul," *Jive at Five—The Style-makers of Jazz 1920s–1940s,* New World Records, 274.

26. Coleman Hawkins (the Fletcher Henderson Orchestra), *A Study in Frustration,* Columbia Records, C4L–19; Lester Young (with the Count Basie Orchestra), *Lester Young Memorial Album,* Epic Records, SN 6031.

arrangements. The soloists had more opportunity to stretch out than the soloists in the more heavily orchestrated New York bands. Few of the Basie arrangements were very complicated; good intonation and well-drilled performances were not nearly as important as was the creation of a rolling, surging rhythmic swing. Kansas City jazz was dancing jazz, and the beat was the most important element. The revolutionary work of the Basie rhythm section made the Basie band something special. Their ability to generate a free-flowing, almost-alive pulse undoubtedly helped Young develop a rangy horizontal, i.e., melodic, playing style.[27]

Sometimes it is hard for young jazz enthusiasts to see how older players have influenced contemporary favorites, but the influences are there. Young's lines and Hawkins's tone can both be heard in Coltrane's recordings. Young's rhythmic and melodic outlooks can be heard on Ornette Coleman and Eric Dolphy records. In fact, it would not be an overstatement to say that every contemporary saxophonist is indebted to Young, Hawkins, and Parker.

The overall contributions of different swing bands to the development and future of jazz were varied. Benny Goodman's contribution was drive with an intense 4/4 rhythmic feeling. The Casa Loma Band featured ensemble arrangements specializing in the call and response pattern. Duke Ellington offered new sounds and colors built around the individual talents of his musicians and introduced larger forms into jazz. Glenn Miller proved that unerring precision was a possibility in jazz. Lionel Hampton played with chaotic swing. Bob Crosby preserved and expanded Chicago Style Dixieland music. Stan Kenton used more complex harmonies and brought recognition to such innovators as Shelly Manne, Shorty Rogers, Gerry Mulligan, and others too numerous to list. Count Basie contributed a type of relaxed ensemble setting with longer solo opportunities. Woody Herman aided the growth of jazz by continually adapting each new trend. His bands were always proving grounds for rising young instrumentalists. Herman surprised many people by adding a woman trumpet player in the 1940s. Billie Rogers of course played with as much strength and swung as hard as anyone else in the band.

There were good bands that pursued the showmanship aspect of the business with great energy; a typical example is Cab Calloway.[28] This aspect of performance was at low ebb in jazz at one time, causing

record executive Irving Townsend to proclaim, "For some reason, jazz thinks it doesn't need showmanship; it couldn't be more wrong."[29] In general, the many other swing bands of the period duplicated those already mentioned.

Swing Combos

The small combo idea was never entirely discarded. Most large bands also had a small group made up of the better jazz players in the band. The smaller combo played during intermissions of the large band, and sometimes the small group built up its own personal following. In his band, Goodman had a trio, quartet, quintet, sextet, and even septet, depending upon the personnel in his band.[30] (S, Benny Goodman Sextet, "I Found a New Baby," side 6, band 2; "Blues Sequence" with Charlie Christian, side 6, band 3; Benny Goodman Trio, "Body and Soul," side 4, band 3) (NW, "I Found a New Baby," 274, side 1, band 7) Artie Shaw's small "band within a band" was called The Gramercy Five and featured Johnny Guarnieri on harpsichord. Woody Herman had The Woodchoppers, Tommy Dorsey had The Clambake Seven, and so on. Throughout the swing years, Fifty-second Street in New York, with its numerous night clubs, was a real gathering place for small combos.

In July, 1944, Norman Granz organized a jazz concert at the Los Angeles Philharmonic Auditorium to aid in a fund for the defense of some Mexican-Americans who had been sent to San Quentin after a killing in Los Angeles. This concert was recorded and was the first commercial recording made in a public place instead of in a studio. It was a **jam session** recorded live, and it started a whole new phase in recording history. Jazz at the Philharmonic, as Granz's recording and touring package became known, was an extremely successful venture.

27. Don Heckman, "Pres and Hawk, Saxophone Fountainheads," *Down Beat 30*, no. 1 (January 1963): 20.

28. Cab Calloway Orchestra, "Pickin' the Cabbage," *Jammin' for the Jackpot*, New World Records, 217.

29. Irving Townsend, "The Trouble with Jazz," *Down Beat 29*, no. 7 (March 1962): 14.

30. Benny Goodman, *The Great Benny Goodman; Carnegie Hall Jazz Concert;* Benny Goodman Sextet, "I Found a New Baby," "Blues Sequence" (with Charlie Christian), Smithsonian Collection of Classic Jazz; Benny Goodman Trio, "Body and Soul," Smithsonian Collection of Classic Jazz; "I Found a New Baby"; *Jive at Five*, New World Records, 274.

The Demise of Swing

Because of the draft for military service and problems of transportation, the Swing Era came to an abrupt end at the beginning of World War II. Swing bands could not function unless they could play one-night stands. Though the bands took a financial loss on location jobs, they were necessary for radio time, a chance to record, and a chance to rest from the rigors of traveling. Then the bands went on the road again to recoup their losses. But World War II meant no gasoline and no automobile tires for civilians, and therefore all unessential travel came to a halt in this country. One other event contributed to the shutdown of employment for musicians. The federal government levied a 30 percent cabaret tax, and most cabarets simply closed their doors.

Summary

Swing is still with us, however, and much of the jazz we hear today stems directly from the developments of this eight- or ten-year period. The Swing Era must also be credited with two beneficial side effects: it absolutely rescued the record industry, and it allowed the musical instrument industry to grow to its present strength.

Trumpeter Ray Anthony has founded an organization called "Big Bands 80s" whose objectives include the restoration of big bands as an important factor in the popular music scene. They supply arrangements to schools and act as a clearing house for the sale of big band records. They have printed a catalogue of 1,200 LP albums (the catalogue is available at 9288 Kinglet Drive, Los Angeles, 90069).

To reiterate: no style ever really dies out. For years Eddie Condon ran a nightclub that featured nothing but Chicago Style Dixieland.[31] The Early New Orleans Dixieland revival of the late 1930s was mentioned previously in chapter 5.[32] Swing is still played all over the world. Not only is nostalgia of swing a salable product, but swing itself is a most communicative style of jazz.[33] There are books on the market today about the Swing Era alone.[34] It is indeed hard to be completely objective about this literature when one finds he is a part of that being discussed. The books are generally both interesting and informative. There are even books on the activities of just the Glenn Miller Band during the Swing Era,[35] and other books about this band are being written at this time. Bands like Basie's, Ellington's, and Herman's have certainly proven that the big bands can swing as hard and maintain all the vitality demonstrated by the smaller groups of the day. The organized, written arrangements are capable of creating an energy all their own. The controversy begun with Henderson's band, that one ensemble was superior to another, is no longer appropriate.

Additional Reading Resources

Allen, Walter C. *Hendersonia: The Music of Fletcher Henderson and His Musicians.*

Charters, Samuel B., and Kunstadt, Leonard. *Jazz: A History of the New York Scene.*

Dance, Stanley. *The World of Swing.*

Dexter, Dave. *The Jazz Story,* pp. 56–87, 105–20.

Feather, Leonard. *The Book of Jazz,* pp. 174–91.

Harris, Rex. *Jazz,* pp. 168–74.

McCarthy, Albert. *Big Band Jazz.*

Russell, Ross. *Jazz Styles in Kansas City and the Southwest.*

Schuller, Gunther. *Early Jazz: Its Roots and Musical Development,* pp. 242–317.

Shapiro, Nat, and Hentoff, Nat, eds. *The Jazz Makers,* pp. 175–86, 218–26.

Simon, George. *Glenn Miller.*

————. *Simon Says.*

————. *The Big Bands.*

Stearns, Marshall. *The Story of Jazz,* pp. 120–54.

Ulanov, Barry. *Handbook of Jazz,* pp. 15–26.

Walker, Leo. *The Wonderful Era of the Great Dance Bands.*

Note: Complete information including name of publisher and date of publication is provided in the Bibliography.

Additional Record Resources

(Big Bands '80s Record Library.)

Calloway, Cab. *Sixteen Calloway Classics.* Columbia Records, J–10.

31. *History of Classic Jazz,* vol. 9.

32. *History of Classic Jazz,* vol. 10.

33. Live Concert, *Music Made Famous by Glenn Miller,* Warner Brothers Records, W 1428; *Those Swingin' Days of the Big Bands,* Pickwick Records, TMW-002; *The Great Band Era; The Big Bands Are Back Swinging Today's Hits,* RCA Victor Records, RD4–112 (XRIS–9501).

34. George Simon, *The Big Bands* (New York: Macmillian Co., 1967); George Simon, *Simon Says* (New Rochelle, N.Y.: Arlington House, 1971).

35. John Flower, *Moonlight Serenade* (New Rochelle, N.Y.: Arlington House, 1972).

Casa Loma Band. *Glen Gray's Greatest Hits.* MCA Records, 122.

Jammin' for the Jackpot. New World Records, 217.

Jive at Five. New World Records, 274.

Little Club Jazz. New World Records, 250.

The World of Swing. Columbia Records, F6–32945.

Suggested Classroom Activities

1. In what ways did Fletcher Henderson influence the development of jazz in the Swing Era?

2. Describe the role of the music arranger in this era.

3. Explain why swing bands produced a fuller sound.

4. What jazz trombonist is considered the outstanding trombone virtuoso of the era?

5. Certain limitations were placed on the recordings of swing bands of the record industry. What were these limitations?

6. Identify the band that was the most popular as well as the most successful.

7. What were some factors that resulted in the end of the Swing Era?

8. Was swing music primarily for listening or for dancing?

9. In order to enhance your aural perception of the big-band sound, listen to several recordings of thirty-seven top bands playing ten years of top tunes from the album *The Great Band Era* manufactured especially for *Readers Digest* by RCA.

10. Now listen to the swing band recordings in the album *Jazz* (Folkways Records FJ2808, vol. 8, Big Bands) and compare the arrangements of these earlier bands with the band sounds in the *Readers Digest* album.

11. The swing era produced many outstanding soloists, among them Benny Goodman and his clarinet. Listen to his Sextet playing "I Found a New Baby" (S, side 6, band 2) and identify the instrument that follows Benny Goodman's clarinet solo.

12. Listen to Duke Ellington's "Ko-Ko" (S, side 7, band 2). Toward the end of the recording you will hear another outstanding soloist on an instrument that was not considered a solo instrument. Can you identify the name of the instrument?

Listening Guide

From Taped Demonstration 14

Swing

:00 Introduction on solo drums using tom toms

:04 Ensemble chorus (saxes on melody, brass on riff) (full rhythm section keeps 4/4 rhythm)

:17 Drum solo on tom toms

:20 Clarinet solo (one chorus backed by trombones on riff)

:34 Ensemble chorus (same as first chorus except a tone higher)

:49 Ensemble chorus (same except for another ½ tone higher for still more intensity)

1:01 Clarinet solo break

1:03 End

From Smithsonian Collection (side 5, band 8)

Count Basie
"Taxi War Dance"

:00 Introduction consists of 4 measures piano solo (Count Basie) in a boogie-woogie pattern followed by 4 measures brass

:09 1st chorus—Tenor sax solo (Lester Young) for 16 measures (rhythm plays 4/4 except piano plays accents throughout the record)

:27 8 measures as bridge of chorus, still tenor sax solo

:36 8 measures to finish up the chorus, same as first 8 measures of this first chorus

:48 2nd chorus—Trombone solo (Dickie Wells)— 32 measure chorus with the same chords for the bridge that were used in the first chorus

1:24 3rd chorus—4 measures of brass

1:28 4 measures of tenor sax solo (Buddy Tate)

1:33 Repeat of the above 8 measures

1:43 8 measures of piano solo on the bridge chords

1:51 4 measures of brass

1:56 4 measures of tenor sax solo

2:01 4th chorus—4 measures of full ensemble (piano playing boogie-woogie pattern)

2:06 4 measures of tenor sax solo (Lester Young)

2:10 Repeat of above 8 measures

2:19 8 measures of piano solo on bridge chords

2:28 4 measures full ensemble

2:33 4 measures tenor sax solo

2:38 2 measures brass, 2 measures tenor sax (Buddy Tate), 2 measures bass solo (Walter Page), 2 measures drums (Jo Jones)

2:47 Full ensemble ending

2:50 End

10
Bop
(1940–1950)

Bop jazz was sometimes called *bebop* or *rebop,* but common usage shortened it to bop. In spite of some of the explanations of the origin of these words, the answer probably is that players sang the words *bebop* and *rebop* to an early bop phrase, as shown in example 25.

Example 25

The Shift to Bop

Bop was a revolt against the confines of the larger bands. The short, stylized solos typical of the large bands of the Swing Era minimized the opportunity for exploratory expression. Soloists not only desired more freedom for experimentation, but also searched for a fresh and different approach to jazz. The young players were tired of reading written arrangements, tired of the clichés of swing, tired of the limitations of opportunity for improvisation, and so on. They also felt that many musicians with little creativeness were earning more than their share of fame and wealth and that the time had come for many changes. (As an introduction to bop, listen to the cassette demonstration 15 included with this book.)

Most bop players turned naturally to small combos. A quintet seemed to be the size Charlie Parker found most comfortable. It is interesting that the combos resembled, in appearance at least, the earlier dixieland bands—that is, a rhythm section with a sparse (by comparison to swing) front line. Without a doubt, the bop combo reflected Kansas City jam sessions. Regardless of claims, bop or any other style of music surely does not "begin" at any one place and at one time. It could not, for example, have been decided in October, 1940, at Minton's Playhouse in New York's Harlem, that bop was to be the next jazz style.

Many unrelated events brought bop about quite naturally. Just as Early New Orleans Dixieland jazz solidified in New Orleans years before, bop solidified in New York in the early 1940s. Charlie Parker said that an alto saxophone player from Dallas named Buster Smith was playing the beginnings of this free style. In the Southwest, Charlie Christian surely played saxophone-type lines on the guitar. In the St. Louis area, Jimmy Blanton was innovating on the bass. All this activity meant that the bop style developed not only in New York, but also in Kansas City, St. Louis, Oklahoma City, and other cities.

Bop Arranging

The shift to bop embraced the most radical changes in the development of jazz to this point. The draft and

Example 26

transportation difficulties during World War II favored the smaller band necessary for these new experimentations. In contrast to the musical arrangements of the Swing Era, notations for the bop bands were usually confined to **unison** lines for the melodic instruments. A standard format for performing tunes in the bop manner was to play the first chorus in unison (trumpet and saxophone usually), then the improvised choruses, followed by the unison chorus again. Therefore, if the tune had a chorus of thirty-two bars and a form of AABA, the first eight bars (A) would be composed, the second eight would be a repetition of the first eight (A), the third group of eight bars would be improvised (B), and the last eight bars would again be a repetition of the first eight bars (A). All of it added up to thirty-two bars and constituted the first chorus and last chorus. Therefore, all that had to be planned ahead was one eight-bar strain, the A part.[1]

Musical Expansion

For greater freedom of expression, these players used **extended harmonies** in their improvised choruses. The development of new harmonic resources for the jazz musician followed closely upon the heels of experimentations by classical composers. At the turn of the century, harmonies were enriched through the successive inclusion of higher members of the **overtone series** (see example 26). This resulted in an extensive use of **ninth, eleventh,** and **thirteenth chords** and beyond. Use of the flatted fifth became so ordinary that from this point on it was considered to be another "blue note" just as the third and seventh tones of the scale had been.

It was not until the Bop Era that the use of **higher harmonics** and their resultant complex harmonies became prevalent. Harmonic sonorities that were complex enough to be designated as polychords were used

extensively. This harmonic construction can be best understood as a combination of two conventional chords. As long as these chords have a close relationship, such as common tones, they are perceived as one chord in the same key instead of in two separate keys.

In example 27, an A-major chord is placed directly over a G seventh chord.

Example 27

This type of sound was common to bop, and since the tones of the A-major chord are all contained in the higher harmonics of the G seventh chord, the players considered these extended harmonies and did not think of the sound as being in two different keys.

Substitute chords became important during the Bop Era. For example, C to C₇ to F could just as well be played C to G♭₇ to F, and it sounded more interesting at the time. The players were greatly stimulated by fresh chords inside of old progressions. An example follows.

Bop playing in general employed faster tempos.[2] (S, Dizzy Gillespie and Charlie Parker, "Shaw 'Nuff,"

1. Charlie Parker, "Yardbird Suite," *Bird Symbols,* Charlie Parker Records, PLP–407.

2. Dizzy Gillespie and Charlie Parker, "Shaw 'Nuff," Smithsonian Collection of Classic Jazz; Charlie Parker, "KoKo," Smithsonian Collection of Classic Jazz; Dizzy Gillespie and Charlie Parker, "Shaw 'Nuff;" Charlie Parker, "KoKo;" Dizzy Gillespie, "Things To Come," *Bebop,* New World Records, 271; "Wee," *Jazz at Massey Hall,* Fantasy Records, 6003.

	B♭	Gm7	Cm7	F7	Gm7	E dim.	Cm7	F7	B♭
	↓	↓	↓	↓	↓	↓	↓	↓	↓
or	B♭9M7	D♭7	Cm7	B9	B♭9M7	Gm9	Cm7	F13	B♭9M7
	B♭9M7	E9	E♭M7	A♭13	B♭9M7	etc.			

side 7, band 6; Charlie Parker, "KoKo," side 7, band 7) (NW, Dizzy Gillespie and Charlie Parker, "Shaw 'Nuff," 271, side 1, band 3; Charlie Parker, "KoKo," side 1, band 8; Dizzy Gillespie, "Things To Come," side 1, band 5) To create excitement by merely increasing the tempo would have been impractical with the large, unwieldy bands of the Swing Era. Bop was the first style of jazz that was not specifically for dancing. While the early jazz players used primarily quarter notes with four-tone chords or chords of the seventh, the bop players often played sixteenth note rhythms with harmonies of greater complexity. One of the unusual phrasing idioms in bop occurred when there was a series of eighth notes:

[musical notation: series of eighth notes]

The bop players accented the note in between the beats:

[musical notation: series of eighth notes with accents on offbeats]

Compare the swing style:

[musical notation: swing-style dotted rhythm with triplet equivalents marked "3"]

Therefore, if the phrase were counted "one and, two and, three and, four and," the players would accent the "ands." Also at first, bop phrasing was heavily influenced by Kansas City-type short riffs; but soon the statements, both planned and improvised, became longer and less repetitive.

There was more tension in the music of this era than in the music of the Swing Era. Jazz, as well as the other arts, has always been influenced by the mood of the times, and this country was entering a war. The musical tension, then, was created by **tonal clashes,** unusual harmonies, and fast tempos with complex rhythms. To play bop well, the musicians had to have a good knowledge of harmony plus great technical facility. Even with these attributes, the hectic tempos and rapidly moving chords of many of the works caused some experienced players to merely run the chords (**arpeggios**) instead of creating interesting lines.

One of the major changes that occurred during the Bop Era was repertoire. The building of repertoire in bop was accomplished mainly by using the chords

of a **standard tune** as the framework on which to compose a new melody. An example of this kind of borrowing is found in the selection "Ornithology," which is a melody improvised from the harmonies in the composition "How High the Moon."[3] Miles Davis and Thelonious Monk both recorded tunes based on "All God's Children Got Rhythm." Davis called his "Little Willie Leaps," and Monk's is titled "Suburban Eyes." Chords from "What Is This Thing Called Love" became "Hot House," "Indiana" became "Donna Lee," "Whispering" became "Groovin' High," "I Got Rhythm" became "Anthropology," "Koko" is from the chords to "Cherokee," "S'Wonderful" became "Stupendous," and so on. Twelve-bar blues had such titles as "Relaxin' at Camarillo," "Parker's Mood," "Now's the Time," "Congo Blues," and others. In previous eras, the melody was usually stated in the first chorus, and improvisation began after that. The bop innovators, however, often disregarded the initial statement of the melody and began their improvisation at the beginning of the selection. Besides changing the harmonies, melodies, and rhythms, the bop players changed the approach to phrasing from neat **symmetrical** phrases to phrases that seemed uneven and unnatural compared to earlier jazz.

The Bop Rhythm Section

The assigned parts played by individual members of the rhythm section also underwent radical changes. Instead of the regular 4/4 steady rhythm heard in swing music, the drummer now used the bass and snare drums mainly for accents and punctuations. He usually maintained an overall sound by playing eighth-note rhythms on the top cymbal. If the accents were not spontaneous, then they were played on either the fourth beat of the bar or the fourth beat of every other bar. The more spontaneous punctuations were called **bombs** and had to be done with great discernment in order to aid the impetus instead of being a distraction. The piano player changed from playing 4/4 steady rhythm to chordal punctuations. Count Basie had played in this style for some time. These punctuations were played at specific moments to designate the chord changes and thus added to the overall musical excitement. With the advent of the amplifier, the guitar became a melody instrument and took its place with the trumpet, saxophone, and others. This left the sole responsibility for the steady pulse of the beat to the string bass. Although the string

3. Al Casey, "How High the Moon," *The History of Jazz,* vol. 4, Capitol Records, T796; Charlie Parker, "Ornithology," *Bird Symbols,* Charlie Parker Records, PLP–407.

bass part now had a more interesting line, the line was secondary to the job of maintaining a rhythmic pulse.

The beauty of the bop rhythm section was that the individual members were freed from duplicating each other's role. In the swing style, all four players were forced mainly to keep the pulse because the bands were quite large and because the public wanted to feel the pure, unornamented, uncomplicated beat in order to dance. These bop approaches were, in general, not really new, as shown by Basie's piano work, Jimmy Blanton's bass playing with Ellington, and Charlie Christian's guitar work with Benny Goodman's orchestra. The bop players also added rhythm players from Cuba who not only aided the pulse assigned to the bass player, but also brought new rhythmic excitement into jazz through improvised **cross-rhythms.** This addition pointed out the fact that the more intricate aspects of the West African musical tradition had been kept alive much more in Cuba than in the United States. Of course, Latin rhythms, as they were considered, were not new to jazz. For instance, there is a tango section in Handy's "St. Louis Blues," written about thirty years earlier.

The Performers

Much of the leadership of this era must be attributed to Charlie Parker's fluid alto sax, Dizzy Gillespie's virtuosic trumpet playing, Thelonious Monk's melodies, and the brilliantly accented drumming of Kenny Clarke and Max Roach. The early bop sessions at Minton's Playhouse emerged from a band led by drummer Kenny Clarke. Charlie Parker was not there at first, but came later. Ex-bandleader Teddy Hill applied the Kansas City formula to Minton's style. He was the manager and hired a good contemporary nucleus of players with whom the performers of this advanced jazz enjoyed jamming. The musicians who played regularly at Minton's devised ways to discourage the unwanted from sitting in on the jam sessions. They would play tunes at such fast tempos, and play what at the time were such strange chords, that those musicians not really in the clique simply could not compete.

As Armstrong influenced many jazz musicians by 1930, Charlie Parker influenced almost all jazz musicians by 1950. Whereas Armstrong generally took the original melody and changed it subtly, Parker often merely implied the melody. Charlie Parker died in 1955, when he was less than thirty-five years old; yet he is considered to be one of the most significant of all jazz figures. The most notable followers of Parker are Sonny Stitt, Phil Woods, Jackie McLean, and Cannonball Adderley. (Parker is discussed at length in chapter 20.)

Dizzy Gillespie, as talented a trumpet player as he is a showman, has combined great technique with fresh thoughts and extensive harmonic knowledge. Along with Parker, he was a leader in the style of jazz that he and his contemporaries labeled *bop.* Gillespie's trumpet playing stems from Louis Armstrong by way of Roy Eldridge. (In passing we must note that not nearly enough is ever said about the versatile playing of Eldridge. He had played in a very fiery style for many years before bop came along.[4]) Dizzy Gillespie's playing was so modeled on the talents of Eldridge that when Eldridge left the Teddy Hill band Gillespie was very naturally hired to replace him. Gillespie's first recorded solos were with this band in 1937. "King Porter Stomp" and "Blue Rhythm Fantasy" reflect the Eldridge influence most directly, and "Things to Come" was probably his most important record.[5] (NW, side 1, band 5) There is no doubt that Gillespie was the most talked about bop musician at that time.

The reactions to Gillespie's style of playing ranged all the way from unqualified enthusiasm to pure indignation. Today he is highly regarded all over the world, and his contributions to modern jazz trends cannot possibly be disputed.[6] (S, Dizzy Gillespie, "I Can't Get Started with You," side 7, band 5; Dizzy Gillespie and Charlie Parker, "Shaw 'Nuff," side 7, band 6) (FJ, "Groovin' High," Vol. 11)

The period from 1944 to 1947 was noted for the great jazz groups that worked in the clubs on Fifty-second Street in New York City. The first actual bop band on Fifty-second Street was formed by Dizzy Gillespie and bassist Oscar Pettiford in January of 1944. The Earl ("Fatha") Hines band had experimented in 1942 and 1943, but until the Gillespie-Pettiford band in 1944, bop had been confined mainly to Harlem's after-hours clubs such as Monroe's and Minton's, and to occasional improvised solos in big bands by such performers as Howard McGee, Charlie Parker, or Dizzy

4. Roy Eldridge, *Dale's Wail,* Verve Records, MGV–8089.

5. Dizzy Gillespie, "Things To Come," *Bebop,* New World Records, 271.

6. Dizzy Gillespie, "I Can't Get Started," Smithsonian Collection of Classic Jazz; Dizzy Gillespie and Charlie Parker, "Shaw 'Nuff," Smithsonian Collection of Classic Jazz; Dizzy Gillespie and All Stars, "Leap Here," *Jazz Story,* vol. 5; "Groovin' High," *Folkways Jazz,* vol. 11; *Dizzy Gillespie,* RCA Victor Records, LPV–530; *Essential,* Verve Records, 68566; *The Greatest Names in Jazz,* Verve Records; "Carombola," *History of Jazz,* vol. 4; Dizzy Gillespie, *Dizzy Gillespie: Composer's Concepts,* Mercury Em Arcy Records, EMS–2–410; Dizzy Gillespie, *Dizzy Gillespie and Stan Getz,* Verve Records, VE 2–2521; Dizzy Gillespie, *Benny Carter and Dizzy Gillespie,* Pablo Records, 231–0781; Dizzy Gillespie, *Bahiana,* Pablo Records, 262–5708.

Dizzy Gillespie. *Courtesy of Ray Avery.*

Gillespie. These choruses seemed out of context in the big swing bands—Cab Calloway's, Andy Kirk's, and so forth.

In 1945, Dizzy Gillespie organized his first big band. He preferred the larger band at a time when all other bop advocates were performing in combos. His first big band, called Hep-Sations of 1945, was short-lived. Gillespie became interested in Afro-Cuban rhythms after having performed with Cuban orchestras around New York City. In 1947 he added Chano Pozo to his band to bring Latin American and West African rhythms to jazz. With the addition of Chano Pozo the gap between bop and the 4/4 meter of swing became more apparent. The followers of Gillespie's trumpet excursions included Fats Navarro, Kenny Dorham, Miles Davis early in his career, Clifford Brown, Thad Jones, Donald Byrd, Pete and Conte Condoli, Freddie Hubbard, Wynton Marsalis, and Jon Faddis.

It should also be noted that Gillespie was the first to take a jazz band on tour for the United States State Department. His band, composed of both black and white musicians, helped relieve diplomatic tension in some parts of the world.

Both Charlie Christian and Jimmy Blanton became national figures on the jazz scene late in 1939. In the short span of time between 1939 and 1942 (both died of tuberculosis in 1942), Christian and Blanton changed entirely the concept of playing their respective instruments—Christian, the guitar, and Blanton, the bass.

Charlie Christian played mostly around Oklahoma City, Kansas City, and St. Louis before joining Benny Goodman when he was only nineteen years old. As influential as he was, speculation remains as to what he would have contributed had he not died prematurely. Charlie Christian's guitar playing influenced all future jazz, and he must be placed in the same category as Gillespie, Parker, Lester Young, and Jimmy Blanton. He elevated the guitar from a strictly rhythm instrument to a solo melody instrument equal to other instruments. This is not to say that other guitarists did not play extremely capable solos, but Christian, who came along about the same time as the introduction of the amplifier, was by far the strongest influence. Though he was involved in a new extension of chords, Christian's main innovation was that he played solos with long lines like those for a saxophone.

It is possible that most guitarists felt that the big moving chords of Eddie Lang, George Van Epps and other earlier players were beyond them. Also, the most perfect listening conditions were necessary for hearing guitar solos. Christian's single-note lines and the advent of the amplifier opened the door for many talented players such as Wes Montgomery, Barney Kessel, George Benson, and Pat Metheny. It should be understood, however, that Christian's approach to solos—single-note lines instead of great moving chords—had been played earlier by the talented Belgium player Django Reinhardt. But there were few Reinhardt recordings at that time to document his technique.

Even in Charlie Christian's original and modern guitar playing, the blues influence was the most predominant feature. But unlike other blues guitarists, Christian pioneered the use of the amplifier as early as 1937 in Oklahoma City. He joined the Benny Goodman band in 1939 in New York City. It was at this time that, after his performances every evening with Goodman, he became a regular performer at Minton's. The fact that he died in 1942 meant that he had very little time to develop his impressive legacy. The most mentioned of his recordings today are "Solo Flight" with the Benny Goodman orchestra, "Gone with What Wind" with the Benny Goodman sextet, and "Profoundly Blue" with the Edmond Hall quartet.[7] (S, Benny Goodman with Charlie Christian, "Blues Sequence," side 6, band 3)

Until Jimmy Blanton joined Duke Ellington in 1939, the bass player played either two or four notes to a bar and played very simple lines at that, mainly the roots and fifths of the chords. There was hardly ever a bass solo; solos demanded more technique from players as well as some entirely new techniques from recording engineers. In the Ellington band Blanton excited the jazz world with his solo "Jack the Bear" and his duets with Ellington—"Mr. J. B. Blues" and "Pitter Panther Patter." Blanton satisfied his listeners with the bass parts that he played, but while accomplishing this, he also played tasteful and interesting lines. He used eighth notes and sixteenth notes without ever sounding clumsy on the instrument, and he also proved that he could bow well. Though he died early, Blanton laid the foundations for all bass players who followed. Because of the path opened by Blanton, bass players were able to assume responsibility for keeping the pulse for the whole combo while weaving their way among the new, advanced chords. Blanton's solo on Duke Ellington's "Jack the Bear" was considered for a long time to be the greatest bass solo on record.[8] (NW, "Pitter Panther Patter," 274, side 2, band 8)

One of the fine bass players to follow Blanton was Oscar Pettiford, who, with Dizzy Gillespie, formed the first bop band to appear on Fifty-second Street in 1944. There have been many great bass players to be sure, but two must be singled out: Ray Brown and Charlie Mingus. Brown progressed so quickly that he had been out of high school only two years when he joined the famous Dizzy Gillespie sextet in 1946. Brown's style seems modern today, and even though he sounds relaxed, he displays great technical ability and fine musicianly taste. The musicianship of Mingus was ever present as he included *ostinato* figures, **pedal points,** and **double stops** even during accompaniment. When Mingus soloed you were aware that he was also a good contemporary composer.

Ever since jazz musicians began hearing Thelonious Monk, they realized that he was an important pianist and jazz composer. Works written by Monk have to be considered "compositions" as opposed to the "lines" written by Charlie Parker, for example. Under some lines, the harmony can be changed, and over some chord progressions new lines can be invented. But with Monk's works, it seems necessary to use both his lines and his harmony. When Monk improvised, he did not simply play variations; he fragmented lines sometimes and at other times he elaborated on them. He often started with a basic phrase and, like Sonny Rollins on the tenor sax, played the phrase in almost every conceivable manner. However, he received recognition for his composing before he was accepted as an innovating pianist. An example of Monk's strong influence is the effect he had on John Coltrane. When Coltrane joined Monk's combo he had to struggle with the repertoire. But after his experience in the group, he had the opportunity to become a really great musician and a most important influence himself. It was as if Monk were able to open Coltrane's ears and to point out possible

7. Benny Goodman Sextet with Charlie Christian, "Blues Sequence," Smithsonian Collection of Classic Jazz; *Charlie Christian,* Columbia Records, CL 652, G–30779; Charlie Christian (Edmond Hall's Quartet), "Profoundly Blue," *Three Decades of Jazz (1939–1949);* Charlie Christian, *Solo Flight,* Columbia Records, CG–30779; Charlie Christian, *The Harlem Jazz Scene,* Archive of Folk Music, 219E.

8. Jimmy Blanton (Duke Ellington's Orchestra), "Jack the Bear," *Historically Speaking—The Duke,* Bethlehem Records, BCP60; Duke Ellington and Jimmy Blanton, "Pitter Panther Patter," *Jive at Five—The Style-makers of Jazz 1920s–1940s,* New World Records, 274.

Thelonious Monk. *Courtesy of Ray Avery*

directions as yet unconceived of by the saxophonist.[9] (S, Thelonious Monk, "Misterioso," "Criss Cross," "Evidence," "Smoke Gets in Your Eyes," "I Should Care," side 9, bands 4, 5, 6, 7, 8; Miles Davis All Stars, "Bags' Groove," side 10, band 1) (NW, "Misterioso," 271, side 2, band 4) Thelonious Sphere Monk died in February of 1982.

Bud Powell, a seemingly logical piano heir to Art Tatum's reign, was one of the key figures in the development of bop. He was a regular on Fifty-second Street in the 1940s, playing with groups like John Kirby's and Dizzy Gillespie's. Unfortunately, Powell was constantly plagued by mental illnesses, beginning when he was only twenty-one years of age. In spite of this, repressings by both Verve and Blue Note Record companies, as well as recordings with Parker and Gillespie, attest to his contributions. [10] (S, Bud Powell, "Somebody Loves Me," side 8, band 5) (NW, "Un Poco Loco," 271, side 2, band 2)

Trombone playing did not contribute to the beginning of the bop style. Trombone players who had the virtuosity to play this style were not sufficiently interested at first. It required a highly developed technique

plus understanding. J. J. Johnson proved to trombonists that the style was possible on the instrument. Kai Winding, Frank Rosolino, and many others quickly followed his lead.

When large bands used these bop harmonic and melodic developments, this jazz was labeled "progressive" jazz. At first, the only contributions in this direction were solos in big bands by such musicians as Gillespie and Parker, but soon entire bands were dedicated to these new directions. The progressive band

9. Thelonious Monk, "Misterioso," "Criss Cross," "Evidence," "Smoke Gets in Your Eyes," "I Should Care," Smithsonian Collection of Classic Jazz; Miles Davis All Stars, "Bags' Groove," Smithsonian Collection of Classic Jazz; Thelonious Monk, "Misterioso," *Bebop,* New World Records, 271; *Thelonious Monk,* Prestige Records, 24006; *Brilliant Corners,* Riverside Records, RLP 12–226; *Monk's Dream,* Columbia Special Products, JCS-8765; *The Thelonious Monk Orchestra at Town Hall,* Riverside Records, 1138; Miles Davis' Album, "Bags' Groove, Take 1," *Bags' Groove,* Prestige Records, 7109; *Misterioso,* Columbia Records, CS-9236.

10. Bud Powell, "Somebody Loves Me," Smithsonian Collection of Classic Jazz; "Un Poco Loco," *Bebop,* New World Records, 271; *The Amazing Bud Powell,* vols. 1 and 2, Blue Note Records, 81503–4.

Stan Kenton. *Courtesy of Ray Avery.*

surely many frustrations, including limited audience appeal for the new music, bans on recording by the musicians' union, and lack of sympathy, cooperation, and encouragement from record companies when there was no ban. At times Eckstine's band was a financial success, but when the orchestra disbanded, Eckstine was left somewhat in debt. Gillespie was the musical director of Eckstine's band. Their first records sold mainly because of Eckstine's fine vocals. In fact, Eckstine's vocals, along with those of Sarah Vaughan, were the band's best means of communication with both the public and the recording executives. In 1944 when Gillespie left the Billy Eckstine band, he was first replaced by Fats Navarro and then by Miles Davis, who remained until the orchestra disbanded in 1947. Miles Davis first joined this band for a short stay in 1944. George Hoefer of *Down Beat* has described what happened:

Trumpeter Anderson was taken seriously ill shortly after the band's arrival in St. Louis and was hospitalized. On the night the band opened at the Riviera, the first customer was a high school student with a trumpet under his arm. Gillespie asked him if he had a union card, and Miles Davis, 16, of East St. Louis, said that he did. The music director told him to go up on the stand and see what he could do.

"Miles," Eckstine later said, "he sounded terrible." Davis recalled, "I couldn't read the book, I was so busy listening to Bird and Dizzy." He played a few nights with the band and then headed for Juilliard in New York.[13]

The band eventually recorded a variety of jazz for National Records including up-tempo works, ballads, and blues. Eckstine can even be heard on valve trombone solos. The trend was for vocalists to be more successful attractions than bands, and Eckstine surely must be considered one of the finest singers to come out of jazz or any other background.

Stan Kenton, who was continually an influential pioneer in jazz, had been working as a pianist in Los Angeles before organizing his first band in Balboa, California, in 1941. Kenton stated that he soon became aware of the adventurous excitement of jazz players and began to base his repertoire on the talents of the

leaders included Stan Kenton (who even adopted the label "progressive"),[11] Woody Herman, Earl Hines, Billy Eckstine, Boyd Raeburn, and bands led by Dizzy Gillespie himself. The Boyd Raeburn band played music as far removed from the earlier swing bands as could be envisioned.

Billy Eckstine, having built a following as a ballad singer with Earl ("Fatha") Hines, formed a band which had almost every leading bop player at one time.[12] (NW, Billy Eckstine, "Good Jelly Blues," 284, side 1, band 6) Between 1944 and 1946 his female singer was Sarah Vaughan. The Earl Hines and Billy Eckstine bands of this type reached their peak during a record ban, and hence there is not much recorded documentation of them. Record bans occur when the musicians' union strikes against the record companies. Eckstine's band dates from June, 1944, to February, 1947. There were

11.   Stan Kenton, *Kenton in Stereo,* The Creative World of Stan Kenton, ST 1004.

12.   Billy Eckstine Orchestra, "Good Jelly Blues," *Jazz in Revolution—The Big Bands in the 1940s,* New World Records, 284.

13.   George Hoefer, "The First Big Bop Band," *Down Beat* 32, no. 16 (July 1965): 21.

Woody Herman. *Courtesy of Ray Avery.*

excellent musicians who passed through his band. Great credit should be accorded Kenton for having never compromised what to him was art for the comfort and safety of more commercial aspects of big bands. Kenton added Jack Costanzo to play Latin rhythms in 1948, furthering this direction in contemporary jazz.[14]

By 1944, Woody Herman had lost his dixieland trend and some of his Ellington influence as additions in his band began showing a heavy bop emphasis. For example, for a while his trumpet section was composed of Sonny Berman, Neal Hefti, Pete Condoli, and Conrad Gozzo.[15]

There were vocals, but the bop players primarily thought instrumentally. Earlier players played as they would have sung, seeming to work over a melody. Bop players were much more involved with working over the chord progressions.

Summary

By 1946, bop was being heard even in some commercial dance bands. Today, most good amateur or semi-amateur players improvise in the bop style. Even most name jazz players perform in a manner directly related to the bop school. Some more than others show the effects of having worked through the cool and funky styles since bop, but the phrases, harmonies, and the approach still seem to be quite clearly bop derived.

Bop did not have a chance to emerge gradually for public listening as had other styles previously. By the time the differences between the union and the record industry were resolved, bop was well advanced. One reason for its slow acceptance by listeners was that the public was saturated with bad publicity about bop that made the music appear more like a passing fad than an advancement in the development of jazz. An example is the way in which the followers of Gillespie imitated his dark glasses, goatee, and beret. Fan magazines even began advertising "bebop ties." After World War II, when bop started to be heard by more of the public, the radical changes from swing caused great consternation. Some of the older jazz players accepted the advancements, but most rejected bop, feeling that it lacked the more desirable jazz characteristics—emphasis on pulse, theme and variations approach, and so on. However, the real opposition appeared to stem from jazz critics, which seems to be the case as each new innovation arrives on the jazz scene. The adverse reaction to bop resulted in the revival of simpler forms of jazz like Early New Orleans Dixieland. Oddly enough, Parker and Gillespie were not terribly far from the early roots of jazz. Parker's earliest recordings were blues numbers; Gillespie's earliest recording was "King Porter Stomp," written by Jelly Roll Morton.

These changes in jazz, like the changes in classical music, were reactions against the preceding jazz styles. Musicians were constantly searching for new means of expression. As a consequence, they intentionally played melodic lines with unusual intervals. The absence of an easily recognizable melody has been one of the main obstacles to the acceptance of bop by the general public. The complexities of this style of jazz demand deeper concentration and more attentive listening. Rex Harris suggests that bop should not be dismissed at first hearing: "No worthwhile form of music will yield its secret so readily as that."[16]

Additional Reading Resources

Berendt, Joachim. *The New Jazz Book*, pp. 17–19, 61–70.

Dankworth, Avril. *Jazz: An Introduction to Its Musical Basis*, pp. 68–75.

Dexter, Dave. *The Jazz Story*, pp. 121–31.

Feather, Leonard. *The Book of Jazz*.

————. *Inside Jazz*.

Francis, André. *Jazz*, pp. 107–15, 124–30.

Harrison, Max. "Thelonious Monk." *Musician and Musicians*, London, May, 1982.

Hodeir, André. *Jazz: Its Evolution and Essence*, pp. 99–115.

Keepnews, Orin. "The Monk of Jazz: Memories of Thelonious, The Legendary Pianist," *Washington Post*, February 18, 1982.

Shapiro, Nat, and Hentoff, Nat, eds. *The Jazz Makers*, pp. 332–48.

Stearns, Marshall. *The Story of Jazz*, pp. 155–72.

Williams, Martin T. *The Jazz Tradition*, pp. 187–213.

Wilson, John S. "Thelonious Monk, Created Wry Jazz Melodies and Harmonies." *The New York Times*, February 23, 1982, p. D20.

Note: Complete information including name of publisher and date of publication is provided in the Bibliography.

14. Stan Kenton, *Cuban Fire*, The Creative World of Stan Kenton, ST 1008.

15. Woody Herman, *The Thundering Herds*, vol. 1, Columbia Records, C3L–25.

16. Rex Harris, *Jazz* (Baltimore, Md.: Penguin Books, 1952), p. 188.

Additional Record Resources

Art Blakey and the Jazz Messengers, "Straight Ahead," Concord Jazz Records CJ–168.

Bebop. New World Records, 271.

Be-Bop Era. RCA Victor Records, LVP–519.

Eckstine, Billy. *Mister B and the Band—The Savoy Sessions.* Savoy Records, SJL–2214.

The Genius of Bud Powell. Verve Records, VE2–2506.

Giants of Jazz. Atlantic Records, 2–905.

Gillespie, Dizzy. *Big 4.* Pablo Records, 23107.

———. *The Great Dizzy Gillespie.* Counterpoint Records, 554.

———. *In the Beginning.* Prestige Records, 24030.

Greatest Jazz Concert Ever. Prestige Records, 24024.

Jazz at Massey Hall. Fantasy Records, 86003.

Jazz in Revolution—The Big Bands in the 1940s, New World Records, 284.

Kenton, Stan. *The Kenton Era.* Creative World of Stan Kenton, 1030.

Monk, Thelonious. *Genius of Thelonious Monk.* Prestige Records, 7656.

———. *Memorial Album.* Milestone Records, M-47064.

———. *Straight, No Chaser.* Columbia Records, CS-9451.

Strictly Bebop. Capitol Records, ML–11059.

Suggested Classroom Activities

1. Explain the term *bop.*
2. In what ways was this direction in the development of jazz a change from the Swing Era?
3. Compare the arrangements of bop music with those of the Swing Era.
4. What is meant by "extended harmonies"?
5. Why were bop ensembles able to employ a faster tempo than swing bands?
6. Why is the word *tension* most appropriate in describing the feeling of bop music?
7. In what manner did the percussionist obtain the effect of accent and punctuation?
8. Listen to Dizzy Gillespie's rendition of "Things to Come" (*Dizzy Gillespie,* Galaxy Series, Long play 4811), and in your own words describe your reactions to the music.
9. An excellent example of the true bop sound is found on the album *Jazz at Massey Hall* (Fantasy 6003), in the selection "Wee" as played by Charlie Chan, Dizzy Gillespie, Bud Powell, Max Roach, and Charles Mingus. Name the instrument featured in the solo spot that follows the short introduction. Do you hear the ascending and descending melodic playing of the string bass? Is the instrument bowed or plucked? Which instrument improvises next? What would you say about the range of tones this instrument realizes? What instrument is third? Finally, what instrument takes over in the wild, exciting climax?
10. Listen to Charlie Parker's Re-Boppers playing "KoKo" (S, side 7, band 7) which is not the same as Ellington's blues "Ko-ko." "KoKo" borrows its chord changes from the song "Cherokee" and is a classic example of the true bop style of playing. Listen carefully to the interplay between the saxophone and trumpet as they toss the melody back and forth to the accompaniment of the exciting drummer Max Roach. As you listen, follow the musical analysis on the next page.

Listening Guide

From Taped Demonstration 15

Bop

:00 Ensemble chorus (trumpet, alto sax, and electric guitar in unison) (bass and drums keep 4/4 rhythm plus accents on piano)
:11 Trumpet solo (2 choruses, very frantic style)
:33 Solo break on drums
:35 Ensemble chorus (same as first chorus)
:48 End

From Smithsonian Collection (side 7, band 7)

Charlie Parker's Re-Boppers

"KoKo"

:00 Introduction—unison alto sax (Charlie Parker) and muted trumpet (Dizzy Gillespie), drums with brushes using many accents (Max Roach)
:06 Muted trumpet solo, drums continue as before
:12 Alto sax solo, drums the same
:19 Alto sax and muted trumpet in parallel harmony, drums the same

:25 1st chorus—alto sax solo, drums on a fast 4/4 rhythm plus accents, bass playing a very fast walking style (Curley Russell), piano enters with his own chordal punctuations. If the piano seems a trifle late, that is because that is also Gillespie, he had to put his trumpet down.

:50 Bridge of first chorus—change of chords

1:04 Last part of first chorus

1:15 2nd chorus—still Parker on alto sax

1:40 Bridge of second chorus

1:54 Last part of second chorus

2:07 Drum solo—very intricate as far as the pulse is concerned (this gives Gillespie time to go from piano to the trumpet)

2:27 Alto sax and muted trumpet in unison, drums now on cymbals

2:34 Muted trumpet solo, drums the same

2:40 Alto sax solo, drummer a bit lighter on cymbals now

2:45 Alto sax and muted trumpet in parallel harmony (a reminder of the introduction for the sake of continuity)

2:49 End

11
Cool
(1949–1955)

The bop style was a reaction against swing, and the cool style of playing was a reaction against the complexities of bop. "Conservatism and understatement were the keys to this era. Jazz assumed . . . the form of a restrained chamber music."[1] The shock treatment of ten brass and five saxes would have been entirely out of place. What was needed was truly a chamber orchestra. Chico Hamilton, a drummer, was surprisingly a leader in the new direction.[2] Of course, Hamilton was no ordinary drummer, as indicated by his subtle rhythmic control and use of different drum pitches and timbres. One of his surprises was that he featured Fred Katz on cello.[3] (As an introduction to cool jazz, listen to the cassette demonstration 16 included with this book.)

It is often thought that the violin and other stringed instruments do not make satisfying jazz sounds because these instruments, except for the plucked (**pizzicato**) bass, cannot be played percussively because they are usually bowed. This attitude reveals an oversight of some good jazz talent such as Jean Luc Ponty, Noel Pointer, Leroy Jenkins, Joe Venuti, Stuff Smith, Eddie South,[4] (NW, Joe Venuti, "My Honey's Loving Arms," side 1, band 1; Eddie South, "Hejre Kati," side 1, band 3; Stuff Smith, "Knock Knock," side 1, band 9, 250) Ray Nance, and Stephane Grappelly.[5] Edgar Redmond, a woodwind player, has put forth a great effort to enlighten music educators along this line and has produced a very good album to prove his point.[6]

The **tonal sonorities** of these conservative players could be compared to pastel colors, while the solos of Gillespie and his followers could be compared to fiery red colors. Cool was a new ". . . kind of jazz which could be quite easily arranged . . . by conservatory trained musicians with a real feeling for contrapuntal jazz in an extended form."[7] By the extended form, Stearns refers to the fact that this new style was not restricted to twelve-, sixteen-, and thirty-two-measure

1. Barry Ulanov, *Handbook of Jazz* (New York: Viking Press, 1959), p. 158.

2. Chico Hamilton, *The Best of Chico Hamilton,* Impulse Records, A–9174; *Easy Livin',* Sunset Records, SUS–5215.

3. *Chico Hamilton Quintet,* Pacific Jazz Records, PJ–1209.

4. Eddie Lang and Joe Venuti, "Farewell Blues," *Encyclopedia of Jazz on Records,* Decca Records, DXSF–7140; Joe Venuti, *The Daddy of the Violin,* BASF Records, BASF–MPS 2120885–0; Joe Venuti, *Stringing the Blues,* Columbia Records, C2L–24; Joe Venuti's Jazz Four, "My Honey's Loving Arms," Eddie South, "Hejre Kati"; Stuff Smith, "Knock Knock," *Little Club Jazz,* New World Records, 250.

5. Stephane Grappelly, *Django,* Barclay Records, 820105; Django Reinhardt Record, *Djangology,* RCA Victor Records, LPM–2319; *Violin Summit: 1966,* BASF Records, 20 626.

6. *Edgar Redmond and The Modern String Ensemble,* Disque Phenomenon Records, DP 2696.

7. Marshall Stearns, *The Story of Jazz* (London: Oxford University Press, 1958), p. 170.

Example 28

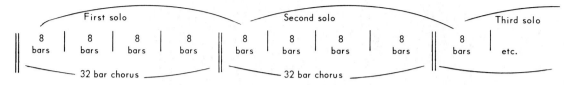

choruses. Cool players devised a way to go even further than bop players in the direction of freedom from the square-cut divisions of jazz music. For example, in playing a thirty-two-bar chorus, the soloist would play a little into the next player's chorus, causing the second soloist to play into the third soloist's chorus in order to play thirty-two bars, and so on (see example 28). This helped the music flow as a continuous entity and erased the conception of a block type of form. By 1950, the acceptance of the long-playing record made possible the recording of longer works and longer improvisations.

This music sacrificed excitement for subtlety, and the players underplayed their variations. André Hodeir analyzed cool music according to three principal characteristics: "First, a sonority very different from the one adopted by earlier schools; second, a special type of phrase; and finally, an orchestral conception that . . . is not its least interesting element."[8] These three characteristics deserve examination. The most pronounced difference from the preceding eras was the more delicate **attack** used by the cool players. Little or no vibrato was used, and the wind players had a tendency to use the **middle registers** rather than the extremes. The delicate attacks used in the Cool Era and the lack of vibrato caused the playing to resemble that of classical playing, although relaxation was more salient to this style of jazz than to the classical performances.[9] It should also be noted that more and more schooled players were entering the jazz field.

In general, cool phrasing did not permit the player to deviate far from the original line. Some critics consider this backtracking rather than an advancement. Even with their melodic charm these lines often lacked the richness and boldness of music of the Bop Era. The cool players conceived their harmonic parts polyphonically. This approach gave the instrumentalist an independence of line not found in the Swing Era.

Changes

The chamber-type orchestral groups or combos were usually composed of from three to eight players. The introduction of instruments not previously associated

with jazz changed the overall sound. The flute became important as a jazz instrument, as did the French horn, oboe, and cello. Important flute players include Paul Horn,[10] Buddy Collette, Herbie Mann,[11] Bud Shank, Frank Wess, and others. The soft sounds of the French horn fit beautifully with the general feeling of cool jazz. Nevertheless, there has been a scarcity of jazz French horn players. However, Willie Ruff, Johnny Graas,[12] Junior Collins, and Julius Watkins can be mentioned.

Playing jazz on a double-reed instrument is still not common. Bob Cooper began playing jazz on the oboe while he was with Stan Kenton. Today, good fresh blues and other jazz formats can be heard on the oboe on records by Yusef Lateef[13] and Rahsaan Roland Kirk. The oboe and other double-reed instruments, new to jazz, fit in very well with the more standard instruments (trumpet, trombone, saxophone) when the standard instruments are played in a cool manner as individual instruments instead of as parts of a section. The tuba was brought into jazz for the first time since the very early dixieland period, and was given slow-moving melodic lines instead of the familiar bass parts of marches.

The **flügelhorn** worked its way into the jazz scene mainly through the efforts of Miles Davis, Clark Terry, and Art Farmer.[14] The flügel, as it is often called, is in the same key and pitch as the B flat trumpet and cornet. It has a larger bore and as a consequence has a darker, more mellow sound; it is also easier to play at a low

8. André Hodeir, *Jazz: Its Evolution and Essence* (New York: Grove Press, 1956), p. 118.

9. Woody Herman, "Summer Sequence," *The Thundering Herds*, Columbia Records, C3L–25; "Early Autumn," *The History of Jazz*, vol. 4.

10. Paul Horn, *Profile of a Jazz Musician*, Columbia Records, CL 1922.

11. Herbie Mann, *Latin Mann*, Columbia Records, CL 2388; *Today*, Atlantic Records, SD 1454; *Stone Flute*, Embryo Records, SD 18035.

12. Johnny Graas, "Mulliganesque," *Encyclopedia of Jazz*, vol. 4.

13. Yusef Lateef, *Eastern Sounds*, Prestige Records, PR 7319.

14. Art Farmer, *Art*, Argo Records, 678.

Modern Jazz Quartet: John Lewis, piano and director; Connie Kay, drums; Percy Heath, bass; Milt Jackson, vibraphone. *Courtesy of Ray Avery.*

pitch and harder to play at a high pitch than the trumpet. The most enjoyable examples are the Clark Terry-Bob Brookmeyer recordings that team flügelist Terry with the very talented and tasteful valve trombonist Brookmeyer.[15]

The cool players established that jazz need not be confined to 4/4 and 2/4 meters and that choruses need not always be divided symmetrically. Many new meter signatures came into use in jazz, including 3/4, 5/4, 9/4, and others. Successful jazz compositions often used an interchange of signatures within a selection. Pianist Dave Brubeck stimulated interest by laying one rhythm, or more, over another, creating both polyrhythms and **polymeters.**[16] Don Ellis has, of course, carried the use of meters new in jazz much further (discussed further in chapter 15).

This school of jazz moved closer to classical music, even to the point of adopting such forms as rondos and fugues.[17] Sometimes the use of classical forms in jazz has been categorized as **third stream music.** Sometimes, however, the Modern Jazz Quartet (and other groups) used the fugue and similar forms just to play good, swinging, subtle jazz and gave no thought to third stream music. It should be noted that

the Quartet played classical forms quite precisely. For example, the fugues they played were truly baroque in form except that the exposition parts were improvised.

Critics who feel that the Cool Era lacked excitement should note that these players were seeking a more subtle means of jazz expression. The Modern Jazz Quartet, while being subtle, had the strength and vitality necessary for longevity; it lasted from 1951 to 1974, then reassembled in 1981.

The public seemed quite divided in its attitude toward cool players. Some people felt that the musicians were bored and arrogant, that they were disdainful and cold. Others considered the cool players to be creative, hard-working, serious musicians, not clowns trying to be impressive. They understood that the players were in fact saying, "like my music for itself."

15. Clark Terry, *Bobby Brookmeyer Quintet,* Mainstream Records, 320.

16. Dave Brubeck, *Time Out,* Columbia Records, CL 1397.

17. Modern Jazz Quartet, "A Fugue for Music Inn," *The Modern Jazz Quartet at Music Inn,* Atlantic Records, 1247.

The Performers

Cool developed gradually, as did previous styles. Saxophonist Benny Carter underplayed his attacks, Teddy Wilson played the piano with a delicate touch, Benny Goodman stopped using the thick vibrato of Jimmy Noone and other clarinetists. Miles Davis's solo on Charlie Parker's "Chasin' the Bird" in 1947 and John Lewis's piano solo on Dizzy Gillespie's record of "Round Midnight" in 1948 anticipated the Cool Era. However, it took Lester Young to prove that great swing could be generated without using any of the more violent aspects of jazz.

Near the end of the 1940s there were two large bands that seemed to have entirely different feelings and directions, yet both were quite influential in the beginnings of cool—Claude Thornhill's band from about 1946 to 1949 and the Woody Herman band of 1947 to 1949. Both were instrumental in directing the trend away from the hot feel toward the cool feel.

Woody Herman is the type of bandleader who always seems to make changes in his personnel that are responsible for keeping the band up to date. He formed a band in Los Angeles in 1947 after he had disbanded for three months. This band had a saxophone section that changed the concept of sax sections that followed. He hired Sam Marowitz on alto, Stan Getz, Zoot Sims, and Herbie Stewart on tenors, and Serge Chaloff on baritone. From this group (not using alto sax) came the famous "Four Brothers" sound. This was a tightly knit, beautifully blended section of four excellent jazz players who again disproved the theory that good improvisors are too individualistic to coordinate well. The tune "Four Brothers," incidentally, was written by another talented reed player, Jimmy Giuffre. Another boost for the cool advocate was the recording by the Herman band of Ralph Burns's "Early Autumn." This record alone was enough to launch the career of Stan Getz.[18]

The Claude Thornhill band, in addition to a tuba and a French horn player, had such talented musicians as Lee Konitz on alto sax, Gerry Mulligan on baritone sax and as arranger, and Gil Evans also as arranger.[19] (NW, Claude Thornhill, "Donna Lee," 284, side 1, band 6) The nucleus of this band made the first Miles Davis-Gil Evans records. One of the several recording bans was lifted in December of 1948, and the way was open for the three recording sessions in 1949 and 1950 for an album that was eventually called *The Birth of the Cool*.[20] (S, "Boplicity," side 9, band 1) An excerpt of a question-and-answer session with Gerry Mulligan throws a little light on these events:

Question: *Was the fact that so many men on the Miles Davis dates came from the Thornhill band coincidental?*
Mulligan: *No, the Thornhill orchestra was a tremendous influence on that small band. Because the instrumentation, when you get down to it, was a reduced version of what Claude was using at the time.*
Question: *Was this an attempt to get away from the conventional bop format?*
Mulligan: *No, the idea was just to try to get a good little rehearsal band together. Something to write for.*
Question: *Then it was more or less regarded as a workshop experiment?*
Mulligan: *Yes. As far as the "Cool Jazz" part of it, all of that comes after the fact of what it was designed to be.*[21]

As for his part in these recordings, Miles Davis believes that at the time he was interested in nothing more original than playing with a lighter sound; it was more expressive as far as he was concerned. At any rate, the recordings of this nine-man orchestra did set the tone for the Cool Era. Mulligan wrote "Jeru," "Venus de Milo," "Rocker," and "Godchild"; Gil Evans contributed "Boplicity" and "Moon Dreams"; John Lewis wrote "Move," "Budo," and "Rouge"; and John Carisi wrote "Israel."

The George Shearing Quintet also influenced the beginning of cool. Shearing, a classically trained pianist originally from England, can play in any style of jazz or classical music that he cares to. One of his favorite approaches is to play bop-type thoughts in a very subtle manner, thus making a good transition from one era to the next.[22]

The leading exponents of cool jazz were Lester Young, Miles Davis (from about 1949 on), and Stan Getz, one of the few tenor saxophone players who compares well with Young in this style.

18. Woody Herman, *The Thundering Herds.*

19. Claude Thornhill, "Snowfall," *The Great Band Era*, RCA Victor Records, RD4–25 (RRIS–5473); Claude Thornhill Orchestra, "Donna Lee," *Jazz in Revolution—The Big Bands in the 1940s*, New World Records, 284; *The Memorable Claude Thornhill*, Columbia Records, KG–32906.

20. Miles Davis, *The Birth of the Cool*, Capitol Records, DT 1974; "Boplicity," Smithsonian Collection of Classic Jazz.

21. Leonard Feather, "Cool," in *Jazz* (Los Angeles: Pacific Press, 1959), p. 26.

22. George Shearing, *Best of George Shearing*, Capitol Records, ST–2104; *Touch of Genius*, MGM Records, E 90.

Gerry Mulligan. *Courtesy of Ray Avery.*

Lester Young

Lester Young not only started a new style of playing tenor sax, but was also the epitome of an entirely new concept of jazz—hence his nickname Prez, president of the Cool Era of jazz.[23] Lester Young was born in Mississippi and matured during the 1930s in Kansas City where the jam sessions prepared him for all competition. Young first attracted attention when he was with the Count Basie band,[24] but there was much opposition to his playing at first. The big bands were very much oriented to the full-bodied Coleman Hawkins approach to tenor sax. Young seemed light and airy, even out of place, in the big Basie band. However, the younger players were more than impressed. Lester Young, the model for cool tenor saxophonists, played softer than Coleman Hawkins and was more abstract and subtle. Young himself was influenced the most by

Rudy Wiedoeft (a nonjazz concert artist), Frankie Trumbauer, and Jimmy Dorsey. Oddly enough, all were white alto saxophone or C melody saxophone players instead of black tenor saxophone players.

Young joined the Basie band for the second time in 1936 and stayed with him through 1940. During this time, he recorded 105 sides with Basie, plus many others with outside small groups. His first job as a leader was in 1941 on Fifty-second Street in New York City. However, he did return to the Basie band for a few months in 1943 and 1944 and, in 1944, was drafted into the army. Young was associated with Norman Granz's *Jazz at the Philharmonic* from 1946 until his death on March 15, 1959. Young had a beautiful, light, pure sound, but his biggest asset was his phrasing. He would carry melodic thoughts to their conclusion regardless of the bar lines. He recorded many solos with the Count Basie band that are available in repressings. But those that are most cherished by his army of admirers are the small combo records, including those backing Billie Holiday vocals.[25]

Miles Davis

Miles Davis first came into New York in 1945 to study at Juilliard. He has said that when he started he played like anyone he could imitate, but states that Clark Terry was his main influence. It seems that no matter what Davis plays on his horn, it has a rather sad feeling to it. There is no doubt that he plays with the sound that he desires and that he simply would not trust his personal thoughts to any other type of sound. He seems to have a highly developed sense of communicative simplicity. At first, Davis could neither play high, loud, nor very fast. When he first arrived on the New York scene, he was young enough to be still in the process of developing strength in his lip muscles. But he felt that he could think better anyway if he were playing with a light sound; he was more relaxed with that approach. The critics of his bop efforts with Parker in 1945 should remember that eighteen-year-old Davis was only in his formative years.

Today, many fans are annoyed that Davis continually changes. These fans claim that just when they have become oriented to one style of his, the next time they hear him he seems to have changed to a different style. It is true that the only real constant in his career

23. Lester Young, *Prez,* Mainstream Records, 56012.

24. *Lester Young Memorial,* Epic Records, SN 6031.

25. *The Essential Lester Young,* Verve Records, V–8398; *Giant of Jazz,* Sunset Records, SUM–1181.

Lester Young. *Courtesy of Dave Dexter, Jr.*

is his unpredictability. Davis, though, is a contemporary musician who is always searching for a new, fresh, exciting way to play his music. He does not feel obligated to older fans; after all, they can buy his previous albums and thereby preserve the style that they prefer. Incidentally, these fans usually feel that the collaboration of the talents of Davis and Gil Evans is one of the highlights of music history. For interesting contrasts, listeners should compare the feelings on such Davis albums as *Sketches of Spain,* done with Gil Evans, and *Bitches Brew,* done with an electrified rhythm section as well as with an amplification of Davis's trumpet.[26] (S, "Summertime," side 10, band 2)

Summary

Cool is a style of jazz that even the general public can agree is beautiful music. Very few players have contributed more to this beauty than tenor saxophonist Stan Getz. Getz was very heavily influenced by Lester Young, but, as time went on, he was able to establish an identity of his own that is quite distinctive. His *bossa nova* excursions brought together a very moving Brazilian rhythm with pure tone and melodic charm, a combination that was readily accepted throughout the world.[27]

26. Miles Davis, *Sketches of Spain,* Columbia Records, CL1480; Miles Davis, *Bitches Brew,* Columbia Records, GP 26; "Summertime," Smithsonian Collection of Classic Jazz.

27. Stan Getz, *Jazz Samba,* Verve Records, V–8432; *Jazz Samba Encore,* Verve Records, 68523.

Miles Davis. *Courtesy of Les McCann.*

As cool jazz drifted farther and farther from bop and all other preceding styles, it reached the apex of subtlety when Jimmy Giuffre, playing low-register clarinet instead of tenor sax, decided to do away entirely with the steady pulse of jazz. Giuffre claimed that the beat of the music could be implicit instead of explicit. But when the listener experiences Giuffre's trio (clarinet, bass, and guitar) playing "Happy Man," the pulse can be felt quite readily—even though no instrument is relegated to the pulse alone.[28]

A word should be said here about *west coast jazz*. This term usually refers to Gerry Mulligan's pianoless band and his associates in California. The term itself has been generally dropped with the realization that this was merely a part of the cool movement. Miles Davis, Lester Young, and Claude Thornhill were located on the east coast, and it is quite easy to list players on the west coast who were much more involved in a hotter approach to jazz. Communication being what it is, it is hardly likely that any style of jazz was fostered exclusively in one area.

In considering cool jazz in retrospect, one realizes that the major problem of performing in this style is that no matter how cool the jazz becomes it must always have warmth—a problem the best musicians solved beautifully.

Additional Reading Resources

Berendt, Joachim. *The New Jazz Book*, pp. 19–24.

Cole, Bill. *Miles Davis.*

Francis, André. *Jazz*, pp. 130–49.

Hodeir, André. *Jazz: Its Evolution and Essence*, pp. 116–38.

Shapiro, Nat, and Hentoff, Nat, eds. *The Jazz Makers*, pp. 243–75.

Stearns, Marshall. *The Story of Jazz*, pp. 167–72.

Williams, Martin T. *The Jazz Tradition*, pp. 219, 233.

Note: Complete information including name of publisher and date of publication is provided in the Bibliography.

Additional Record Resources

Baker, Chet. *Cool Burnin'*. Prestige Records, PR 7496.

Davis, Miles. *Basic Miles*. Columbia Records, C 32025.

————. *Greatest Hits*. Columbia Records, CS–9809.

————. *Greatest Hits*. Prestige Records, S–7457.

————. *Miles Ahead*. Columbia Records, CL 1041.

————. *Miles Davis at Filmore*. Columbia Records, G 30038.

————. *Miles Davis*. Prestige Records, 24001.

————. *Walkin'*. Prestige Records, 7608.

Desmond, Paul, and Mulligan, Gerry. *Two of a Mind*. RCA Victor Records, LSP–2624.

Evans, Gil. *Out of the Cool*. Impulse Records, A–4.

Getz, Stan. *Best of Stan Getz*. Verve Records, V6–8719.

————. *Stan Getz Years*. Roost Records, RK–103.

Greatest Names in Jazz. Verve Records, Pr 2–3.

Modern Jazz Quartet. *European Concert*. Atlantic Records, 2–603.

————. *European Tour*. Atlantic Records, SD 20603.

————. *The Last Concert*. Atlantic Records, 909.

————. *Modern Jazz Quartet*. Prestige Records, 24005.

Mulligan, Gerry. *What Is There to Say*. Columbia Records, 32 16 0258.

Mulligan, Gerry, and Baker, Chet. *Timeless*. Pacific Jazz Records, PJ–75.

Nica's Dream. New World Records, 242.

Young, Lester. *The Aladdin Sessions*. Blue Note Records, BN–LA456–H2.

————. *Complete Lester Young on Savoy*. Arista Records, SJL–2022.

————. *Young Lester Young*. Columbia Records, J 24.

Suggested Classroom Activities

1. What are some words that might be used to describe the feeling and tone of the Cool Era?

2. How does the cool type of tonal attack and vibrato influence the descriptive terms of activity 1?

3. What instruments became important in this era that were not prominent previously?

4. What instrument used in early dixieland music became more prominent and was used melodically in this era?

28. Jimmy Giuffre, "Happy Man," *Seven Pieces*, Verve Records, MG V–8307.

5. What new meters were used in place of 2/4 and 4/4?

6. Define the terms *polyrhythm and polymeter.*

7. Who were the leading exponents of cool jazz?

8. Two selections that are good examples of this jazz era are "Jeru" and "Moon Dreams" from the album *Miles Davis—Birth of the Cool* (Capitol Records, DT1974). Compare and contrast these selections by answering the following:

   a. Are the instruments played mostly in the middle range or do you hear extremely high and low pitches?

   b. Do the instrumentalists use vibrato in solo spots?

   c. Compare the percussion rhythm with that of the Bop Era. How do you react to the rhythmic pulse of "Moon Dreams"?

9. An example of the use of alternating meters is "Three to Get Ready" in the album *Time Out— The Dave Brubeck Quartet* (Columbia, CL 1397). After the short waltzlike melody, the meter alternates between 3/4 and 4/4. Listen carefully and clap lightly two measures of three (heavy-light-light, heavy-light-light) followed by two measures of four (heavy-light-light-light, heavy-light-light-light) and continue to alternate.

10. Listen to "The Morning After" and "I Want to Be Happy" from the album *Chico Hamilton Quintet* (Pacific Jazz Enterprises, PJ—1209), and identify by sound two instruments used in jazz for the first time.

Listening Guide

From Taped Demonstration 16

Cool

:00 Ensemble chorus (flute lead and flügelhorn harmony) (bass, guitar, and drums keep a relaxed 4/4 rhythm while piano plays fill-ins)

:27 Flute solo (one chorus) (listen also for piano fill-ins)

:55 Ensemble chorus (same as first chorus)

1:26 End

From Smithsonian Collection (side 9, band 1)

Miles Davis

"Boplicity"

:00 1st chorus (no introduction)—Trumpet lead (Miles Davis), bass and drums play a relaxed 4/4 rhythm throughout, piano plays gentle chordal punctuations

:27 Bridge—change of melody and chords

:42 Last part of 1st chorus

:56 2nd chorus—baritone sax solo (Gerry Mulligan), rhythm section continues as before

1:24 Bridge—sax unison with French horn, trombone, and tuba

1:35 Trumpet solo

1:42 Last part of 2nd chorus—slight variation on the original 8 measures of the tune, ensemble

1:58 3rd chorus—trumpet solo, sustained harmonic background

2:25 Bridge—piano solo (John Lewis) sustained harmonic background for ½ of solo (saxes, trombone, French horn, tuba)

2:40 Ensemble with the original melody

2:57 End

12
Hard Bop—
Funky
(circa 1954–   )

At first, this style was called Funky Hard Bop Regression, but the style changed considerably and the title was shortened to funky. The word **funky** refers to the rollicking, rhythmic feeling of the style. The term **hard** means a performance that is more driving and less relaxed than cool jazz. The phrase **bop regression** implies a return to the elements of the bop style. "The funky idiom represented an attempt by the jazzman to rediscover his emotional roots. . . ."[1]

It may well be true that musical styles swing back and forth like a pendulum. But it must be kept in mind that the swinging of the music pendulum is not smooth. The swing toward complexity is fairly gradual. The players of the Swing Era added more musicians; the bop players played with extended harmonies and complicated melodies; the cool players brought in new instruments, time signatures, extended forms; and so forth. But the funky style that followed seemed to revert quite suddenly to the most basic of music elements, for example, the "amen chords" from religious services. (As an introduction to the funky style, listen to the cassette demonstration 17 included with this book.)

The term funky is often used interchangeably with soul during this period. Both the funky and soul styles are also associated with the music prevalent in the black churches. The term soul certainly has a connection to the church and perhaps speaks of the intended emotional content of the music. On the other hand, funky has a more earthy association. Emotional and earthy are both appropriate descriptors of this music.

Funky was a rawboned type of playing, with a highly rhythmical melody and a less complex harmony than that of the preceding era. This music had a happy sound and lacked tension and frustration. These performers used bop elements that were generally simplified because of having passed through the Cool Era. Today, the simplification has gone even further. Most of the bop sounds have been dropped in favor of elements that tend toward gospel jazz.

Contributing to the development of the funky and gospel styles, no doubt, was the new black awareness developing in the United States. During this social development, blacks found the black church, its harmonies and blues inflections, a link to their roots.

Some authors go so far as to suggest that the funky style was an effort among blacks to recapture jazz as their own expression.[2] Even if this intent did exist, the funky idiom quickly spread throughout the jazz world and was soon played from school bands to professional ensembles independent of race.

Perhaps even more than an ethnic reaction, the funky idiom can be seen as a reaction to the cool intellectualism many found in music of the cool period. The lively emotionally exuberant nature of the funky

1.   Martin T. Williams, "Bebop and After: A Report," in *Jazz,* eds. Nat Hentoff and Albert McCarthy (Holt, Rinehart & Winston, 1959), p. 297.

2.   James Lincoln Collier, *The Making of Jazz,* Dell Publishing Co., Inc., New York, 1978, pp. 435–453.

Example 29

Example 30A

Example 30B

style stands in strong contrast to the measured and controlled expression of the cool players. Unlike the cool style, which looked to European compositional techniques, the funky style adopted the truly American, and oral, idioms found in gospel and blues.

In addition to stylistic differences, the distinction between cool and hard bop was also geographical. The cool style was often called "west coast" jazz because it seemed centered in California. Shelly Manne even suggests that a more relaxed life style in California might have been a factor in the development of the relaxed cool jazz style, contrasted with the more driving bop style he found typical of New York jazz.[3]

The Music

The funky idiom embraces homophonic harmonic construction. Although the lines appear to be invented independently, as can be seen in example 29, they are actually planned homophonically. The lower note is played because of the sound of the specific interval produced when it is played against the melodic note above it. Example 29 also points up the excessive use of the fourth and fifth intervals. Another identifying feature is the use of many blue notes, the E-flats and B-flats in example 29.

Although these blue notes are not really the same as the original blue notes heard by church singers, their prevalent use in this style is meant to create the same effect. The original blue notes were slightly mistuned notes (very often the third and seventh of the scale) in a major key. This mistuning created a disagreement between the major key and the almost minor blue notes sung against it. In an effort to recreate the blues sound, many pieces in this period were actually played in a minor key.

Performers

The homophonic construction of the Swing Era and that of the Funky Era are compared in examples 30A and 30B. Swing music was harmonized in a closed manner, as shown in example 30A by the blocks of chords. The funky players, while planning their music homophonically, developed a more open, loose setting, as demonstrated in example 30B.

This style was introduced by pianists but was quickly adopted by all instrumentalists. The funky style

3. Shelly Manne, from an interview with Reginald Buckner, *Jazz: American Classic,* video tape # 7.

Horace Silver. *Courtesy of Ray Avery.*

was brought to public notice by pianist Horace Silver and a group led by drummer Art Blakey called the Jazz Messengers.[4] Horace Silver made many records with his own combo.[5] (NW, "Stop Time," 271, side 2, band 6) Most pianists who play funky style music admit that Silver was the progenitor.

Berendt mentions Silver as the beginning:

The pianist-composer Horace Silver—and along with him a few others—has broken through with a manner of playing known as "funky": slow or medium blues, played hard on the beat, with all of the heavy feeling and expression characteristic of the old blues. Jazz musicians of all persuasions and on both coasts have thrown themselves into funk with notable enthusiasm.[6]

A good example of a big band playing in a funky manner is "Hey, Pete" on Dizzy Gillespie's album entitled *Dizzy in Greece.*[7] This album contains part of the music that Gillespie performed on the first State Department sponsored tour in jazz history. It is also excellent proof that the talented Quincy Jones could write

good funky blues works for big bands. In addition, the album demonstrates the fact that the funky melodies were more riff-like and rhythmically and melodically more simple than in bop.

Critic Don Heckman has some different insights into these changes as he writes about the jazz of the 1960s:

Perhaps the most significant was the music that was called, variously, funk, soul, etc. Its roots in modern jazz could be traced to Horace Silver's efforts to

4.   Horace Silver (Art Blakey), *A Night at Bird Land,* Blue Note Records, 1521, vol. 1; *Horace Silver and the Jazz Messengers,* Blue Note Records, 1518.

5.   Horace Silver, *Blowing the Blues Away,* Blue Note Records, 4017; *Song for My Father,* Blue Note Records, 4185; Horace Silver, "Stop Time," *Bebop,* New World Records, 271.

6.   From the *Jazz Book: From New Orleans to Rock and Free Jazz,* translated by Dan Morgenstern, copyright 1975 Lawrence Hill & Co., Westport, Connecticut.

7.   Dizzy Gillespie, "Hey Pete," *Dizzy in Greece,* Verve Records, MEV—8017.

Les McCann. *Courtesy of Ray Avery.*

translate the Blues-based forms, riffs, and rhythms of the Midwestern and Southwestern bands of the late '20s and early '30s into the idiom of the contemporary small group. Its roots in Negro society were less well defined but also important.

Silver's work, however, was soon modified, simplified, and repeated—over and over. And few of the imitators understood the delicate balance of elements that was crucial to the music's artistic success. As often happens, the values Silver was seeking to express were discarded by most of his imitators in favor of the superficialities—the simple rhythms, the reduction of blues changes to their most simple form, and the distortion of Gospel-derived techniques.

The relationship between this music, which was considered by many to be a genuine expression of the Negro past, and the growing civil-rights movement was very close.[8]

The fact that funky music was a culmination of all previous styles leads one to conclude that this jazz must have been extremely complex music strictly for musicians. On the contrary, the return to jazz roots indicated by the less complex harmonies, excessive use of blue notes, and simpler rhythmic feeling enhanced

8. Don Heckman, "Ornette and the Sixties," *Down Beat* 31, no. 20 (July 1964): 59.

communication between players and listeners. It is interesting that on early Horace Silver recordings the bop concept is prominent and the afterbeat accent hardly discernible. In the funky style the bop elements faded gradually as the accented afterbeat developed.

The Hammond organ had been only rarely used before 1951 (Fats Waller and Count Basie) when Wild Bill Davis surprised everyone by performing real blues-oriented works on it. Jimmy Smith proved the real potential of the instrument. For one thing, he used a larger variety of organ stops (effects) than any other player in the jazz field—and with incredible technique. The instrument was accepted wholeheartedly in the Funky Era.

Certainly one of the best funky piano players was Carl Perkins, who died much too soon to leave a legacy.[9] Les McCann paid tribute to Perkins by naming a tune after him.[10] Another notable funky artist is Ramsey Lewis.

André Previn adopted the funky style when he came on the jazz scene. There was considerable controversy concerning the worth or at least the sincerity of Previn's interpretation when he first entered the jazz field. Previn, however, continued to listen to good players and to associate himself with an excellent rhythm section (Shelly Manne, Red Mitchell, and others), and his playing improved rapidly to the point where it was no longer controversial. Today, Previn is capable of leading an entire tour as a jazz pianist, a classical pianist, or a classical conductor. He is, at this writing, the conductor of a symphony orchestra.

Just about the time that jazz musicians were deciding that they wanted to get back to communicating with the public (about 1953), a reputable critic of symphonic music, opera, and so on, Henry Pleasants, wrote a scathing book emphasizing that present-day composers of so-called serious music had lost touch entirely with their dwindling audience. "He [the contemporary 'serious' composer] finds it difficult to admit that he is simply not producing music that provokes a sympathetic response in his listeners. He forgets that it is the purpose of music to provoke such a response, and that all superior music in the past has provoked it."[11] The funky players agreed with Pleasants. Communication at the immediate level was truly important.

Gospel Jazz

Gospel jazz is an extension of the funky style. If a distinction is to be made between funky and gospel, it can be found in gospel's more triadic use of harmonies, very much like those associated with the improvisational singing of hymns. As the name implies, gospel jazz uses elements from, and has a definite feeling of, early gospel music.[12] A primary example of these elements is the constant use of the amen chord progression (I, IV, I) (**the plagal cadence**). To hear extensive use of the amen chords listen to Les McCann's "Fish This Week."[13] In spite of the fact that this style is a return to prejazz music, gospel jazz has also been influenced by all preceding jazz styles including their harmonies, forms, and advanced musical techniques.[14] Rhythm, as well as emotional intensity, is highlighted in gospel jazz.

Many selections of this form of jazz can just as easily be performed in a church as in a nightclub. One is Les McCann's "A Little 3/4 for God and Company."[15] Big gospel bands sometimes perform in a handclapping, "shouting Baptist" manner as they enact a scene of baptism in a work such as "Wade in the Water."[16]

The first edition of this textbook spoke of this type of jazz as "soul jazz"; since then, the term has been used *ad infinitum*. If *soul* means *sincerity,* then certainly Armstrong's first recordings, or those of Jack Teagarden, must be included in this category. And no performer was more sincere than Mahalia Jackson. But the term began to have some racial and revolutionary connotations. Therefore, as the music reverted more and more to church roots, the authors have seen the label for this kind of jazz gradually change to "gospel jazz."

Charles Mingus

Charles Mingus is, perhaps, the most difficult player/composer of the bop and post bop era to categorize. His musical output covers a wide berth of idioms and styles, from his earliest work with Armstrong and Kid Ory to

9. Carl Perkins, "Too Close for Comfort," *Jazz Pianists Galore,* World Pacific Records, JWC–506.

10. Les McCann, "For Carl Perkins," *Les McCann Plays the Truth,* Pacific Jazz Records, 3075.

11. Henry Pleasants, *Serious Music and All That Jazz,* p. 26. Copyright © 1969 by Henry Pleasants. Reprinted by permission of Simon & Schuster, a Division of Gulf & Western Corporation.

12. Les McCann, *The Truth,* Pacific Jazz Records, 2.

13. McCann, *The Truth.*

14. The Jazz Brothers, "Something Different," *The Soul of Jazz,* Riverside Records. S-5.

15. McCann, *The Truth.*

16. Johnny Griffin, "Wade in the Water," *The Soul of Jazz,* Riverside Records, S-5.

Charles Mingus. *Tony Lane Courtesy Fantasy Records.*

the later, almost free, compositions like "Pithecanthropus Erectus."[17] His efforts became centrally important during the hard bop days. His connection to that idiom may not be, at first, stylistically apparent. However, his compositional intent was to create a direct and immediate emotional statement. His legacy to this jazz tradition lies in the manner in which he tried to convey that emotion.

He attempted to channel the creative energies of his players into a unified statement. While he relied on the individual strengths of his players, he also expected them to work toward a common emotional statement during a performance. This approach differs from the traditional bop approach which encouraged players to seek very individual statements during their improvisations.

An example of Mingus's emotional intent can be heard in his recording of "Haitian Fight Song."[18] He has been quoted that it could also have been called "Afro-American Fight Song."[19] He goes on to state that to play it successfully, he must think about prejudice, hate and persecution. In this regard, Mingus shows his tie to the funky movement and its relationship to the developing black rights activities.

A more direct tie to the gospel idiom can be found in his 1959 recording of "Better Git It in Your Soul" from his album "Mingus Ah Um."[20] In this recording, the reference to the gospel church is made clear.

Mingus's ties to both the swing and bop traditions can be heard in his composition "Hora Decubitus."[21] (S, "Hora Decubitus," side 10, band 5) The 1963 recording of this piece shows the balance between individual statement and collective intent Mingus was able to inspire in his players. The emotional level is high from the beginning to the end of the performance. Only an ensemble that is both loose and secure could successfully support the different solo styles of Booker Ervin (tenor saxophone) and Eric Dolphy (alto saxophone).

Sonny Rollins

Tenor saxophonist Sonny Rollins exercised a great deal of influence during the late 1950s. He captured the attention of many of the day's players with his melodic style of improvisation. He often improvises from a melodic line with apparent disregard for chord structure.[22] As previously stated, an improvising player in the Swing Era usually had only a few measures in which to express his ideas. Rollins, on the other hand, often

17. Charles Mingus, *The Best of Charles Mingus,* Atlantic SD 1555.

18. Charles Mingus, *The Best of Charles Mingus,* Atlantic SD 1555.

19. James Lincoln Collier, *The Making of Jazz* (New York: Dell Publishing Co., Inc. 1978), p. 446.

20. Charles Mingus, "Mingus Ah Um," Columbus CS 8171.

21. Charles Mingus, "Hora Decubitas," Smithsonian Collection of Classic Jazz.

22. Sonny Rollins, *Sonny Rollins at Music Inn,* Metro Jazz Records, E 1011.

Sonny Rollins. *Courtesy of Leonard Feather.*

improvises for twenty or thirty minutes in order to develop his musical thoughts. He invents a short phrase and elaborates on it, expanding the idea in every conceivable direction as Mozart, Haydn, and Beethoven did. The concept is at least five hundred years old.

Rollin's playing shows cool and bop influences repeatedly. For two choruses of "Limehouse Blues" he shows great economy of notes, playing only what he thinks the listener need hear. Then the bop influences become apparent, plus an occasional funky phrase.[23] On his recording of "St. Thomas," his solo flows extremely well as he establishes a short melodic thought and elaborates on it, changing it in every way that he can.[24] By little phrases he continually brings the listener back to thoughts that he has played earlier. Listen to "Doxy" to hear this approach.[25]

An interesting aspect of Rollins's career was that after he had become a top nightclub attraction he became dissatisfied with his performance. He retired for two years, from the summer of 1959 to the fall of 1961 (and again in 1969), in order to practice. (Stories are that much of this practicing took place on top of the Williamsburg Bridge in New York City.) Such retirement action takes great courage and dedication. The consensus seems to be that Rollins's absence did bring his coordination to real excellence.

23. Sonny Rollins, "Limehouse Blues," *Sonny Rollins at Music Inn,* Metro Jazz Records, E 1011.

24. Sonny Rollins, "St. Thomas," *Saxophone Colossus.* Prestige Records, LP 7079.

25. Sonny Rollins, "Doxy," *Sonny Rollins at Music Inn* and *On Man in Jazz,* RCA Victor Records, LPM/LSP-2612.

The key in Rollins's advancement is thematic improvisation rather than either improvisation on a chord progression or variations on an established melody. Rollins is more concerned with fragments of a piece than with the whole melody itself. He uses these fragments for his own personal expression. Many musicians use this approach, but Rollins seems to have brought it to a recognizable and viable level.

This *thematic* or *motivic* approach can be heard in the way Rollins works the theme of "St. Thomas."[26] Rollins's recording of "Blue 7" is a clear example of how he (sometimes humorously) dissects a melodic line.[27] (S, "Blue 7," side 10, band 3) It is sometimes noted that this approach stems from the piano playing of Thelonious Monk—at least as far as Rollins is concerned. Therefore, another example of the thematic approach is Monk's development of a little three-note motif in "Bags' Groove."[28] (S, "Bags' Groove," side 10, band 1) Most musicians who had observed Monk's approach considered it valid but pianistic. After Rollins demonstrated that it was feasible and logical on a saxophone (which can be played only one note at a time), an entire school of wind players followed his lead.

Straight-ahead Jazz

The hard bop school often explained its development as a return to the basics of jazz. It saw the new instrumentation and compositional devices used by cool musicians as gimmicks rather than valid developments of the jazz tradition. Their call was, therefore, back to a "straight-ahead" jazz that was more improvisatory and emotionally based. "Mainstream" was another term often applied to this return-to-basics movement. This was more than a mere revival of an older tradition; it was a recognition by jazz musicians that they had a guiding jazz tradition.

The function of the jazz tradition becomes even clearer in the following jazz periods when the development of new musical styles push harder on the very definition of jazz. Straight-ahead jazz (and later called, ironically, "progressive jazz") still remains a beacon of the jazz tradition. It is embodied in players like Wynton Marsalis who not only speaks respectfully of past jazz styles, but is, himself, a respected performer of "mainstream" jazz.

Wynton Marsalis brings the hard bop period full circle. Like so many other strong players in this tradition, Marsalis worked in his youth under the tutelage of Art Blakey in the Jazz Messengers. Blakey's group, first established in 1955, can boast some of the most prominent players in this genre: Horace Silver, Freddie

Wynton Marsalis. *Courtesy Carl Baugher.*

Hubbard, Wayne Shorter, Lee Morgan, Hank Mobley, Kenny Dorham and both Marsalis brothers, Branford and Wynton.

Blakey describes his efforts to pass on the jazz tradition. "I look for the new guys, and I just give them a place to hone their art and they grow. They do it themselves. I just give them a chance. All they need is a little guidance, a little direction, and they're gone. When they get big enough, I let them go and get their own thing. Then I find some more."[29]

26. Sonny Rollins, "St. Thomas," *Saxophone Colossus.*

27. Sonny Rollins, "Blue 7," *Saxophone Colossus;* "Blue 7," Smithsonian Collection of Classic Jazz.

28. Thelonious Monk (Miles Davis record), "Bags' Groove (Ta 1)," *Bags' Groove,* Prestige Records, 7109.

29. Art Blakey, "Art Blakey in His Prime," *Down Beat,* July 1985, p. 21.

The straight-ahead jazz legacy can be heard on *Art Blakey and the Jazzmessengers, 'Album of the Year'*.[30] The composition by pianist James Williams, "Soulful Mister Timmons," is particularly noteworthy because of its gospel and blues references. Like much music of the hard bop period, this piece has a newly composed opening and ending. This differs somewhat from the bop period in which standard tunes were the vehicle for improvisation.

Additional Reading Resources

Blanco, Charles, *Sonny Rollins: The Journey of a Jazzman.*

Williams, Martin T., ed. *The Art of Jazz,* pp. 233–38.

Note: Complete information including name of publisher and date of publication is provided in the Bibliography.

Additional Record Resources

Adderley, Cannonball. *Mercy, Mercy, Mercy.* Capitol Records, T 2663.

———. *The Best of Cannonball Adderley.* Capitol Records, SN 16002.

———. *The Cannonball Adderley Quintet Plus.* Riverside Records, 9388.

Holmes, Richard "Groove." *The Best of Richard "Groove" Holmes.* Prestige Records, 7700.

Lewis, Ramsey. *The In Crowd.* Cadet Records, S–757.

———. *The Best of Ramsey Lewis.* Cadet Records, S–839.

Morgan, Lee. "Sidewinder." *Three Decades of Jazz (1959–1969).* Blue Note Records, LA 158–60.

Rollins, Sonny. *Blue 7.* Prestige Records, LP 7079.

———. *Sonny Rollins* (two vols.). Blue Note Records, 1542/1558.

———. *Taking Care of Business.* Prestige Records 24082.

Silver, Horace. *Best of Horace Silver.* Blue Note Records, 84325.

Smith, Jimmy. *Jimmy Smith's Greatest Hits.* Blue Note Records, BST 89901.

———. "Back at the Chicken Shack." *Three Decades of Jazz (1959–1969).* Blue Note Records, LA 158–60.

Art Blakey. *Courtesy Carl Baugher.*

Suggested Classroom Activities

1. In terms of rhythmic feeling, what does the word *funky* mean?

2. How would one describe the emotion or feeling of the music of the Funky Era?

3. What electronic instrument became popular in this era?

4. Listen to the excellent example of the funky style, "The Preacher," on *Horace Silver and the Jazz Messengers* (Blue Note Records, BLP1518). Give your reactions to the total sound. Is the melody

---

30. Art Blakey, *Art Blakey and the Jazzmessengers, 'Album of the Year',* Timeless SJP 155, 1981.

recognizable? Do you hear the amen-chord progression? Which of the two solo instruments, trumpet or saxophone, plays blue notes? Do you hear the musical conversation between the piano and ensemble near the end of the music?

Listening Guide

From Tape Demonstration 17

Funky

:00 Introduction (piano solo and bass solo alternate measures)

:06 Ensemble chorus (flügelhorn lead and alto sax harmony) (piano, bass, guitar, and drums play 2/4 rhythm)

:28 Flügelhorn solo (one chorus) (listen for drums accenting 2nd and 4th beats)

:51 Ensemble chorus (same as first chorus)

1:16 End

From Smithsonian Collection
(side 10, band 5)

Charles Mingus

"Hora Decubitus"

:00 Bass solo in octaves (Charles Mingus), establishing the intended directions for intensity, tempo, and motive.

:12 Baritone sax (Jerome Richardson) plays the motive with the rhythm section.

:36 Starts unison and adds chords.

:48 Brass section joins in background.

1:14 Tenor sax solo (Booker Ervin), strong walking bass and piano on chordal punctuations throughout.

1:36 Ensemble backing enters.

1:50 Tenor sax solo finishes up without ensemble backing.

2:03 Ensemble short break leading into alto sax solo.

2:07 Alto sax solo (Eric Dolphy)

2:25 Ensemble backing as earlier.

2:38 Alto sax solo with ensemble backing.

2:50 Ensemble short break leading into trumpet solo.

2:53 Trumpet solo (Richard Williams)

3:00 (Under the trumpet solo) Listen particularly for the piano chords, walking bass, and the punctuations prominent in the drums.

3:15 Ensemble backing enters.

3:38 Ensemble.

3:50 Saxes lead.

4:03 Ensemble—saxes over brass.

4:14 Long ending—very free.

4:36 End.

From Smithsonian Collection
(side 10, band 3)

Sonny Rollins

"Blue 7"

:00 Bass (Doug Watkins) plays a walking solo.

:14 Drums (Max Roach) enter lightly, with mainly 2nd and 4th beats on the foot cymbals.

:43 Tenor sax (Sonny Rollins) enters establishing the theme.

1:07 Piano (Tommy Flanagan) enters, solves any key problem listeners may have had due to Rollins' angular solo lines.

2:57 Piano solo—the I, IV, and V chords can be detected quite easily.

3:57 Tenor sax returns—very short interlude, just a clue to designate that the piano solo is over and that the drum solo should start.

4:07 Drum solo—lightly and steadily on the foot cymbals (on beats 2 and 4) while playing intricate syncopated work on the snare drum, bass drum, and tom-toms.

6:23 Drummer rather splashes a definite clue that he has finished his solo.

6:23 Tenor sax solos again.

7:05 Tenor sax softens to accentuate the walking bass as in the beginning.

8:09 Piano and drums soften to feature the bass.

8:30 Piano drops out, leaving just the walking bass and afterbeats on the foot cymbals.

9:19 Tenor sax solo re-enters—4 bars, starting a series of trading fours with the drums.

9:26 Drum solo—4 bars.

9:33 Tenor sax solo—4 bars.

9:40 Drum solo—4 bars.

9:47 Tenor sax solo—4 bars.

9:55 Drum solo—4 bars.

10:02 Tenor sax solos again.

10:44 Tenor sax softens and plays sustained notes.

11:11 End.

13
Free Form—
Avant Garde

Most new developments in jazz have been extensions of earlier traditions which only modify the musical structures and idioms defined by preceding styles. **Free form,** also known as **free improvisation** or even the **new thing,** breaks sharply with its musical predecessors. It is actually easier to describe what free form is not rather than try to find descriptors for the limitless number of expressions of which it is capable. Most free form efforts operate in a medium that is not defined by the harmonic and rhythmic forms prescribed by earlier jazz practices.

Even with the new approach taken by bop, the song structure, with its repeating harmonic form, was maintained. The songs were characterized by a steady rhythmic meter that varied very little throughout the course of the performance. If a tune were in 4/4, it was likely to remain there until the performance was finished. Although the melody to the tune was often absent during the improvised solo areas, the harmonies remained the same. There was therefore a formal and unchanging structure that supported each player's improvisation.

Free form improvisation sheds these structures of harmonic repetition and rhythmic regularity, allowing the players to react without restrictions to one another. The musical material for the improvisation comes extemporaneously from the players rather than from a commonly known tune. The greatest empathy possible is necessary for this means of performance to be successful. Also, the old axiom, the more freedom allowed, the more discipline necessary, is pertinent to this style. Without discipline, a performer might merely make unusual and unrelated sounds instead of reacting in a muscial way to the other players.

Listen to demonstration 18 on the cassette included with this book for an example of how two players might interact in a free music environment.

In an age when the finished product is the only criterion for judgment, it is refreshing to have a situation where it is the process, not the product, that is really important. However, this one fact makes free form jazz, at first, difficult to understand. The listener must conscientiously observe and attempt to empathize with the players in order to appreciate the excitement of this process. It is often easier to understand this style first in a live performance situation in which the listener can more readily become involved with the players than on a record.

This type of music can be compared to action painting or nonrepresentational painting, such as a Jackson Pollock work. Listen to Red Mitchell (bass) and Shelly Manne (drums) as they attempt to communicate with Ornette Coleman (and vice versa) on "Lorraine."[1] Alto saxophonist Joe Harriott, sometimes called an abstractionist, claims to have worked in this idiom before there could have been any Ornette Coleman influence.

1. Ornette Coleman, "Lorraine," *Tomorrow Is the Question,* Contemporary Records, M3569.

122

It would not be illogical to feel that the seeds of free form jazz existed from the beginnings of jazz itself. The very nature of improvisation places great emphasis on spontaneous musical creativity. To some degree, in every jazz performance, there is an element of improvisation, if only in the rhythm section where the specific notes are left to the player's discretion. The balance between fixed compositions and improvisatory development has shifted throughout jazz's history. Free form jazz proves to be the fullest expression of spontaneous composition, in which improvisation takes a dominant role.

The leading players and composers in this medium come to it from different musical and philosophical backgrounds. These backgrounds add a distinctive stamp to each of their efforts. As we shall see, the traditional musical structures of harmony and rhythm are only two of the many possible glues available to musicians. The effectiveness of free form performance rests in the individual and collective compositional strengths of the players. The unique musical characteristics of the players carry over into the performance itself, instilling it with its own unique expression. It is no surprise that the dominant musical voice in each ensemble establishes the trademarks that unify and narrow the infinite possibilities of free form jazz for each ensemble. These trademarks, in turn, help us distinguish the performances of Cecil Taylor from those of Ornette Coleman or John Coltrane.

Free form jazz did not just suddenly appear with Ornette Coleman's "Free Jazz" recording. Composers like Charles Mingus had already pushed hard on the musical fabric, forcing it into a freer expression. As early as 1956, Mingus had recorded "Pithencanthropus Erectus" and shocked the listening world with his daring use of some free playing. In much the same way, Coltrane broke into a free style as a natural result of his own harmonic and melodic extensions. It was Ornette Coleman who drew the sharpest line between the traditional jazz idiom and his new expression, **free jazz.**

Ornette Coleman

One of the most controversial free jazz players is saxophonist Ornette Coleman. Critics who have examined his work fall into one of two distinct groups. One group is composed of staunch admirers, while the other group views his work as unworthy of any consideration. These adverse opinions are due to Coleman's disregard for tradition.[2] (S, "Lonely Woman," "Congeniality," "Free Jazz," side 12, bands 1-3) It is said that he refuses to comply with restrictions normally imposed by rhythm and meter, chord progressions, or melodic continuity, and that he desires the freedom to play any thought that occurs to him at any time, regardless of context. There are many misunderstandings concerning Coleman's playing. One is that he turns to free form because he is incapable of anything else. To say that Coleman "doesn't sound good" is too loose a statement. Questions immediately arise: good compared to what? Compared to other saxophonists? Compared to European scales and harmony? Coleman shows on "Part 1" that he can play both melodically and rhythmically.[3] (S, side 12, band 3)

Despite the free playing in this cut, much of the melodic rhythms are consistent with those used by traditional jazz players. The melodic lines still swing in a hard bop fashion, but their relationship to the independent bass line is harmonically vague. The steady meter in this cut is not necessarily typical of free jazz performances, but works well as a support for Coleman's solo and the responses by the other horn players.

In fact, Coleman is very melody oriented. Coleman phrases freely. He feels no obligation to contain or extend his musical thoughts so that they fit neatly into a certain number of measures, which is logical since he does not use defined chord progressions. Also, he is not involved in keeping a certain pulse; after all, his music is not for dancing. Coleman's melodies have pitch relationships even for the uninitiated, but his metrically invented phrases are placed over a free rhythm with no identifiable chord progressions, and this approach tends to lose those who have not listened to free form. The shift from a steady pulse to a free-flowing rhythm can be traced first to Lester Young and then to Gerry Mulligan and others as they attempted to avoid constraint within the *bar lines.*

Because there is no chord progression, some players feel free enough to avoid a key center and play with an atonal feel. This sense of not being in a key is not quite the same as the **twelve-tone system** of Schoenberg, where each tone has equal importance and no key center is implied. Rather these players seem to have no home base, which many listeners evidently need. However, there is no reason to argue about atonality in jazz. Remember that many of the roots of jazz, such as the field holler, were in no specific key. Some authorities consider the lack of a steady pulse or beat to be a new rhythmic concept, while others consider it no concept

2. Ornette Coleman, "Lonely Woman," "Congeniality," "Free Jazz," Smithsonian Collection of Classic Jazz; *Tomorrow Is the Question,* Contemporary Records, M3569.

3. Ornette Coleman, "Free Jazz," Smithsonian Collection of Classic Jazz, "Part 1," *Free Jazz,* Atlantic Records, 1364.

Ornette Coleman. *Courtesy Carl Baugher.*

at all. One of the more appreciated concepts of this new music is the way in which musical thoughts and attitudes from the entire world are incorporated. Obviously, these young musicians feel that older musical concepts are too rigid, too predictable, and certainly too cliche laden.

Coleman was the first jazz player to go all the way into harmonic freedom. This idea had been examined earlier by classical composers, but in an entirely different way. Coleman's approach was through improvisation. To say that Coleman was the first is only partially true. Actually he was only the first to receive widespread recognition. At the time Coleman organized a quartet in 1957 in Los Angeles, Cecil Taylor was playing in a free manner at the Newport Jazz Festival. Charlie Mingus had invented free sounds even earlier. The term **free form** first appeared on a Coleman album with Eric Dolphy entitled *Free Jazz*.

Faulty intonation has been one of the criticisms leveled at Coleman. It could be that the fault lies in the well-tempered scale of European classical music. Reference could be made to the blue areas or blue notes and questions could be raised about the cultures that do not subscribe to the European concept. Possibly in any emotional music in which notes are constantly pushed this way or that way, there is faulty intonation.

Martin Williams quotes Coleman on this issue: "You can play sharp in tune and flat in tune," pointing out that the intonation for any note is dependent on the musical context.[4]

Cecil Taylor

Unlike Coleman, pianist Cecil Taylor did not have an extensive background in blues bands. His contribution, instead, was an integration of a conservatory technical facility and European based compositional practices. However, like Coleman, he is interested in a free improvisatory arena for the players. Taylor is often considered an "**avant garde**" expression of third stream jazz. His music is perhaps a more effective fusion of classical compositional practices and jazz improvisation than the traditional third stream itself. Taylor was able to blend his conservatory background and the raw energy typical of the freest improvisation into a seamless whole. Taylor has found an intersection in which his music can be heard as either classical or jazz, depending on the vantage point of the listener. Unlike Coleman's groups, traditional jazz idioms are not commonly heard although the spirit of jazz improvisation is clearly evident. "Enter Evening," recorded in 1966, is an example of Taylor's free form style. Notice how the players react to one another in a manner not only free of harmony and meter, but also free from many of the usual jazz melodic idioms.[5] (S, side 11, band 2) Taylor's use of an oboe and bass clarinet in the ensemble is consistent with the third stream's earlier use of traditionally classical instruments.

The variety of musical textures used in Taylor's music can be heard on "Idut" and "Serdab."[6] (NW, *Cecil Taylor,* No. 201) "Idut" is a very high energy composition made up of fragmented and punctuated statements that are characteristic of much of Taylor's percussive style. He often approaches his piano as a drummer might, striking clusters of notes for their percussive effect. The sequence of musical textures leads the listener through a series of energy levels that are shaped by Taylor's compositional skill. Throughout these pieces the interchange between musicians is the propelling force. What any one player does at any one time is seldom as important as the composite musical statement. It is often helpful when listening to this type of free form music to step back from the detail of individual players and listen instead to the whole musical fabric, woven by the players collectively. Notice that many of the transitions between musical areas are carried by Taylor himself as he sets up each new collective effort.

"Serdab" offers the listener some contrasting musical textures, although there are still several high energy sections. In this composition, the players have several occasions to work out melodic ideas individually although the composite sound is still dominant. In several of the more open areas, Taylor is quite willing to use traditional jazz idioms, only to move quickly back into a more dense percussive style. The interchange between players is more clearly audible in the less dense areas in which the melodic fragments are given more length and often accompanied by other similar (or contrasting) melodic lines.

Cecil Taylor's music often requires stamina from listeners and players alike. His concerts are notorious for their long uninterrupted compositions. Holding such long compositional structures in a free form manner attests to Taylor's strength as a composer. "3 Phasis," a single piece, runs over fifty seven minutes, spanning two sides of a record. (NW, No. 303)[7] The fact that this recording was the last of six efforts that day to record this piece demonstrates the ensemble's intensity and stamina. Perhaps more than any other trait, it is Taylor's intensity that identifies his music, an intensity more typical of jazz than the European counterpart with which it was fused. Few composers have been as successful as Taylor at blending the two musical worlds so completely.

John Coltrane

Saxophonist John Coltrane, despite his relatively short career, charted one of the most direct and continuous courses from the **modal jazz** of the Miles Davis quintet

4.   Ornette Coleman, Smithsonian Collection of Classic Jazz, liner notes, 1973, p. 43.

5.   Cecil Taylor, "Enter Evening," Smithsonian Collection of Classic Jazz.

6.   Cecil Taylor, "Idut" and "Serdab," New World Records, 201.

7.   Cecil Taylor, 3 Phasis, New World Records, NW 303.

to his own late albums, rich with free improvisation. Rather than declare an independence from traditional form and harmonic practice, as Coleman did, Coltrane extended the traditional harmonic chords until they no longer functioned tonally. The resulting **atonal** medium offered Coltrane a free environment in which he could develop his melodic ideas.

Coltrane used the modal jazz approach as a springboard for his characteristic melodic extensions. His melodies were often based on modes played over slow moving harmonies. Rather than using the lower notes of a chord (i.e. the root, third or fifth), Coltrane centered his melodies on higher **harmonics** such as the ninth, eleventh and thirteenth. The result was a more complex harmonic sound that could, when pushed harder, develop into atonal passages characteristic of free form jazz. The slow moving harmonies of modal jazz actually contained the seeds of atonality because they fostered a melodic approach toward improvisation and allowed time for the player to explore more complex harmonic extensions. Coltrane uses this modal jazz approach on his recording of "Alabama."[8] (S, side 12, band 4) Notice the relationship of his melody to the harmonic underpinning. He is able to consistently maintain an extended distance from the basic harmony. The opening and closing statements use only one chord over which Coltrane plays a modal melodic line.

Coltrane's sense of melody is displayed in one of his most celebrated performances on a Rogers-Hammerstein tune, "My Favorite Things," performed with his quartet.[9] His solo on this recording shows how he applied his modal and extended harmonic techniques to the more traditional song form. As his solo develops, it becomes so extended harmonically that it seems only vaguely related to the ongoing and apparently frozen harmonic center below it. There are several points at which the quartet collectively weaves musical textures not dissimilar to those heard in Ornette Coleman's free expressions.

Coltrane completes his transition toward free form in performances like "Manifestations" in which his later quartet operates in a very free interchange.[10] Even with the freedom allowed the players, Coltrane's guiding influence can be heard. The long but disjunct melodic lines, frozen harmonic centers and emotional intensity characterize the later Coltrane performances. (Coltrane is discussed at length in chapter 20.)

Anthony Braxton

The jazz and classical avant garde streams are in many ways practically indistinguishable. The **chance** music promoted by John Cage, although free as far as harmony, timbre, and meter are concerned, finds its cohesion in the intellectual restrictions imposed by the composer. Without the traditional musical idioms as support for the free use of sound and rhythm, compositions are based on the composer's ability to creatively mold the musical elements into an understandable whole. As we have seen in the highly emotional music of Mingus, Coleman, and Coltrane, the emotional theme and the players' collective understanding of it can be used to hold large expanses of music together. The classical approach toward new music is often based, not on emotional unity as such, but on an intellectual premise that explores and develops new musical areas.

Cecil Taylor maintained a careful balance between emotional and intellectual composition. Multifaceted woodwind player, Anthony Braxton, also maintains this kind of balance. His compositions are based on well crafted notions about timbre and time relationships, yet develop freely in an improvisational environment.

Braxton spent the middle sixties in Chicago, which was developing into one of the most influential cities in the world for new music. Richard Abrams formed an organization called the Association for the Advancement of Creative Music (AACM) which benefited from the participation of many important new music figures: Leo Smith, Abrams' Experimental Band, the Art Ensemble and, perhaps the most influential, Braxton himself. It is difficult to characterize the nature of the music AACM fostered because it was so experimental. However, a common consensus existed that the composers/performers should be free to explore not just traditional elements of pitch and meter but also the more general notions of sound and time. All sounds are considered appropriate musical material and their placement in time completely free.

Braxton has been productive as an author as well as a composer. He has written a great deal about his view of creativity in music and bases his musical compositions on well developed theories. His 1974 album, *Anthony Braxton, New York, Fall 1974*, offers several examples of his compositional approach.[11] Each cut

8. John Coltrane, "Alabama," Smithsonian Collection of Classic Jazz.

9. John Coltrane, *The Best of John Coltrane*, Impulse Records, AS-9200-2.

10. John Coltrane, *The Best of John Coltrane, His Greatest Years*, Impulse Records, AS-9223-2.

11. Anthony Braxton, *Anthony Braxton, New York, Fall 1974*, Arista Records, AL 4032.

Anthony Braxton. *Courtesy Carl Baugher.*

from the album is represented with an enigmatic geometric design which guided the performance. Contrast the almost bop-like idiom of "Side One, Cut One" with the much freer "Side Two, Cut Three." The first side clearly reflects a jazz heritage in its use of meter and melodic inflection. The second side, however, has very few obvious ties to traditional jazz. Although similar to Taylor's more classical approach, Braxton's music presents a more specifically composed image than that of Taylor. This is not to say that Braxton lacks the improvisational energy characteristic of Taylor's or Coleman's music. Braxton has often performed fully improvised solo concerts which would be difficult to match in technique or intensity. His music, however, tends to show the more measured qualities associated with more fully composed music. "Side Two, Cut One" demonstrates Braxton's ability to maintain such a controlled, yet free sounding, environment. His clarinet lines are effectively intertwined with the timbres produced by Richard Teitelbaum on the Moog synthesizer.

The Free Jazz Controversy

Some performers who gain recognition today make no pretense to any connection with past musical styles. They specify that they play "emotion," which is entirely different from playing lines, keys, modes, and rhythms.[12] Players of free form are considered the most radical musicians since the Bop Era. They feel that music in general and jazz in particular should show the emotion of the player, and that the older types of jazz do not adequately show today's deep emotion. Coleman and other free form players think that jazz should also express feelings not previously reflected. After an interview with Archie Shepp, Leonard Feather wrote, "Shepp's music—impassioned, fierce, often atonal, almost totally free of rules of harmony, melody and tone that have governed most music of this century—reflects the turmoil and frustrations that bedevil him."[13] Whether free form is "hate music," "love music," or whatever, it is still a means of expression.

We suspect that it is mainly the critics and musicians who simply cannot go along with these new expansions who call free form jazz "hate music." Of course, it was mainly the jazz critics who chose to label it "hate music." Some of the music on Coltrane's recordings is in fact quite religious. There were many jazz critics who would neither support nor condemn free form for fear of eventually being proven wrong or at least foolish. No matter what it is called and even though many claim it to be chaotic, this music has found an audience.

Free form players thrive on controversy. Those free form advocates who acknowledge that this style has not developed a large following argue that a person should have the right to fail. But failure is not always the result for free form players. There are even those who are financially successful—witness Ornette Coleman's Guggenheim Foundation Grant.

Because of the lack of adherence to established rules, the question is often asked if free form is jazz and, indeed, if it is music. Each listener must decide. At a time when free form was still fairly new in jazz (in comparison to most styles), Dan Morgenstern took a perceptive look at the controversy:

But is it jazz? Some of the main elements are lacking. There is little of what we have come to know as "swing." *There is often none of the formal organization found in most jazz—rhythm section and melody instruments, solo versus ensemble, strict time, etc. Yet, the sound and feeling is often of a kind peculiar to jazz as we have become accustomed to it, and it is certainly not "classical" music in any sense of that ill-defined word. Whatever it may be—and one often has the feeling that even the musicians don't quite know what they have hold of; it is a music in flux, if anything—it must not be burdened with comparisons that are unwarranted.*

To accuse a drummer of not swinging when he doesn't want to achieve swing in the sense that his critic has in mind is unfair and pointless. To demand adherence to formal patterns that the musicians are obviously rejecting is as foolish as taking a painter of geometric abstractions to task for being nonrepresentational.[14]

Summary

In spite of the debate as to whether the performance is jazz, the free form manner of expression proves to be the ultimate in improvisation. Coleman was the leader in this direction, but followers extended this experimentation much further—notably Eric Dolphy and Ken McIntyre.[15]

Coltrane was a tremendous help in furthering the careers of other contemporary free jazz players like Archie Shepp and Pharaoh Sanders. Coltrane and Coleman were at the top of most musicians' polls in the mid-1960s, especially in Europe.

McCoy Tyner played piano for Coltrane for almost six years (1960 to 1965), and it took him almost eight years after that to free himself to the point where he was an individual expressing his own thoughts. When he started his group, they played set forms. Later they became much more flexible and free.[16]

12. Albert Ayler, *Bells*, E.S.P. Disk, 1011.

13. Leonard Feather, "Archie Shepp Jazz: Portrait in Passion," *Los Angeles Times*, 10 April 1966, p. 23.

14. Dan Morgenstern, "The October Revolution—Two Views of the Avant Garde in Action," *Down Beat 34*, no. 30 (November 1964): 33.

15. Eric Dolphy, "Out to Lunch," *Three Decades of Jazz (1959–1969)*; Ken McIntyre and Eric Dolphy, *Looking Ahead*. Prestige Records, 8247.

16. McCoy Tyner, *Sama Layuca*, Milestone Records, M9056; McCoy Tyner, *Together*, Milestone Records, M-9087; McCoy Tyner, *Reflections*, Milestone Records, M-47062.

There are contemporary groups who deserve special mention because of their highly experimental nature: the Archie Shepp Quintet, the New York Art Quintet, the Albert Ayler Quintet, and the Jazz Composers Workshop (later Jazz Composers Orchestra) with Carla Bley and Mike Mantler. There is also a great deal of this type of activity in Europe. There have been innovators of avant garde jazz in Los Angeles, but the main strongholds are New York and Europe. The problem is a real "catch 22" situation. The club owners won't hire these musicians until they have recordings, record companies are reluctant to give them a recording date until they have proven that their music is commercial enough to appeal to the expanding jazz audience.

It appears as though the freer aspects of jazz, at least, have somewhat reduced the freedom acquired in the sixties. Most successful recording artists today construct their works in this way: beginning with a strain with which listeners can relate, following with an entirely free portion, and then returning to the recognizable strain. The pattern may occur several times in a long selection, giving listeners pivotal points to cling to. At this time, listeners accept this—they can recognize the selection while also appreciating the freedom of the player in other portions. Players, meanwhile, are tending toward retaining a key center for the seemingly free parts. It is as if the musician has learned that entire freedom is not an answer to expression, that the player needs boundaries, bases, from which to explore. Some players with this attitude are Miles Davis, Cecil Taylor, John Klemmer, Keith Jarrett, Chick Corea, Pharaoh Sanders, McCoy Tyner, Alice Coltrane, Wayne Shorter, Anthony Braxton, Don Cherry, and Sun Ra.

Arista Records, a relatively new recording company, devotes most of its energies to this new type of free form jazz. Company executives say this effort is for both prestige and integrity, implying their confidence in the honesty and validity of this means of expression in spite of opposition. The company has also released some avant garde jazz recorded in Europe (Anthony Braxton, for example) so that Americans as well as Europeans can become aware of these artists. Strangely, Europeans have always appreciated this American art form more than Americans. Perhaps efforts such as those of Arista will win the stamp of validity for free jazz.

The free form player places the importance of individuality of self-expression considerably ahead of popularity or acceptance by general audiences. His or her claim to musical artistry is often through music unrelated to any previous approach to music.

Additional Reading Resources

Budds, Michael J. *Jazz in the Sixties.*

Jost, Ekkehard. *Free Jazz.*

Note: Complete information including name of publisher and date of publication is provided in the Bibliography.

Additional Record Resources

Art Ensemble of Chicago. *Urban Bushman,* 2-ECM/Warner Brothers Records, ECM 2–1211.

———. *The Third Decade,* ECM/Warner Brothers Records, 25014–1.

Ayler, Albert. *Vibrations.* Arista Freedom Records, AL 1000.

Braxton, Anthony. *New York, Fall 1974.* Arista Records, AL 4032.

Cherry, Don. *Old and New Dreams.* Black Saint Records, BSR–0013.

———. *El Corazon,* ECM/Warner Brothers Records, ECM 1–1230.

Coleman, Ornette. *At the "Golden Circle" Stockholm.* Blue Note Records, 4225.

———. *Science Fiction.* Columbia Records, KC 31061.

Handy, John III. *Quote, Unquote.* Roulette Records, R 52124.

Jazz Composers Orchestra. JCOA Records, 1001/2.

Murray, David. *Morning Song.* Black Saint Records, BSR–0075.

Sanders, Pharaoh. *Deaf Dumb Blind.* Impulse Records, AS 9199.

———. *Journey to the One.* Theresa Records TR 108/109.

Shepp, Archie. *Four for Trane.* Impulse Records, A–71.

———. *On This Night.* Impulse Records, A–97.

Taylor, Cecil. *Silent Tongues.* Unit Core Records, 30551.

———. *Unit Structures.* Blue Note Records, 84237.

World Saxophone Quartet. *W.S.Q.* Black Saint Records, BSR–0027.

Suggested Classroom Activities

1. What relationship exists between the attitude one has toward free form jazz and one's understanding of the way the musical elements are used by the performer in expressing his musical thoughts?
2. Explain two variations of free form technique used by performers playing this type of jazz.
3. Describe the fundamental difference between John Coltrane and Anthony Braxton in their approaches to free jazz.

Listening Guide

**From Smithsonian Collection
(side 12, band 3)**

Ornette Coleman

"Free Jazz"

- :00 Introduction
- :10 Melody from which to improvise later played in unison at this point
- :22 Alto sax solo (Ornette Coleman), listen for two basses and the accenting on the drums
- 1:10 Back-up horns enter
- 3:33 Horns play independently
- 4:10 Alto sax plays faster, one bass is bowing
- 4:45 Ensemble players now playing very independently
- 5:05 Peak
- 5:30 Alto sax solos again
- 5:40 Everybody is improvising
- 6:10 Alto sax solos again
- 6:43 Everybody is improvising
- 7:45 Everybody plays fast for a moment
- 9:46 Original motive played here in unison
- 10:00 Fade
- 10:03 End

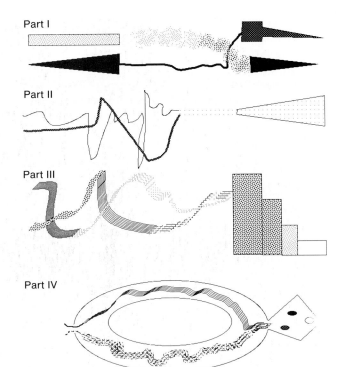

Part I

Part II

Part III

Part IV

Free Form Demonstration 18

Dialogue, Ann LaBerge: flute, David Megill: alto saxophone

- :00 Part I, saxophone player sings while playing
- :06 Flute player uses breath articulations while saxophone plays soft melodic fragments
- :17 Flute player sings while playing
- :25 Part II, interchange of repeated notes, flute player uses flutter tongue technique
- :39 Exchange of short punctuated notes between players
- :54 Part III, more lyric tone used by both players, glissando in flute
- 1:10 Gradually picks up more melodic speed as short melodic motives are passed back and forth
- 1:25 Sharp change from soft low tones to louder less lyric sound
- 1:36 Soft consonant ending
- 1:41 Part IV, soft rapid exchange of melodic ideas which grow in intensity and volume
- 1:57 Short very loud and overblown notes exchanged as piece ends
- 2:05 End

14
Crossover—Fusion

The evolution of musical styles is often metaphorically referred to as a collection of streams which share a common source but have branched to create individual and separate identities. However, unlike its river analogue, once a musical stream has branched from its source, it is still subject to the influences of all other musical streams around it. Musical streams, in essence, share a common riverbed, the cultural milieu of the day. Because they often share listeners, performers, and critics, elements of each style tend to *cross over* into one another, creating even newer streams. Musical crossovers are certainly not new to jazz. Its players have borrowed from anywhere and everywhere throughout its history. The terms, crossover and fusion, however, became especially prevalent during the late 1950s and into the 1970s, after rock 'n roll had captured the attention of the public, opening new doors for the development of jazz itself.

The fact that jazz's art status was certain led many to question whether it was foul play to assimilate the characteristics of other clearly delineated musical styles. How classical can jazz become and still remain jazz? Likewise, where does one draw the line between the jazz and rock expressions? Questions such as these have unsettled, time and again, our efforts to firmly fix a definition of jazz. As frustrating as this constant assimilation of other idioms is for historians, it is also the driving force behind the evolving jazz musical stream. The very fact that jazz is unique and indigenous to America demonstrates the multiplicity of cultural influences at work here, and absent, in the same proportions, anywhere else. Jazz is a carefully blended style which depends on its past, and depends now, on the fertile crossovers from the various musical styles around it.

The degree to which the crossover occurs, how much, and in what directions, all influence any newly emerging musical style. Sometimes, the crossover is one sided, in which one stream assimilates much but exports little. In contrast, a more equal fusion can occur which creates a new style capable of being claimed by each of the contributing streams. Third stream music is more typical of the former. Jazz has continually borrowed from the European classical model but the reverse, the classical use of jazz idioms, has been only sporadic and not long lasting. Jazz/rock fusion has proven to be a more equal exchange. Successful rock groups like Blood Sweat and Tears or Sting can be found that have borrowed jazz idioms and even players for their predominantly rock sound. Jazz groups, as early as the Ramsey Lewis Trio, have, in turn, imported the more frozen harmonic structure and rhythmic insistence, typical of rock, to open new doors for improvisational freedom.[1]

1. Julie Coryell and Laura Friedman, *Jazz-Rock Fusion,* New York, Delta Books, 1979, p. ix.

The two most predominant jazz crossover areas of the 1960s and 1970s occurred with the classical and rock streams. Since that time, the rock stream has itself become even more multifaceted, creating new opportunities for jazz crossover. Listen to demonstration 19 on the cassette included with this book for an example of crossover between the jazz, rock, and pop styles. The crossover with classical music was complete enough to generate its own name, third stream, and establish its own champions.

Third Stream

Throughout jazz's history, composers have struck a balance between the fully composed pieces typical of European models and more open improvisatory structures characteristic of the oral tradition. The cool era marked a move toward the more fully composed and formally defined works. The hard bop period was, in contrast, a call for a return to the more individual and spontaneous oral tradition. Third stream jazz can be seen as an extension of the cool compositional style and linked to Gunther Schuller who participated with Miles Davis on the *Birth of the Cool* album. In fact, the phrase "third stream" is usually attributed to Schuller although writer John S. Wilson is also credited with inventing it.

Schuller was a French horn player with the Metropolitan Opera in New York City and has composed both classical and third stream pieces. From 1967 to 1977, he was the director of the New England Conservatory of Music in Boston. He therefore brought much of his classical training to his efforts in third stream jazz. Schuller's "Abstraction" as well as Larry Austin's "Improvisation for Orchestra and Jazz Soloists" are good examples of early third stream music.

Third stream jazz shares both the instrumental sound and instrumental variety first employed during the cool era. The jazz musicians play their instruments in a manner closely resembling the technique used by symphonic players, a technique that employs a precise tonal attack and a minimum of vibrato. Third stream, also like cool, introduces more exotic and typically classical instruments, such as the French horn, oboe, bassoon, and cello.

The harmonies used in third stream music are similar to those associated with contemporary jazz; however, musical forms such as the fugue, canon, theme and variations, and other extended types were borrowed from classical music.[2] The use of these forms by third stream composers resulted in a return to a more polyphonic type of composition. Classical music markedly differs from jazz in its use of meter and rhythmic pulse. Although present in both, jazz has always given it great prominence. Third stream jazz often uses a more classical notion of rhythm which gives more weight to the melodic and harmonic activity than to a strong rhythmic pulse. For this reason, some contend that third stream music cannot be considered jazz.[3]

Robert Freedman's "An Interlude" is an example of a third stream composition that uses classical models of *polytonal* and *polymodal* techniques.[4] Leon Dallin defines a polytonal composition as one that emphasizes clearly two or more tonal centers at the same time.[5] Polymodal music uses two modes (i.e. major and minor) with the same tonic, or two forms of the same chord simultaneously. Dallin calls it dual modality.

Jazz, as an art form, has also been embraced by the classical art world through commissions of jazz works for performance by symphony orchestras, for example, Brubeck's *Dialogues for Jazz Combo and Symphony Orchestra*,[6] Rolph Lieberman's *Concerto for Jazz Band and Symphony Orchestra*, and John Graas' *Jazz Symphony No. 1*. These compositions fall into two distinct groups:

1) compositions that contain jazz elements intended for performance by large symphonic orchestras using traditional instrumentation, and,

2) *concerto grosso* approaches which place a small jazz group of seven or eight players within a large symphonic orchestra.

Too often, however, the concerto grosso format offers a little jazz and a little of the classical ensemble but no integrated effect. John Lewis's "Sketch" is an example of a third stream composition which combined the Modern Jazz Quartet and the Beaux Arts String Quartet.[7] During this performance neither of the two groups seem to lose their identities but an integrated feeling is still created. The Modern Jazz Quartet

2. Harold Shapero, "On Green Mountain," *Modern Jazz Concert*, Columbia Records, WL 127.

3. Gunther Schuller, "Transformation," *Modern Jazz Concert*.

4. Robert Freedman, "An Interlude," *Jazz in the Classroom*, Berklee Records, BLPIA.

5. Leon Dallin, *Techniques of Twentieth Century Composition* (Dubuque, Iowa: Wm. C. Brown Company Publishers, 1974), p. 132.

6. The New York Philharmonic Orchestra with the Dave Brubeck Quartet, conducted by Leonard Bernstein, *Bernstein Plays Brubeck Plays Bernstein*, Columbia Records, CL 1466.

7. The Modern Jazz Quartet, *Third Stream Music*, Atlantic Records, 1345.

Gunther Schuller (standing) and Dizzy Gillespie. *Courtesy of Ray Avery.*

during the late 1950s proved to be a pivotal group between cool and third stream. John Lewis' classical training can be seen in the composed nature of their ensemble passages and the formal compositional structures used. John Lewis' use of Renaissance brass sounds and his own characteristic improvisatory style offers yet another third stream blend in his composition "Piazza Navonna."[8] (NW, 216, side 2, band 4) In a manner similar to John Lewis' "Sketch," Chuck Mangione has also merged his jazz quintet with a symphony orchestra as well as a full choir on the album *Land of Make Believe.*[9]

Upon a closer inspection of third stream techniques, particularly the use of more fully composed compositional forms, we find that composers throughout the history of jazz have been importing classical techniques. Scott Joplin used quite strict forms for his rags and Jelly Roll Morton was a master of the compositional concept of theme and variations. It is only during the third stream period that such a conscious effort to assimilate classical music idioms was so evident. Duke Ellington's music certainly reflects the power of a classical compositional approach in a strictly jazz medium.

8. The Modern Jazz Quartet, "Piazza Navonne," New World Records, 216.

9. Chuck Mangione, *Land of Make Believe,* Mercury Records, SRM 1–684.

The Sauter-Finegan Orchestra was an earlier attempt to bridge the gap between jazz and classical music. The orchestra was originally organized strictly as a recording orchestra and was strongly influenced by the impressionistic music of Debussy and Ravel. Eddie Sauter was as well-known an arranger for the Benny Goodman Orchestra as Bill Finegan was for the Glenn Miller Orchestra. Their most ambitious effort was the Lieberman work. It was extremely well received when performed and recorded with the Chicago Symphony Orchestra.

The Stan Kenton orchestra showcased several third stream compositions. William Russo's compositions for this orchestra were often bold and adventuresome in their blend of classical, avant garde, and jazz elements.[10] (NW, "Mirage," 216, side 1, band 4, "Eldon Heath," 216, side 2, band 1)

"All About Rosie" from the *Modern Jazz Concert* album demonstrates how George Russell has developed an extended jazz (or third stream) work from a children's song-game.[11]

Yet another approach to third stream music is the actual use of classically composed music in a larger jazz work, or, the complete statement of a classical work with jazz interpretation. The Swingle Singers used many of Bach's pieces and Hubert Laws effectively recorded Stravinsky's *Rite of Spring*.[12]

Jazz in Classical Composition

Classical composers were actually first in their efforts to cross over the classical/jazz line. The most lasting and popular attempt to include jazz idioms in classical music occurred in France in the 1920s. Composers like Darius Milhaud, in his travels to America, actually got firsthand knowledge of the New Orleans jazz style as heard in Harlem.[13] As a result of his trip to the United States, he composed a work, *La Création du Monde*, about which he writes, "I adopted the same orchestra as used in Harlem, and I made wholesale use of the jazz style to convey a purely classical feeling.[14]

Rhythmic and harmonic jazz elements were consciously used in France as exotic music references to the free spirited music of the American Negro. This interest in jazz was also promoted among literary leaders such as Jean Cocteau. In his essay, *Le Coq et l'arlequin,* he holds up American jazz as an example of the virtue of indigenous and more accessible music which should be assimilated by classical composers.

Ernst Krenek, an Austrian composer, looking to the success of jazz in Paris, wrote a "jazz opera," *Jonny Spielt Auf,* that was popular all over Europe. It was translated into 18 languages and performed in over 100 cities. The leading character was, appropriately, a Negro jazz musician. Stravinsky's *Ragtime for Eleven Instruments* is another example of a classical composer adopting jazz idioms for use in a classical composition. Stravinsky crossed over in the reverse direction when he wrote the *Ebony Concerto* for the Woody Herman band. This piece is unique in that it is written by a classical composer for a traditional jazz ensemble.

In America, composers like Gershwin and Gould also worked in a classical medium reflecting jazz influences. These composers remained classical in their form and style, but made use of the jazz idioms in a generalized sense. Claude Bolling's *Suite for Flute and Jazz Piano* serves as a clear example of this type of fully composed, yet jazz imbued, composition. On his own recording of this piece with the renowned classical flutist, Pierre Rampal, the use of jazz inflections and idioms helps create a spirit of improvisation even though the composition is completely notated.[15]

These classical works, although greatly influenced by jazz, are not considered to be third stream because they originate from, and maintain their allegiance to, the classical idiom. The deciding feature seems to be the direction in which the crossover moves. A composer associated primarily with jazz, but who uses classical models or idioms, is considered a participant in the third stream. Classical composers, on the other hand, who fuse jazz expressions in their works are generally excluded. The reasoning for this most likely rests in the fact that the third stream is a notion belonging primarily to jazz historians. Despite the shading in terminology, it is worth noting that the crossover between the classical and jazz worlds is a two-way street. Both stylistic streams have been enriched by their association with one another. As we saw in the previous chapters, these two musical streams will again interact as the avant garde school of jazz emerges.

10. William Russo, "Mirage" and "Eldon Heath," New World Records, 216.

11. George Russell, "All About Rosie," *Modern Jazz Concert.*

12. Swingle Singers, *Bach's Greatest Hits,* Philips Records, 200–097; Metropolitan Pops Choir with Robert Mandel, *More of the Greatest Hits of Bach,* Laurie Records, LLP 2023; The Jacques Loussier Trio, *Play Bach Jazz,* London Records, 3289; Hubert Laws, *Rite of Spring,* CTI Records 6012; Nina Simone, "Love Me or Leave Me," *Little Girl Blue,* Bethlehem Records, 6028.

13. Darius Milhaud, *Notes without Music,* Alfred A. Knopf, 1953, New York, p. 136.

14. ibid., p. 148.

15. Claude Bolling, "Suite for Flute and Jazz Piano," Columbia Records, M33233.

Jazz/Rock Fusion

By the late 1960s, rock had captured the attention of America's listeners. It was quickly becoming the most influential musical style in the United States, perhaps even the western world. Jazz found in this popular music yet another opportunity for the assimilation of new musical idioms, sounds and concepts. This crossover with rock is most commonly referred to as *jazz/rock fusion* or just **fusion**. Although fusion is not new to jazz's development, it became a popularized notion during the 1960s and the term itself became specifically associated with groups that crossed over the jazz/rock line.

Miles Davis proved to be a central figure in the development of jazz/rock fusion. After his impact with the "Birth of the Cool" record, he continued to effect change in the development of jazz. His albums, *In a Silent Way* in 1969 and *Bitches's Brew* the following year, added an impetus to the jazz/rock crossover movement that is still being felt. The list of personnel that worked with Davis during these years reads like a Who's Who of jazz/rock fusion for the 1970s and 1980s: Herbie Hancock, Chick Corea, Wayne Shorter, John McLaughlin, Joe Zawinul, Tony Williams, and Lenny White. These musicians later formed, or participated in, the most influential fusion groups of the 1970s and early 1980s, particularly Chick Corea with Return to Forever, Joe Zawinul and Wayne Shorter with Weather Report, and John McLaughlin with the Mahavishnu Orchestra.

Jazz, throughout its history, has always cut a careful course between an orally developed tradition and the more schooled literate tradition characteristic of European classical music. As third stream jazz was a move toward the literate classical tradition, jazz/rock fusion at first offered a balancing gesture toward the more improvised oral tradition. Rock in the '50s and '60s had a raw energy that offered a new rhythmic backdrop for jazz improvisation. Although the harmonic activity in rock was somewhat primitive with respect to jazz, its rhythmic intensity offered a different type of cohesion for extended jazz improvisation.

In addition to the newer electronic instruments and greater amplification, jazz also borrowed the new and increasingly complex rock rhythms. These rock patterns make use of straight eight notes instead of the uneven eight notes more typical of swing or bop. It is not uncommon for fusion groups to use both straight and swing eights simultaneously, with rock patterns in the rhythm section as soloists play bop lines against it.

The changes in the rhythm section are as definite as those made in the bop era when the means of displaying the pulse was also revolutionized. Rock and jazz/rock bass players now usually play an electric bass or bass guitar instead of a traditional stand-up string bass. This allows them to play faster, invent more complex lines and use electronic **effects** to alter their sound. The bass player also takes a more prominent position in the ensemble, often offering solo lines as well as basic harmonic support.

The rhythm guitar in most fusion groups plays the chordal punctuations that had been previously assigned to the piano, and the drums, like the bass, move to a more prominent position in the ensemble. Don Ellis explained the manner in which the drummer plays in this idiom:

> In the drums, whereas in bebop the sound went to the cymbals, in rock music, (although the cymbals are still used) the opposite has happened, and the basic patterns have gone back to the drums. One of the reasons, I suspect, is that because of the high level of volume at which a great deal of rock is played the cymbals give no definition to the time and merely add a blanket to the overall sound. So the burden of time-keeping has now come back to the snare and bass drums. This also gives it a more solid rhythmic feel. For anyone who likes to swing hard, I think this is a definite step in the right direction.
>
> The patterns the snare drum and the bass drum are playing, instead of being sporadic, are now more regular in the sense that they are played continually.[16]

In later fusion groups, the rhythm section is further expanded with multiple keyboards and electronic effects for most all the other instruments. The commitment to a dominant rhythm section is a central feature of most jazz/rock fusion.

Miles Davis, *Bitches' Brew*

The early use of electronic instruments can be heard on Miles Davis' *Bitches' Brew*.[17] Dave Holland shares his bass role with Harvey Brooks who plays electric bass. John McLaughlin plays electric guitar, not necessarily new to jazz, and Joe Zawinul, Larry Young,

16. Don Ellis, "Rock: The Rhythmic Revolution," *Down Beat* 36, no. 24 (1969):32.

17. Miles Davis, *Bitches' Brew*, Columbia Records, GP 26.

Chick Corea. *Courtesy K. ABE*

and Chick Corea join in with electronic piano. Outside of the horn players, Wayne Shorter on soprano sax, Bennie Maupin on bass clarinet and Miles Davis on trumpet, the ensemble is completed with three drummers, Lenny White, Jack DeJohnette, and Charles Alias, and a percussionist, Jim Riley. Like rock groups, Davis gives the rhythm section a central role in the ensemble's activities. His use of such a large rhythm section offers the soloists wide but active expanses for their solos. The title cut from this record offers a good example of how the soloists can interact with the rhythm section. They sometimes hold sustained lines in contrast to the rhythm section's activity and at other times they act as just another member of the rhythm section and only add punctuated statements.

The harmonies used in this recording move very slowly and function modally rather than in a more tonal fashion typical of mainstream jazz. Each harmonic

center appears almost frozen as the players, both independently and collectively, pull away from it only to return and reaffirm it. The home key is established more by insistence than by the traditional tonal chord relationships. The static harmonies and rhythm section's collective embellishment create a very open arena for improvisation. The musical result flows from basic rock patterns to hard bop textures, and at times, even passages that are more characteristic of free jazz. The cut entitled "Spanish Key" offers a more direct example of how a fusion rhythm section can establish a steady rhythmic drive over slowly moving harmonies. The harmonic changes occur so seldom that they create major articulation points in the composition.

Chick Corea, Return to Forever

One of the most prominent and popular fusion groups of the 1970s and 1980s, Return to Forever, was led by Chick Corea, formerly with Miles Davis. Corea, a well-schooled piano player, began to use the electronic piano while with Davis. After working with his own avant garde group, Circle, he formed Return to Forever in 1970. His move to electronic piano soon led to a complete involvement with synthesizers of all kinds.

Corea's music demonstrates a virtuosic skill in both technique and ensemble. His themes are often quite angular and complex rhythmically, yet quite accessible to the listener. Despite their complexity, his records prove to be commercially successful. His music flows smoothly between **up tempo** jazz, complex rock, and a more commercial rock style.

Return to Forever's 1977 album, *Musicmagic*, demonstrates Corea's ability to fuse many quite distinct musical styles into a single composition.[18] The title cut moves from a very smooth commercial sound through jazz interludes, to "funky" rock passages. The fusion trademark of an active rock rhythmic underpinning supporting a soloist with jazz phrasing above it, appears throughout the cut. Corea opens and closes the arrangement with acoustic piano but uses an electronic piano and synthesizers throughout the body of the piece.

Chick Corea's later albums become more and more electronic as the instruments themselves become more accessible and more complex. With the advancing technology, outstanding keyboard players like Corea often experiment with much smaller groups, replacing the usual complement of musicians with sophisticated electronic instruments. Unlike the seven musicians who performed for *Musicmagic*, Corea used

18. Return to Forever, *Musicmagic*, Columbia 34682.

only two to three at one time for his 1986 album, *Elektric Band*.[19] The title proves to be a play on words, on the surface, a reference to a poem called "Elektric City," and secondarily to the heavy use of electronic instruments. Even his drummer, Dave Weckl, uses an electronic drum set (Simmons) and drum synthesizer (Linn) on some of the cuts.

Corea wields this equipment quite effectively. His virtuosic keyboard technique and compositional skill showcase the potential for the new technology. His approach is still quite similar to that heard in the Return to Forever albums, rhythmically complex themes, tight ensemble, colorful orchestrations and virtuosic display. His selection, "Got A Match," from the *Elektric Band* album offers an effective juxtaposition of jazz and rock phrasing. The solo areas again use the high energy rock backdrop with a more typically bop solo in the foreground.

Joe Zawinul, Wayne Shorter, Weather Report

Like Chick Corea, Joe Zawinul and Wayne Shorter worked with Miles Davis when *Bitches' Brew* was recorded. Also like Corea, they formed one of the most commanding fusion bands of the 1970s and 1980s, Weather Report. A special chemistry seems to have existed between Zawinul and Shorter that gave their band a distinctive and popular sound. In an article by George Varga, Zawinul credits an even earlier Miles Davis recording with influencing his writing style: "The record was 'Birth of the Cool,' and it had a great impact on me. I like to write in that sound-spectrum style."[20] A majority of the writing during Weather Report's fifteen year existence was done by Zawinul and his respect for the composed approach to jazz typical on "Birth of the Cool" can be heard in his own compositions. Like Corea, Zawinul is an accomplished pianist who moved comfortably into the electronic medium of synthesizers.

Weather Report's 1980 album, *Night Passage*, offers several examples of fusion at different points along the jazz/rock line.[21] "Rockin' in Rhythm" is based on an Ellington tune and uses synthesizers to fill out a saxophone section sound under Shorter. The rhythm and style remain predominantly swing with very little borrowed from the rock idiom. "Fast City" offers the soloists an energetic arena for a type of virtuosity often associated with fusion groups. The thematic material is again rhythmically complex and punctuated with ensemble motives. Very often even the bass player, Jaco Pastorius, joins the ensemble in the complex unison lines.

Zawinul and Shorter's last record together as Weather Report, *This is This,* came out in 1986 and showed another personnel shift.[22] Victor Bailey on bass and Mino Cinelu, percussionist-vocalist who had been playing with Weather Report, remained, but Peter Erskine returned on drums and, more importantly, John Scofield on guitar was a new addition. Scofield is to be Shorter's replacement as the group continues work as Weather Update.

Zawinul also came out with a solo album in 1986, *Dialects,* on which he uses four synthesizers and four drum machines.[23] The only other performers on the album are four vocalists, one of which is Bobby McFerrin. "All the pieces are improvised," Zawinul told George Varga, "each sound is a personality. It's like a conversation in which I'm the focus."[24] Each piece on the album represents an exotic theme such as "6 A.M./Walking on the Nile" and "The Great Empire" (Japan). Although there is often a rhythmic rock underpinning to the pieces, the musical idiom shifts sharply from piece to piece, reflecting the exotic themes. The compositions might better be thought of as jazz/rock tone poems similar in concept to classical overtures or music for film.

Jazz in Rock

In 1971, Irving L. Horowitz, a professor of sociology at Rutgers University, wrote the following about the merging of jazz and rock:

Many recent bands [Blood, Sweat and Tears, Chicago, and Cold Blood, for example] are highly reminiscent in their instrumentation of such earlier groups as Miles Davis' Tentet in the late '40s. And the loud, brassy arrangements are direct descendants of Count Basie. A promising new group, Ten Wheel Drive, provides a mixture of Big Mama Thornton blues and

19. Chick Corea, *Elektric Band,* GRP Records GRP–A–1026; compact disc GRP–D–9535

20. George Varga, *The San Diego Union,* March 9, 1986.

21. Weather Report, *Night Passage,* ARC Records, CBS Inc., 36793.

22. Weather Report, *This is This,* CBS Records, CK–40280 (compact disc).

23. Joe Zawinul, *Dialects.* Columbia, FCT 40081.

24. George Varga, *The San Diego Union,* March 9, 1986.

Wayne Shorter   Joe Zawinul

Weather Report. *Courtesy Randee St. Nichols.*

a tenor sax reminiscent of Coltrane, all set to tight arrangements that remind one of the Jazz Messengers with Art Blakey and Horace Silver.[25]

Rock from its beginnings shared much in common with jazz, particularly its strong commitment to rhythm. In its earlier days, rock, like jazz, based much of its music on the twelve bar blues progression. (NW, 249, *Shake Rattle & Roll,* "Every Hour," side 1, band 9)[26] However, it was not until the late '60s that groups like Blood Sweat and Tears and Chicago (Chicago

Transit Authority) consciously incorporated jazz instrumentation and idioms into their work. By that time the rock harmonic idiom was becoming more modal and the rhythmic patterns more complex. The jazz crossover was therefore most apparent in the added instrumentation, saxophones, trumpets, and trombones, to the

25. Irving L. Horowitz, "Rock on the Rocks—Bubblegum Anyone?" Reprinted from *Psychology Today,* January, 1971. Copyright © 1971 by Ziff-Davis Publishing Company. All rights reserved.

26. Little Richard, "Every Hour," *Shake Rattle and Roll,* New World Records, 249, side 1, band 9.

more usual guitars. These horns did more than back up the traditional rock band. They were an integral part of the ensemble and even given open areas for jazz solos.

The musicians in the group Chicago say that they incorporated jazz first but that the *Blood Sweat and Tears* album was produced ahead of their own album. Both bands used horn players and more composed ensemble practices. "Spinning Wheel," from the *Blood Sweat and Tears* album, was a particularly popular example of their type of jazz/rock fusion. Bobby Colomby's drumming on this album proves to be a forerunner of the drumming heard in prominent fusion groups in the seventies and eighties. This particular piece worked its way into the jazz community when Maynard Ferguson used it as a basis for an exciting arrangement for his own band.[27]

The material for the *Blood Sweat and Tears* album shows both classical and jazz crossover. The use of traditional jazz tunes like "God Bless the Child" on the one hand and an Eric Satie theme from "Trois Gymnopedies" potentially qualify this album as both fusion and third stream.[28]

More recently, Sting has formed a band that attempts to fuse the worlds of rock and jazz. His approach was to import top jazz players and place them in a rock medium. The jazz players were already established jazz musicians, Branford Marsalis, formally with Art Blakey, Daryl Jones, who worked with Miles Davis, Kenny Kirkland, keyboard player for Wynton Marsalis, and Omar Hakim, drummer for Weather Report. After working with many young jazz players, Sting picked those whom he "considered to be the best young jazz musicians in the world—on the understanding that we weren't going to play jazz. What I wanted was a flavor. I didn't want to go off and give Branford 120 bars to explore a theme; I was gonna say, "You're going to have 16 bars and you're going to burn from the first bar."[29]

Sting's credentials as a rock musician and songwriter were established while he was with the very popular rock group Police. His new band is a hybrid counterpart to most other fusion groups which are led by prominent jazz leaders. While he imported jazz into a rock medium, bands like Weather Report and Return to Forever imported rock idioms into a jazz medium.

As Sting formed and rehearsed his new group he recorded the process on video tape and produced a movie documentary which offers some insight to the excitement and dilemma associated with crossover bands. The concluding filmed concert shows a blend of both rock and jazz material. A couple of the numbers are blues in the traditional jazz sense while other songs, written originally for Police, are adapted for the newer jazz/rock medium.[30]

Jazz/Pop/Rock

Popular music is, without a doubt, the fastest changing of all musics today. Because of the short life of so many of the emerging styles, their impact on jazz is difficult to immediately assess. At the height of Disco's popularity, it was tempting to say that no music would be free from its influence, but now, several years after its decline, very little of its impact is being felt. It certainly strengthened the move toward a greater use of synthesizers and a refinement in studio techniques, but as a musical idiom it has almost entirely vanished.

Despite the unstable nature of popular music, several notable jazz musicians have taken active roles in its creation. Their jazz heritage and notoriety often carry the jazz label into the new medium even when the music has very little recognizable jazz in it. Herbie Hancock and Quincy Jones are two such figures. Both composers have worked in the most diverse musical fields, from jazz to film scores, primarily in the rock idiom.

Herbie Hancock is particularly interesting because of his earlier association with the Miles Davis quintet. While working on his many other projects he has found time to reorganize this earlier group, with himself on piano, Ron Carter on bass, Tony Williams on drums and Freddie Hubbard taking the place of Davis. The group called itself VSOP and featured mainstream jazz. VSOP 2 followed with the Marsalis brothers several years later.

While maintaining his jazz definition with excursions of this kind, he is also producing albums with the Rockit band. Hancock says of these efforts, "Most people who come from a jazz background and do anything in an area of electric or pop music still maintain a lot of the character of jazz in their pop stuff. So it's a true fusion kind of thing. I did that for a while, but I've been trying to take the pop stuff more into the pop area, and leave out the jazz. I think I've pretty much succeeded at that, because the last few records I don't consider jazz records at all."[31] What Hancock does carry to these later albums is the technical skill and

27.   Maynard Ferguson, "Spinning Wheel," *M. F. Horn II*, Columbia KC 31709, CBS 65027.

28.   Blood Sweat & Tears, *Blood Sweat and Tears*, Columbia CS9720.

29.   Art Lange, *Down Beat*, December, 1985.

30.   Sting, *Bring on the Night*, Karl/Lorimar Feature Films, A&M Films, a division of A&M Records Ins., 1985, YHS 344. The music can be heard on *The Dream of the Blue Turtles*, A&M Records.

31.   Howard Mandel, *Down Beat*, July, 1986.

Herbie Hancock. *AP/Wide World Photos*

approach more typical of an accomplished jazz player. The music of his album *Sound-System* falls more into the category of a **beat** or **breaker music,** a rather specific type of music for a popular dance known as break dancing.[32] Hancock may have very well accomplished what he had intended, to clearly leave the jazz out.

Not all musicians have attempted to draw such clear stylistic lines in their work. George Benson was among the first to blur the lines between jazz and popular music with his record *Breezin,* the first such record by a jazz-associated musician to go platinum and hold first place in pop, jazz and r&b at the same time.[33] Chuck Mangione has also gained a similar popularity with his fusion groups, his most popular piece being his 1978 instrumental "Feels So Good."

Miles Davis' 1985 album, *You're Under Arrest,* is a rather unusual blend of pop and jazz.[34] He even rearranges a song written and performed by Cindi Lauper, a very prominent pop music star at the time. Davis also uses a studio mix on the record which is much more consistent with that used in popular rock, the bass drum and bass guitar are placed well out in front of the other instruments on the recording. Despite this more commercial sound, the musical approach is similar to Davis' earlier albums, which tend to place the soloists in sharp contrast to a steady rhythmic underpinning.

Spyro Gyra, led by saxophonist Jay Beckenstein, offers a type of jazz/rock fusion that places itself somewhere between the complexities of groups like Weather Report and a more pop style. Their album, *Morning Dance,* presents pieces in a light, sometimes Latin, jazz style.[35]

The list of crossover musicians, all at different points on the jazz/rock/pop line, is long and growing as fast as the music itself changes. Ramsey Lewis, David Sanborn, Grover Washington, Herbie Mann, Billy Cobham, Freddie Hubbard, Bob James, Tom Scott, George Duke, and Eddie Harris are all musicians who have contributed to this dynamically changing field. To know which of these will leave legacies remains for time to decide. Demonstration 19 on the cassette with this text is an example of the jazz/rock/pop fusion very popular during the 1980s.

Latin Jazz

Another important area of jazz crossover involves the music of Latin America. The resulting blend of Latin rhythms and jazz is often referred to as *salsa.* When translated the term means "a hot, piquant sauce." This term was adapted to *soulsa* to describe a further crossover of Latin jazz and soul music. Salsa is recognized today as a distinctive style by the jazz community as a whole. An example of infectious and sensitive salsa is *Machaca* featuring Clare Fisher and Salsa Picante.[36]

Latin rhythms have been a part of the jazz scene almost from the beginning. In fact, this element can be traced back easily to prejazz (see chapter 3). Jelly Roll Morton often used the tango as a means of expression. There is a tango section in W. C. Handy's "St. Louis Blues." Dizzy Gillespie and Stan Kenton both featured Latin rhythms in the forties. And the bossa nova in the 50s and 60s brought Brazilian rhythms to public notice.

Kenton disbanded briefly in the 1950s, and many of his musicians were absorbed by Rene Touzet and his band. Touzet used what were primarily vocal musical patterns on which the rhythm section could build to ecstatic heights. The jazz-oriented, powerful brass section from Kenton's band soon made these patterns a driving force.

Reggae, a Jamaican brand of rhythm and blues, is another major influence. Artists as diverse as Paul Simon, Eric Clapton, Elton John, and Stevie Wonder use reggae's captivating beat. Audiences are now showing their willingness to accept the "real thing" in reggae. Like jazz with rock, jazz with reggae has gained public acceptance.

Because the interrelationships between Latin, African, and Cuban rhythms are so technical and complex, it is impossible to fully distinguish between them. Yet they each offer distinctive elements as they fuse with jazz.

Jazz even has a defector from Cuba among its ranks; saxophonist Francisco (Paquito) D'Rivera, who is possibly one of the foremost new contributors in the type of jazz that displays both Cuban and American cultures.[37] He had been playing in Cuba with musicians who eventually organized a group called *Irakere.* This band plays fiery jazz, rock, and Cuban sounds combined.

In New York City especially, Latin bands mix Afro-Cuban rhythms, jazz improvisation, and other contemporary jazz thoughts with exciting results.

32.   Herbie Hancock, *Sound-System,* Columbia, 39478.

33.   George Benson, *Breezin',* Warner Brothers Records, BSK–3111.

34.   Miles Davis, *You're Under Arrest,* Columbia Records, FCT 40023.

35.   Spyro Gyra, *Morning Dance,* Infinity Records, INF9004.

36.   Clare Fischer and Salsa Picante, *Machaca,* Discovery Records, DS–835.

37.   Paquito D'Rivera, *Paquito Blowin',* Columbia Records, FC 37374

Carlos Santana, Willie Bobo, Tito Puente, Johnny Pacheco, and Willie Colon are recognized leaders in the field, but Ray Barretto, an energetic percussionist, receives the most publicity. His audiences are mainly bilingual and are very much at home with jazz and such rhythms as the mambo.

Carlos Santana is a dynamic leader whose playing of both Latin music and jazz is accepted by fans of both idioms. If it were possible to hear only two examples of this exciting music, we suggest that they be Santana's *Caravanserai* and Barretto's *Carnaval*.[38]

Summary

Crossover is a very general term that applies to the fusion of any two types of music. As we have seen, jazz has fused or crossed over quite successfully with classical, rock, commercial, and Latin. The vitality of jazz will certainly not let it stop here. As new musics develop, jazz will no doubt continue to import those qualities from them that it finds interesting and useful. As jazz becomes an ever increasing musical force, it will also export a larger number of those idioms it has developed throughout its history. We will always know that jazz is successfully crossing over as long as we have those newly emerging styles that tend to defy category, styles that help shape our developing jazz tradition.

Additional Reading Resources

Coryell, Julie, and Friedman, Laura. *Jazz-Rock Fusion.*

Megill, Donald D. and Demory, Richard S. *Introduction to Jazz History.*

Note: Complete information including name of publisher and date of publication is provided in the Bibliography.

Additional Record Resources

Adderley, Cannonball. *Cannonball Adderley Quintet and Orchestra.* Capitol Records, ST–484.

Chicago Transit Authority. *Chicago.* Columbia Records, KGP24.

———. *Chicago Transit Authority.* Columbia Records, GP8.

Dankworth, Johnny and the London Philharmonic Orchestra. *Collaboration.* Roulette Records, SR 52059.

Evans, Bill. *Bill Evans Trio with Symphony Orchestra.* Verve Records, V6–8640.

Feldstein, Saul. *Jazz-Rock.* Alfred's Music Records.

Hancock, Herbie. *Maiden Voyage.* Blue Note Records, 84195.

James, Bob and Sanborn, David. *Double Vision.* Warner Brothers Records, 25393–4.

Jones, Quincy. *Walking in Space.* A & M Records, SP 3023.

Lewis, John. *European Windows.* RCA Victor Records, LPM–1742.

Lewis, Ramsey. *The In Crowd.* Argo Records, LP–757.

Leviev, Milcho. *Music for Big Band and Symphony Orchestra.* Philippopolis Records, PH–101.

McCann, Les. *Beaux J. PooBoo.* Limelight Records, LS–8625.

Martin, Skip. *Scheherajazz.* Somerset Records, P–9700.

New Wave in Jazz. Impulse Records, A–90.

Outstanding Jazz Compositions of the Twentieth Century. Columbia Records, C 2S 831/C2L 31.

Russell, George. *Jazz in the Space Age/New York, New York.* MCA Records, 2–4017.

———. *Outer Thoughts.* Milestone Records, M–47027.

Schuller, Gunther. *Jazz Abstractions.* Atlantic Records, S–1365.

Stoltzman, Richard. *Begin Sweet World.* RCA Victor Records, 1–7124.

Suggested Classroom Activities

1. Present-day jazz is a potpourri of many years of continuous development. Name the sources and kinds of music jazz musicians adopt today.

2. What are some characteristics of third stream music? Name the jazz era it stemmed from.

3. Select two recordings in your school record library that you think would be good examples of jazz/rock. Give reasons for your selections.

4. What is meant by the terms "crossover" and "fusion" as they relate to jazz/rock? Be specific.

38. Carlos Santana, *Caravanserai,* Columbia Records, KC 31610; Ray Barretto, *Carnaval,* Fantasy Records, 24713.

5. Who led the way for a fusion of rock rhythm and free form jazz?

6. In a jazz/rock percussion section, what rhythmic role is assigned to the snare and bass drums in contrast to the electric bass or bass guitar? Why?

7. Identify two of the earliest rock 'n' roll groups that featured jazz solos.

8. Listen to the Modern Jazz Quartet playing with a string quartet to produce third stream music in the selection "Sketch" from the album *Third Stream Music* (Atlantic 1345). How would you describe the total effect? What musical elements seem to be most prominent in the string quartet's part? What jazz elements are most prominent in The Modern Jazz Quartet's part?

Listening guide

Crossover Demonstration 19

FunkMaster Be Jammin', Lawrence Hopkins

:00 Synthesized bass and drum introduction, angular rock rhythms
:16 Synthesized flute-like melody enters
:35 Melody continues as brass-like melodic figures become more predominate
:56 Rhythm break with only drums
1:01 Short punctuated brass-like sounds support an improvised solo which uses a breath controller to create horn-like articulations
1:40 End

From New World Collection (# 216, side 2, band 1)

William Russo

"Eldon Heath"

0:00 Brass counterpoint lines in a free flowing meter. Vague tonal area.
0:28 Transition melodic figures in brass
0:45 Sax/brass ostinato, more metric
1:03 Trombone solo with ostinato background
1:40 Soft & increasingly loud low brass punches. Fading ostinato.
2:07 Cymbal roll leading to rhythm section and brass in tempo with jazz phrasing and accents
2:36 Saxophone solo with very light rhythm. Long tone chordal support in other instruments. Muted trumpets.

3:09 Strong brass chords
3:15 Trombone solo returns
3:22 Sax and brass ostinato return
3:47 End

Miles Davis

"Bitches Brew"

Columbia Records, GP 26 CS 9995

:00 Bass solo
:07 Keyboard striking a chordal cluster with percussion
:13 Bass solo
:22 Keyboard cluster with percussion
:28 Guitar enters
:32 Bass solo
:37 Keyboard cluster with percussion
:40 Trumpet enters (Miles Davis) with much reverberation—Section goes between trumpet entrances and keyboard clusters
2:45 Bass solo
2:50 Bass clarinet enters establishing its motive
3:27 Steady rhythm, bass clarinet and keyboard prominent, guitar playing punctuations
3:43 Trumpet solo fully integrated with the ensemble
6:10 Trumpet gives way to keyboard and guitar, plenty of heavy rhythm on drums
7:16 Softens (Davis says "Like that—nice")
7:40 Keyboard, guitar, and drums building again, keyboard and drums very rhythmic
8:20 Softens again, showing that music should have highs and lows
8:42 Trumpet enters
10:20 Rhythmic feel changed to suit Davis' new explorations
11:06 Trumpet out
11:18 Soprano sax solo backed by forceful rhythm
12:12 Soprano sax fades
12:15 Only rhythm with sparse keyboard interjections, but building from there
13:05 Everyone softens to build again, keyboard featured
14:17 Keyboard clusters and bass solo alternates several times as in the beginning of the selection
15:22 Trumpet again with lots of reverberation, alternating with the clusters as near the beginning of the selection

16:45 New subtle rhythmic feel to back bass solo
17:31 Add bass clarinet, intensity building again
18:37 Trumpet enters, driving forward
19:27 Trumpet exits, group softens only to rebuild
20:22 Trumpet enters rather subdued but quickly reaches out further
21:15 Bass alone—joined by drums, guitar, keyboard, soon an ensemble with these players and the bass clarinet—a long rhythmic interlude
23:15 Bass alone—alternating with keyboard clusters several times
23:52 Trumpet enters forcefully, as at the top of the selection, jabbing at openings
26:03 End

Chick Corea

"Musicmagic"

Columbia Records, AL 34682

  :00 Introduction—acoustic piano (Chick Corea)
  :06 Flute enters
  :20 Piano interlude
  :31 Flute reenters
  :42 Piano alone
1:09 Ritard and hold
1:10 Low bass note on synthesizer and trombone
1:17 Brass enters
1:20 Keyboard with special effects
1:44 Guitar featured

2:05 Hold and introduction to newer section
2:20 Ensemble
2:33 Fretless sound
2:50 Guitar solo
3:21 Fender Rhodes solo
3:30 Mellotron introduction for vocal
3:43 Vocal duet—swinging background with ensemble
4:35 Hammond organ solo—very funky
5:25 Stop time plus Fender Rhodes
5:36 Fender Rhodes solo
6:23 Brass enters
6:30 New section
6:41 Brass enters
6:48 Repeat of sound from 6:30
7:02 Fender Rhodes solo over stop time, then straight funky solo
7:52 Brass enters
8:24 Drum solo over stop time
8:32 Vocal returns
8:50 Soprano sax over vocal
9:01 Soprano sax solo
9:17 Acoustic piano solo
9:28 Brass enters
9:34 Ensemble
9:52 Piano solo
10:02 Ensemble
10:20 Piano solo
10:25 Ending
10:48 End

15
Big Band Legacy

The big band has often been compared to classical music's symphonic orchestra. Like the orchestra, the big band has offered jazz musicians an ensemble of relatively fixed instrumentation for which to compose. The characteristic common to most large ensembles is the carefully composed arrangements which hold the many players together. Because of the immense popularity of the big bands during the Swing Era, the grouping of those ensembles, saxophone, trumpet, and trombone sections with a rhythm section, became the established instrumentation for large jazz groups. Although the instrumentation was more or less standardized, the music for those ensembles was not. The most successful bands very often had identifiable leaders that placed their individual stamp on the musical product.

Ghost Bands

Because the big bands spanned such a long period from the very early bands of the twenties to contemporary big bands of the eighties, their development reflects much of jazz's history. The bands of the Swing Era enjoyed a prominence and popularity in America seldom if ever felt by other jazz styles. As a result of this popularity, a nostalgia for that style still exists today. This nostalgia has helped keep several bands actively playing and recording even after the death of their leaders. Central among these bands are the contemporary Miller and Dorsey bands. These bands most often perform the

original arrangements that made them popular during the Swing Era. When new arrangements are written, they are generally restricted to the same stylistic trademarks typical of the original bands. Critics and historians have often referred to these groups as *ghost bands* because of the absence of their leaders and in most cases, a completely new personnel.[1]

Transition Bands

Several of the big bands that began working in the twenties, thirties, or forties, performed successfully into the seventies and eighties. These bands vary as to how much stylistic change they have undergone throughout their long careers. Prominent among these bands are those of Duke Ellington (now directed by his son Mercer), Count Basie (now under the direction of Frank Foster), Woody Herman, Stan Kenton, Maynard Ferguson, Gil Evans, Ray Charles, Dizzy Gillespie, Les Brown, Harry James, Buddy Rich, and Tex Beneke. Not all these bands are still playing and those that are, even without their original leaders, cannot properly be called ghost bands. They constantly introduce new material and are not as tightly bound to the nostalgic expectations of their listeners.

1.   Glenn Miller, *In the Digital Mood,* GRP Records, GRP–A–1002. This record is a re-recording of original arrangements with the new digital technology.

Count Basie's band had a long playing career with Basie at the helm and maintained a rather consistent jazz style. What changes did occur were introduced by contemporary soloists. However, Basie felt that the responsibility for innovation rested with the writers, not the performers. After Basie's death, his band was led briefly by Thad Jones and now by Frank Foster, both former members of the band. The new arrangements written by both these men were not necessarily restricted to the original Basie style.

Like Basie's band, Woody Herman's retains a hard swinging style; however, Herman flirts somewhat with newer musical styles.[2] Maynard Ferguson's band has strongly embraced the rock idiom and maintains a large audience.[3] Buddy Rich's band, like both Ferguson's and Herman's spent a majority of its time touring. Due to the size of the groups, touring proved to be very expensive and extremely taxing on the musicians. Despite these limitations, the fact that these bands continue to be so active attests to the interest audiences still have for the big band medium.

The most varied musical styles during this transition period for big bands were heard in the Ellington and Kenton bands. Kenton explored a more expanded instrumentation with French horns and often took on a truly symphonic sound during the late fifties and early sixties.[4] (NW, "Mirage," No 26, band 4) It is noteworthy that he specified in his will that there be no ghost band under his name after his death.[5] Ellington used the big band medium to experiment with new compositional structures not before associated with big bands. (See chapter 20 for a profile of Ellington.)

Contemporary Large Bands

Not all of today's big bands were carried over from earlier periods. The medium has remained vital enough to support the development of new bands by leaders like Thad Jones and Mel Lewis, Toshiko Akiyoshi and Lew Tabackin, Don Ellis, Doc Severinsen, Quincy Jones, Louis Bellson and Ed Shaunessy. While several of these bands exhibit new and very individualized styles, many of them maintain a close tie to the swinging style of the Basie and Herman bands.

Particularly interesting are the compositions by pianist Toshiko Akiyoshi which feature both a modern and culture-crossing style.[6] She often rates among the top jazz composers in each year's *Down Beat* critics' poll. The Thad Jones-Mel Lewis orchestra, an east coast ensemble, began as a rehearsal band which offered musicians a chance to play arrangements for their own enjoyment.[7] It was not long, however, before the freshness of the arrangements and competent playing brought the

band to national prominence. Both the Akiyoshi and Thad Jones-Mel Lewis bands are characterized by carefully crafted arrangements that helped expand the big band idiom. Although the musicians are of the highest caliber, they play supporting roles to the more dominant statements of the composers themselves.

Don Ellis

Trumpeter Don Ellis offered one of the most radical yet captivating approaches for big bands. During his study at the University of California at Los Angeles, he studied with talented Indian musicians like Ravi Shankar who taught at the university in 1965. Ellis and Harihar Rao (from India) formed what they called The Hindustani Jazz Sextet. It should be noted here that possibly the most intricate rhythmic system is that from India. The amalgam of jazz elements, the **raga,** and certain Eastern rhythms produced truly extraordinary jazz music. A raga is a melodic form, a succession of notes. There are thousands of ragas. Ellis was also intrigued by the Indian tala, a rhythmic series that contains 3–108 beats. The particular tala to be played at a given moment is, of course, predetermined, but the rhythmic possibilities are almost endless. Keep in mind that these Indian musical fragments derive from speech patterns. This is also true in the African musical culture.

In Ellis's belief that young children in some countries sing and dance in meters unnatural to jazz is the implication that meter is a matter of conditioning, a difference between cultures.

Ellis directed a successful large band that featured many unusual meters such as 19/4 and 11/8.[8] Ellis subdivided the measures; for example, the very title of the selection in 19/4 meter is the subdivision "332221222." Ellis recorded a number called "New

2.   Woody Herman, *Woody Herman and His Big Band, "50th Anniversary Tour,"* Concord Jazz, CJ–302–C.

3.   Maynard Ferguson, *Live From San Francisco,* Palo Alto, 8077.

4.   Stan Kenton, "Mirage," Avant Garde and Third Stream Jazz, New World Records, No. 216.

5.   From a conversation with the authors.

6.   Toshiko Akiyoshi and Lew Tabackin, *Kogun,* RCA Victor Records, 6246.

7.   Thad Jones and Mel Lewis, *Central Park North,* Solid State Records, SS 18058; "Mel Lewis and the Jazz Orchestra," Tel-Arc Records 10044. (First album since Thad Jones left.)

8.   Don Ellis, "332221222," *Don Ellis Orchestra Live at Monterey,* Pacific Jazz Records, P-J-10112; Don Ellis, "Upstart," *The Don Ellis Orchestra Live in 3⅔/4 Time,* Pacific Jazz Records, PJ-10123.

Toshiko Akiyoshi. Full Shot *Courtesy Tom Capi* Insert *K. ABE*

Don Ellis. *Courtesy of Ray Avery.*

Nine," in which the subdivision (the manner in which the measures are counted and played) varies: 2223, 2232, 2322, 3222, and 333.[9] His "Blues in Elf" (in 11/4) is counted 3332.[10] Ellis's "Indian Lady" is in 5/4 and touches on gospel, rock, and free improvisation.[11]

Ellis was an excellent trumpet player, and also soloed well on drums. Not only did Ellis advance rhythmic techniques, become an educated and acknowledged performer of jazz/rock, and introduce interesting uses for electronic devices, but he also devised a trumpet with an extra valve that allowed him to play quarter tones. Such pitches may seem odd when compared to the well-tempered twelve-tone European scale, but in Eastern cultures they are quite suitable. Ellis died in 1978.

9. Don Ellis, "New Nine," *Monterey,* Pacific Jazz Records, P–J–10112.

10. Don Ellis, "Blues in Elf," *Tears of Joy,* Columbia Records, G 30927.

11. Don Ellis, "Indian Lady," *Electric Bath,* Columbia Records, CL 2785.

Ellis' interest in Indian music was also shared by other jazz musicians. In England, saxophonist Joe Harriott and his jazz quintet collaborated with John Mayer and a quintet of Indian musicians to record an interesting album called *Indo-Jazz Suite*.[12] On "Raga Megha," Harriott improvises over an authentic raga format. It may be fairly easy to play a given raga, but mastery of improvisation is certainly very difficult.

Elements other than rhythms have been borrowed from Indian music. Yusef Lateef makes both scales and ragas part of his personal expression, using them as points of departure for improvisation.

The School Scene

The rise of jazz/rock has whetted the enthusiasm of many young players who might otherwise not have taken quite so readily to jazz. One of the problems today is the lack of organizations to serve as proving grounds for young musicians. There is no better way for them to improve and refine their playing than to work with and learn from the more experienced musicians.

In 1976, there were reported to be at least twenty thousand jazz bands in the United States just in high schools and junior high schools, and this number is growing. The type of music that is in style with these bands is a swing band format with a rock rhythm section.

One of the most rewarding aspects of teaching is the exciting visits by true jazz artists who not only perform at a stimulating and inspiring level, but also communicate their messages verbally to the uninitiated. Such an outstanding personality is the talented pianist Marian McPartland. Her visits, talks, clinics, and performances (all seem to be intertwined) show a skill for improvisation seldom matched plus a most valid means of describing her thoughts and musical directions. Incidentally, McPartland is authoring a book about the women who have made instrumental jazz their careers.

In 1965, only twenty-five colleges gave accredited courses in different phases of jazz. In 1971, the number of colleges offering jazz courses was approximately five hundred. By 1976, jazz researchers had simply stopped counting. From 1978 to 1979, the number of four-year colleges that were involved in what they called "commercial music" doubled their course offerings.

The National Association of Schools of Music recently approved a jazz studies major that is now being offered in many colleges and universities. At least 75 of these offer bachelor's degrees in jazz studies, at least 20 offer master's degrees, and at least 3 have doctoral programs. Duke University was privileged to have the excellent pianist/arranger/composer/teacher Mary Lou Williams on its faculty. She was awarded Duke's coveted Trinity Award for her accomplishments at that university. Famed trombonist/composer/arranger Melba Liston is now teaching at a college in Jamaica. Many more schools are heading in this direction.

All movements are begun by individuals. In the school jazz band movement, great credit should be given to the following: Gene Hall for his work in Texas and other areas, Matt Betton for work in the Midwest, Bob MacDonald for his efforts in Southern California, and Stan Kenton for his clinics. Music publishers and instrument manufacturers should be grateful to these musicians, as well as to the National Association of Jazz Educators, for their exciting, hard work. The National Association of Jazz Educators has organized the teaching of all facets of jazz at all levels of education. This group aids others in the schools who are trying to work with jazz. Although they have accomplished much, they realize that work in the field has barely started.

A controversy has been brewing for some time within the National Association of Jazz Educators. One faction feels that the ideal performance vehicle for students is the big band. The attitude of this group is that there are not many mature, or even good, improvisers at the school level, and that with a large band (and there are excellent models to draw from) more students would be involved, or better yet, fewer students would be discouraged from having a jazz experience. This group points to the esthetic musical values to be attained by playing fine musical arrangements with good balance, intonation, and so forth. The other faction believes in the development of the individual by participation in a small combo setting. They maintain that this situation is the only way to learn to improvise, hence, achieve self-expression through jazz. If it is possible, the authors recommend that students involve themselves with both large bands and combos; so much can be gained from participation in both settings. With a good arrangement, a large band generally sounds acceptable in competitive situations, whereas a small group taxes individual talents, which are very exposed. Instructors should realize that the most important jazz players throughout the history of this music have in general been the best improvisers; this art can best begin today in the school situation.

12.   Joe Harriott and John Mayer, *Indo-Jazz Suite,* Atlantic Records, SD 1465.

Two notable exceptions to schools offering jazz studies, and these are generalities, are music conservatories and black colleges. To qualify that, we must mention that there is very extensive, excellent jazz work done at Eastman School of Music and at the New England Conservatory. Some black colleges are overcoming the misguided notions they have about jazz being sinful and from more humble beginnings than European classical music. Black administrators have told us that their music departments must prove themselves by European standards and then can teach anything that they wish.

The performance of jazz is by far the most important aspect for most jazz educators; the history and theory of jazz take a backseat. Some schools have more than one jazz ensemble. North Texas State has more than ten very fine bands. Although the authors realize the risk of singling out a few of the many fine college jazz bands, at least five more should be mentioned: the bands at the University of Miami, the University of Illinois, the University of Indiana, Berklee College, and the Eastman School of Music. Many fine college jazz bands have taken international tours. These tours have been very successful, except that there is no financial profit involved.

The National Association of Jazz Educators met with executives of the John F. Kennedy Center for Performing Arts in December 1971 in Washington, D.C. As a result of the meeting, the Association was given authority, responsibility, and funding for the American Jazz Festival first held in May, 1972. This is a nationwide event and all colleges having jazz activities are invited to participate. Festivals (by both school groups and strictly professional players) are now an established part of the jazz scene.

Stan Kenton believed that the future of almost all creative music in the United States lay in the hands of the universities.[13]

Additional Record Resources

Akiyoshi Toshiko/Tabackin Lew Big Band. *Insights*. RCA Records AFL 1-2678.

Herman, Woody. *Giant Steps*. Fantasy Records, 9477.

————. *Thundering Herd*. Fantasy Records, 9452.

Severinsen, Doc. *Doc Severinsen's Closet*. Command Records, RSSD-950-S.

Vig, Tommy. *The Sound of the Seventies*. Milestone Records, 9007.

Suggested Classroom Activities

1. Should a school jazz combo listen to and play large band arrangements in addition to those it regularly performs? Why or why not?

2. In what ways do the contemporary large bands differ from the large swing bands?

3. Describe the differences in the way performers react to one another in big bands and in small ensembles.

4. Discuss the different roles played by the composer/arranger in small group ensembles and in big bands.

13. Stan Kenton, "Big Band Jazz: Look to the Colleges," *Down Beat* 29, no. 25 (September 1962): 19.

16

Jazz in Television and Motion Pictures

Motion Pictures

Since the beginning of sound movies, composers have attempted to compose, and critics have attempted to write about, a combination of jazz and classical music for this medium. Some European composers like Ravel were constantly amazed that American composers had not drawn more from jazz sources. Gershwin was headed in this direction; in fact, movie composers borrowed heavily from Gershwin to set urban scenes. However, too many American composers have been reluctant to borrow from the obvious folk source, jazz, knowing full well that European composers whom Americans respect and often emulate have borrowed from folk sources for centuries. Early European composers even used the soloists' ability to improvise; not so in America. The result of this apparent inhibition has been that when American classical musicians attempt this mixture of jazz and classical music, the results have been fairly awkward. The styles seem to have been juxtaposed but not integrated well.

As pointed out earlier in the text, Gunther Schuller coined the label "third stream music." This music, however, has not remained in serious favor with the public except as it appears as background music on television and in motion pictures. For about the first thirty-five years of the movie industry, jazz was not considered right for movie music; music that was closer to classical meant a loftier, more ideal image for that industry. For example, when Benny Carter broke into film scoring, he was used mainly to write backup arrangements for black singers. Any hint of jazz was used to indicate something on the order of a sexy woman. The artists who perform today on the sitar have an "image" problem because television and movie composers overused the instrument for setting scenes that involved drug users.

Jazz began to break through its image dilemma toward the end of the 1950s. One conjecture is that a newer generation of executives who had grown up during the Swing Era came into power in the television and movie industry. They did not make the error of associating jazz with the seamier aspects of life, because they remembered their own good times with big band music and saw no reason to keep out this enjoyable means of expression.

Jazz performers have been a part of the movies for years. Bessie Smith made the film *St. Louis Blues* in 1929. In 1934, Duke Ellington and his orchestra were in Earl Carroll's *Murder at the Vanities*. Louis Armstrong appeared in movies in the late 1930s and early 1940s. In fact, many movies have been made that center on a jazz player or an entire jazz band. There have been movies based on the lives of Bix Beiderbecke, Scott Joplin, Red Nichols, Billie Holiday, Louis Armstrong, and others. During the Swing Era, Glenn Miller made two films featuring his band: *Sun Valley Serenade* with Sonja Henie, and *Orchestra Wives*. Jimmy Stewart played the title role in *The Glenn Miller Story* a dozen years after Miller's disappearance during World

War II. Movies were made featuring Paul Whiteman, Benny Goodman, Tommy Dorsey, Artie Shaw, Gene Krupa, and many others.

In the early 1960s the public began hearing jazz used in films as background music to establish scenes and moods. Elmer Bernstein used Shorty Rogers's "Giants" in *The Man with the Golden Arm,* and Johnny Mandel used Gerry Mulligan's "Quartet" in *I Want to Live.* Both films, however, did deal with unpleasant aspects of life: the first was about a drug addict and the second about a woman accused of murder. Nevertheless, these creative composers used jazz throughout the entire pictures for dramatic purposes—certainly a step forward.

Henry Mancini's movie score for a romantic comedy, *Breakfast at Tiffany's,* proved the feasibility of jazz as background music for movies. This film was followed quickly by Mancini's scoring of the Pink Panther films, *Two for the Road,* and even the African adventure *Hatari.* Duke Ellington scored *Anatomy of a Murder* in 1959, *Paris Blues* in 1961, and *Assault on a Queen* in 1966.

Mancini truly opened the door for television scoring with his jazz-oriented music for the "Peter Gunn" and "Mr. Lucky" series. In addition to his wonderful scorings using jazz, the talented, eclectic Mancini uses classical music, rock, electronics, and anything else that his good taste allows. His up-tempo sequences sound similar to contemporary large bands, while his more romantic underscoring is quite reminiscent of the Cool Era of jazz.

It is possible to mention only a few of the outstanding artists who have contributed to the field of television and motion picture scoring. Quincy Jones wrote the television scores for "Ironside," "Sanford and Son," "The Bill Cosby Show," and many well-known films. Patrick Williams scored the music for "The Mary Tyler Moore Show," "The Bob Newhart Show," and "The Streets of San Francisco." One of the latest film scores by Williams was the movie *Cuba,* whose score is replete with Afro-Cuban rhythmic sounds. Lalo Schifrin wrote the score for "Mission Impossible," "Mannix," and such movies as *Bullitt* and *Dirty Harry.* Oliver Nelson scored for the television shows "Matt Lincoln," "Longstreet," "The Six Million Dollar Man," "It Takes a Thief," "The Name of the Game," and many films. Benny Carter scored television specials such as "Bob Hope Presents" and "The Sarah Vaughan Special," and his film credits include *A Man Called Adam, Buck and the Preacher,* and *Louis Armstrong: Chicago Style.* Among Pete Rugolo's credits are "Thriller," "The Fugitive," and "Run for Your Life."

Billy May's work was heard on "Naked City," Earle Hagen's on "The Mod Squad." Resourceful arranger/composers like the highly respected Dave Grusin and Billy May have done much "ghostwriting." Composers whose time pressures have placed them in an impossible position will call in ghostwriters to do the assignment for them. Billy May wrote a great amount of music for producer Jack Webb, often receiving no screen credit. John Barry combined the Mancini style of jazz with the English approach to rock for the James Bond films. It has become quite natural to hear the infectious creations of jazz trumpeter Harry "Sweets" Edison on Nelson Riddle's scores. For the film *The World of Insects,* Lalo Schifrin wrote no score; instead, he let the players improvise from sequences, clusters, twelve-tone rows, and motifs. Marvin Hamlisch won an Oscar for the music for *The Sting,* although the score consisted mostly of Scott Joplin ragtime tunes. Andre Previn furnished the music for *The Subterraneans* by calling a group of his friends to the studio to improvise behind the scenes of this low-budget movie. His friends included Gerry Mulligan, Art Farmer, Art Pepper, Shelly Manne, and Red Mitchell.

Sometimes the composer must write in such a way as to make the producer feel secure about his product, and film producers seem to want their offerings to the public to have the most contemporary sounds available. This situation, along with the mood of the specific scenes to be underscored, will on occasion cause a talented composer to write certain music that he might not otherwise invent. In our opinion the score for *Star Wars,* written by the talented John Williams, is an example of this situation.

Television

One of the authors was in an orchestra that recorded weekly for "The D.A.'s Man," one of the early television dramatic shows that used jazz-oriented background music. The show was produced by Jack Webb, and the fine scoring was done by Frank Comstock, formerly with Les Brown's band.

Jazz players have found quite remunerative employment on staff bands for talk shows and variety shows. For example, the personnel of Doc Severinsen's band on the "Tonight Show" include some of the best jazz players in the world. Fine jazz could be heard on Dean Martin's variety show—Bob Hardaway improvised on the tenor saxophone over the credits in such an exciting way that musicians would listen to the show specifically to hear Hardaway's creativity. One of the authors was on the staff of the American Broadcasting

Company for sixteen years and played for many series of variety shows with good jazz players.

There are films and television shows based on the talents of individual jazz personalities. Leonard Feather has listed over sixty such films in his book *The Encyclopedia of Jazz in the Seventies*.[1] Producer Jimmy Baker is in the process of donating 150 television shows to UCLA. The shows are called *Stars of Jazz;* these excellent works highlight top artists.

One of the great advantages of scoring a film with jazz, as far as the producers were concerned, was that a smaller musical group could be used—representing quite a financial savings. Also, repairs in the studio (new cuts or additions to the film) could be accommodated much more easily, sometimes involving merely the improvising skills of the players. Consequently, a new breed of musicians evolved out of this situation, musicians who can play any type of music at any time under the pressure of recording.

Today, there is an organization named "The Orchestra," comprised of about one hundred of the best and most well-rounded musicians in the world. The organization was established by two men, Jack Elliott and Dr. Allyn Ferguson, who are intelligent, contemporary, musical, and imaginative. (Allyn Ferguson, has since pulled away, leaving it to Jack Elliott.) These two men collaborated in writing music for television shows such as "Charlie's Angels" and "Barney Miller." They also use jazz often in their film scoring. For example, Benny Goodman's "Sing, Sing, Sing" plays a very important part in the movie *Birds of Prey*. In George Burns's movie *Just You and Me, Kid,* earlier jazz styles set mood and plot. Elliott and Ferguson have gathered together musicians from the movie and television studios, augmented their own compositions with those of David Grusin, Billy May, Robert Farnon, Lyn Murray, Hugo Friedhofer, Roger Kellaway, Patrick Williams, Sam Nestico, Greg McRitchie, Michel Legrand, and others, and performed concerts—with overwhelming success. Offerings of bookings are coming much faster than they can be accommodated. The Orchestra's debut performance was at the 1979 Academy Awards. The reason for this success is simple: the most versatile musicians ever assembled are playing music written by the very best of contemporary American composers. There is no thought of whether the results are jazz or third stream or something else; but it is not difficult to imagine the thrill of a moving Bud Shank improvisation in the middle of a symphonic setting. Ferguson has assured the authors that recordings will soon be available.

With the new music technology of the 1980s, the compositional approach for film and television has again changed. By this time, rock had become one of the most commercially available musical styles. It could be heard in elevators and supermarkets as the musical support for everyday activities. It also became the most commonly used musical style for film and television. The reason for this may not rest solely on the public's musical taste but also on matters of convenience and cost. Much of the music is synthesized with very sophisticated equipment that may not even require a professional studio. The synthesizers and drum machines allow one person to create an entire musical score in a layered fashion. One part after another can be played and recorded as the final product is built up.

As jazz groups offered a smaller and less expensive approach to film music in the 60s and 70s, the new technology reduced the musical groups even more. Live players often only added (**overdubbed**) parts to an otherwise synthesized score. Herbie Hancock and Quincy Jones are two composers normally associated with jazz that write a great deal of music for film. Hancock was involved in film music as early as 1966 with the score for Michaelangelo Antonioni's *Blow Up*. His more recent scores were for *Death Wish* in 1975 and *A Soldier's Story* in 1984. A composer of Hancock's versatility is very difficult to categorize. Because of his jazz background it is tempting to view all his music as belonging to the jazz tradition. However, because music for film and television often requires an alignment with pop and commercial music, his music for film is more pop oriented. Hancock's musicianship and electronic expertise make him one of the best at crossing the lines between musical styles currently popular in film.

In 1986 Hancock collaborated with other jazz musicians on a French film, *'Round Midnight*. Hancock wrote the score for the film and served as its musical director.[2] The cast boasts several established jazz musicians, many of which served as both musicians and actors: saxophonist Wayne Shorter, vocalist Chet Baker, vibraphonist Bobby Hutcherson, guitarist John McLaughlin, drummer Billy Higgins, bassist Pierre Michelot, singer Lonette McKee and, in the leading role, saxophonist Dexter Gordon.

Unlike many earlier films about jazz, this film attempted to portray a truly realistic picture of the American and French jazz communities. Wayne Shorter commented on the film's potential: "Everybody was guarding against one thing. They didn't want

1. Leonard Feather, *The Encyclopedia of Jazz in the Seventies* (New York: Horizon Press, 1976), pp. 382–86.

2. Dexter Gordon, *Other Side of 'Round Midnight*. Blue Note, CDP–7–46397–2.

the movie to leave that old, negative impression. I think we finally have a film that does justice to the subject."[3]

In 1987, the Motion Picture Academy presented its Oscar to Herbie Hancock for the best motion picture score written in 1986. In his acceptance speech, Hancock lauded such earlier jazz inspirations as Bud Powell, Charlie Parker, Dizzy Gillespie, Thelonious Monk, and others. Gordon was nominated for the award for best male actor for 1986. At this same ceremony, an Oscar was awarded for the documentary film on the story of Artie Shaw's life, entitled *Artie Shaw, Time Is All I've Got.*

Summary

Television and movie composers are not attempting to write concert music. They are writing music to establish moods, set scenes, cause reactions, whether the music is intended to convey sadness or joy, light or darkness, fear or courage. That is their goal, that is what they have trained themselves for. Fortunately for those involved in jazz, these talented artists realize that this kind of music can express any emotion and is readily accessible to the listening audience.

Additional Resources

The Cotton Club, Embassy Home Video, VHS–1714.

3. Leonard Feather, *Los Angeles Times/Calendar,* September 29, 1985.

17

Vocal Jazz

Of all the contributions made to music by Americans, the one most taken to heart by the entire world is American popular music. It has been a vital part of our heritage stemming from the British colonies of North America where our first popular composer, William Billings, wrote the first great war song during the Revolution. The African slaves brought their rhythms and musical practices. Of course, immigrants brought with them their ballads, dances, and melodies from their countries. All of these were fused into something new—a distinct art form that reflected the American way of life to the world.

Many different kinds of songs became popular during the first half century of American independence. There were songs that emerged from the Revolution, many based upon melodies that came from England. There were the singing commercials of street vendors who sold wares from their wagons. There were popular songs that described everyday experiences: about city living, country living, politics, and love. Most popular were the sentimental ballads.

Spiritual Singing

Besides being a type of folk song, the spiritual made its contribution to the development of the popular song and to vocal jazz. The singing of the blacks attracted little attention in the period before the Civil War. But it was the singing of spirituals by the blacks that began

to arouse interest and widespread attention after the war. It is interesting to note that the first collection of American spirituals was published in 1867 entitled *Slave Songs of the United States*.[1] The collection contains many errors in notation because, in the words of the editors, "Their notations could only approximate, not accurately reproduce, the characteristic traits of the music in actual performance."[2]

It isn't our purpose here to discuss the historical development of spirituals. We will describe the influence of the singing of spirituals upon the development of vocal jazz.

The singing of spirituals was primarily in group activity performed in a religious setting or on a plantation. There is evidence that spirituals were used in work situations. A good example is "Michael, Row the Boat Ashore," one of the songs found in the 1867 collection. Often there would be a song leader with the chorus joining in the refrain (call and response pattern). The blacks participated in camp meetings singing the same hymns and revival songs as the whites. The blacks practiced a ceremony following religious services that had a direct influence on the preservation of the spiritual in its traditional performance style. This

1. William Francis Allan, Charles Pickard Ware, and Lucy McKim Garrison, *Slave Songs of the United States* (Peter Smith, 1867).

2. Gilbert Chase, *America's Music from the Pilgrims to the Present* (New York: McGraw Hill Book Co. Inc., 1955), p. 243.

was the ceremony called the *shout* or *holy dance*. A group of singers and shouters would stand to one side singing the spiritual and clapping hands with great fervor while another group would shuffle and dance in a circle with a monotonous thumping of their feet. It was through this rhythmic intensity of performance that the "swing" element in the spiritual was kept alive.

It is important to recognize the two main courses of events occurring in the development of spirituals in the middle 1800s. One movement adopted the forms and techniques of European art music while the other conserved the traditional folk character by retaining the characteristics of the African tribal influences. The former spread rapidly through harmonized arrangements sung by choirs and concert performances by trained soloists. The latter was the style much like the shout or holy dance, cultivated by those living in rural areas or small communities that attracted little attention from outsiders. This type of Afro-American vocal singing used traits that are fundamentally of African origin.

Gospel Singing

In 1950 Mahalia Jackson recorded "Move On Up a Little Higher" and the Ward Singers recorded "Surely, God Is Able." Both sold over a million copies—establishing gospel music in the mainstream of American music.

In 1921, at a convention of black Baptists, Thomas A. Dorsey was so inspired by the leading gospel singers that he decided to devote his life to the composition and singing of gospel music. His five-hundred-odd songs became so popular that he was designated "The Father of Gospel Music" by the publication *Black World* in 1973.[3] His composition "There Will Be Peace in the Valley," was written for Mahalia Jackson. He also composed the most popular gospel song of all time, "Precious Lord, Take My Hand."

To be better understood, gospel music has to be experienced in person. By tradition, when gospel music is performed in black churches, it is important that the audience respond. In fact, the performer's skill is measured by the amount of active support or "talking back" that comes from the listeners. Often a singer becomes so "caught-up" by the intensity of the moment, that he or she begins to improvise and embellish the melodic lines by tone bending, sliding, adding tones—all enhancing the intense feeling generated by mutual emotional release.

By 1940, gospel music became so popular in the Holiness Churches that these singers were prompted to become professionals and to go on tours. Sister Rosetta Tharpe was singing before as many as 30,000 people in stadiums and parks by 1948. She has an unusual ability to raise audiences to new emotional heights through her moaning techniques and shaking head.

Some gospel ensembles consist of male groups who sing unaccompanied and supply their rhythm by slapping their thighs or hands in time to the music. Other gospel groups are composed of women with piano accompaniment who clap their hands for rhythmic accentuation.

The melody of a gospel song can be embellished in several ways. These techniques are mostly used by individual soloists or a soloist backed by a vocal ensemble. One of the most popular techniques is the use of a passing tone, one that is inserted between two tones a third apart. Another is to add one tone, either above or below the last tone of the phrase. Another is the use of several "extra" tones sung in rapid succession either stepwise or by skips.

Gospel singing has been freely adapted by performers of other types of music. In a sense, it is a synthesis of many American vocal styles dating back at least to the Fisk Jubilee Singers as mentioned in chapter 3.

Singing Work Songs

Afro-American songs were not all spirituals. Some black songs were born on the banks of the Mississippi to the accompaniment of work tasks associated with the river boats. Others were born in the mines of Virginia, in the cotton fields of the South, in the labor gangs of prison camps in Texas and Georgia.

The singing of these songs had one thing in common. They were sung without instrumental accompaniment and were associated with a monotonous, regularly recurring physical task. Also, their singing was sprinkled with grunts and groans inspired by the physical effort of straining muscular activity. Many years later these sounds became a distinguishing feature of vocal jazz and instrumental jazz.

Publishing Popular Music

Before continuing a discussion of the genre that produced vocal jazz, a brief description should be made of the printed outlet for such music, namely, the sheet music publishing industry.

3. Horace Clarence Boyer, "An Overview; Gospel Music Comes of Age," *Black World*, Vol. 23, no. 1 (November 1973).

Before 1880, the most important song publishers were located in such cities as New York City, Chicago, Pittsburgh, Detroit, Milwaukee, and San Francisco. By the middle of the 1890s, however, Union Square of New York City became the center of the largest concentration of song publishers in the country.

The method of selling their songs to the public was unique even for those days. The song pluggers would do almost anything to get an audience. They would visit the shops selling sheet music and play the tunes on the piano all day long. Others would travel by truck through the city streets singing their songs through megaphones to attract the people.

By 1900 the "Street of Song" moved from Union Square in New York City to 28th Street between Fifth and Sixth Avenues. This location of the music publishing industry was baptized Tin Pan Alley by a journalist who heard a piano being played with strips of paper stuffed between the piano strings producing a tinny effect. It was in Tin Pan Alley where the song plugger was king, demonstrating newly published songs on the piano, and where the million-copy sale of sheet music became a common event.

About 1930 with the advent of recordings, radio, and talking motion pictures, Tin Pan Alley with its techniques of writing and selling songs became obsolete.

Singing the Blues

After the Civil War, the blues developed as a form of Afro-American folk song. It was created by rural black singers in solo form with guitar and/or harmonica accompaniment. These itinerant singers converged on the cities of the South and Middle West in the 1890s in search of work. Eventually the influence of women blues singers in the cities made its impact upon Tin Pan Alley as another type of American popular song—the blues.

A composer of early published blues, W. C. Handy, introduced this type of folk song as "the blues." The blues became popular not only as Handy's creation but also in the performances of such blues singers as Ma Rainey and her pupil Bessie Smith. Gertrude "Ma" Rainey recorded 50 records.[4]

Both Ma Rainey and Bessie Smith were professional vaudeville singers who took great pride in their ability to sing popular songs. Vaudeville blues was popular music composed by Tin Pan Alley professionals. The song style used by these singers was smooth, with well enunciated words, and a somewhat dramatic overall delivery.

Usually the women who sang vaudeville blues did not accompany themselves on a guitar or other instrument. The accompaniment was provided by a small jazz combo in which the piano played the underlying beat and a solo horn improvised on the fill-ins during a pause in the vocal line. If the accompaniment was provided by a solo pianist, the style of playing consisted of a stride bass line with improvised fill-ins.

Bessie Smith

Bessie Smith was born in Tennessee in 1894. She made her first recording, "Downhearted Blues," in 1923, and it sold 800,000 copies to an almost exclusively black public. She became the best known blues singer of the 1920s. Bessie Smith had a large voice and showed a wonderful talent for personal interpretation of lyrics. Even today, when one listens to the recordings available, it is easy to feel the deep emotion that she communicated to her contemporaries. Her repertoire was varied, and her personal feelings show on her recordings—sometimes sad, other times happy and full of humor.

Bessie Smith would interpret any given song by reshaping it to her own special vocal style and to her own feelings about the text. She would infuse the melodic line by embellishment—melodic and rhythmic changes with a special type of word emphasis. It was through her unique style of singing that she not only became known as the Empress of the Blues, but served as a model for blues and jazz singers who followed.

By the end of her first recording year, 1923, Bessie had sold over two million records, and by 1927, four million Bessie Smith records had been sold. She recorded 160 songs and literally saved the Columbia Record Company from bankruptcy at that time. Bessie Smith also made a movie short—quite a breakthrough for a black singer whose market was primarily ethnic. She earned a great deal of money and spent a great deal. By 1930, public interest in her began to wane—some say because she would not adjust to more modern song material. But listening to Bessie Smith records, one can feel that the blues was very personal to her, and that she sang these songs with great sincerity.[5] (S, side 1, bands 4 and 5) She died, penniless, in 1937 as a result of an automobile accident. At the time of her death

4. *Ma Rainey,* Milestone Records, M–47021.

5. Bessie Smith, "Saint Louis Blues," "Lost Your Head Blues," Smithsonian Collection of Classic Jazz; *Empty Bed Blues,* Columbia Records, G30450; *The Empress,* Columbia Records, G30818; *The Bessie Smith Story,* Columbia Records, Cl 855.

Bessie Smith. *Courtesy of Columbia Records and the estate of Carl Van Vechten.*

about ten million of her records had been sold. With her great gift of communication, Bessie Smith set the standard for all future singing of the blues.

Bessie Smith was always selective when it came to choosing her accompanying musicians, among whom were Clarence Williams, Fletcher Henderson, Louis Armstrong, Don Redman, Coleman Hawkins, James P. Johnson, Jack Teagarden, Benny Goodman, Charlie Green, and Buster Bailey.

Billie Holiday

Billie Holiday must be considered apart from others in the jazz field. It is true that many artists defy categorization, a fact we applaud, but Billie Holiday crossed musical lines while sticking with her individual singing style. She sang many blues tunes like "Fine and

Mellow" and could compete most admirably with this one vehicle. If the blues is a "feeling," she used the blues on most of her songs. But Holiday was also deeply into the popular field with beautiful renditions of songs like "Lover Man" and "Travelin' Light." But if popular music means selling a great number of records, she never really entered the popular field. There can never be any doubt, however, that she was a singer of jazz.

There is a kind of jazz song style that is neither all improvised nor all embellishment, but a little of each. The French jazz critic André Hodeir uses the term **paraphrase** to describe this song style. Singer Billie Holiday excelled at both paraphrase and invention.

Early instrumentalists copied singers (or at least oral stylings). In a reverse way, Billie Holiday's singing style seemed to stem mainly from her favorite instrumentalist, tenor saxophonist Lester Young.

Billie Holiday. *Courtesy of Ray Avery.*

Besides Young, she was undoubtedly influenced by Bessie Smith and Louis Armstrong. Singers are influenced by their background, but the background does not always lead to a predictable conclusion. Leonard Feather speaks of this unpredictability:

It would be a gigantic oversimplification to pretend that social conditions alone shaped her life, formed her vocal style, led to her death. Ella Fitzgerald had to endure a family background and childhood not greatly different from Billie's. Each was a product of a breaking or broken family; both suffered through years of poverty; both were at the mercy of Jim Crow. In Ella's case these conditions led to a career that started her on an upward curve at the age of 16, to a success story that has never been touched by scandal, and to the achievement of economic security and creature comforts far beyond her most optimistic childhood aspirations. Yet during the same time span, these *conditions in Billie's case led to marijuana at 14, a jail term as a prostitute at 15, and heroin addiction from her middle 20s.[6]*

One of the most frustrating aspects of Billie Holiday's career must have been that regardless of the fact that musicians *en masse* were her fans, the public was unwilling to accept black and white musicians performing together on the same bandstand. Because of this attitude, some of her best employment situations were short-lived. Musicians enjoyed hearing her sing blues, lovely ballads, novelty tunes, and gripping stories of lynching like "Strange Fruit."

Billie Holiday was born in Baltimore in 1915 but matured on the streets of New York. She recorded with

6.   Leonard Feather, "Billie Holiday: The Voice of Jazz," *Down Beat 29,* no. 3 (February 1962): 18.

Benny Goodman as early as 1933, but her best recordings were in 1935 with a select group of New York musicians. Most of these records are available now on repressings by Columbia Records. She died in 1959, having worked with many bands, including Count Basie's, Artie Shaw's, and Paul Whiteman's. She earned a lot of money during her career but died possessing only seventy cents. Saddest of all, she never realized how many people loved her and her singing.

It is said that Billie Holiday matured listening to recordings of Bessie Smith and Ethel Waters. But, as stated before, the instrumentalists she seemed to admire most were definite influences; they would be Louis Armstrong and Lester Young. To these wonderful models she added her own feelings, her own life-style, and the results were truly most intimate and personal.

Billie Holiday did not record as many blues tunes as many fans think. Her style and her conceptions often led listeners to feel that she was singing blues when the song was some fairly banal pop tune. Most successful female singers, knowingly or unknowingly, have been influenced by the jazz singing of Billie Holiday.[7] (S, "He's Funny That Way," "All of Me," side 4, bands 6 and 7) (NW, "I Can't Get Started," 295, side 1, band 1; "The End of a Love Affair," 295, side 2, band 8)

Ethel Waters

Ethel Waters made a name for herself in the early 1920s by making records and appearing in black nightclubs. Her repertoire broadened from blues to jazz style of singing and then to pop. She made records with such swing bands as Benny Goodman and the Dorsey Brothers. She starred in successful Broadway musicals and appeared in films and television shows.

She was born an illegitimate child and married when she was fourteen for the first time. Starting as a cleaning lady, she managed to work her way up as a singer in Harlem nightclubs and in vaudeville. Her singing style influenced such singers as Mildred Bailey, Connie Boswell, Ella Fitzgerald, Pearl Bailey, Lena Horne, and Sarah Vaughan. She died in 1977.

Listen to her famous recording of "Stormy Weather" and you will feel very deeply the mood she projects of a woman who has lost her man. This recording is a good example of how she sings emphasizing the consonants n, m, and 1.

She was different from most blues singers. She noted, herself, that she was not a shouter. Her singing style was smoother than most blues singers while her tones and vibrato were unique.

Contemporary Jazz Singers

The first recorded example of the wordless vocal jazz style called scat singing was by Louis Armstrong in his recording of "Heebie Jeebies" in 1926. Dispensing with the lyrics completely, the singer substitutes either nonsense or real syllables for the words. Many jazz and popular singers display virtuosity in this style of singing.

Sarah Vaughan played piano with the Earl Hines Orchestra and later became a featured vocalist. As a pianist, her knowledge of harmony greatly influenced her ability to sing scat as well as ballads.

Sarah Vaughan has sung for presidents and toured the world with rhythm sections, a cappella choirs, jazz combos, large jazz bands, and symphony orchestras. One of her best albums to date was recorded in Brazil; in fact, it is called *I Love Brazil*, recorded in 1977.[8] (S, "Dancing in the Dark," "Ain't No Use," side 8, bands 6 and 7) (NW, "Key Largo," 295, side 2, band 1) This musician has influenced many singers, but she herself has been considerably influenced by those musicians with whom she has worked. This most impressive list includes Dizzy Gillespie, Earl "Fatha" Hines, Charlie Parker, Miles Davis, Clifford Brown, Herbie Mann, Cannonball Adderley, Count Basie's Band, Thad Jones, Jimmy Rowles, Michel Legrand, and Bob James. It is no wonder that her creative vocalizing is so steeped in jazz.

Another vocalist worth mentioning is Betty Carter, formerly with the Lionel Hampton Band. Carter is an excellent scat singer. With her rapid execution of nonsense syllables interspersed with the actual lyrics, she almost sounds like an instrumentalist playing rapid sixteenth note patterns.

Betty Carter feels that she is the keeper of a dying flame—the true jazz singer. She agrees that the great jazz singer is linked to the instrumental approach to performing, the lyrics seem to become mere vehicles. Carter shows a profound influence of Charlie Parker

7. *Billie Holiday, The Golden Years*, Columbia Records, C31–21 and C3L40; *The Billie Holiday Story*, Decca Records, DXSB7161; *Lady Day*, Columbia Records, CL637; *Billie Holiday*, Mainstream Records, s/6000; *Strange Fruit*, Atlantic Records, 1614; "He's Funny That Way," "All of Me," Smithsonian Collection of Classic Jazz; "I Can't Get Started," *When Malindy Sings*, side 1, band 1; "The End of a Love Affair," *When Malindy Sings*, New World Records, 295.

8. Sarah Vaughan, "Dancing in the Dark," "Ain't No Use," Smithsonian Collection of Classic Jazz; *Sarah Vaughan*, Archive of Folk Music, FS–250; *Sarah Vaughan*, Trip Records, 5501; *Live in Japan*, Mainstream Records, 401; *Swings Easy*, Trip Records, 5511; *I Love Brazil*, Pablo Records, 2312101; "Key Largo," *When Malindy Sings*, New World Records, 295.

and also Sonny Rollins. These influences probably account for her rhythmic daring, her virtuosity. These bop artists are easily detected in her highly creative scat singing.[9] (NW, "Moonlight in Vermont," "Thou Swell," "Can't We Be Friends?," 295, side 2, bands 2, 3, 4)

The popular and talented Ella Fitzgerald has proven that popular singing and jazz singing can be merged with good taste. "A Tisket, A Tasket" was a good swing tune she recorded with Chick Webb in the 1930s. Later, she showed the bop influences by scat singing that style to "How High the Moon" recorded in 1948. She wanted to prove that bop performed with the voice could be comparable to instrumental renditions. Even though she is a contralto singer, using her head voice she is able to sing almost three octaves. It is a brilliant example of the voice imitating an instrument. One of the authors has recorded with Ella Fitzgerald. Her style, tone, and intonation produced no criticism from anyone except the singer herself. By 1982, Ella Fitzgerald had won 10 Grammy Awards and the *Down Beat* readers' poll 22 times.[10] (S, "You'd Be So Nice to Come Home To," side 4)

Al Jarreau attempts to imitate the precise sounds of specific instruments with his voice. A recent album of Jarreau's is *Breaking Away*.[11] Particularly intriguing is Jarreau's tricky breathless lyricization of Dave Brubeck's instrumental "Blue Rondo à la Turk," which won for Jarreau the Grammy Award for the best male jazz singer of 1981.

Vocal jazz flowered during the big bands in the Swing Era. Singers had to be well versed in a wide range of styles in order to hold their positions as soloists. They had to be able to realize the earthy sounds of the blues, the dreamy sounds of love ballads, as well as that indefinable *swing* technique.

It is interesting that many of the better jazz singers are known primarily for their instrumental prowess. Obvious examples are Louis Armstrong and Jack Teagarden. On the other side of the ledger, there are some excellent instrumentalists who are known primarily for their singing. For example, much of the listening public is not even aware of the talented piano work of Sarah Vaughan or Nat Cole.

Mel Torme, sometimes referred to as the "consummate jazz/pop vocal master of our time," continues to thrill audiences on records and live in clubs and concerts. Alto saxophonist Phil Woods makes great contributions on the 1975 Torme album *Live at the Maisonette;* it received a NARAS nomination. However, a more highly recommended effort is *Mel Torme and Friends*.[12]

Anita O'Day is often called a "pure jazz singer," intimating that jazz is her unadulterated means of expression. She enhances each song with more new directions of shape, volume, and thought than it had previously been accorded. Her earlier exposure was with the Gene Krupa Band, then with Stan Kenton, then on to become one of the prime innovators in vocal jazz.[13]

Sheila Jordan uses melismatic twists with such poignancy that her means of manipulating lyrics may mark her as the outstanding jazz singer of the 1980s. She is considered to be a "musician's singer," in fact, she often functions as an instrumental voice.[14]

Joni Mitchell reached deeply into the field of jazz with her *Mingus* album.[15] And, using excellent jazz personnel for her backup, she completed a notable album called *Shadows and Light*.[16] Joni Mitchell was known as a composer before being recognized as a singer. She stated that her first real influence was the great Lambert, Hendricks, and Ross Trio.

Urszula Dudziak sings with echoes, tapes, and synthesizers. Her husband, Michal Urbaniak, contacted Dr. Robert Moog who directed him to a laboratory in New Jersey; results: the electric violin. The couple perform on each other's albums with influences going both directions and allowing good exposure for both artists. Her vocal pyrotechnics are truly astonishing. She surprises listeners with her electronic harmonizer. She sings one note and the harmonizer produces harmonics to the original note. An excellent example is her album called *Future Talk*.[17] By way of

9. *Finally,* Roulette Records, 5000; *Betty Carter,* Bet-Car Productions, MK 1001; *Betty Carter Album,* Bet-Car Productions, MK 1002; *Now It's My Turn,* Roulette Records, 5005; *Ray Charles and Betty Carter,* ABC-Paramount Records, 385; "Moonlight in Vermont," "Thou Swell," "Can't We Be Friends?," *When Malindy Sings,* New World Records, 295.

10. *Best of Ella Fitzgerald,* MCA Records, 4047; *Ella in Berlin,* Verve Records, 64041; *Fine and Mellow,* Pablo Records, 2310829; Ella Fitzgerald and Count Basie, *A Perfect Match,* Pablo Records, 2312110; Ella Fitzgerald and Joe Pass, *Fitzgerald and Pass . . . Again,* Pablo Records, 2310772; "You'd Be So Nice To Come Home To," Smithsonian Collection of Classic Jazz, vol. 4.

11. *Breaking Away,* Warner Brothers Records, 3576.

12. *Mel Torme and Friends,* Finesse Records, W2X–37484.

13. *Anita O'Day,* Glendale Records, 6001; *Anita O'Day Sings the Winners,* Verve Records, 8283.

14. *Playground,* ECM Records, 1–1159; *Portrait of Sheila,* Blue Note Records, BST–89002.

15. *Mingus,* Asylum Records, S–505.

16. *Shadows and Light,* Asylum Records, BB–704.

17. *Future Talk,* Inner City Records, 1006.

tapes and the harmonizer, she sounds like as many as four singers at once with no overdubbing. Mostly she sings wordlessly, transcending the need for language as a tool for understanding and appreciation.

Lorez Alexandria is an example of a good jazz singer who refuses to adopt the latest fads as they go rushing past. As a consequence, her popularity has never caught up with her talent as displayed in the rather hard to locate album *A Woman Knows*.[18]

In the *Down Beat* readers' polls, vocal groups have been taking their place with instrumentalists and vocal soloists since 1944. The Pied Pipers won for the first six years, then the Mills Brothers for three years, then the Four Freshman and the Hi-Los; from 1958 through 1963, it was Hendricks, Lambert, and Ross Trio, then three years of the Double Six of Paris. The category was then altered to include non-jazz groups. A group that has hovered near the top a few times that now demands that they be taken even more seriously is Manhattan Transfer. They have always employed jazz overtones and used many excellent jazz instrumentalists on their recordings. However, their *Extensions* album[19] came as a revelation with the arrangement of "Birdland" and the lyrics by Jon Hendricks, arranged by the groups own Janis Siegal; the album included lyricization of "Body and Soul" by the great bop singer, Eddie Jefferson. This version was a harmonized transcription of Coleman Hawkins' famous 1939 improvisation.

The tradition of Lambert, Hendricks, and Ross began in the 1950s. They developed to a high degree the art of taking old jazz records and setting lyrics to just about everything on them including not only the tunes themselves, but also the improvised solos; this technique is being labeled a "vocalese art." Annie Ross was replaced by Yolande Bavan; now Hendricks uses his wife Judith, his daughter Michelle, and Bruce Scott. Their work is a contemporary form of onomatopoeia.[20]

Manhattan Transfer's 1985 album, *Vocalese*, marshalls impressive jazz forces in the vocalese style.[21] It makes use of players like McCoy Tyner, Dizzy Gillespie and the entire Basie band as well as singers like Jon Hendricks and Bobby McFerrin. "To You," from this album demonstrates the vocalese art. The music comes from a Basie and Ellington session, *First Time*, and the solo is one originally played by Butter Jackson on trombone. The lyrics for the solo were written by John Hendricks and sung by Alan Paul who described the technique. "It was hard, but Jon said if you're doing somebody's solo you've got to do it right . . . I really listened to Butter's solo and the certain way he shaped the sounds, and Thad Jones came up and said 'Yeah, Butter!' "[22]

Bobby McFerrin has proven to be a singer of unusual talent. He follows in the scat singing tradition of Louis Armstrong, Ella Fitzgerald, Mel Torme and Clark Terry. His scat ability involves more than improvised syllables with jazz inflections; he also makes percussive sounds as accompaniment to his improvisations. McFerrin is particularly effective in solo performance. He is able to recreate all the essential parts of a jazz standard by himself. By dividing his time between the melody and the bass line, he is able to give the impression that both are present all the time. He complements the performance with percussive sounds created by striking his chest while he sings. He demonstrates his versatility effectively on his album, *Spontaneous Inventions*.[23]

There is a great upsurge of jazz vocal groups in schools at this time. Some jazz groups begin in college and upon graduation become professionals. An example is an excellent Los Angeles based 19-member group. They were originally known as the Pierce College Jazz Choir; on leaving college, they became the L.A. Jazz Choir. Like most of the organizations of this type, the singing of ballads with beautiful chords seems to be their forte.

Summary

Vocal jazz means different things to different people. To some, vocal jazz, at least in the school environment, means choreography, showtunes, or the latest pop/rock/disco. To others, it may mean the sound of Singers Unlimited,[24] the Hi-Los,[25] or Lambert, Hendricks, and Ross. However, in our opinion, the use of choreography must come a distant second; the real emphasis should be on musical style. The vocal jazz performers should use jazz techniques and concepts. It is only a matter of time before almost every high school and university will offer some type of vocal jazz ensemble.

18. *A Woman Knows*, Discover Records, DS800.

19. *Extensions*, Atlantic Records, SD 19258.

20. *The Best of Lambert, Hendricks and Ross*, Columbia Records, KC–32911.

21. Manhattan Transfer, *Vocalese*, Atlantic 7 81266–1.

22. Michael Bourne, *Down Beat*, November, 1985, p. 24.

23. Bobby McFerrin, *Spontaneous Inventions*, Blue Note, BT 85110.

24. *Friends*, Pausa Records, 7039.

25. *Back Again*, Pausa Records, 7040.

Bobby McFerrin. *Courtesy Carl Baugher.*

The identification of a jazz singer dates back to the late 1920s with Al Jolson; the jazz community quite naturally never took the label seriously regarding the talented Jolson. It is easy to look back and state that Louis Armstrong, Jack Teagarden, Billie Holiday, and Ray Charles, of course, were jazz singers; they phrased in the jazz idiom on jazz materials. Today, it is more of a problem. The usually dependable hindsight is of no help in solving the immediate dilemma. Is a singer a jazz singer if the repertoire is associated with jazz? If jazz interpretation is employed? Is improvisation the main dividing line as is often stated about instrumentalists individually or bands collectively? One of the best examples of such a discussion is Ella Fitzgerald. She surely belongs to this elite grouping of sensitive vocal talent; yet she often records albums composed of strictly popular sounds done with beautiful timbre, intonation, and personal phrasing. The same can surely be said of Cleo Laine. The rationale has to be that even our best jazz singers do not always sing jazz, any more than our finest jazz instrumentalists always perform in this genre. Once again, each listener must make his or her own decisions.

It is, of course, impossible to go into detail about all the important jazz singers. Talent like that of Louis Jordan, Clark Terry and his scat singing, Jackie Cain and Roy Kral and others makes up a list that is impressive. Then, of course, there are always new jazz singers on the horizon.

Additional Reading Resources

Albertson, Chris. *Bessie*.

Chilton, John. *Billie's Blues*.

Holiday, Billie, and Dufty, William. *Lady Sings the Blues*.

Pleasants, Henry. *The Great American Popular Singers*.

Smith, Charles Edward, "Billie Holiday." *The Jazz Makers*, pp. 276–95.

Additional Record Resources

Bailey, Mildred. *Greatest Performances 1929–1946*. Columbia Records, C31–22.

Carmen McRae and the Great American Music Hall. Blue Note Records, LA–709–H2.

Jazz Singers. Vol. 4, Folkways Jazz Series. Folkways Records, FJ2804.

Jefferson, Eddie. *The Jazz Singer*. Inner City Records, 1016.

Jordan, Sheila. *The Crossing*. Blackhawk, 50501.

Mean Mothers/Independent Women's Blues. Rosetta Records, RR1300.

Sorry But I Can't Take You/Woman's Railroad Blues. Rosetta Records, RR1301.

The Blues. Vol. 2, Folkways Jazz Series. Folkways Records, FJ2802.

The Essential Jimmy Rushing. Vanguard Records, 65/66.

Washington, Dinah. *Dinah Jams*. Trip Records, TLP–5500.

When Malindy Sings—Jazz Vocalists 1938–1961. New World Records, 295.

Suggested Classroom Activities

1. Describe the differences between a folk song and a popular song.

2. Select a blues melody with text. Have each student or the class as a whole learn to sing the blues song; then, gradually with each repetition, add some new element of either the melody or rhythm. Have all the other students listen actively and critically to those changes made. A tape recorder can be a very good aid for the participants.

3. Select three or four different recordings of vocal jazz singers. Encourage students to listen for the specific techniques used by the artist to achieve her or his effects. Encourage students to copy the jazz phrases on paper or reproduce them with their singing voices.

4. Feel the excitement of a gospel selection by responding physically while listening. This may be accomplished through syncopated hand-clapping that is an integral part of gospel performance. Respond to the music by tapping the foot on beats one and three, and hand clapping on beats two and four.

5. After listening to Ella Fitzgerald's "One Note Samba" on the Album *Fitzgerald and Pass*, select a song that is very familiar, such as "De Lovely" or "Great Feelin'," by Scott Fredrickson and make up your own scat rendition. Try to select a variety of vowels and consonants that do not follow the familiar *shoo-bee-doo-bee-doo-bee-doo*. Create a musical line with form and sense to it. After the scat syllables have been created, repeat the song and start to make creative alterations by changing the rhythmic patterns. Next, alter the melody. Perhaps a portion of melody can be sung as written and another portion can be altered.

18

Jazz and the New Technology

All art forms respond in some way to dominant cultural developments. The intersection of music and technology is certainly not new; however, it was probably never as active as during the 1950s to 1980s. Jazz found this period characterized by impressive technological developments in audio production. Always quick to assimilate new elements from the world around it, jazz was among the first art musics to incorporate the new technology.

Outside of the advancements in instrument manufacturing, the first major impact technology had on jazz resulted from the advancements in recording. The early recordings, although of poor quality by today's standards, offered traditionally provincial jazz styles a much larger audience. New Orleans style could be heard anywhere the early records could be found, not just in the central metropolitan areas to which the musicians usually traveled. In the early part of this century, Milhaud was able to carry back records of Harlem's New Orleans style jazz to Paris; at that same time only a handful of bands themselves actually made the trip to Europe. Without records and radio, Europe's fascination with early jazz would not have occurred.

Jazz's own development has been influenced by the increased ease and use of recording. The development of the art form depends on the reaction of performers to one another's work. What would jazz be like if Armstrong's *Hot Five,* Parker and Gillespie's 1945 records, or Miles Davis' *Birth of the Cool* recordings

were not easily available to other musicians? A consistent tradition depends on the knowledge new players have of their predecessors. The fact that musical styles are not limited to specific geographical locations testifies to the effective role recordings play in the development of the jazz tradition.

The Recording Medium

The recording medium has changed dramatically since the early days of phonographs which involved recording directly on wax cylinders. In the late 1940s, the recording process made one of its most dramatic steps with the creation of the wire and magnetic tape recorders. The wire recorder (a thin wire which was magnetized to store the sound impressions) was short-lived for several reasons, one being that the wire could not be edited easily. Magnetic tape recording, however, was much more flexible and soon became the dominant recording medium. Although recorded on tape, the music was eventually transferred to a vinyl phonograph record for marketing. The tape recorder made the recording process more accessible to listeners and performers alike, and in the 1950s became a normal component in home stereo systems. The convenience of the later cassette tape recorder soon made it, in many cases, even more popular than records themselves. Because music was so easy to transport and play back, the breadth of musical material being recorded and promoted also began to broaden.

Until the early sixties, the recording style remained much the same; a group of musicians would gather, play, and record a piece from start to finish as many times as was necessary until the performance was satisfactory for a record. Or, more often, a recording was just made at a live performance and later transferred to record. The resulting recording reflected the normal playing abilities and collective strengths of the performers as well as the unexpected triumphs or mistakes associated with the live performance.

With the advent of **multiple track recording** (the ability to record several different parts, each on a separate track but synchronized), new performing styles began to develop. A single musician could essentially be a complete band. By recording one instrument after another (called *overdubbing* or *multi-tracking*), a performer can build up a very complex piece of music all alone. As a result, there are some groups that perform only in the studio and produce albums, but would find it difficult to produce the same music in a live concert situation. Bill Evans, on his solo album, *New Conversations,* uses multi-tracking to combine two acoustic pianos and one electric piano into monologues, dialogues, and trialogues with himself.[1] Even with the restriction of having to play the second and third parts in synchronization with his first part, Evans is able to maintain an improvisational style. Joe Zawinul's solo album, *Dialects,* is also exemplary of one performer's ability to build complex musical structures through the use of sophisticated multi-tracking techniques.[2]

A more recent effort to improve the quality of recording involves a process called "direct to disc." This process bypasses the tape recording stage (which introduces a new level of **noise**) and records directly on the disc used to **master** the recordings. Very few electronic effects are ever used while recording, and there is no opportunity to go back and change anything after the recording is done. The direct to disc process is, therefore, most useful for music that does not traditionally require any **editing** or special treatments, classical or jazz being the greatest beneficiaries. This method of recording stands in sharp contrast to the patchwork approach possible in the recording studio, where the various musical parts, which are not likely to be recorded on the same day, can later be edited to correct specific problems.

Digital Recording

The eighties marked another dramatic change for the recording medium. Rather than a tape which holds magnetic imprints of the sound waves, sounds are analyzed and converted to numeric information suitable for storage and use by a computer. This **digital** information can be processed in what appears to be an infinite number of ways by computers themselves or by specially designed musical devices (**effects**). Traditional vinyl records can be made from these digital recordings or the information can be stored on **compact discs** (CD). The information on these discs, still digital in format, is read with the use of laser beams during playback. The compact disc player is able to interpret the digital information and convert it into the musical sounds first recorded. As with all the previous improvements in the recording process, the development of compact disc players has produced a marked improvement in the quality of the finished recording. Chick Corea's *Elektric Band* album was digitally mastered, meaning it was recorded with digital equipment and then put on a traditional vinyl record. The album is also available on compact disc.[3] Although it is possible to put traditional recordings (**analog** as opposed to digital) on CD, the greatest clarity is achieved when the entire process is digital, both recording and playback.

Since its earliest days, the digital recording process has developed much further and dropped dramatically in cost. It is now quite common to find digital recording studios in most all major cities and compact disc players in many homes. The major advantage of this new digital process comes from both the ability to process the information during the recording process and the durability of the disc. Digital information is essentially nothing but numbers and can be processed in any fashion suitable with numbers. Sounds can virtually be added together, subtracted, read forward or backward, and even edited at the microsecond level. A sound, when analyzed digitally, is broken down most commonly into 40,000 to 50,000 parts or **samples** each second. The computer is able to transform and manipulate these samples individually or collectively. It will take quite a while to fully realize all the possibilities inherent in the digital treatment of sounds.

Amplification—Loudness

With advancements in electronics, the nature of the concert hall has also changed. Traditionally, a large hall

1. Bill Evans, *New Conversations,* Warner Bros., BSK 3177.

2. Joe Zawinul, *Dialects,* Columbia Records, FCT 40081.

3. Chick Corea, *Elektrik Band,* GRP Records, GRP–A–1026, (Compact Disc, GRP–D–9535).

usually required a large ensemble. The success of the big bands in the large ballrooms demonstrates a good match of group and hall size. Amplification and electronic instruments opened new possibilities for performances by small groups before large audiences. A small group could effectively play to a very large audience if enough of the proper amplification equipment could be utilized. However, with the development of amplification also came a new notion of loudness in performance. In an acoustic environment, loud is most usually accompanied by a change in timbre, for example, a loud trumpet sounds different from a soft one. In contrast, a change in the setting of a volume knob does not carry a similar shift in timbre. Listeners normally associate the change in timbre that accompanies louder playing with a parallel increase in intensity. It cannot be denied that there is a certain visceral response to higher volumes which carries with it a new kind of intensity for both the player and the listener. Rock, because of its early use of amplified instruments, has dealt the longest with the dilemma of finding intensity in amplified loudness. The rock singing style often pushes the voice to its limit in an effort to create the intensity not supplied by the volume knob. The musical instruments do much the same with electronic effects such as **distortion** units. Many in the jazz audience are actually lost because of their distaste for excessive volume. However, as jazz audiences grow to include those who are already comfortable with the louder volume of rock, the volume of electronic jazz groups also tends to increase.

Jazz approached its use of greater volume more slowly and deliberately than did rock. Fusion groups have been the first jazz groups to experiment with volume levels more typical of rock. A clear distinction is still made between acoustic and electronic groups in jazz. *Down Beat* magazine's yearly critics' poll offers separate categories for each. Arguments can be offered in support of both approaches. The new colors available through the use of electronics are often countered with a loss of intimacy associated with acoustic groups.

The use of amplification has also redefined the notion of balance within an ensemble. In acoustic settings, the players adjust their individual volumes to create shifts in balance, but soft instruments are always at a disadvantage when loudness is needed. By selectively amplifying different instruments new ensemble balances can be created. Miles Davis's album, *You're Under Arrest,* shows an interesting change in instrumental balance.[4] The bass drum is given a very prominent position in the mix. Even a very strong drummer would find it difficult, if not impossible, to create the same balance without the use of amplification. Vocalists and instrumentalists with softer volume

capabilities like flutist Hubert Laws are now able to perform with much louder groups and to much larger audiences.

Stanley Jordan has turned the electronically amplified guitar to a unique advantage. With the use of amplification, Jordan developed a touch technique on the fingerboard of the guitar that allows him to play complex contrapuntal lines not normally possible on a guitar. By using both hands to press the strings to the fretboard, he is able to create individual notes without having to pluck the strings. The normally very soft sound of the string hitting the fret is amplified enough so that the strings do not need to be strummed or picked. Without amplification this playing technique would be virtually impossible. The result is so startling that guitar players have had to re-evaluate the very potential of the instrument. Jordan's album, *Magic Touch,* even contains a notice to the listener that there is only one guitarist playing all the parts without the use of recorded overdubs.[5]

Synthesizers

Most dramatic in the technology of instruments in the seventies and eighties was the growing accessibility of synthesizers. No longer restricted to high budgeted academic research institutions, synthesizers are appearing on the stage and bandstand. Although capable of an infinite number of sounds yet to be created, the first performance oriented synthesizers were designed to replicate existing acoustical instruments. It soon became cheaper to buy a string or drum synthesizer than to hire the players themselves. Needless to say, the response from all musicians about the opportunities offered by the synthesizers was not all favorable. It was not uncommon for musicians' unions to forbid the use of synthesizers in order to promote the use of live players.

Restrictions such as this proved fruitless in the face of the excitement felt by other musicians about the prospects for the new equipment. Rather than making the musician's task easier, the new devices required a more complex understanding of the sounds that make up music. The first electronic instrument outside of the guitar to be adopted by the jazz community was the electronic piano, and the Fender Rhodes in particular. This instrument dominated the keyboard world for many years during the seventies and early eighties, eventually to be replaced by Yamaha's very popular

4. Miles Davis, *You're Under Arrest,* Columbia, FCT 40023.

5. Stanley Jordan, *Magic Touch,* Blue Note, BT 85101.

Stanley Jordan. *Courtesy David Barr.*

DX7 synthesizer. Although the Rhodes does not sound at all like a real piano, it was adopted and granted full status by the jazz and commercial music communities. The Fender Rhodes proved to be the doorway to even more complex electronic keyboards for many of the later synthesists like Chick Corea and Joe Zawinul, both of whom started to use the Rhodes while working with Miles Davis. George Duke and Jan Hammer also used the Rhodes before branching out to newer keyboards.

The adoption of Fender Rhodes' electronically produced sound proved to be just the tip of the iceberg. Jazz and commercial music listeners were soon presented with a new world of sounds never before heard. In fact, a trademark of fusion jazz is often the use of unique sounds only possible with the help of synthesizers. Zawinul proves that exotic sounds are not the only use for a synthesizer on Weather Report's *Night Passage* album. By accompanying Wayne Shorter's saxophone line on Ellington's "Rockin' in Rhythm"

Chick Corea. *Courtesy of Glen Wexler*

with a synthesized line, he is able to create a pseudo-saxophone sound similar to a big band saxophone section.[6] While reminiscent of the big band saxophone section sound, it maintains a unique timbre appropriate to the more electronic sound typical of fusion jazz. The stylistic gap is bridged by Shorter's saxophone lead which lends an acoustic authenticity to the synthesizer support.

Synthesizers have mushroomed in diversity and complexity and tend to fall into two categories, performance or composition models. The former are usually more limited but consequently easier to manipulate during a live performance. The composition models, like the Synclavier and Fairlight systems offer the composer/performer a great deal of flexibility but are more suitable for the studio than the stage. They require a substantial background in sound synthesis as well as a great deal of programming time.

The inclusion of synthesizers in new ensembles has become so complete that their model names are often listed on records in the same fashion as the players themselves. A keyboard player is often credited on each cut with a list of the synthesizers used. For example on the first cut of Chick Corea's *Electrik Band* album,

Corea's name is followed by the name of five different synthesizers. Different model synthesizers are felt to have personalities as different from one another as a trumpet is from a trombone.

Computers and Effects

In addition to the synthesizers themselves, there are many other instrumental devices available for use both in the studio and live performance. Most notable are the **sequencers** and **samplers.** Sequencers are able to store musical melodies and play them back at various speeds and pitches. Samplers allow the musicians to capture an acoustic sound and use it as if it were a separate voice on the synthesizer. Sampling is essentially a digital recording of a sound which the computer then adjusts to fit all the keys on a synthesizer. It is therefore possible to record even a spoken phrase and then play it back on the synthesizer with a different pitch for each key.

6. Weather Report, *Night Passage,* CBS, 36793.

Once a sound is created or sampled, computers like the Fairlight system are capable of making microscopic alterations. At this point, the possibilities seem limitless. So much so, that new never before heard sounds may become the norm, if not a requirement, for electronically based ensembles.

The increased use of synthesizers has also placed a strain on the traditional use of notation. These new instruments are capable of creating sounds outside our standard notational capabilities. Jazz has always made great use of inflections difficult to notate, but the new instruments have in many cases made the notation useless. It is ironic that the high technology represented by synthesizers has, at the same time, promoted the oral tradition. The explosion of possibilities for timbre cannot be shown in musical notation, only passed on as the aural sensation it is. The synthesizer, like all the instruments that preceded it, proves to be most viable in the hands of creative musicians working from the sounds heard in their imaginations.

Synthesized sounds have often been accused of sounding impersonal and mechanical. The computer is capable of creating sounds so steady that they are immediately recognized as synthesized. In an effort to solve this problem, a great battery of musical treatments, called effects, have been created to soften and enhance the quality of synthesized sounds. These effects range from simple **reverberation** units to complex **harmonizers** and **vocoders.**

Don Ellis was among the first to use early effects like **tape loops** and **pitch dividers.** The divider isolates an undertone or overtone from the amplified instrument sound and plays it along with the natural instrument sound. The most common use involves setting the divider so that it plays along with the natural instrument, but an octave below it. Tape loops were used to create very slow echoes while playing. A phrase was played and recorded on a loop which keeps playing back the phrase while the soloist continues to solo above it. Listen to Don Ellis' trumpet cadenza on "Open Beauty."[7] Here he uses the divider and plays in octaves with himself, adding echo and reverberation with the tape loop. Harmonizers now do what dividers, loops, and reverberation units did but can also accompany the melodic line with any pitch desired and treat the sound digitally as well.

Our familiarity with musical sounds can lead us to think sounds are simpler than they really are. To simulate the complex characteristics of music, a great deal of computing time is required. Most synthesizers intended for use in live performance cannot spend the necessary computing time for complex sounds and still be immediately responsive to the performing musician.

With the help of effects, applied to the sound after it is created by the synthesizer, sounds can be given the subtle characteristics more typical of acoustic instruments. Herbie Hancock uses a popular effect called a vocoder which allows him to sing into a microphone and combine the syllables he pronounces with the pitches he plays on the synthesizer.[8] The vocal effects heard on Zawinul's *Dialect* album also make use of a vocoder.

It is the very individual and expressive solo style of jazz players with which the new technology must compete for acceptance in the highly personalized world of jazz. Judged by the many rapid advancements since Dr. Robert Moog designed his early synthesizers, the still young technology should have no trouble finding the expressive voices required by performers.

Musical Instrument Digital Interface

The advantages of the new electronic devices are most fully realized when they can be synchronized for live performance. The ability to synchronize more than one unit together has only recently been standardized. The manufacturers of the various equipment have developed a standard for communication between computers and synthesizers called the Musical Instrument Digital Interface or just **MIDI.** All the musical actions on any particular instrument can be described in MIDI code (in many ways very similar to Morse code), actions such as which key is pressed, the speed of the keypress, and when the key was released.

Most synthesizers today are equipped with MIDI capabilities that allow them to be played from other keyboards, to be hooked to a **drum machine,** sequencer or computer for synchronization, or even to be used to play other synthesizers remotely. This is particularly useful to musicians who prefer live performances but could not possibly operate all their equipment at one time. One approach a musician can take is to play several of the parts to be used in performance and store them in a sequencer. With the help of MIDI interfaces, new parts played live can be synchronized to the earlier stored parts during the performance itself. Although this process helps coordinate a large amount of equipment it also limits the flexibility of the performance. It is difficult for a preprogrammed song to be responsive

7. Don Ellis, "Open Beauty," *Electric Bath,* Columbia Records, CL2785.

8. Herbie Hancock, *Feets Don't Fail Me Now,* Columbia Records, 35764.

to the personality of the other players or even the audience. With any new technology comes a new jargon and music synthesis has its jargon with phrases like **real time.** To play a synthesizer and hear immediate results is considered to be in real time. To program a composition for a computer or overdub tracks on tape is not. Live performances can have a blend of both. Previously recorded music (on tape or in a sequencer) can be created before the performance and later used during a real time performance as part of the total group sound. In this way the art worlds of the stage and studio begin to merge.

Studio Performance/Composition

Because of the advancements in recording and synthesizers, the studio has become as viable a performing arena as the concert stage. The new studio technology and its freedom from real time constraints offers musicians a different compositional approach. Robert Irving III speaks of some of those possibilities in *Down Beat's* interview after his work on Miles Davis' *You're Under Arrest* album:

"In general, we use signal processing to try to give every instrument a different room sound. We use digital reverb chambers to simulate different room sounds for each instrument—even the high-hat [foot operated cymbal] has its own sound—then combine it with analog reverb in the mix."[9]

He also speaks of Davis going back after the initial recording and doing the trumpet "punches" (plugging in or replacing trumpet lines in the recording) and then doubling Davis' lines with his synthesizers. This type of overdubbing is only possible in the studio. The dilemma with such an approach arises when the same music must be performed on tour. To pre-record parts that were overdubbed can create a stiff undynamic live performance. Working successfully in both arenas proves to be no easy task.

Jazz has historically been characterized by its spontaneity and improvisational approach; the studio may at first appear to compromise both these characteristics. When the final product does not represent the entire group reacting to one another in real time, how can there be spontaneity? The patchwork approach toward performance certainly places a higher emphasis on the compositional approach. Although the solo areas are freely improvised (but not necessarily at the same time as the backup is recorded), the effectiveness of a piece rides on its compositional strength. This approach might best be likened to music of the big bands

during the Swing Era in which the ensemble composition was also very specific and created prior to the performance. Performing tours often serve to ready the groups for their final studio work. The material to be recorded is tested and refined while on tour and then taken into the studio where it is enhanced for the bigger-than-life sound expected on record.

Zawinul describes his compositional approach for his solo album, *Dialect,* on which he used four synthesizers and four drum machines: "all the pieces on the album were originally just things I sat down and improvised. Then I replayed them, wrote them down note for note and recorded them again to achieve the best possible sound and mix."[10] This approach, like so many today, benefits from the exchange between playing and recording. Improvisation is not necessarily forsaken in the studio, only stored for later listening. By placing a time barrier between performers and listeners, the studio approach tends to promote a more crafted performance style. It takes a good understanding of both the studio and the music to align the technical requirements of the studio with the expressive intent of the musicians.

The studio also introduces a new member to most ensembles, the engineer/producer. The producer may quite often come from the performing ensemble itself; however, the engineer may not necessarily be a performing musician. He must, therefore, know the studio equipment as well as any of the players know their instruments and also be sensitive to the music being performed. Any shortage of skill or knowledge in either area will alter the final musical product.

Summary

The merger of technology and the jazz tradition has not occurred without its controversies. Some critics sense an impersonality in the technology that robs jazz of its freely improvisational tradition. With any new development, there is often excess while experimentation occurs. Jazz has, no doubt, suffered its excesses, excesses of volume and electronic overkill. However, the fact that there is so much experimentation in the jazz community with the new technological achievements is a testimony to the ongoing vibrancy still at work in jazz. When the technological dust settles, jazz, as it has so

9. Robert Irving III, Down Beat, August 1985, p. 54.

10. Joe Zawinul, Los Angeles Times Calendar Section, March 2, 1986.

often in the past, will find its proper response. Jazz remains a history of individuals expressing themselves with the tools at hand. When the tools change, so must the music.

The power of the recording studio and its influence on jazz performance and composition will certainly continue. For many jazz performers the studio is becoming a performance arena equal in importance to the concert stage. How lasting the influence of our technological explosion is on the development of jazz will only be known when our future becomes history.

Demonstrations 20 to 23 are examples of some of the technical equipment available to the studio and live performance musician. Demonstration 20 is an excerpt of the synthesized drum track from the crossover demonstration 19. Lawrence Hopkins created these sounds on a programmable drum synthesizer ("drum machine"). The entire piece was programmed into the drum synthesizer which, in turn, played the program back during the actual performance (in this case in the recording studio).

Demonstration 21 is an excerpt of the synthesized bass line for the same piece. The sound is actually a composite of several synthesizers, all playing the same musical line. Demonstration 22 is, again, several synthesizers programmed for the brass-like sounds of the crossover demonstration 19.

Demonstration 23 is an excerpt of the flute-like melodic line. This line was played "live" while all the others were played back from a sequencer (actually a computer) which coordinated all the synthesizers by means of MIDI control. For the melodic line Hopkins used a breath controller which allows him to use his breath to control the synthesizer to create articulations very similar to those used by jazz horn players.

The final demonstration, 24, is a repeat of the crossover demonstration 19 in its entirety so that you may listen for the excerpted sounds from the previous demonstrations.

Additional Reading Resources

Baird, David. *From Score to Tape.*

Friend, David; Perlman, Alan R.; Piggott, Thomas G. *Learning Music with Synthesizers.*

Drake, Russell; Herder, Ronald; Modugno, Anne D. *How to Make Electronic Music.*

Feather, Leonard. *The Book of Jazz,* pp. 245–62.

Hentoff, Nat, and McCarthy, Albert. *Jazz,* pp. 327–42.

Muro, Don. *An Introduction to Electronic Music Synthesizers.*

Stearns, Marshall. *The Story of Jazz,* pp. 227–30.

Note: Complete information including name of publisher and date of publication is provided in the Bibliography.

Additional Record Resources

Synthesizer Recordings

Hammer, Jan. *Melodies.* Nemperor Records, 35003.

Hancock, Herbie. *Sunlight.* Columbia Records, 34907.

———. *Sound System.* Columbia Records, FC 39478.

Mahavishnu Orchestra. *Birds of Fire.* Columbia Records, KC 31996.

———. *Inner Worlds.* Columbia Records, PC 33908.

Weather Report. *Heavy Weather.* Columbia Records, PC 34418.

Weather Report, Columbia Records, C 3066.

Wonder, Stevie. *Songs in the Key of Life.* Tamla Records, T 13–34062.

Direct to Disc Recordings

Herman, Woody. *Road Father.* Century Records, CRDD–1080.

Herman, Woody, and Phillips, Flip. *Together/Flip and Woody.* Century Records, CRDD–1090.

Miles, Barry. *Fusion Is.* Century Records, CRDD–1020.

Torme, Mel, and Rich, Buddy. *Together Again—For the First Time.* Century Records, CRDD–1100.

Woods, Phil. *Song for Sisyphus.* Century Records, CRDD–1030.

Suggested Classroom Activities

1. In producing a tone, how does the synthesizer function in contrast to an electric piano? In contrast to an acoustic piano?
2. Give the title of a recording that uses the synthesizer.
3. For an exciting new sound, listen to "Open Beauty" as played by the Don Ellis Orchestra on the album *Electric Bath, The Don Ellis Orchestra* (Columbia, Stereo CS 9585). In this composition Ellis weaves a psychedelic effect by using an electric piano with reeds and brasses. What electronic effect was used to create the sound of many parts occurring at one time?
4. Who was noted for his mix of electronics and the singing voice?
5. Name the musician who was highly successful while identified with a particular style of jazz and now is associated with electronics. Has his entrance into electronics changed his earlier style of jazz playing? If so, how?
6. What is digital recording?
7. Discuss the influence the recording studio has on the improvisational nature of jazz.

Listening Guide

Demonstration 20, synthesized drum excerpt from crossover demonstration 19, Yamaha RX11 drum machine.

Demonstration 21, synthesized bass excerpt from crossover demonstration 19, Yamaha TX7, two DX7s and Roland JX-8P synthesizers.

Demonstration 22, synthesized brass figures from crossover demonstration 19, Yamaha TX7, two DX7s and Roland JX-8P synthesizers.

Demonstration 23, synthesized flute excerpt (with digital delay) from crossover demonstration 19, Two Yamaha DX7s with breath controller.

Crossover Demonstration 24

FunkMaster Be Jammin', *Lawrence Hopkins*
In addition to the above listed synthesizers, an Atari computer was used to sequence the song and control the timing while overdubbing during the recording.

:00 Synthesized bass and drum introduction, angular rock rhythms
:16 Synthesized flute-like melody enters
:35 Melody continues as brass-like melodic figures become more predominate
:56 Rhythm break with only drums
1:01 Short punctuated brass-like sounds support an improvised solo which uses a breath controller to create horn-like articulations
1:40 End

19

Jazz Esthetics and Criticism

Historical criticism is normally a latecomer to any developing musical line. Jazz has, in the last decades, become a music of independent distinction with a developing tradition all its own. The many commentaries and musical criticisms that have accompanied the developing jazz tradition can be viewed as a collective body that expresses the historical development of the art form itself.

Throughout its history, jazz has had many valuable contributions by patrons, critics, and historians. These individuals have in their own way influenced the evolution of the music itself. As jazz develops as an art form, it becomes ever more susceptible to the dictates of its own tradition. This notion is particularly noticeable in the verbal expressions of performers like Wynton Marsalis, who openly states that today's jazz performers are responsible to their tradition and should reflect it in their work.

This is not, however, a notion universally shared among all jazz performers. As the innovative efforts of frontier jazz groups and individuals stretch out in all directions, the performers and composers may feel burdened by what they might call the baggage of the past. To better understand these discrepancies of opinion among both performers and historians, it is wise to understand the frame of reference from which the musical authorities speak. Any statement of musical value reflects the viewpoint from which it is made. Those

evolutionary developments that lead to a favored style might be viewed as exciting innovations, while those that lead away as decadent expressions. Innovation for one person might therefore be decadence for another.

It is in such an environment that jazz has developed into a recognized art form, complete with its own history. This history is interpreted and elucidated by a body of critics and historians as diverse as the styles they describe and often judge. As a critic/historian gains credibility, he or she also gains influence on, and a responsibility toward the developing musical frontiers. This influence can be viewed as an historical feedback that can influence newly emerging styles. Jazz of the early 1980s and the interest in a return to bop serves as an example of this type of influence. Bop of the 1980s is often referred to as a "pure" or "straight ahead" expression of the jazz tradition. By shifting our musical viewpoint back to the 1950s, we find that this bop style was considered quite extreme and hardly responsible to the tradition of its day, but in light of the free jazz of the 1960s, bop offers a secure anchor to the past.

As another example, consider the innovations of form that Jelly Roll Morton offered the jazz community. He introduced new ways of composing for ensembles based on variation within the formal structure.[1] (S, "Dead Man Blues," side 1, band 8) From the

---

1.   Jelly Roll Morton, "Dead Man Blues," *Smithsonian Collection of Classic Jazz.*

perspective of his time, the implementation of his new techniques in form was a liberating device. Compare then the free form jazz of the 1960s. Here the innovation was considered the destruction of form to liberate the performance.[2] (S, "Free Jazz," side 12, band 3)

Controversy is a companion of any developing tradition. Change from the polished sounds of a familiar style to the roughness characteristic of experimental efforts is seldom smooth. The history of jazz music does not always present a continuous or even predictable evolutionary continuum. The amount of controversy that surrounds a new effort is often an indication of just how different the experimentation is from its immediate past. Consider the controversy that surrounds Ornette Coleman's use of free form jazz with the above mentioned innovations of Morton. Morton's innovations did not make a clean break with the ragtime influences still at work but fused new elements with that tradition. Coleman's work is much more of a clean break with its immediate past. Such sharp breaks with past tradition are often surrounded by strong controversy (see chapter 13).

The influences that shape a new style may, in fact, not even originate from the music itself. Were the seeds for the blues in its musical predecessors, the cultural situation, or both? Because the influences on the music vary throughout its history, a universal definition of jazz, good for all time, is difficult to establish. Historians are still battling with definitions that might successfully encompass such divergent forms as "cool," "free," and "big band" jazz. We agree that they all represent valid expressions of jazz, but still find it difficult to extract a precise and common definition.

Despite the elusive character of a fixed definition, most all performers, historians, critics, and patrons of jazz base their response to the music on some kind of working definition that may not always be conscious. To fully appreciate the work of today's musicians, it is helpful to develop such a working definition, which is subject to change. This definition should respect the efforts of the past yet still remain open to the experimentations necessary for a healthy and continuous evolution. There is a danger in this, however. Jazz expressions should not be considered valid only if they can be clearly explained in terms of a working definition. Historically, explanations have always followed the music they describe. It may be more proper to allow the working definition to evolve with the music it is meant to define.

An Historical Perspective

A feature of an historical perspective is often a high respect for innovation. In any effort to appear innovative and thereby take a place in the developing history, players and critics are sometimes led into theoretical areas that seem only remotely related to its tradition. In other words, does one play to shape history, or is history only inadvertently shaped by ones playing? The answer probably lies somewhere between the two extremes and varies among players and critics. The dilemma a critic faces here is how to support artistic experimentation while, at the same time, holding the resulting compositions and performances accountable to the developing jazz tradition. Jazz artists are sometimes criticized for not pushing to innovate even when their music is universally loved.

Values, like our respect for innovation, can also distort our view of past accomplishments in jazz. For example, while the information explosion of the seventies and eighties might foster a respect for the new and experimental, that respect might prove to be an obstacle when listening to earlier stylistic periods. The criteria at work in free compositional music typical of Ornette Coleman's collective free jazz would be inappropriate to apply to the workings of the big band arrangements of the 1940s.

Jazz Controversies

To better understand jazz's evolutionary flow, it is helpful to look at some of the periods of controversy which centered around various individuals and their music. In the largest overview, jazz history could be reduced (although somewhat simplistically) to just a few large periods: the Jazz Age (1920s), the Swing Era, Bop, Cool, and Eclectic eighties. Rather than static, each of these periods can be described as an evolution to the next. The fact that these period descriptors are generally understood by the jazz community implies that the periods are at least minimally distinctive historically.

The transitions between these periods are generally the most controversial times in jazz's evolution. The movement toward bop is particularly interesting because it can be viewed as one of the important transitions in the developing art form. It was during this

2. Ornette Coleman, "Free Jazz," *Smithsonian Collection of Classic Jazz*. Also see Martin Williams, *The Jazz Tradition*, Oxford University Press, 1983.

Nat Hentoff. *Courtesy of Sylvia Plachy*

time that jazz began to leave its traditional boundaries of dance music entertainment to be played for its own sake.[3] This move coincided with the New Orleans revival which waved a banner of traditionalism as a reaction, first, to the commercialization of swing, and later to the modernism of bop.

Charles Mingus offers a unique example for this argument in his composition, "Eclipse," which has an avant garde flavor but espouses a return to the more contrapuntal New Orleans style, and therefore opposes the more harmonic style of swing. He is also supporting

a concern of many jazz musicians of that time for a return to a smaller chamber music format in contrast to the larger and less flexible groups often found in swing.[4] (NW, 216, "Eclipse," side 1, band 5)

The traditionalists versus the modernists is an argument that accompanies the development of all art forms. In the 1980s we see the same forces at work, although less vociferous. The traditional school, championed by performers like Wynton Marsalis, looks to

3. Dan Morgenstern, liner notes to *Bebop,* NW #271.

4. Charles Mingus, "Eclipse," New World Records, 216.

Art Lange. *Courtesy Herb Nolan.*

the bop period for its inspiration. The modernists, on the other hand, advocate experimentation, unfettered by traditional protocol, an example being the Art Ensemble of Chicago. It is in the balance of these two forces that jazz evolves. The excitement and unpredictability of experimentation is guided by the integrity of jazz's past tradition.

Historian versus Critic

The roles played by historians and critics, although quite similar, vary in several important ways. The historian attempts to clearly and objectively present a description of the events and performers in jazz. The evolutionary line of the history described will be determined by what the historian considers the most influential forces at work at any given time. Historians attempt to point out these influences but not make judgment about their worth. This proves to be a nearly impossible task because errors of exclusion and personal tastes can greatly distort an historian's objective intention.

Critics, while also aware of prevalent jazz influences, attempt to evaluate the worth of a new influence on the developing tradition. Critics may decide to evaluate specific performances or broad stylistic developments. Again, personal taste can shape the nature of the criticism. Although critics have often been accused of being biased and unfair, their responses are expected to reflect their personal taste as well as rate the performance. With such a responsibility comes both recognition and abuse. A critic is often allowed the flamboyance and pointed statements not tolerated of an historian. Nat Hentoff, himself a critic, offers insight to what might be expected of a critic when he discusses a critic he found exciting.

"From the first time I read him . . . Frazier was an influence on me. Not his style; that was too calculatedly personal to be adapted by anyone. It was his spirit . . . his refusal to tone himself down, to be more "balanced," to be "objective," to be "responsible." That was for sidemen in symphony orchestras, not for a horn man in the front line whom people were eager to read because he took chances, because he went outside the chords, because they had no way of knowing what this elegant wild man would do next."[5]

5. Nat Hentoff, *Boston Boy,* Alfred A. Knopf, New York, p. 133, 1986.

Martin Williams. *Photo by George de Vincent*

Leonard Feather. *Courtesy of Leonard Feather*

The critics that endure, like the star performers in jazz, are the ones that offer the excitement Hentoff speaks of but also show a respect and understanding for the evolving jazz tradition. Critics that speak of only one style and crusade for it at the expense of other styles will usually become only a footnote in the history they wish to shape. Those who carry an historical consciousness with their criticisms add a credence to their work that helps support the personal judgments they offer.

A critic's prominence carries a heavy responsibility. A new performer's fragile career can sometimes be launched or destroyed by a critic's response. The responsibility must, however, also be shared by the reader who judges the validity of the critic's remarks. It is often too easy for the reader to trust the critic's reputation rather than seek out enough information to make a personal judgment. It is good practice to read a number of reviews by any critic to discover the critic's personal preferences. These preferences can then be taken into account when later reviews are read.

Very prominent critics have been known to change their opinions of a particular performer or even a jazz style in general. Critics are not independent from their readers, and, like performers, cannot operate effectively in direct opposition to their audience. Sometimes critics will change their opinion of a particular style or performer because the jazz climate demands it, or because they simply change their own mind after repeated listenings. In extreme cases, critics might discover that they had based their arguments on false or nonmusical premises. Good and honest critics can make such shifts gracefully and not lose their integrity in the eyes of their readers.

Joachim-Ernst Berendt. *Courtesy of Joachin-Ernst Berendt*

André Hodeir. *Courtesy of André Hodeir*

Many times, performers may feel that they have been judged unfairly by either a particular critic or critics at large. It becomes the listener's (and reader's) responsibility to decide whether the performer is misunderstood or being unfairly treated.

Prominent Critics

Like Nat Hentoff, there are many notable jazz critics at work. The most prominent are usually associated with major publications and larger metropolitan areas. *Down Beat* magazine, centered in Chicago and currently edited by Art Lange, has been a major springboard for many critics. Hentoff was at one time the New York editor for that same magazine. Martin Williams is also notable for his work with the Smithsonian Institute and has authored many books on the history of jazz. The *New Yorker* benefits from Whitney Balliet's writings and on the West Coast Leonard Feather writes regularly for the Los Angeles *Times*.

Notable jazz criticism is also found outside of the United States. In Germany, Joachim Berendt has gained a strong reputation as well as André Hodeir in France.

These writers are characterized by a large output of material that has appeared in many forms from dictionaries to comprehensive histories. Their work is also broad in scope and often deals with the nature of jazz as well as the criticism of specific performers or events. In the last decade, particularly since the 1950s, jazz criticism, like the music it mirrors, has gained a new respectability. As jazz continues to develop as an art form, the jazz critic becomes a more active ingredient in the evolution of emerging jazz styles.

Suggested Class Projects

1. Find and compare the criticisms of two critics on the same or similar performance.
2. Look for a change of mind by a single critic.
3. Select a single controversy in jazz and describe it showing both points of view; for example, New Orleans revival, bop versus swing, free versus straight ahead jazz.

Listening Guide

**From Smithsonian Collection
(side 1, band 9)**

Jelly Roll Morton

"Dead Man Blues"

:00 Introduction—a funeral march—trombone lead
:14 Ensemble—listen for the standard blues chord sequence over the established dixieland instrumental format
:35 Clarinet solo
:57 Trumpet solo
1:20 2nd chorus of trumpet solo
1:41 Clarinet trio, accents by the rest of the band on the fourth beat of every other measure
2:02 Clarinet trio with trombone playing a solo legato line
2:23 Ensemble
2:45 Tag played by the clarinet trio
2:49 End

From New World Collection (#216, side 1, band 5)

Charles Mingus

"Eclipse"

:00 Cello solo. Loose arhythmic support and atonal horn statements
:28 Vocal enters. More metric feel. Cello plays a counter melody to the vocal. More traditional chordal support but still extended harmonies
1:30 Instrumental interlude. Faster tempo with loose sounding counterpoint

1:45 Bass and cello play counterpoint lines which build up as other instruments enter. Atonal feeling which results from the counterpoint
2:26 Vocal enters with cello obligato. More traditional harmonic support
2:51 End.

**From Smithsonian Collection
(side 2, band 8)**

Louis Armstrong

"Hotter Than That"

:00 Introduction by the ensemble
:09 Trumpet solo (Louis Armstrong)
:25 Trumpet break
:27 Trumpet solo
:41 Clarinet break into solo
:43 Clarinet solo
:59 Clarinet break
1:01 Clarinet solo
1:17 Scat singing backed by guitar only
1:31 Vocal break
1:33 Scat singing—note rhythmic complexity
1:49 Guitar and voice alternate short breaks
2:07 Piano interlude
2:12 Trombone solo
2:27 Trumpet break
2:29 Ensemble (standard established dixieland format)
2:35 Trumpet break
2:40 Ensemble
2:42 Guitar break
2:44 Trumpet break
2:46 Guitar break
2:50 End

20

Six Out of Many

If we make a list of truly great jazz men, it should begin Louis Armstrong and Duke Ellington. Armstrong—the intuitive improviser—and Ellington—the creator who held improvisation and written part, soloist and orchestra, in delicate balance in his work, a balance in which each contributed to a total development, a whole greater than the sum of its parts.[1]

Louis Armstrong (1900–1971)

If the one most influential musician in the entire span of jazz had to be chosen, the choice would be Louis Armstrong. The other five artists discussed in this chapter made permanent contributions to be sure, but if jazz is considered from the very beginnings, the selection would be Armstrong.

Daniel Louis Armstrong was born on July 4, 1900, as close as any researcher has been able to discover. He was born in a poor neighborhood in New Orleans. Armstrong's parents were separated when he was very young. His father worked in a factory and his mother was a cleaning woman. Armstrong was placed in the Colored Waifs Home for boys at the age of thirteen years because he playfully fired a revolver in the air while celebrating New Year's Eve, and he remained there for 1½ years. At the Waifs Home, Peter Davis taught him to play the bugle and then the cornet. He joined the band and the chorus and played for social affairs outside the home.

After leaving the home, he first played with an orchestra of youngsters under Joe Lindsay. The king of New Orleans trumpet players around 1917 was Joe Oliver. Oliver took an interest in Armstrong and made him his protégé. When Oliver left for Chicago in 1918, he placed Armstrong in his chair with a band directed by trombonist Kid Ory. Armstrong stayed with Ory for eighteen months and then joined Fate Marable's orchestra on a Mississippi steamboat in 1920. He was briefly married when he was eighteen years old. In 1922, Oliver sent for Armstrong to join him in Chicago at the Lincoln Gardens. Armstrong married Lil' Hardin (the second of four wives) in 1924. She was the pianist with Oliver, but she encouraged Armstrong to organize his own band. However, Armstrong always remained grateful to Oliver and considered him his idol.

Another of Armstrong's early idols was B. A. Rolfe, a white virtuoso trumpeter who later conducted a Paul Whiteman-type radio orchestra, and who was never associated with the mainstream of jazz. Armstrong heard in Rolfe a good tone and sensible control of melodic thoughts. In Armstrong's opinion, both of these elements are missing in the performance of most contemporary jazz players.

One of Armstrong's greatest thrills was at his first recording session when the engineer placed him twenty

1. Martin T. Williams, *Jazz Masters in Transition* (London: Macmillan & Co., 1970), p. 39. Copyright © by Martin Williams.

Louis Armstrong. *Courtesy of Ray Avery.*

feet behind the other musicians (including King Oliver) because Armstrong's tone was so powerful. Armstrong left the Oliver band in 1924, and the band declined. (Oliver did make some good recordings in 1926 and 1927.)

Armstrong joined Fletcher Henderson at the Roseland Ballroom in New York City in 1924. At this time he recorded frequently with Clarence Williams's Blue Five accompanying singers. With Henderson, he accompanied Bessie Smith and Ma Rainey. He was a remarkable influence in the Fletcher Henderson band. Because of his spirit and inspiration, he was a true catalyst.

In 1925 he returned to Chicago and was billed as the World's Greatest Trumpet Player. Also in 1925, he started to record under his own name. The next four years are notable for the Hot Five and Hot Seven records. With these records (classics in this music), jazz was turning from ensemble-oriented music to solo-oriented music.

By 1926, Armstrong was considered the greatest trumpet player that had ever lived. His tone, stamina, range, creativeness, and technique were envied by all jazz performers. At that early age, he became the ideal, the model of how to play jazz improvisation.

In 1929 he headed for New York City again—this time with his own band. Here he continued to record and play nightly on radio as well, which helped to spread his fame. In 1930 he was in Hollywood, and in 1931 he returned to Chicago. Then he went to England and Europe, where he was, of course, a tremendous success. Armstrong was the first jazz player to achieve international fame.

Armstrong's career remained very solid throughout the Swing Era and even included several motion pictures. He had a large swing band that was usually led by someone else—Louie Russell, for example. The band was usually only a showcase for the talents of Armstrong himself. His big band phase was not as productive nor nearly as creative as the earlier and later small band phases. He seemed to be most comfortable with the small band format.

His career hit a new high in 1947. He returned to using a combo, which included at one time or another Jack Teagarden, Earl Hines, Cozy Cole, Barney Bigard, Sid Catlett, Arvell Shaw, Dick Cary, Billy Kyle, Joe Darrensbourg, Tyree Glenn, and Trummie Young. With his All Stars, Armstrong toured the world in the 1950s and 1960s and became known as the Ambassador of Good Will. As late as 1964, he had his biggest record success, "Hello Dolly." Fortunately he lived to be both wealthy and famous. He died July 6, 1971.

Armstrong was the first great jazz soloist. Here is Martin Williams's assessment of Armstrong (with which most other writers agree):

Armstrong's music has affected all our music, top to bottom, concert hall to barroom. No concert composers here or abroad write for brass instruments the way they used to, simply because Armstrong has shown that brass instruments, and the trumpet in particular, are capable of things that no one thought them capable of before he came along. Our symphonists play trumpet with a slight, usually unconscious vibrato that is inappropriate to Beethoven or Schubert because Armstrong has had one.

"Louis changed our whole idea of the band," said Henderson's chief arranger at the time, Don Redman. So did he change everyone's idea of every band, and every soloist's idea of himself. From that, the era and the style took its name: swing. From the Henderson band itself came the Benny Goodman style, and, directly or indirectly, most of the popular big bands of the Swing Era. American music was not the same after it became swing, and what made it different was the influence of Armstrong.[2]

In the 1920s, playing high C on the trumpet was extraordinary. Armstrong, however, often amazed his audiences by playing 100 high Cs (with the band shouting out the count on each one). Then Armstrong would soar upward to a high F. In the twenties and thirties that alone was an incredible feat, but Armstrong would follow this display with an outstanding version of a blues or some tune of the day. The moment was one to be remembered.

Armstrong was also considered one of the best jazz singers. He was very concerned with pleasing his audiences, and he became a great showman and even a comedian. Too often, praise for Armstrong is divided between Armstrong the artist and Armstrong the entertainer, as if artists do not entertain. It is almost inconceivable that the man who was probably America's greatest natural musician, the man who was so personally responsible for a way of playing and listening to music, should be remembered as an affable clown. Is it possible that without Armstrong there would have been no jazz? There may have been jazz, but it truly would have developed in an entirely different way than it did. Armstrong always felt that even if music was one's whole life, it was meaningless if it could not be presented to and appreciated by the public.

It must be gratifying to their fans to know that during their lifetime both Armstrong and Ellington received the public acclaim they deserved. Armstrong was undoubtedly one of the best-known and most highly respected musical personalities in the world. He was probably the first to be recognized as an artist—about 1925—in a music that was at that time considered merely entertainment.

Today's researchers benefit greatly from the fact that Armstrong's recordings are a real documentation of his career and his permanent worth. The most mentioned solos are "West End Blues," "Savoy Blues," "Potato Head Blues," "Hotter Than That," "Weather Bird," "Muggles," "Beau Koo Jack," "I'm Not Rough," "Cornet Chop Suey," "Struttin' with Some Barbeque," "Heebie Jeebies," and "Mahogany Hall Stomp."

In Armstrong were combined well-developed technique, rhythmic feel, intuition, good tone, and high register, as well as personal warmth and an ability to communicate. Each solo, no matter how deep into improvisation, sounds cohesive and well planned but still spontaneous. In spite of being a great improviser, Armstrong's chief talent was his ability to inject rhythmic feeling into a melodic line, whether that melodic line was an improvised line or a written line. The tunes that he recorded were often quite banal until he transformed them into a worthwhile listening experience.

He was a genius at improvisation, and his improvisations showed more than anything else that simplicity leads directly to communication. As great as his trumpet playing was, Armstrong's chief asset was his ability to communicate.

2. Martin T. Williams, "For Louis Armstrong at 70," *Down Beat* 37, no. 13 (July 1970): 22.

Although he often seemed gregarious and extroverted, Armstrong could play a blues that was lovely and sad at the same time. Almost every player who improvises plays phrases that can be traced back to Armstrong and his influence. Somehow, he almost single-handedly set the stage for the jazz soloist, maybe the stage for jazz itself. Most musicians agree that Armstrong was the leader that all other jazz players followed. ". . . Daniel Louis Armstrong, the man from whom has flowed so much good music and so much good-will that the world will never fully realize just how deeply it is in his debt."[3] Armstrong's approach to jazz and to life has never been out of style. Somehow Armstrong made everybody happy!

Duke Ellington (1899–1974)

Just as Armstrong crystallized and popularized the solo aspect of jazz, Duke Ellington, more than any other single musician, proved that orchestrating jazz was an art of the highest level. However, it should be pointed out that Ellington's music was always a combination of solo and ensemble playing. He, like Basie, drew the thoughts of his soloists together into the orchestral whole, accomplishing the feat from the piano. On the other hand, the musicians playing for Ellington did not lose their identity. The Ellington orchestra was always made up of the *individual* talents of his players. It cannot be emphasized enough that listeners are always aware of the personalities of the players (Johnny Hodges, Lawrence Brown, Rex Stewart, Harry Carney, and so on). Yet the band always sounded like Ellington regardless of changes in personnel over the years. This is one of the most important aspects of the band: allowing individuals to retain their own identity and to expand and explore their own directions. Ellington's band always sounded like a well-knit unit expressing the feelings and personality of Ellington.

Edward Kennedy ("Duke") Ellington was born in Washington D.C., on April 29, 1899. He did not come from a poor family, as did Armstrong, and he had educational advantages that many musicians his age lacked. He received his nickname from a high school friend. He was a better than average young painter and won a scholarship to study at the Pratt Institute in Brooklyn, New York. His art career was superseded, of course, by music.

Ellington listened to and was influenced by ragtime piano players in the Washington area. It is possible to hear ragtime and stride in Ellington's extended piano solos, especially at the faster tempos. The influences of Fats Waller, Willie ("The Lion") Smith, and James P. Johnson are evident. Ellington played piano,

but most jazz writers agree that the orchestra was his real instrument. By the age of seventeen he had a five-piece combo called The Washingtonians.

In 1919, Ellington's son Mercer was born. He became a trumpet player, composer, and arranger—a talented musician in his own right. Mercer now leads the Ellington band.

Ellington, with his drummer Sonny Greer and saxophonist Toby Hardwicke, made an abortive attempt to move to New York City in 1922 to join the orchestra of Wilbur Sweatman. Financial problems caused Ellington to return to Washington until Fats Waller encouraged him to try to move again in 1923. This time Ellington and his friends went to work in New York's Harlem where Ellington began his exceptional career as a leader, pianist, and composer-arranger.

Around 1926, the Ellington personnel began to solidify, and, as a consequence, his style, his sound, was established. Personnel changes were rare from then on. Complete sections of the orchestra remained constant for an entire decade. It is no wonder that they worked so very well together. Baritone saxophone player Harry Carney joined the band in 1926 when he was seventeen and remained in the orchestra until he died in 1974. Johnny Hodges joined the band in 1928, and, except for a period from 1951 to 1955, stayed with the band until his death in 1971.

A move that really established the orchestra was the booking at the Cotton Club in Harlem from 1927 to 1932. Ellington's influence from that point on has always been quite definite. His musical pictures were considerably ahead of their time, and the band could swing. Ellington's band at this time featured what were called "Jungle Sounds," with much "growling" on the instruments. As a consequence, the very elaborate floor shows of the Cotton Club were designed around the music that the band played. Once again, the sounds of the individuals were woven into the tonal colors of the entire group, an attribute that was evident throughout Ellington's career.

Ellington had four rather different styles that pervaded his repertoire. One was the previously mentioned "jungle style" built around the raucous playing of Bubber Miley, and then of Cootie Williams on trumpet and Tricky Sam Nanton on trombone. Ellington also had a "mood style" that is identified with the beautiful ballads played by saxophonist Johnny Hodges. Some of the selections like "Solitude" are well known to the public, but other works like "Prelude to a Kiss" and "Lotus Blossom" are known and loved

3. Leonard Feather, "The Real Louis Armstrong," *Down Beat* 29, no. 5 (March 1962): 23.

Duke Ellington. *Courtesy of Ray Avery.*

mostly by musicians. Another Ellington style could be called his "concerto style," in which he featured Cootie Williams on trumpet or Jimmy Hamilton or Barney Bigard on clarinet. The other style was a rather "standard style" in which he approached his arrangements in much the same manner as other large bands. However, he always sounded exactly like Ellington, something no one else could accomplish.

In 1933 the Depression prompted Ellington to make what turned out to be a most successful trip to Europe. He returned home a recognized international attraction. When Ellington first went to England, he was surprised to find out how well known he and other American jazz players were. He realized the importance of jazz as an American export, but also was aware

that popularity at home somewhat determined his effectiveness abroad. There is no need to expound on his success during the Swing Era. His band was by far the most colorful of the large bands during a time when large jazz bands were attracting a multitude of followers. Ellington may not have been quite as popular with the public as he could have been because he did not receive the radio coverage that some bands enjoyed and did not concern himself as much with the popular tunes of the day as other bands did.

In 1943, Ellington gave the first of a series of annual concerts in Carnegie Hall in New York City, introducing the longer forms into jazz that became a recognized part of his repertoire (an example is "Black, Brown, and Beige," fifty minutes in length). He seemed to expand his thinking without altering his music. Ellington's recording of "Reminiscing in Tempo" in 1935 foreshadowed later directions. He used the concerto form in jazz to write "Barney's Concerto" (for clarinetist Barney Bigard) and "Cootie's Concerto" (for trumpeter Cootie Williams).

Ellington toured constantly, which kept his image alive in the entire world. He recorded historically important works written by him and Billy Strayhorn. The collaboration of Ellington and Strayhorn led to some of the most charming music possible in any category of the art. Sometimes while composing a piece of music, it would occur to either of these musicians that a specific member of the orchestra was in need of a work on which he would be featured, and this fact would influence the composition. Sometimes it worked just the opposite: the work being composed would need a specific player in order to be interpreted to the greatest advantage.

Ellington's innovations include the following: the wonderful ensemble sound (developed using individuals in the band), the larger forms in jazz (which often ignored the three-minute limit on recordings that dictated the repertoire of most bands), his more than skillful orchestration, the use of voices as instruments (as far back as 1927 with singer Adelaide Hall on "Creole Love Song"), and many, many innovative jazz tunes starting with "Mood Indigo" (first recorded as "Dreamy Blues" in 1930), "Sophisticated Lady" (1933), and "Solitude" (1934). Ellington often changed the titles of his tunes: for example, "Rumpus in Richmond" was changed to "Harlem Air Shaft." This puts the liner notes on some albums in a very suspicious light since some record company employee tried to explain the final title as if it were Ellington's idea of daily life in New York's Harlem.

Those listeners who challenge all changes disturbed Ellington—to a point. His later music was sometimes compared unfavorably with that which he had played in the past. Ellington's answer to the "time test" (comparing jazz to other music) was that he was not interested in writing or playing music for posterity; he wanted his music to sound good at the very moment that it was performed.

The earliest Ellington recording available is an album called *The Birth of Big Band Jazz*. These sides were recorded in 1923 (some writers place the date at 1925). The album called *Early Ellington* comprises recordings made between 1927 and 1931. Most writers feel that Ellington's greatest recordings were made between 1940 and 1942, with such records as "Jack the

Bear," "Warm Valley," "Cotton Tail," "Chelsea Bridge," "Take the A Train," and "C Jam Blues," and so on. Ellington recorded more than 150 albums even though well over half can no longer be purchased. However, the Smithsonian Institution has helped to resolve this situation with sets that fill many of the would-be gaps in collections of Ellington music.[4]

True, Ellington did perform his "standards"—he was almost required to. But it cannot be said that his repertoire did not have good variety. He performed in so many different situations (dance halls, large clubs, theaters, festivals, concert halls) that he had to be diversified.

It is worth noting that Ellington, while feeling that his music was always primarily black music, never felt ethnic ties to the point of using only black musicians in his band—as witnessed by the white drummer Louie Bellson.

It appears as if the talents and influences of Duke Ellington will always be with us. Today there are Ellington Societies, The Duke Ellington Cancer Fund, even Duke Ellington Boulevard in upper Manhattan and a play on Broadway entitled "Sophisticated Ladies" featuring Mercer Ellington conducting the Duke Ellington Orchestra performing his father's music. Ellington's style of arranging and composing is taught at the Berklee College of Music in Boston. In Washington, D.C., students attend Duke Ellington High School of the Arts. At UCLA, guitarist Kenny Burrell teaches a course called "Ellingtonia."[5]

Ellington's band, his music, and his recordings are proof of his belief that though jazz borrowed from any and every source available, it still remained personal. His ensemble was an integrated whole; yet, no one's orchestra has ever been based so much on the talents of its individuals. Some jazz writers actually credit Ellington's success to his brilliant sidemen. The sidemen themselves, however, always point to Ellington's composing, arranging, piano playing, and leadership in general. In 1962, Leonard Feather wrote of Ellington: "We see him today as the most challenging, most provocative, most brilliant, and most irreplaceable paragon in the sixty-year history of jazz."[6] That statement is still true.

4. *Ellington '38*. Smithsonian Records, R003. *Ellington '39*. Smithsonian Records, R010.

5. Kenny Burrell, *Ellington Is Forever, Vols. 1 and 2*. Fantasy Records, 79005 and 79008.

6. Leonard Feather, "The Duke's Progress," *Down Beat* 29, no. 12 (June 1962): 19.

Benny Goodman. *Courtesy of Popsie and Phoebe Jacobs.*

Benny Goodman (1909–1986)

Rave reviews for an artist (who was probably the universal symbol of jazz thirty-five years earlier) dominated the media in 1975. It is true that when Benny Goodman played a concert, many of his listeners experienced great feelings of nostalgia, but, on the other hand, some who thoroughly enjoyed his mastery of the clarinet, his vibrant rhythm feel, and his effervescent improvisations were too young to feel any nostalgia for his music. He was truly a master of his art.

Benny Goodman was born May 30, 1909, in Chicago, the eighth of eleven children of an immigrant tailor. Just as jazz is a product of America, Benny Goodman's rise from poverty to global fame is a typical American story.

His early musical training was in a synagogue orchestra and at Hull House in Chicago. He next studied privately with Franz Schoepp of the Chicago Symphony Orchestra. By the time Goodman was sixteen, word of his excellent musicianship had spread even to California, and Ben Pollack asked him to join his band. He had built a considerable reputation by the time he left the Pollack band in 1929 at the age of twenty. For the next five years he played on radio and for recording companies in New York City.

In 1934 Goodman organized his first band for a theater restaurant, the Music Hall, owned by Billy Rose. At the same time, Goodman played on a series of Saturday night, three-hour radio shows. The two jobs coincided with his association with Fletcher Henderson who created most of the musical arrangements that were such an integral part of Goodman's success.

In the winter of 1934–35 Goodman began a tour across the United States that seemed to consist of one failure after another. No one appeared to know or care about his band. The farther the band traveled from New York City, the more worried became Goodman, the band, his bookers, and the manager of the Palomar Ballroom in Los Angeles—their destination. In fact, it has often been rumored that had the manager been able to locate Goodman during that tour he would have canceled the booking. Fortunately, the booking was not canceled. Goodman opened at the Palomar Ballroom in May of 1935 and was an immediate success. Whether the swing type of jazz started earlier than this is beside the point. Goodman's engagement at the Palomar is designated by most jazz writers as the beginning of the Swing Era.

Goodman's band played a hard-driving type of swing in comparison to other bands at that time. He often rehearsed the band without the rhythm section—reasoning that if an arrangement could swing well and have momentum without the rhythm section, the music would offer much more when the rhythm section was added. The band also played a soft, more subtle jazz—a chamber music sort of jazz—by using trios, quartets, quintets, and so forth.

The Goodman trio consisted of Teddy Wilson on piano, Gene Krupa on drums, and Goodman on clarinet. The group was enlarged to a quartet in 1936 with the addition of the exuberant Lionel Hampton on vibraphones, and in 1939 it became a sextet when Charlie Christian on guitar and a bass player were added. These smaller groups also included at various times Red Norvo, Cootie Williams, Roy Eldridge, and George Auld. The small units played during the intermissions of performances by the large band and also recorded separately. Some fans consider these recordings to be as important as those of the large band.

In 1938, the Benny Goodman band became the first swing band to play a concert in Carnegie Hall. Record sales of his Carnegie Hall concerts alone grossed more than a million dollars and continue to sell today.

Mention should be made of Goodman's classical solo work. He commissioned and recorded a solo clarinet composition by Béla Bartók, commissioned clarinet concertos by Aaron Copland and Paul Hindemith, and performed works by Mozart, Debussy, Brahms, and other composers with such distinguished orchestras as the Boston Symphony, the Rochester Symphony, the NBC Symphony, the Cleveland Symphony, the Budapest String Quartet, and the American Art Quartet. Goodman was one of the few musicians who moved easily between classical music and jazz—with distinction in each field.

In 1955 Universal-International Studios made a motion picture based on his life, and Goodman himself recorded the music and acted as musical director.

Goodman toured in many parts of the world on behalf of the State Department. In 1956 he played to sellout audiences in Hong Kong, Singapore, Tokyo, and Bangkok. In 1958 and 1959 his overseas tours took him to Belgium, Germany, Sweden, Denmark, France, Switzerland, Austria, England, Australia, Central America, South America, and Alaska, and his reception was as great as ever each time. The Goodman band was chosen to be the first band to make a State Department tour of Russia. His triumph there was proof of his artistry, the durability of the swing style, and the worldwide popularity of this American music. Benny Goodman enjoyed a truly international popularity. The mere announcement that he was to perform in a country caused great excitement among the jazz enthusiasts there, a fact probably more true about Goodman than about any other living musician.

Since the middle 1960s, Goodman appeared regularly at jazz festivals and even at some of the more plush night spots. At the end of the 1960s, he toured the United States with both jazz and classical groups and recorded in the United States and England.

Through the 1970s, Goodman continued to tour Europe, the United States, and Canada. Sometimes he appeared with a full band, sometimes with a sextet, and sometimes with members of his original quartet. The reception was the same: he was the King of Swing, a jazz immortal, and an international celebrity to jazz fans of all ages.

Goodman was the first band leader to force the issue of integration. Black musicians and white musicians jammed together in after-hours clubs and recorded together, but neither the white public nor the black public would go to see a "mixed" band. In 1936 when Goodman hired Teddy Wilson and Lionel Hampton, he had to pretend that they were not regular members of his band but only an act. Finally, he simply acknowledged that these musicians were part of his band and gave notice that the public would have to see and hear his music on his terms. He stated very simply in a nonpolitical way that he was not selling prejudice or integration but music.

Goodman continued to play jazz in a most exemplary manner and led the world on clarinet. He performed a concert at Carnegie Hall in 1974, thirty-six years and eight months after his first concert there. The authors saw and heard Goodman at a jazz festival in 1975 where he received a standing ovation as he walked on stage. As he played he proved conclusively that he truly deserved the applause.

Besides being the King of Swing, and besides almost single-handedly cutting through racial barriers in music, Goodman was instrumental in making it possible for jazz musicians to earn a decent wage. He brought jazz out of back rooms into the best night spots, into the greatest theaters where young people screamed and danced in the aisles. Still, for a man whose name is synonymous with the Big Band Era, Goodman was extremely low-key, never flamboyant. His playing was a combination of great wit, precise musicianship, beautiful subtleties, and never-ending swing.

Down Beat magazine nominated Benny Goodman to its All Time Jazz Hall of Fame, and the National Academy of Recording Arts and Sciences placed his recording of "Sing Sing Sing" in its Hall of Fame. He collaborated on four books: *The Kingdom of Swing,*

Charlie Parker. *Courtesy of Orrin Keepnews.*

BG—Off the Record, BG—On the Record, and *Benny: King of Swing.*[7] Goodman inspired musicians when he was only sixteen years of age and in the mid 1980s, he still inspired them. He was unique. Goodman did not follow the changing fads in jazz. He attributed his continued overwhelming success to the fact that he simply played "good" music. Benny Goodman died in June, 1986.

Charlie Parker (1921–1955)

Charlie Parker, called "Yardbird"—or more often simply "Bird"—was born August 29, 1921, in Kansas City, Kansas. He moved to Kansas City, Missouri, at the age of seven. As a youngster, he listened a great deal to saxophonists Lester Young and Buster Smith. An important predecessor of Parker, Smith was from the Kansas City School. After Benny Moten's death, Smith was at first coleader with Basie of Moten's group.

7. Benny Goodman and Irving Kolodin, *The Kingdom of Swing* (New York: Frederick Ungar Publishing Co., 1939); Benny Goodman and D. R. Connor, *BG—Off the Record* (Fairless Hills, Pa.: Gaildonna Publishers, 1969); Benny Goodman, D. R. Connor, and W. W. Hicks, *BG—On the Record* (New Rochelle, N.Y.: Arlington House, 1969); Stanley Baron, *Benny: King of Swing* (New York: William Morrow & Co., Inc., 1979).

As far back as 1932, Buster Smith recordings fore-shadow Charlie Parker. There is no doubt about the strong influence that altoist Smith and tenor saxophonist Young had on young Charlie Parker. But what is surprising is that Parker himself credited five white saxophonists with being the greatest early influences on his playing: nonjazz players Rudy Wiedoeft and Rudy Vallee, and jazzmen Frank Teschemacher, Jimmy Dorsey, and Bud Freeman. He definitely surpassed all of these players.

In 1936, Parker used to stand around in the alley behind the Reno Club in Kansas City and listen to the Basie band. At fifteen years of age he was learning in the same way that most jazz players learned their trade: he listened and attempted to imitate. Parker was always curious about advanced harmony, and he worked for and studied with a graduate of the Boston Conservatory, Tommy Douglas, who was ahead of his time in this direction in 1935. Parker's studies with pianists and guitarists furthered this knowledge. He became intensely interested in the use of the higher harmonies of chords as structures on which to improvise new melodies. This approach became one of the mainstays of the bop movement, and many new tunes were created from old chord progressions.

When saxophonist Budd Johnson heard eighteen-year-old Parker in Chicago, he noted that Parker already had some of the element of bop—such as double time—in his repertoire.

Parker first came to New York in 1939 where he searched out jam sessions and every other opportunity to listen and learn, supporting himself by washing dishes and other menial jobs. The first combo job that Parker played in New York City was at Clark Monroe's Uptown House on 134th Street. He left town afterward with the Jay McShann band. The first recorded solos of Charlie Parker are on transcriptions made by the Jay McShann band in 1940 at a Wichita, Kansas, radio station. The McShann band, besides being blues-based, was also riff-oriented like Basie's. It was McShann who brought Parker back to New York in 1942, this time as a mature musician. Today it is hard to locate recordings of Parker with McShann. Folkways pressed "Hootie Blues," recorded in Dallas in 1941, and Decca pressed "Sepian Bounce," recorded in New York in 1942.[8] (FJ, Jay McShann, "Hootie Blues," Vol. 10)

By 1942, mainly because of jam sessions at Minton's Playhouse, Charlie Parker and Dizzy Gillespie had become the most talked about musicians in the new style of jazz called bop.

In 1942, saxophonist Budd Johnson was urging Earl Hines to hire Charlie Parker from the blues-oriented band of Jay McShann. In December 1942,

Johnson himself left Hines. Billy Eckstine then talked Hines into hiring Parker and buying a tenor sax for him even though Parker much preferred to play alto sax. The Hines band collapsed, but Eckstine held most of the avant garde players together by hiring them for his own band. In 1944, as this band started a tour toward St. Louis, a trumpeter became ill and was replaced temporarily by a young teenager named Miles Davis. Thus the association between Davis and Parker began.

The key musicians each produced certain ideas independently and when they came together in New York they discovered their affinities and stimulated each other to further effort. Over a period of several years this produced a synthesis of new elements based on old that became known as modern jazz, or bop.[9]

Parker's first job as leader was at the Spotlight Club on New York's Fifty-second Street in 1944 after he had left Eckstine. His most mature jazz statements are generally conceded to be those recorded in 1945 under his own name as leader: "Koko," "Now's the Time," "Billie's Bounce," "Meandering," "Warming Up a Riff," and "Thriving from a Riff." On these records he shows a rich, expressive tone and unprecedented rhythmic freedom in his phrasing.

Parker's success was demonstrated by the fact that after World War II he was sometimes paid $1,200 a week by the same people who had hired him earlier for $2 a night.

Parker spent seven months in Camarillo State Hospital in California in 1946. By 1949, due to a combination of ulcers, drugs, and alcohol, his playing began to decline. He was not considered reliable by booking offices, so employment began to be a problem. Some musicians never see the dope and alcohol problems affecting them, but Parker was very much aware of the fact that his career had been ruined by these mistakes. He constantly advised against such indulgence. Sonny Rollins tells of conversations along this line with Parker:

Bird befriended quite a few guys. Sonny Stitt before me. With us and a few other cats, especially saxophone players, it was like a father thing. When we were hung up personally, we went just to talk to him, just to see him. The purpose of his whole existence was

8. Jay McShann, "Hootie Blues," *Folkways Jazz*, vol. 10; Jay McShann, "Sepian Bounce," *Encyclopedia of Jazz*, vol. 3, Decca Records, DL 8400 and *Encyclopedia of Jazz on Records*, vol. 3.

9. Max Harrison, *Charlie Parker* (New York: A. S. Barnes & Co., 1961), p. 17.

music and he showed me that music was the para-mount thing and anything that interfered with it I should stay away from. Later on I was able to take advantage of his advice, but he died before I had a chance to see him and tell him I had.[10]

In 1950, Parker recorded with strings (as did Gillespie). It was the fulfillment of a dream for Parker, but his fans screamed that he had "gone commercial."

When Parker's young daughter Pree died of pneumonia, he seemed to decline for the last time both musically and physically. He died March 12, 1955, less than thirty-five years old.

One of the trying aspects of Parker's career is that he knew that even among contemporary musicians only a few understood his music. Parker's abilities and contributions have, of course, been finally recognized. In fact, it would be extremely difficult to find a musician who is more recognized and so little understood. In 1973, a group called Supersax was featured on an album called *Supersax Plays Bird*.[11] For this album, saxophonist Med Flory and bassist Buddy Clark put together a library of Parker's recorded solos. But Flory and Clark harmonized all of these wonderful improvisations and played them using five saxophones—an almost overwhelming sound. The album won a Grammy Award from the National Academy of Recording Arts and Sciences (NARAS) for the best jazz record performed by a group (as opposed to a large band). Supersax has extended these efforts further since their first recording. In 1974, Onyx Records released an album of the very first works recorded by Parker going back to his work with Jay McShann.[12] This album, called *Original Recordings*, also won a NARAS award for the best solo jazz album. Such public recognition came nearly twenty years after Parker's death.

Most young saxophonists feel that Parker's style and melodic and rhythmic thoughts are the "correct" ways to play. Furthermore, in 1969 a Charlie Parker Center for the Performing Arts was established by a group of teachers, musicians, and civic leaders to provide free music instruction for young players.

In February, 1942, one *Down Beat* reporter stated that Parker had a tendency to play too many notes. In July of that same year, another reporter from the same magazine noted that Parker used a minimum of notes. To say that there was controversy and a lack of understanding of Parker's work even among his peers would be a gross understatement. Some who write and talk about jazz feel that Parker was the most important catalyst in the advancement of jazz. Surely there can be no doubt that he brought to culmination the many innovations of the 1940s and 1950s, more changes than had previously occurred in the history of jazz.

Parker was one of the rare musicians who could play slow blues very well but was also comfortable at extremely fast tempos. A great percentage of what Parker played was based on the blues—"Now's the Time," "Cool Blues," and others.

One of Parker's most impressive assets was his use of rhythmic nuances. "Relaxin' at Camarillo"[13] (NW, 271, side 1, band 6) shows how beautifully these can be applied to the standard blues form. Of course, Parker had an impeccable ear and virtuosity on the alto saxophone that could be exploited unconsciously instead of contrived. When a musician realizes what Parker was able to invent within the six-note phrase in "Embraceable You," the musician hears developments leading to Sonny Rollins and others. Parker used the phrase repeatedly, but he also changed each time, demonstrating a creativeness worthy of Mozart, Beethoven, and others who composed great music from motifs.[14] (NW, 271, side 1, band 7) Most musicians agree that as advanced as Parker's style was, he never seemed to lose sight of the early jazz roots. Some casual observers seem surprised that Parker could appreciate all kinds of music that were performed well, classical music as well as early jazz.

Parker thought that there must be something in jazz improvisation that had not been done before because he thought that he could hear things that he could not play. By working over and over his favorite tune "Cherokee," he finally found that he could play what he had been hearing by developing melodic lines from the higher harmonies of the chords (as described in chapter 10). Parker freed the solo aspect of jazz not only melodically and harmonically but also rhythmically. Those who follow him can benefit from the freedom, not necessarily from copying his actual phrases.

It is true that drummers Kenny Clarke and Max Roach developed new rhythmic approaches; Thelonious Monk, new harmonic approaches; Dizzy Gillespie, new solo directions; and so on. But it did seem to be Charlie Parker who brought all of these elements to maturity in the style known as bop. Parker's playing was the realization of the potential of what was available; Parker's influence, like Armstrong's earlier, extended to all instruments.

10. Harrison, *Charlie Parker*, pp. 64–65.

11. *Supersax Plays Bird*, Capitol Records, ST 11177.

12. Charlie Parker, *Original Recordings*, Onyx Records, 221.

13. "Relaxin' at Camarillo," *Bebop*, New World Records, 271.

14. "Embraceable You," *Bebop*, New World Records, 271.

Parker's achievements are unique and for a continually sick man almost incredible. It is hard to imagine what he would have accomplished given a long and healthy life. In many ways his admirers got more out of his life than Parker did himself but, in the end, he is not a man to be pitied. On all but his darkest days he experienced the joy of creation that is given few men to know and he enriched the lives of all those who could respond to his work.[15]

"To Bird With Love" is by Societo Wizlov (La Cure, 86310, Antigny, France). This epic on Parker is 424 pages, 14½ inches high and 10 inches wide, weighs 8 pounds and costs $147. Never has there been such a dedication to a jazz musician.

John Coltrane (1926–1967)

Saxophonist John Coltrane combined great emotion with excellent musicianship and discipline with freedom. Like Parker, he did not have an extensive career compared to Armstrong and Ellington. His career lasted about twelve years, from 1955 to 1967.

John Coltrane was born in Hamlet, North Carolina, September 23, 1926. He studied saxophone in Philadelphia and began playing professionally in that city. Coltrane started to attain recognition while playing with Miles Davis from 1955 to 1960. In 1960 he formed his own quartet. In 1965 Alice McLeod (Coltrane's wife) joined the group. Coltrane's short career ended with his death on July 1, 1967, at the age of forty.

Musicians disagree about other contemporary players such as Ornette Coleman, but there were few disagreements about John Coltrane. Coltrane was a fine saxophone player (tenor and soprano) in every sense. The prime concern of most musicians is the tone that a player produces. There is no way to imagine a musical sound without considering the quality of the tone. Coltrane produced a large, dark, lush sound from his instrument. A brief listen to "Ogunde" verifies this fact.[16] On the album *Giant Steps* (Coltrane's first album under his own name) his beautiful, solid tone is most evident in "Naima."[17] This record shows his confidence at this time in his career and reveals deeper feeling and conviction than when he worked for Davis. His drive is very apparent on "Cousin Mary."

Coltrane's chief legacy was his beautiful tone and his control of the upper register. (He had equal strength in all registers of the instrument—an unusual trait.) Wayne Shorter, Charles Lloyd, Pharoah Sanders, and Eddie Harris all show traces of this legacy. The influence of Coltrane's very passionate approach appears in unlikely places, like in an occasional near scream from

cool saxophonist Stan Getz. Coltrane said that Sidney Bechet was an important influence on his own playing.

As stated in chapter 13, Coltrane advanced jazz improvisation harmonically through long excursions into the higher harmonics of chords on an instrument that is sounded where a trombone, or a man's voice, is pitched (the tenor saxophone).

Coltrane had great coordination between his fingering of the saxophone and his tonguing. This coordination allowed him such fast technique that he played arpeggios so rapidly that they are referred to as Coltrane's "sheets of sound." His sheets of sound can be heard as early in his career as "All Blues" with Miles Davis, and a little in "Cousin Mary" with his own quartet. Coltrane's creativity with his sheets of sound was actually homophonically constructed music that had been carried to a higher level. He thought of these runs as if they were chords on top of chords. His fast arpeggios have great emotional impact, and he was an expert in the use of sequences.

A logical starting place for those uninitiated in Coltrane's music is Miles Davis's recording of *Kind of Blue*.[18] On "All Blues," "So What," and "Freddie Freeloader," the listener can hear Coltrane when he was working for a fairly conservative leader. Therefore he had not expanded his directions very much and is quite easy to understand and appreciate immediately. It is interesting to compare the Coltrane of this album with Cannonball Adderley. On both "So What" and "Freddie Freeloader," Adderley shows a more direct association with Parker and at the same time plays some very funky-type phrases not to be found in Coltrane's playing. In "Freddie Freeloader," Coltrane is blowing aggressively and melodically at the same time.

Coltrane played rhythmically but counter to that which was being played by what would normally be the rhythm section; so the music became arhythmic. This effect freed the rhythm players to play whatever occurred to them according to the melodic thoughts they were hearing. Coltrane could play "on top of the beat" whenever he wanted to, but he liked to play differently from the rhythm players with the idea that this freed them from having to play with him. His counterrhythms can be heard on both "Countdown" and

15. Harrison, *Charlie Parker,* p. 74.

16. John Coltrane, "Ogunde," *Expression,* Impulse Records, A–9120.

17. John Coltrane, *Giant Steps,* Atlantic Records, 1311.

18. John Coltrane (Miles Davis album), *Kind of Blue,* Columbia Records, CL 1355.

John Coltrane. *Courtesy of Ray Avery.*

"Spiral" on *Giant Steps*. He seemed to fuse melody and rhythm in "The Father and The Son and The Holy Ghost."[19]

Eventually, Coltrane turned toward emphasizing the melodic line above all else. Chords were used only as they related to the melody. Instead of melody being improvised out of harmony, melody was improvised from melody—an approach used by classical composers quite early in the history of music but seldom by jazz performers. Coltrane had the advantage of working with Thelonious Monk. From Monk, he was able to establish a mature, consistent relationship between the chords and his melodic thoughts. Monk stimulated Coltrane's interest in wide intervals, while it is very possible that his interest in various types of scales came from his time with the Miles Davis group.

Coltrane broke away from the format of theme, solos, theme. On his recording of "The Father and The Son and The Holy Ghost," there is no real theme before his solo, and the ensemble portion has no theme at all. This is very disturbing to jazz listeners who expect only traditional approaches to jazz. In "Countdown," Coltrane shows his great coordination. The work sounds free; yet when chords are brought in under his solo, he is exactly where he should be harmonically.

An example of Coltrane's innovation is a selection called "India," recorded before the Beatles received credit for "discovering" Ravi Shankar. In this album one hears influences such as Indian scales and rhythms.

Coltrane opened the path for others like Archie Shepp through his conviction that improvisation could continue past all existing melodic considerations, harmonic considerations, and rhythmic flow. Free form seemed to need another leader besides Ornette Coleman. Coltrane became this leader with his long improvisations (sometimes 40 minutes), his sheets of sound, his tone, and his technique. He was looked upon as a spiritual leader. Coltrane and his followers have often been criticized for playing solos that were too long, but their answer was that they needed the time to explore the music in depth.

At first, Coltrane was admired more as a technically complete musician than as a creative artist. He showed speed as he cascaded chords with his powerful moving tone. But his recording *A Love Supreme* seemed to change the attitude toward his playing.[20] It is a very emotional record that does away with some earlier excesses and is more a work of art than an exhibition. Coltrane tried to explain (in his music) the wonderful things that the universe meant to him. Playing jazz was a spiritual experience to Coltrane, and he always felt that he should share his feelings with his listeners. There is no doubt about his strong religious motivation.

Coltrane continually experimented. Even when listeners were well acquainted with Coltrane's recordings, they would still be constantly surprised and

19. John Coltrane, "The Father and The Son and The Holy Ghost," *Meditations,* Impulse Records, A–9110.

20. John Coltrane, *A Love Supreme,* Impulse Records, A–77.

amazed at each live performance. His fans learned to expect only the unexpected.

In 1965 Coltrane won four *Down Beat* polls: Record of the Year ("A Love Supreme"), Jazzman of the Year, Hall of Fame, and Number-One Tenor Saxophonist.

"Coltrane came, and he made music. He built on existing foundations. He and his music lived in inexorable relation to other lives, other ideas, other musics. But how he built! The musical structures are changed forever because of him."[21]

Miles Davis (b. 1926)

Perhaps no figure in the history of jazz has influenced as many different styles over as long a time as has Miles Davis. His prominence in the jazz scene was not paralleled by the stereotypical attributes, poverty, and prodigious talent normally associated with leading jazz players. He was born of a relatively affluent family in 1926 and was even able to attend Juilliard for a short time in 1944. He has never been a highly polished trumpet player in technical terms but he has had an aggressive nature that has continually pushed him to the forefront of jazz developments. He has reigned there despite dramatic musical changes inside and outside the jazz world.

The forthright approach that has characterized Davis much of his career began as early as 1944, when he convinced Billy Eckstine to allow him to "sit in" with Earl Hines during a tour through St. Louis.[22] At that time, Hines' band, later Eckstine's band, represented the front edge of the big band bop style and no doubt captured Davis' attention. In 1945, after his short stay at Juilliard, Davis sought out Charlie Parker, the leading bop player of the day, and actually roomed with him. His association with Parker gave him an unusually early (for his age) start in the top eschelons of the jazz community. He even took over Fats Navarro's prestigious chair in Eckstine's band when he was only twenty. Before Navarro, this chair was defined by Gillespie himself as the showplace for trumpet virtuosity. Although following in the Gillespie tradition, Davis was not the technician necessary for the bravura bop style. Whether this incongruity between style and ability had anything to do with Davis' later more fragmented and slower melodic style has been much debated.

Davis left Eckstine to play with Parker from 1947 to 1949, at which time he began working with members of the Claude Thornhill band. His association with these players led to the famous "Birth of the Cool" recordings. Davis assumed leadership during the work on this album which featured the cool style initiated by Gerry Mulligan, Gil Evans, and John Lewis. Fronting the band catapulted Davis to a newly found prominence among jazz players which endures today.

By 1954, Davis had begun to develop the playing style which characterizes much of his later work. Rather than the high energy, note-filled melodic lines typical of the bop era, Davis borrowed the softer tone of the cool era and slowed down the melodic activity. His phrasing became fragmented leaving open spaces for just the rhythm section. He set himself apart from the rhythm section by playing scale oriented rather than chord oriented long notes. When responses are made to the energy of the rhythm section, they are usually in the form of short motivic fragments.

By 1958 Davis' playing style was freed further by his use of modal scales and slower moving harmonies. Rather than weave a melody through complex bop or funk harmonies, he suspended his melodies, based on early modes, above the harmony. The lack of harmonic movement and the scalar concept of improvisation seemed to disassociate the melody from whatever rhythmic underpinning there might be. His "Milestones" recording demonstrates this modal and almost **arhythmic** melodic approach.[23] Davis' collaboration with Gil Evans on "Summertime" produced a particularly effective demonstration of the fragmented and plaintive style to be Davis' trademark, (S, side 10, band 2). The backup riffs from the rest of the group plug the open spaces in Davis' solo and Gershwin's slow melody could not be more appropriate for Davis' penchant for long tones.

Davis' 1959 recording of "So What" clearly demonstrates his new modal approach toward improvisation.[24] (S, side 11, band 3) There are really only two different harmonies in the entire piece. During the solos, the first harmony lasts sixteen measures (approximately 25 seconds), the second harmony is ½ step higher and lasts eight measures. The solo chorus is completed with a return to the first chord for another eight measures. The fact that the two harmonies are related by only a ½ step is itself a move away from tradition which would more properly dictate a move of four or five scale tones away for the contrasting harmony. The solos above this almost frozen chord progression are usually marked by an introspective and motivic melodic style.

21. Gordon Kopulos, "John Coltrane: Retrospective Perspective," *Down Beat* 38, no. 14 (July 1971): 40.

22. Lincoln Collier, *The Making of Jazz*, Delta, Dell Publishing Co., Inc., p. 427.

23. Miles Davis, *Milestones*, Columbia Records, PC–9428E.

24. Miles Davis, "So What," Smithsonian Collection of Classic Jazz.

Miles Davis. *Courtesy of Carl Baugher.*

Davis had successfully carried music through the transition from bop to cool and again on to a modal jazz that would launch players like John Coltrane (heard on the "So What" recording). He was to face yet another turn in music with the advent of rock. As rock began to dominate the popular music culture, Davis faced the dilemma confronted by most leaders in jazz, that of maintaining leadership as styles change.

Just as Davis was not held to his bop heritage or trapped in the cool idiom, he would not blindly hold to his modal jazz expression and ignore the growing activity in the rock world.

In 1964 Davis made his move by calling on younger names in jazz, Tony Williams, Ron Carter, Herbie Hancock, and Wayne Shorter. He found players that were not as closely tied to the past bop and funky traditions. His "Nefertiti" shows his early efforts at assimilating some of the rock idioms.[25] But it was his 1969 album, *In a Silent Way,* that first truly addressed the rock issue.[26] He took on John McLaughlin, a guitarist known also to the rock world, to grant a greater integrity to his jazz/rock approach. His next album in 1970, *Bitches' Brew,* brought his effort into focus and with the aid of a Grammy, gained him a great deal of popularity. His rhythm section which was characterized by rock patterns and electronic instruments supported his already well defined modal jazz approach.[27] The cuts on this album even show a relationship to the other quickly developing jazz style, free jazz. The title cut alternates between a free, arhythmic opening theme and hard driving rock solo areas. Davis had again discovered a musical forefront and aggressively placed himself in the middle of it. Jazz/rock fusions were already at hand in other bands, Gary Burton, Billy Cobham (Dreams), Larry Coryell and others, but Davis had created the dominant statement for the developing genre.

Performers of Davis' stature do not make major stylistic moves without generating controversy. Those who hold to previous styles once led by Davis might find his flirtations with newly developing styles somewhat disconcerting. In a career as dynamic as Davis' not all musical efforts carry the same weight in his stylistic evolution. Many albums fall between the gaps of the giant steps made by *Birth of the Cool* and *Bitches' Brew.* These other albums might often lack the surprise and power of the giants, but they show a musician who continues to experiment while also maintaining an individual identity. His 1985 album, *You're Under Arrest,* shows a new interest in commercial music and its allied recording studio sound.[28] The musical mix is more commercial and even some of the musical material is drawn from the popular music scene (a song by pop singer Cyndi Lauper). Despite the new format, Davis is still recognizable through his melodic style, plaintive, fragmented and somewhat isolated from its musical underpinning.

Miles Davis is unique in his ability to sense new directions, assimilate their attributes and then popularize the newly fused style. As a personality, his outspoken nature is sometimes as strident as his music is definitive. In many ways, he is a maverick among jazz musicians. His intensely introspective, if not melancholy, playing style is characterized by expressions that can be perceived as technical blunders when contrasted to the lineage of trumpet virtuosos like Armstrong and Gillespie. Yet these same flaws in techniques offer Davis a personalized style that is conducive to his very intimate expression. His half valve notes and broken pitches

support the glimpse he often gives us of the raw emotional world which often emanates from his music.

Davis' legacy, yet to be completed, is one of melodic phrasing which breaks holes in the solo fabric while freeing the soloist from the bondage of harmonic movement. Rather than long, unbroken lines, the detail of short melodic motives takes centerstage. The melodic lines born of these motives then float above the static harmonic support. Where Davis goes from here will depend on the major influences he feels both culturally and musically. He has always been one to assimilate the dominate influences of the time and in turn dominate them. If past experience is indeed the best predictor of future behavior, then we must assume that Miles Davis will again surprise us with his use of things to come.

Additional Reading Resources

Louis Armstrong

Armstrong, Louis. *Swing That Music.*

Jones, Max, and Chilton, John. *Louis: The Louis Armstrong Story.*

Jones, Max. *Salute to Satchmo.*

Panassie, Hughes. *Louis Armstrong.*

Sanders, Ruby W. *Jazz Ambassador Louis Armstrong.*

Duke Ellington

Dance, Stanley. *The World of Duke Ellington.*

Ellington, Duke. *Music Is My Mistress.*

Ellington, Mercer, and Dance, Stanley. *Duke Ellington in Person: An Intimate Memoir.*

Gammond, Peter, ed. *Duke Ellington: His Life and Music.*

George, Don. *Sweet Man: The Real Duke Ellington.*

Gleason, Ralph. *Celebrating The Duke.*

Schuller, Gunther. *Early Jazz: Its Roots and Musical Development.*

Shapiro, Nat, and Hentoff, Nat, eds. *The Jazz Makers.*

Ulanov, Barry. *Duke Ellington.*

25. Miles Davis, *Nefertiti,* Col. PC 9594.

26. Miles Davis, *In a Silent Way,* Col. PC 9875.

27. Miles Davis, *Bitches' Brew,* Columbia, GP 26.

28. Miles Davis, *You're Under Arrest,* Columbia, FCT 40023.

Charlie Parker

Gitler, Ira. *Jazz Masters of the Forties.*

Harrison, Max. *Charlie Parker.*

Reisner, Robert. *The Legend of Charlie Parker.*

Russell, Ross. *Bird Lives. The High Life and Hard Times of Charlie (Yardbird) Parker.*

Note: Complete information including name of publisher and date of publication is provided in the Bibliography.

Additional Record Resources

Louis Armstrong

Autobiography. Decca Records, DX–155.

Best of Louis Armstrong. Audio Fidelity Records, 6132.

Essential Louis Armstrong. Verve Records, V–8569.

Folkways Jazz. Vols. 2, 4, 5, 7.

Hello Dolly. Kapp Records, 3364.

Louis Armstrong. Audio Fidelity Records, 6241.

Louis Armstrong. RCA Victor Records, VPM–6044.

Louis Armstrong and Earl Hines. Columbia Records, CL 853.

Louis Armstrong in Memoriam. Everest Records, 3312.

Louis Armstrong in the Thirties and Forties. RCA Victor Records, LSP 2971.

Louis Armstrong Jazz Classics. Decca Records, 8284.

Louis Armstrong Plays W. C. Handy. Columbia Records, CL 591.

Louis Armstrong Story. Vols. 1, 2, 3, 4. Columbia Records, CL 851–52–53–54.

Louis Armstrong, V.S.O.P. Columbia Special Products, JEE–20019.

Rare Batch of Satch. RCA Victor Records, LPM 2322.

Rare Items. Decca Records, 79225.

Satchmo at Pasadena. Decca Records, 8041.

Satchmo at Symphony Hall. Decca Records, DXS 7195.

Satchmo on Stage. Decca Records, 8330.

Smithsonian Collection of Classic Jazz. Vols. 2 and 3.

Young Louis Armstrong: The Sideman. Decca Records, 79233.

Duke Ellington

And His Mother Called Him Bill. RCA Victor Records, LSP–3906.

At His Very Best. RCA Victor Records, LPM–1715.

Best of Duke Ellington. Capitol Records, SM–1602.

Birth of Big Band Jazz. Riverside Records, 129.

Duke's Big 4. Pablo Records, 2310703.

Duke Ellington, the Beginning. Decca Records, DL–9224.

Duke Ellington's Concert of Sacred Music. RCA Victor Records, LPM–3582.

Duke Ellington's Greatest Hits. Reprise Records, S–6234.

Duke Ellington, 70th Birthday Concert. Solid State Records, SS 19000.

Early Ellington. Brunswick Records, 54007.

Ellington at Newport. Columbia Records, CS 8648.

Ellington Era. Columbia Records, C3L 27.

Ellington '66. Reprise Records, 6154.

Historically Speaking, the Duke. Bethlehem Records, BCP 60.

New Orleans Suite. Atlantic Records, SD 1580.

Smithsonian Collection of Classic Jazz. Vols. 6 and 7.

This Is Duke Ellington. RCA Victor Records, VPM–6042.

This One's For Blanton. Pablo Records, 2310721.

Togo Brava Suite. United Artists Records, UXS–92.

Benny Goodman

All Time Greatest Hits. Columbia Records, PG–31547.

Benny Goodman. Archive of Folk and Jazz Music Records, 277.

Carnegie Hall Concert. Columbia Records, OSL–160.

The Complete Benny Goodman. Bluebird Records, AXM 2–5515.

From Spirituals to Swing. Vanguard Records, VRS–8523/4.

Great Benny Goodman. Columbia Records, CS–8643.

Greatest Hits. Columbia Records, CS 9283.

Small Groups. RCA Victor Records, LPV 521.

Smithsonian Collection of Classic Jazz. Vols. 4 and 6.

This Is Benny Goodman. RCA Victor Records, VPM 6040.

Charlie Parker

Bird and Diz. Verve Records, V6–8006.

Bird Symbols. Charlie Parker Records, PLP–407.

Bird—The Savoy Recordings (Master Takes). Savoy Records, SJL–2201.

Charlie Parker. Everest Records, FS–254.

Charlie Parker. Prestige Records, 24009.

Charlie Parker. Savoy Records, S5J5500.

Charlie Parker in Historical Recordings. Le Jazz Cool Records, JC102.

Charlie Parker Memorial. Savoy Records, MG–12000.

Charlie Parker Story, vols. 1, 2, 3. Verve Records, V6–8000–1–2.

Echoes of an Era. Roulette Records, RE–105.

Essential Charlie Parker. Verve Records, V–8409.

Genius of Charlie Parker. Savoy Records, MG–12014.

Greatest Jazz Concert Ever. Prestige Records, 24020.

Jazz at Massey Hall. Fantasy Records, 6003.

Original Recordings. Onyx Records, 221.

Smithsonian Collection of Classic Jazz. Vols. 7 and 8.

John Coltrane

Ascension. Impulse Records, A–95.

Ballads. Impulse Records, S–32.

Best of John Coltrane. Atlantic Records, S–1541.

Impressions. Impulse Records, AS–42.

John Coltrane. Prestige Records, 24003.

My Favorite Things. Atlantic Records, 1361.

Selflessness. Impulse Records, AS–9161.

Smithsonian Collection of Classic Jazz. Side 12.

The Mastery of John Coltrane. Volume 1, *Feeling Good*. Impulse Records, 129345/2. Volume 2, *To the Beat of a Different Drum*. Impulse Records, 129346/2. Volume 3. *Jupiter Variation*. Impulse Records, 1A–9360.

Miles Davis

Basic Miles. Columbia Records, PC–32025.

Best of Miles Davis (2). PDL Records, 2–1095E.

Birth of the Cool. Capitol Records, N–16168.

Bitches' Brew (2). Columbia Records, GP–26.

Collector's Items (w. Parker, Mingus) (2). Prestige Records, 24022E.

ESP (w. Shorter, Hancock, Carter, Williams). Columbia Records, PC–9150.

"Four" and More (w. Hancock). Columbia Records, PC–9253.

Green Haze (w. Coltrane) (2). Prestige Records, 24064.

In a Silent Way. Columbia Records, PC–9875.

Jazz Classics (w. Coltrane). Prestige Records, 7373E.

Kind of Blue (w. Coltrane, Evans). Columbia Records, PC–8163.

The Man With the Horn. Columbia Records, PC–36790.

Miles Ahead (w. Gil Evans Orch.). Columbia Records, PC–8633E.

Miles Ahead (w. Parker, Lewis, Silver). Prestige Records, 7822E.

Milestones (w. Coltrane, Adderley). Columbia Records, PC–9428E.

My Funny Valentine (w. Hancock). Columbia Records, PC–9106.

Nefertiti (w. Shorter et al.). Columbia Records, PC–9594.

Porgy and Bess (w. Gil Evans Orch.). Columbia Records, PC–8085.

Quiet Nights (w. Gil Evans Orch.). Columbia Records, PC–8906.

'Round About Midnight (w. Coltrane). Columbia Records, PC–8649E.

Seven Steps To Heaven (w. Hancock). Columbia Records, PS–8851.

Sketches of Spain (w. Gil Evans Orch.). Columbia Records, PC–8271.

Some Day My Prince Will Come. Columbia Records, PC–8456.

Tutu. Warner Brothers, 2549–4.

You're Under Arrest. Columbia Records, FCT–40023.

Appendix A
Scores

Chapter 5: Early New Orleans Dixieland (1900–1920)

Taped Demonstration 10

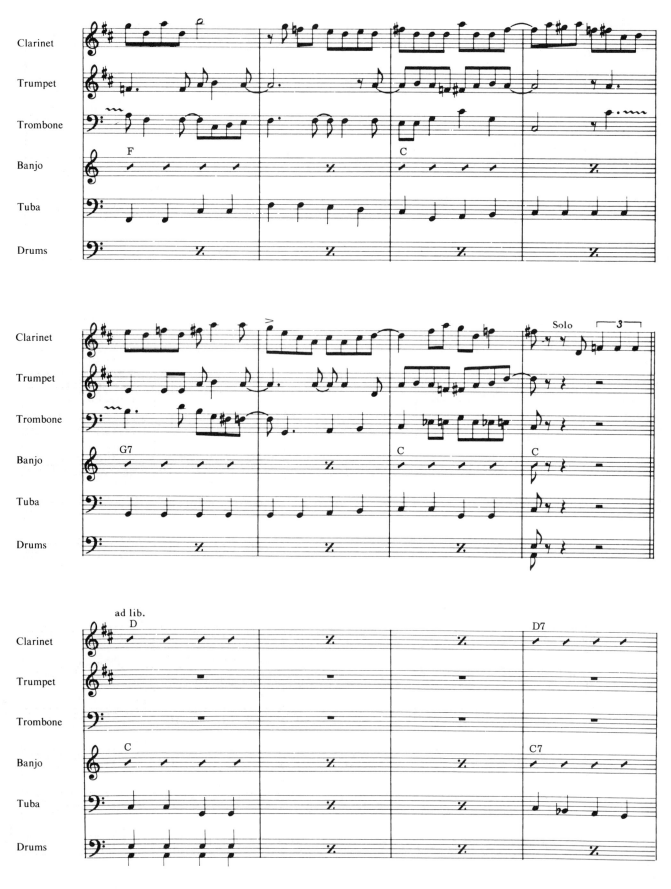

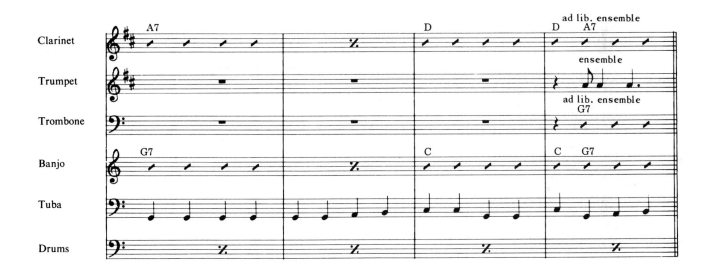

Taped Demonstration 12

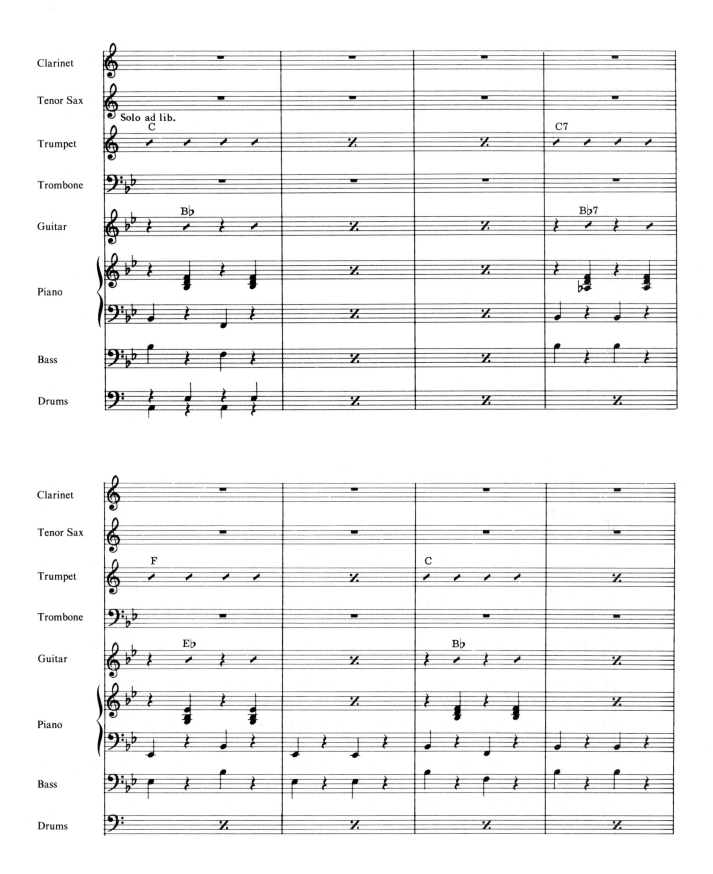

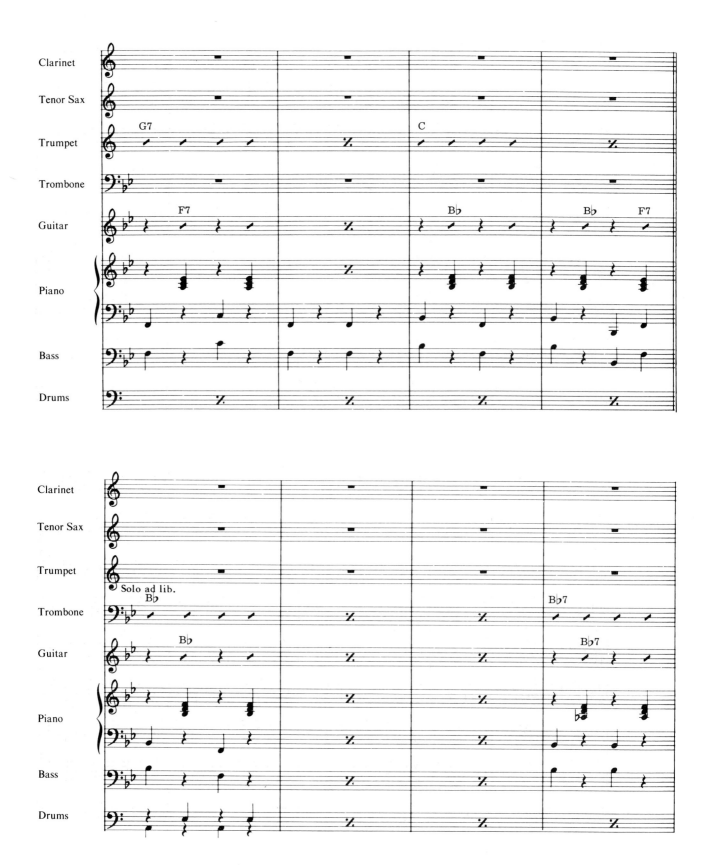

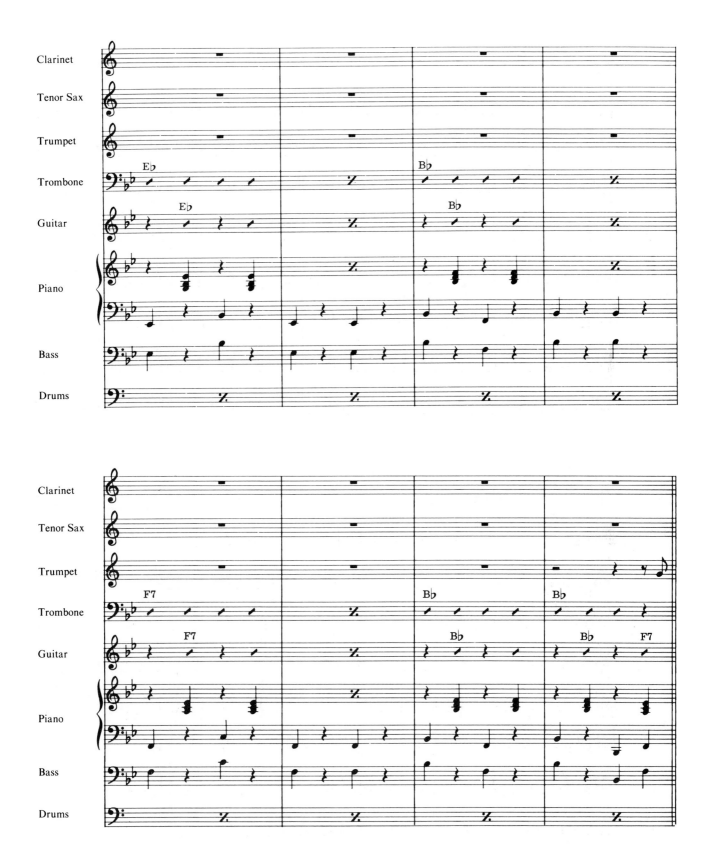

1st Alto Sax
1st Tenor Sax
2nd Tenor Sax
Baritone Sax
1st Trumpet
2nd Trumpet
3rd Trumpet
1st Trombone
2nd Trombone
3rd Trombone
4th Trombone
Guitar
B♭7
E♭7
Piano
Bass
Drums

1st Alto Sax
1st Tenor Sax
2nd Tenor Sax
Baritone Sax
1st Trumpet
2nd Trumpet
3rd Trumpet
1st Trombone
2nd Trombone
3rd Trombone
4th Trombone
Guitar
B♭
F7
Piano
Bass
Drums

Change to Clarinet
1st Alto Sax
1st Tenor Sax
2nd Tenor Sax
Baritone Sax
1st Trumpet
2nd Trumpet
3rd Trumpet
1st Trombone
open
2nd Trombone
open
3rd Trombone
open
4th Trombone
open
Guitar
B♭
Piano
Bass
Tom-Tom Solo
Drs.
Drums

Solo ad lib.
C
C7
1st Alto Sax
1st Tenor Sax
2nd Tenor Sax
Baritone Sax
1st Trumpet
2nd Trumpet
3rd Trumpet
Open
1st Trombone
mp
Open
2nd Trombone
mp
Open
3rd Trombone
mp
Open
4th Trombone
mp
Bb
Bb7
Guitar
Piano
Bass
Drums

1st Alto Sax
1st Tenor Sax
2nd Tenor Sax
Baritone Sax
1st Trumpet
2nd Trumpet
3rd Trumpet
1st Trombone
2nd Trombone
3rd Trombone
4th Trombone
Guitar
Piano
Bass
Drums
F
C
E♭7
B♭

1st Alto Sax
1st Tenor Sax
2nd Tenor Sax
Baritone Sax
1st Trumpet
2nd Trumpet
3rd Trumpet
1st Trombone
2nd Trombone
3rd Trombone
4th Trombone
Guitar
Piano
Bass
Drums
G7
C
C
Open
Open
Open
F7
B♭
B♭
C

1st Alto Sax
1st Tenor Sax
2nd Tenor Sax
Baritone Sax
1st Trumpet
2nd Trumpet
3rd Trumpet
1st Trombone
2nd Trombone
3rd Trombone
4th Trombone
Guitar
F
F
C
C
C
G7
Piano
Bass
Drums
2
2

1st Alto Sax
1st Tenor Sax
2nd Tenor Sax
Baritone Sax
1st Trumpet
2nd Trumpet
3rd Trumpet
1st Trombone
2nd Trombone
3rd Trombone
4th Trombone
Guitar
Piano
Bass
Drums
G7
G7
C
C
C
Db

1st Alto Sax
1st Tenor Sax
2nd Tenor Sax
Baritone Sax
1st Trumpet
2nd Trumpet
3rd Trumpet
1st Trombone
2nd Trombone
3rd Trombone
4th Trombone
Guitar
Piano
Bass
Drums
D♭
D♭7
G♭
2
2

1st Alto Sax
1st Tenor Sax
2nd Tenor Sax
Baritone Sax
1st Trumpet
2nd Trumpet
3rd Trumpet
1st Trombone
2nd Trombone
3rd Trombone
4th Trombone
Guitar
Piano
Bass
Drums
G♭
G♭
D♭
D♭
D♭
A♭7
2
2

1st Alto Sax
1st Tenor Sax
2nd Tenor Sax
Baritone Sax
1st Trumpet
2nd Trumpet
3rd Trumpet
1st Trombone
2nd Trombone
3rd Trombone
4th Trombone
Guitar
Piano
Bass
Drums
Change to Clar.
Solo
A♭7
A♭7
D♭
D♭

Chapter 10: Bop (1940–50)
Taped Demonstration 15

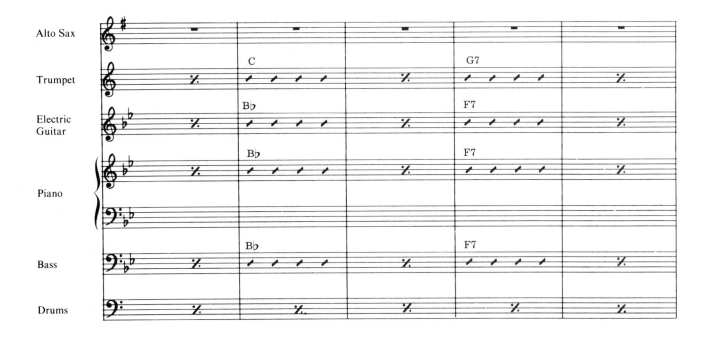

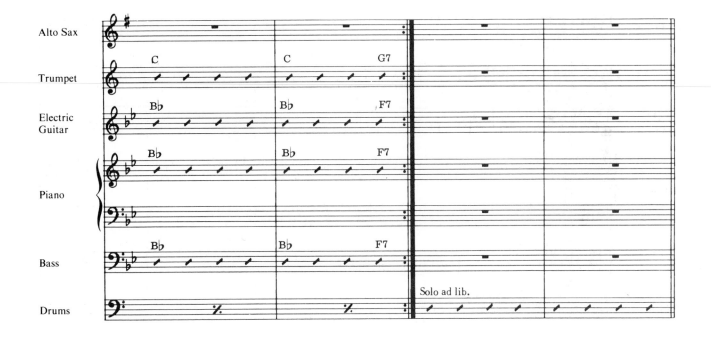

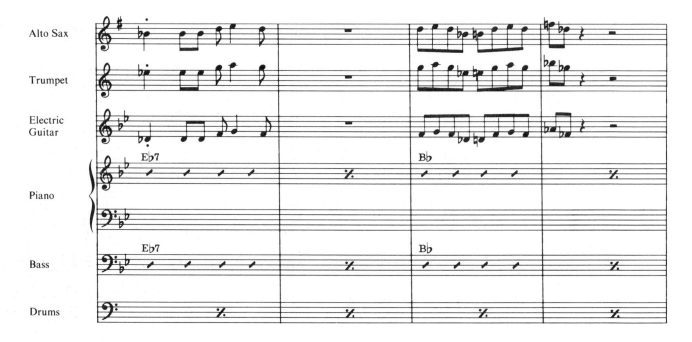

Chapter 11: Cool (1949–55)

Taped Demonstration 16

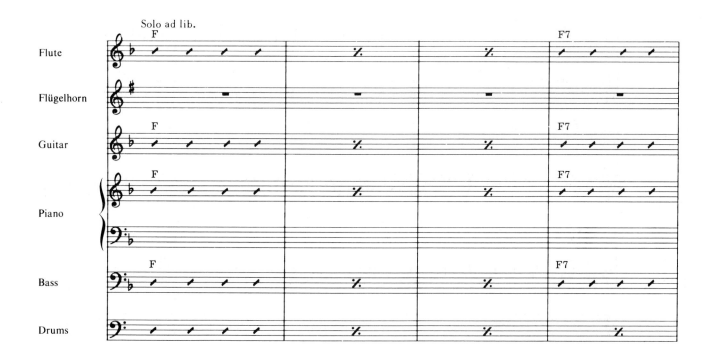

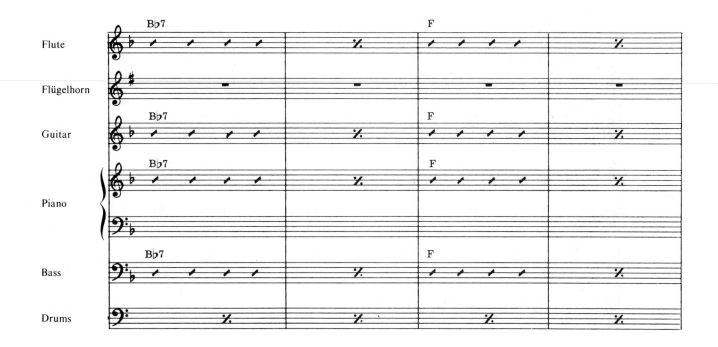

Chapter 12: Funky (circa 1954–63)
Taped Demonstration 17

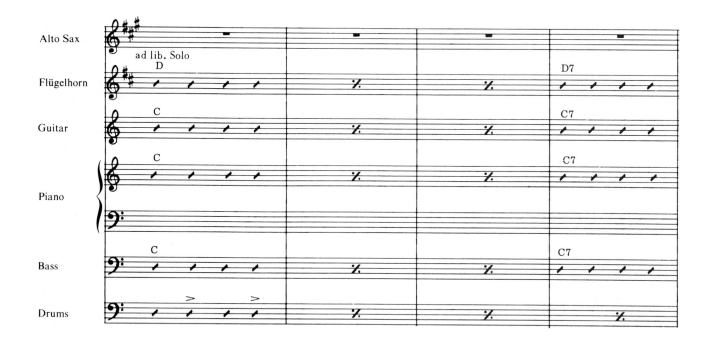

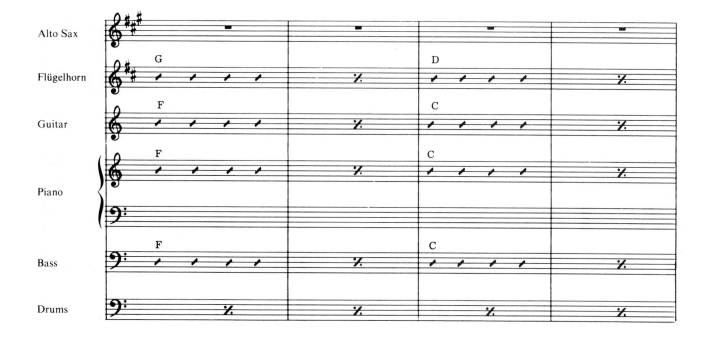

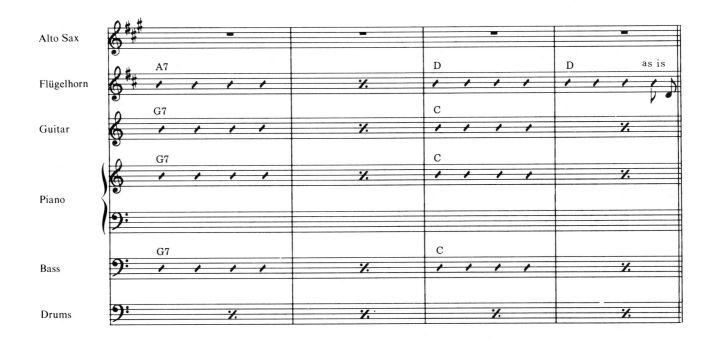

Chapter 13: Free Form
Taped Demonstration 18

Part I

Part II

Part III

Part IV

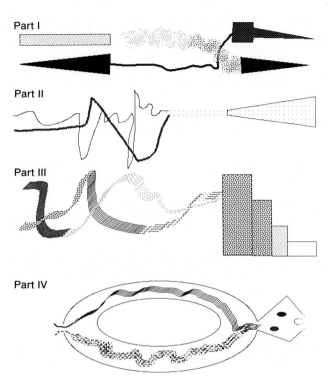

Appendix B
Awards and Films

National Academy of Recording Arts and Sciences Awards for Jazz

The award is given annually for the best jazz record of the year as voted by the National Academy of Recording Arts and Sciences (NARAS).

1966   Wes Montgomery. *Goin' Out of My Head.* Verve Records, V–8642.

1967   Cannonball Adderley. *Mercy, Mercy, Mercy.* Capitol Records, T 2663.

1968   Duke Ellington. *And His Mother Called Him Bill.* RCA Victor Records, LSP–3906.

1969   Quincy Jones. *Walkin' in Space.* A & M Records, SP 3023.

1970   Miles Davis. *Bitches Brew.* Columbia Records, GP 26.

1971   Bill Evans. *The Bill Evans Album.* Columbia Records, 30855.

1972   Gary Burton. *Alone at Last.* Atlantic Records, 1598 (solo).

1972   Freddie Hubbard. *Hub of Hubbard.* BASF Records, 20726 (group).

1972   Duke Ellington. *Togo Brava Suite.* United Artists Records, UXS, 92 (big band).

1973   Art Tatum. *God Is in the House.* Onyx Records, 295 (solo).

1973   Supersax. *Supersax Plays Bird.* Capitol Records, 11177 (group).

1973   Woody Herman. *Giant Steps.* Fantasy Records, 9432 (big band).

1974   Charlie Parker. *Original Recordings.* Onyx Records, 221 (solo).

1974   Oscar Peterson. *The Trio.* Pablo Records, 2310–701 (group).

1974   Woody Herman. *Thundering Herd.* Fantasy Records, F9452 (big band).

1975   Phil Woods and Michel Legrand. *Images.* RCA Victor Records, BGL 1–1027 (big band).

1975   Return to Forever (Chick Corea). *No Mystery.* Polydor Records, 6512 (group).

1975   Oscar Peterson and Dizzy Gillespie. *Oscar Peterson and Dizzy Gillespie.* Pablo Records, 2310740 (solo).

1976   Duke Ellington. *The Ellington Suites.* Pablo Records, 2310–762 (big band).

1976   Chick Corea. *The Leprechaun.* Polydor Records, PD6062 (group).

1976   Count Basie and Zoot Sims. *Basie and Zoot.* Pablo Records, 2310–745 (solo).

1976   Ella Fitzgerald and Joe Pass. *Fitzgerald and Pass . . . Again.* Pablo Records, 2310–772 (vocal).

1977   Count Basie. *Prime Time.* Pablo Records, 2310–797 (big band).

1977 Phil Woods. *Live from the Showboat*. RCA Victor Records, BGL 2–2202 (group).

1977 Oscar Peterson. *The Giants*. Pablo Records, 2310–796 (solo).

1977 Al Jarreau. *Look to the Rainbow*. Warner Brothers Records, 2BZ–3052 (vocal).

1978 Thad Jones and Mel Lewis. *Live in Munich*. Horizon Records, SP–724 (big band).

1978 Chick Corea. *Friends*. Polydor Records, PD1–6160 (group).

1978 Oscar Peterson. *Montreux '77*. Pablo Records, 2308–208 (solo).

1978 Al Jarreau. *All Fly Home*. Warner Brothers Records, BSK–3229 (vocal).

1979 Weather Report. *8:30*. ARC-CBS Records, PC2–36030, C3603 (jazz/rock).

1979 Duke Ellington. *At Fargo, 1940 Live*. Book of the Month Club (big band).

1979 Gary Burton and Chick Corea. *Duet*. EMC-Warner Brothers Records, 1–1140 (group).

1979 Oscar Peterson. *Jousts*. Pablo Records, 2310817 (solo).

1979 Ella Fitzgerald. *Fine and Mellow*. Pablo Records, 2310829 (vocal).

1980 Ella Fitzgerald. *A Perfect Match*. Pablo Records, 2312110 (female vocal).

1980 George Benson. "Moody's Mood" from his album *Give Me the Night*. Warner Brothers Records, HS 3453 (male vocal).

1980 Bill Evans. *I Will Say Goodbye*. Fantasy Records, F–9593 (solo).

1980 Bill Evans. *We Will Meet Again*. Warner Brothers Records, HS 3411 (group).

1980 Count Basie. *On the Road*. Pablo Records, D2312112 (big band).

1980 "Dinorah Dinorah" from George Benson's album *Give Me the Night*. Warner Brothers Records, HS 3453 (instrumental arrangement).

1980 Manhattan Transfer. "Birdland" from their album *Extensions*. Atlantic Records SD 19258 (fusion).

1981 Ella Fitzgerald. *Digital III at Montreux*. Pablo Records, 2308223 (female vocal).

1981 Al Jarreau. "Blue Rondo a la Turk" from his album *Breaking Away*. Warner Brothers Records, BSK–3576 (male vocal).

1981 Manhattan Transfer. "Until I Met You" from the album *Mecca for Moderns*. Atlantic Records, 53491 (group vocal).

1981 John Coltrane. *Bye Bye Blackbird*. Pablo Records, 2308227 (soloist).

1981 Chick Corea and Gary Burton. *Chick Corea and Gary Burton in Concert, Zurich, October 28, 1979*. ECM Records, 2–1182 (group).

1981 Gerry Mulligan. *Walk on the Water*. DRG Records, SL–5194 (big band).

1981 Quincy Jones. "Velas" from his album *The Dude*. A&M Records, 52357 (instrumental arrangement).

1981 Grover Washington, Jr. *Winelight*. Elektra Records, 6E305 (fusion).

1982 Sarah Vaughan. *Gershwin Live!* CBS Records, 37277 (female vocal).

1982 Mel Tormé. *An Evening with George Shearing and Mel Torme*. Concord Jazz Records, 190 (male vocal).

1982 Manhattan Transfer. *Route 66*. Atlantic Records, 54034 (group vocal).

1982 Miles Davis. *We Want Miles*. Columbia Records, 38005 (soloist).

1982 Phil Woods Quintet. *"More" Live*. Adelphi Records, 5010 (group).

1982 Count Basie. *Warm Breeze*. Pablo Today Records, 2312131 (big band).

1982 Pat Metheny Group. *Offramp*. ECM/WB Records, 1–1216 (fusion).

1983 Ella Fitzgerald. *The Best Is Yet To Come*. Pablo Records, 2312–138 (female vocal).

1983 Mel Tormé. *Top Drawer*. Concord Records, CJ-219 (male vocal).

1983 Manhattan Transfer. "Why Not" from *Bodies and Souls*. Atlantic Records, 80104 (group vocal).

1983 Wynton Marsalis. *Think of One*. Columbia Records, FC-38641 (soloist).

1983 Phil Woods Quartet. *At the Vanguard*. Antilles/Island Records, AN 1013 (group).

1983 Rob McConnell and the Boss Brass. *All in Good Time*. Dark Orchid, PAJ 8074 (big band).

1983 Pat Matheny. *Travels*. ECM/Warner Brothers Records, 23791 (fusion).

1984 Joe Williams. *Nothin' but the Blues*. Delos Records, 4001 (vocal).

1984 Wynton Marsalis. *Hot House Flowers*. Columbia Records, FC-39530 (soloist).

1984 Art Blakey. *New York Scene*. Concord Records, CJ-256 (group).

1984 Count Basie. *88 Basie Street*. Pablo Records, 2310–901 (big band).

1984 Pat Matheny. *First Circle*. ECM/Warner Brothers Records, 1278 (fusion).

1984 *Big Band Jazz*. Smithsonian Collection of Classic Jazz. Columbia Special Products, Columbia Records, F6 11891 (historical).

1985 Instrumental soloist—Wynton Marsalis, "Black Codes from the Underground", Columbia 40009

1985 Fusion—David Sanborn, "Straight to the Heart", Warner Brothers 1-25150

1985 Female soloist—Cleo Laine, "Cleo at Carnegie: The 10th Anniversary Concert", DRG 2-2101

1985 Male soloist—Jon Hendricks and Bobby McFerrin, "Another Night in Tunsia", Atlantic 81256-1 (Track from "Vocalese")

1985 Jazz duo or group vocal—Manhattan Transfer, "Vocalese", Atlantic 81266-1

1985 Group instrumental—Wynton Marsalis, "Black Codes from the Underground", Columbia 40009

1985 Big band instrumental—John Barry and Bob Wilber, "The Cotton Club: Original Motion Picture Soundtrack", Geffen 24062

1986 Diane Schurr. *Timeless*. GRP 11105-1030-1 (female vocal).

1986 Bobby McFerrin. *Round Midnight*. Columbia CBS CK-40464 (male vocal).

1986 2 Plus 2. *Free-Fall*. Discovery Records (group vocal).

1986 Miles Davis. *Tutu*. Warner Brothers 7599-25490-1 (soloist)

1986 Wynton Marsalis. *J Mood*. Columbia CBS 7464-40308-1 (group)

1986 The Tonight Show Band with Doc Severinsen. *The Tonight Show Band with Doc Severinsen*. Amherst 3311 (big band).

1986 Bob James and David Sanborn. *Double Vision*. Warner Brothers 7599-25393-1 (fusion).

National Academy of Recording Arts and Sciences Hall of Fame Awards

Honoring Recordings of Lasting Historical or Qualitative Significance Released before Inception of the Grammy Awards in 1958

The following recordings have been voted as winners since the first Hall of Fame Awards were given in 1974.

Ain't Misbehavin'. Fats Waller (piano solo). Victor, 1929.

"And the Angels Sing." Benny Goodman. Victor, 1939.

April in Paris. Count Basie. Clef, 1955.

Artistry in Rhythm. Stan Kenton. Capitol, 1945.

"A-Tisket A-Tasket." Chick Webb with Ella Fitzgerald. Decca, 1938.

Bach: Goldberg Variations. Wanda Landowska. Victor, 1945.

Bach: Goldberg Variations. Glenn Gould. Columbia, 1956.

Bach: Suites for Cello Unaccompanied. Pablo Casals. Victor, 1936/9.

Bach: The Well-Tempered Clavier (Complete) Wanda Landowska. RCA Victor, 1949-54.

Bach-Stokowski: Toccata & Fugue in D Minor. Leopold Stokowski conducting the Philadelphia Orchestra. Victrola, 1927.

Ballad for Americans. Paul Robeson. Victor Records, 1940.

Bartok: Complete Six Quartets. Juillard Quartet. Columbia, 1950.

Beethoven: Piano Sonatas (32). Artur Schnabel. Beethoven Sonata Society/RCA, 1932-1938.

Beethoven: *Quartets For Strings* (16). Budapest String Quartet. Columbia, 1952.

Beethoven: Symphonies (9). Arturo Toscanini conducting the NBC Symphony. RCA Victor, 1950-53.

Begin the Beguine. Artie Shaw. Bluebird, 1938.

Birth of the Cool. Miles Davis. Capitol, 1957.

"Black and Tan Fantasy." Duke Ellington. Victor, 1928.

"Blueberry Hill." Fats Domino. Imperial, 1956.

"Blue Suede Shoes." Carl Perkins. Sun, 1956.

Blue Yodel (T for Texas). Jimmie Rodgers. Victor, 1928.

Body & Soul. Coleman Hawkins. Bluebird, 1939.

Carnegie Hall Jazz Concert. Benny Goodman. Columbia, 1950.

Christmas Song. Nat "King" Cole. Capitol, 1946.

"Cool Water." Sons of the Pioneers. Decca, 1941.

Empty Bed Blues. Bessie Smith. Columbia, 1928.

Four Brothers. Woody Herman. Columbia, 1948.

The Genius of Art Tatum, vols. 1-13. Art Tatum. Verve, 1954-1955.

Gershwin: Porgy & Bess (Opera). Lehman Engel, conductor; Cast: Lawrence Winters, Camilla Williams, and others. Columbia, 1951.

Gershwin: Rhapsody in Blue. Paul Whiteman with George Gershwin. RCA Victor, 1927.

"God Bless America." Kate Smith. Victor, 1939.

God Bless the Child. Billie Holiday. Okey, 1941.

How High the Moon. Les Paul & Mary Ford. Capitol, 1951.

I Can Hear It Now, vols. 1–3. Edward R. Murrow. Columbia, 1948–1950.

I Can't Get Started. Bunny Berigan. Victor, 1937.

"If I Didn't Care." Ink Spots. Decca, 1939.

"I'll Never Smile Again." Tommy Dorsey. Victor, 1940.

In a Mist. Bix Beiderbecke (piano). Okey Records, 1927.

In the Mood. Glenn Miller. Bluebird, 1939.

In the Wee Small Hours (album). Frank Sinatra. Capitol, 1955.

Jelly Roll Morton: The Saga of Mr. Jelly Lord. Circle Records, 1938.

Leoncavallo: Pagliacci. Act I: Vesti La Giubba. Enrico Caruso. Victrola, 1907.

Mahler: *Das Lied Von Der Erde.* Bruno Walter cond. Vienna Philharmonic Orchestra with Kathleen Ferrier & Julius Patzlak. London, 1952.

Mood Indigo. Duke Ellington. Brunswick, 1930.

My Blue Heaven. Gene Austin. Victor, 1928.

My Fair Lady. Original Broadway cast with Rex Harrison & Julie Andrews. Columbia, 1956.

"Nobody." Bert Williams. Columbia, 1906.

Oklahoma! Original Broadway cast with Alfred Drake; orchestra and chorus directed by Jay Blackton. Decca, 1943.

One O'Clock Jump. Count Basie. Decca, 1937.

"Over the Rainbow." Judy Garland. Decca, 1939.

"Pinetop's Boogie Woogie." Pine Top Smith. Vocalion, 1928.

Puccini: Tosca. Maria Callas. Angel, 1953.

Rachmaninoff: Piano Concerto No. 2 in C Minor. Sergei Rachmaninoff (piano), Philadelphia Orchestra, Leopold Stokowski, conductor. Victrola, 1929.

Rachmaninoff: Rhapsody on a Theme of Paganini. Sergei Rachmaninoff (piano), Philadelphia Orchestra, Leopold Stokowski, conductor. RCA Victor, 1935.

"Rock Around the Clock." Bill Haley. Decca, 1955.

Rudolph the Red-Nosed Reindeer. Gene Autry. Columbia, 1949.

September Song. Walter Huston. Brunswick, 1938.

Singin' the Blues. Frankie Trumbauer & His Orchestra featuring Bix Beiderbecke on cornet. Okey, 1927.

"Sing Sing Sing." Benny Goodman. Victor, 1937.

South Pacific. Original Cast with Mary Martin and Ezio Pinza. Columbia, 1949.

Strange Fruit. Billie Holiday. Commodore, 1939.

Take the "A" Train. Duke Ellington & His Orchestra. Victor, 1941.

"Tea for Two." Art Tatum. Decca, 1939.

Villa-Lobos: Bachianas Brasileiras No. 5. Bidu Sayao; Heitor Villa-Lobos cond. Cello Ensemble. Columbia, 1945.

West End Blues. Louis Armstrong. Okey, 1928.

White Christmas. Bing Crosby. Decca, 1942.

"Your Cheating Heart." Hank Williams. MGM, 1953.

Authors' Note

It is quite obvious that many of these recordings are jazz or at least jazz oriented.

Films

The following are suggested films about jazz.

'Round Midnight. Award winning feature film scored by Herbie Hancock and featuring Dexter Gordon on tenor saxophone and many other fine jazz artists.

Audio-Visual History of Jazz (filmstrips). Orrin Keepnews. Educational Audio Visual.

Discovering Jazz (16 mm.). Paul Tanner, Bailey Film Associates, a Division of Columbia Broadcasting System.

An Introduction to Electric Music Synthesizers (filmstrips). Don Muro. Belwin-Mills Publishing Company.

As noted in chapter 16 there is a list of over sixty films featuring jazz artists in Leonard Feather's book *The Encyclopedia of Jazz in the Seventies.*

Appendix C
Discography

Series

The Bass. Impulse Records, 9284 (6 sides).

Big Bands '80s Record Library
(by mail only)
9288 Kinglet Drive
Los Angeles, CA 90069

Capital Jazz Classics. Capitol Records.
    Volume 1 Miles Davis
    Volume 2 Stan Kenton
    Volume 3 Art Tatum
    Volume 4 Gerry Mulligan
    Volume 5 Coleman Hawkins
    Volume 6 Various Artists: All Star Sessions
    Volume 7 Serge Chaloff
    Volume 8 Nat King Cole Trio
    Volume 9 Woody Herman
    Volume 10 Various Artists: Swing Exercise

Collector's History of Classic Jazz. Murray Hill Records, 927942.

The Definitive Jazz Scene, vols. 1, 2, 3. Impulse Records, A–99, A–100, A–9101.

The Drums. Impulse Records, 9272 (6 sides).

Encyclopedia of Jazz on Records. Decca Records, DXSF–7140 (8 sides).

Folkways Jazz Series. Folkways Records, FJ2801–2811.
    Volume 1 The South
    Volume 2 The Blues
    Volume 3 New Orleans
    Volume 4 Jazz Singers
    Volume 5 Chicago No. 1
    Volume 6 Chicago No. 2
    Volume 7 New York (1922–34)
    Volume 8 Big Bands
    Volume 9 Piano
    Volume 10 Boogie-Woogie
    Volume 11 Addenda

Giants of Jazz. Time/Life Records.

History of Classic Jazz. Riverside Records, SDP–11.
    Volume 1 Backgrounds
    Volume 2 Ragtime
    Volume 3 The Blues
    Volume 4 New Orleans Style
    Volume 5 Boogie-Woogie
    Volume 6 South Side Chicago
    Volume 7 Chicago Style
    Volume 8 Harlem
    Volume 9 New York Style
    Volume 10 New Orleans Revival

Jazz Odyssey. Columbia Records, C31–30, 32, 33.
  Volume   1 The Sound of New Orleans
        (1917–47)
  Volume   2 The Sound of Chicago
        (1923–40)
  Volume   3 The Sound of Harlem

Jazz Piano Anthology. Columbia Records, PG 32355 (4 sides).
Jazz: The '60s, Vols. 1 & 2. Pacific Jazz Records, L893–H and L895–H.
The Jazz Story. Capitol Records, W2137–41.
  Volume   1 New Orleans
  Volume   2 North to Chicago
  Volume   3 The Swinging Years
  Volume   4 The Big Bands
  Volume   5 Modern and Free Form

New World Records (100 albums), suggested album numbers:
  204 Loxodonta Africana: The Jazz Sound of Ricky Ford
  210 The Jazz of the Seventies
  216 Mirage: Avant Garde and Third Stream Jazz
  217 Jammin' for the Jackpot: Big Bands and Territory Bands of the 30s
  235 Maple Leaf Rag: Ragtime in Rural America
  240 Where Have We Met Before? Forgotten Songs from B'way, Hollywood, & Tin Pan Alley
  242 Nica's Dream: Small Jazz Groups of the 50s and Early 60s
  248 The Music Goes Round and Around: The Golden Years of Tin Pan Alley 1930–39
  249 Rock 'N' Roll
  250 Little Club Jazz: Small Groups in the 30s
  252 The Roots of the Blues
  256 Sweet and Low Blues: Big Bands and Territory Bands of the 20s
  259 Cuttin' the Boogie: Piano Blues and Boogie Woogie, 1926–1941
  261 Straighten Up and Fly Right: Rhythm and Blues
  269 Steppin' on the Gas: Rags to Jazz 1913–1927
  271 Bebop
  274 Jive at Five: The Style-Makers of Jazz (1920s–1940s)
  275 Introspection: Neglected Jazz Figures of the 1950s and Early 1960s
  279 Yes Sir, That's My Baby: The Golden Years of Tin Pan Alley 1920–1929
  284 Jazz In Revolution: Big Bands in the 1940s
  295 When Malindy Sings: Jazz Vocalists 1938–1961
  303 Cecil Taylor: 3 Phasis

The Saxophone. Impulse Records, 9253 (6 sides).
Smithsonian Collection of Classic Jazz (12 sides).
  (by mail only)
  Smithsonian
  Box 10230
  Des Moines, Iowa 50336
Three Decades of Jazz. Blue Note Records, LA 158–60.
  1939–49
  1949–59
  1959–69

Albums

African Drums. Folkways Records, FE 4502.
Anatomy of Improvisation. Verve Records, 8230.
Art of Jazz Piano. Epic Records, 3295.
The Art Tatum Touch (Paul Smith). Outstanding Records, vols. 1 and 2, 004 and 007.
Basic Miles. Columbia Records, C 32025.
The Be-Bop Era. RCA Victor Records, LPV–519.
The Best of Dixieland. RCA Victor Records, LSP–2982.
Big Bands' Greatest Hits. Columbia Records, CG–31212.
Bix Beiderbecke and the Chicago Cornets. Milestone Records, M–47019 (4 sides).
The Blues in Modern Jazz. Atlantic Records, 1337.
The Blues Roll On. Atlantic Records, 1352.
Boogie-Woogie Rarities. Milestone Records, MLP 2009.
Bop Session. Sonet Records, 692.
Carnegie Hall Concert. Columbia Records, OSL–160.
Chicagoans (1928–30). Decca Records, 79231.
Chicago Jazz Album. Decca Records, 8029.
A Child's Introduction to Jazz. Wonderland Records, 2435.
Classic Jazz Piano Styles. RCA Victor Records, LPV–543.

Classic Piano Styles. RCA Victor Records, LPV–546.

Energy Essentials. Impulse Records, ASD–9228 (6 sides).

Fifty Years of Jazz Guitar. Columbia Records, CG–44566.

From Spirituals to Swing. Vanguard Records, VRS–8523/4.

The Golden Age of Ragtime. Riverside Records, 12–110.

The Great Band Era. RCA Victor Records, RD4–25 (RRIS–5473).

Great Blues Singers. Riverside Records, 121.

The Greatest Jazz Concert in the World. Pablo Records, 2625704.

The Greatest Names in Jazz. Verve Records, PR 2–3.

Guide to Jazz. RCA Victor Records, LPM 1393.

Introspection—Neglected Jazz Figures of the 1950s and Early 1960s, New World Records, 275.

Jazz of the 1920s. Merry Makers Records, 103.

The Jazz Makers. Columbia Records, CL 1036.

Jazz at Preservation Hall. Atlantic Records, 1409 and 1410.

Jazz at the Santa Monica Civic '72. Pablo Records, 2625701.

The Jazz Scene. Verve Records, 8060.

Jazz Scene I. Epic Records, LA–1600.

Jive at Five—The Style-makers of Jazz 1920s–1940s, New World Records, 274.

Kansas City Jazz. Decca Records, 8044.

Mainstream Jazz. Atlantic Records, 1303/S.

A Musical History of Jazz. Grand Awards Records, 33–322.

Never Before . . . Never Again (Joe Venuti/Tony Romero). Dobre Records, DR 1066.

New Orleans Jazz. Decca Records, 8283.

New Orleans: The Living Legends. Riverside Records, 356–57 (s).

The New Wave in Jazz. Impulse Records, A–90.

New York: Fall 1974 (Anthony Braxton). Arista Records, AL 4032.

Piano Giants. Prestige Records, 24052.

Piano Roll Hall of Fame. Sounds Records, LP 1202.

Ragtime Piano Roll. Riverside Records, 126.

The Roots of American Music. Arhoolie Records, 2001–2.

Saxophone Revolt. Riverside Records, 284.

The Soul of Jazz. Riverside Records, S–5.

Steppin' on the Gas—Rags to Jazz 1913–1927. New World Records, 269.

The Story of the Blues. Columbia Records, G 30540.

Thesaurus of Classic Jazz. Columbia Records, C4L 18.

This Is Benny Goodman. RCA Victor Records, VPM 6040.

Appendix D
Videography

The following is a listing of videos available for purchase. They range in quality and amount of live footage by the jazz performers being discussed. When initials appear at the end of a listing it can be matched at the end of this list with the companies that produce or distribute those tapes.

The running time for each tape is given when known. Key personalities are also listed where possible. The quality of these tapes vary greatly due to the newness of the medium. However, despite the shortcomings in the production quality, these tapes offer a first hand look at many of today's (and yesterday's) jazz personalities.

Alberta Hunter: Jazz at the Smithsonian (58 min). **SVS, VF**

All Star Swing Festival (52 min). Benny Goodman, Ella Fitzgerald, Count Basie, Duke Ellington, Dave Brubeck, Dizzy Gillespie, Bobby Hackett, Joe Williams. **VF**

Always for Pleasure New Orleans jazz funeral and Mardi Gras celebrations, 1977, **VF**

An Evening with Ray Charles, (50 min). At Jubilee Auditorium in Edmunton. 1981, **VF**

Anything For Jazz-Jaki Byard (25 min), Bill Evans, Ron Carter. **RF**

Art Blakey: Jazz at the Smithsonian (58 min), Wynton Marsalis. **SVS, VF**

Art Ensemble of Chicago: Live at the Showcase (50 min), **IRL**

Art Farmer: Jazz At The Smithsonian (57 min) **SVS, VF**

Benny Carter: Jazz at the Smithsonian (57 min). **SVS, VF**

Best Of The Big Bands (75 min). Benny Goodman, Buddy Rich, Teddy Wilson, Gene Krupa, Lionel Hampton, Harry James, Jimmy Dorsey, Tommy Dorsey, Count Basie, Les Brown, Stumpy Brown **AE**

Big Bands Vol. 101 (Basie, Hampton and Ellington) (50 min). 1964–65, **VF**

Big Bands At Disneyland: 3 Volume Set, Cab Calloway, Lionel Hampton, Woody Herman **AE**

Big Bands At Disneyland: Cab Calloway, (57 min). **AE**

Big Bands At Disneyland: Lionel Hampton (57 min). **AE**

Big Bands At Disneyland: Woody Herman (57 min). **AE**

Big, Black And Beautiful (60 min). Duke Ellington, Cab Calloway, Count Basie, Lionel Hampton, George Shearing, Nat King Cole. **AE**

Bill Evans: On the Creative Process (20 min). Black and white. **RF**

Bill Watrous (24 min). **SVS**

Blues Alive. Mick Taylor, John McVie, Colin Allen, Albert King, Etta James, Sippie Wallace, Buddy Guy, Junior Wells. **AE**

Blues I (58 min). Leatta Galloway, Linda Hopkins, B. B. King, "Pee Wee" Crayton, Ernie Andrews, Eddie "Cleanhead" Vinson. **AE**

Bob Wilber And The Smithsonian Repertory Company (59 min). 1983 **SVS, VF**

Bobby Hutcherson and Dexter Gordon, (60 min). 1986, **VF**

Born to Swing, Basie Alumni (50 min). **RF**

Buddy Rich: The 'Channel One' Set (55 min). **SVS, VF**

Cab Calloway And His Orchestra. **JCVC 103**

Chick Corea: Very Special Concert (60 min), Lenny White, Stanley Clarke, Joe Henderson **SVS, VF**

Chick Corea/Gary Burton In Tokyo (58 min). **VF, AE**

Chico Hamilton: The Jazz Life (53 min). **SVS, VF**

Claude Bolling: Concerto For Classical Guitar & Jazz Piano (50 min). Angel Romero, George Shearing.

Count Basie Live At The HollyWood Palladium (42 min). **AE**

Crusaders Live: Midnight Triangle (60 min). **MCA**

Different Drummer: Elvin Jones (30 min). **RF**

Dizzy Gillespie (19 min). 1981, **VF, AE**

Dizzy Gillespie's Dream Band (19 min). **VF, AE**

Duke Ellington Goodyear Jazz Concert (27 min). **AE**

EAV history of jazz, Educational Audio Visual, 17 Marble Ave., Pleasantville, NY 10570 **EAV**

Eddie Gale Jazz Unit: High Tech Emergency/Silicon Valley Suite (55 min). **VNP**

Eddie Jefferson: Live at the Showcase (50 min). **IRL**

An Evening With Ray Charles (50 min). **AE**

Fats Waller And Friends. **JCVC 107**

Freddie Hubbard: Studio Live (59 min). **SVS, VF**

Gerry Mulligan (18 min). 1981, **AE**

Grover Washington, Jr.—In Concert (60 min). **AE**

Herbie Hancock And the Rockit Band. **AE**

Jazz: An American Classic Series, a series of period oriented lecture demonstrations by Reginald Buckner. University of Mid America, P.O. Box 82006, Lincoln, Nebraska 68501 **AE**

Jazzball (60 min). Duke Ellington, Artie Shaw, Louis Armstrong, Cab Calloway, Gene Krupa, Red Nichols, Peggy Lee, Buddy Rich and others. **AE**

Jazz Hoofer (28 min), Charlie Parker, Dizzy Gillespie. **RF**

Jazz In Exile (50 min), Phil Woods, Dexter Gordon, Steve Lacy. **RF**

Jazz Then—Dixieland 1, Della Reese, Scotty Plummer, Al Hirt, Woody Herman, Clora Bryant, Johnny Guarnieri. **AE**

Joe Williams: Jazz At The Smithsonian (58 min), 1982 **SVS, VF**

John Carter and Bobby Bradford: The New Music (29 min). **RF**

Johnny Griffin: The Jazz Life (55 min). **SVS, VF**

Last Of The Blue Devils (90 min), Kansas City Jazz, Jay McShann, Joe Turner, Count Basie. **RF**

Lena Horne: The Lady And Her Music (134 min). **AE**

Leroy Jenkins: Solo Violin (50 min). **RF**

Lift the Bandstand (50 min), Steve Lacy. **RF**

Lionel Hampton (24 min). **SVS, VF**

Lionel Hampton's One Night Stand (50 min). Buddy Rich, Mel Tormé, B. B. King, Gene Krupa, Gerry Mulligan, Dusty Springfield, Zoot Sims and more. **AE**

Louis Armstrong And His Orchestra. **JCVC 102**

Louis Jordan And Friends. Meade Lux Lewis, Maxine Sullivan, Nat King Cole. **JCVC 105**

Mahalia Jackson (34 min). **AE**

Manhattan Transfer (1980). **AE**

Manhattan Transfer, *Vocalese,* Atlantic Video, Dept. M, 75 Rockefeller Plaza, New York, N.Y. 10019

Max Roach (19 min). **AE, VF**

McCoy Tyner (53 min). 1986, **VF**

Mel Lewis Orchestra: Jazz At The Smithsonian (55 min), 1982, **SVS, VF**

Mel Tormé And Della Reese. **AE**

Mel Tormé Special (53 min). 1983, **SVS, VF**

Mike Mainieri: The Jazz Life (60 min), Warren Bernhardt, Eddie Gomez, Bob Mintzer, Omar Hakim, fusion **SVS**

Music in Monk Time (60 min). **VAP**

Nancy Wilson (60 min), Chick Corea, Stanley Clark, Lenny White, Joe Henderson, 1982 **SVS**

Nina Simone (57 min). 1984, **VF**

One Night With Blue Note: Preserved (60 min), Vol 1: Herbie Hancock, Bobby Hutcherson, Freddie Hubbard, Stanley Jordan; Vol 2: Cecil Taylor, McCoy Tyner, Art Blakey. 1985 **SVS, VF**

Passing It On-Barry Harris (23 min). **RF**

Piano Players Rarely Ever Play Together (76 min). **SP**

Playboy Jazz Festival, Vol 1 & 2, (91 min each), Vol 1: Freddie Hubbard, McCoy Tyner, Elvin Jones, Red Norvo, Tal Farlow; Vol 2: third stream, Dave Brubeck, Ornette Coleman, Weather Report, Manhattan Transfer, Dexter Gordon, Sarah Vaughn . . . **RCA**

Prime Cuts 4: Jazz And Beyond. Miles Davis, Herbie Hancock, Chuck Mangione, Al Di Meola, Andreas Vollenweider, Hiadshima, Clark/Duke Project and Weather Report. **AE**

Red Norvo: Jazz at the Smithsonian (58 min). **SVS**

Rob McConnell (25 min). **SVS**

San Francisco Blues (60 min). Clarence "Gatemouth" Brown, Clifton Chenier. **SVS**

Spyrogyra (56 min). **AE**

Sun Ra: A Joyful Noise (60 min). **RF**

Talmadge Farlow (58 min) **RF**

Tribute To Billie Holiday (60 min). Nina Simone, Morgana King, Ester Phillips, also some footage of Billie Holiday herself. **AE, VF**

Vocalese Live 1986, Manhattan Transfer, **EAV**

IRL Instructional Research Lab, Univ of Illinois, Box 4348, Chicago, IL 60608.

JCVC Jazz Classics.

MCA MCA Home Video Inc. 70 Universal City Plaza, Universal City, CA 91608.

PHV Paramount Home Video, 5555 Melrose Ave., Los Angeles, CA 90038.

RCA RCA/Columbia Pictures Home Video, 2901 Alameda Ave., Burbank, CA 91505.

RF Rhapsody Films, 30 Charlton St., NYC, NY 10014, offers a catalog of historic jazz documentaries.

SP Stevenson Productions.

SVS Sony Video Software, 9 W. 57th St., New York, NY 10019, 800-847-4164.

VAP Video Arts Productions.

VNP Video Now Productions, 7435 Bolanger Dr., Cupertino, CA 95014.

Distributors:

AE American Express Special Offer Center, P.O. Box 520, Great Neck, NY 10022

EAV Education Audio Visual Inc., 17 Marble Ave., Pleasantville, NY 10570.

VF Viewfinders, Inc., P.O. Box 1665, Evanston, IL 60204

Appendix E
Listening Guides

Glossary

accompanying To perform with another performer or performers usually in a less prominent role; for example, to play the piano accompaniment for a trombone soloist.

amplification The process of electronically making a sound louder.

analog The type of audio signal produced by early synthesizers. Voltage rather than numbers are used to describe the musical sounds.

appoggiatura A musical ornament consisting of a single tone moving to an adjacent tone which is harmonized.

arhythmic Seemingly without meter; music that lacks a definite beat.

arpeggio In which the individual tones of a chord are not sounded simultaneously but performed like a melody (single tones), nearly always starting at the bottom or lowest tone.

arrangement An adaptation of a musical composition (often called *charts* in musical slang). In a written arrangement, the musical arranger writes out the notes he wants each performer to play. In a head arrangement, the arrangement is made up out of someone's head, not written down.

arranger One who writes musical compositions for particular groups of performers.

atonal Lacking in tonal centers; free jazz often has atonal areas which avoid the chord and melodic relationships normally associated with the major-minor system.

attack The manner in which the tone or tones are first sounded.

avant garde A term which refers to composers and performers that break away from traditional practices and push for radical change; used primarily to describe post bop jazz.

ballad A simple song, usually romantic in nature, which uses the same melody for each stanza.

bar line A vertical line drawn down a music staff dividing it into bars or measures.

bar of music A means of dividing music; also called a measure of music.

bass (brass) The member of the brass family sounding the lowest tones; generally referred to as the *tuba*.

bass (string) An instrument that looks like a very large violin; also called the *bass violin*. The string bass is played either by plucking the strings with the fingers *(pizzicato)* or by bowing *(arco)*.

beat or breaker music A musical style characterized by electronic drum machines and a heavy beat; designed for a dancing style called break dancing.

block chords Usually chords with many notes that move in parallel motion.

blue tonalities The alteration of the third and seventh tones of the major scale by a flatting inflection.

bombs Spontaneous punctuations by the drummer.

break A short interruption in the flow of the music; an interlude in which a solo player improvises or an accompanying group interpolates.

bridge The name given to the third eight-bar section in the most common construction of a thirty-two bar chorus. AABA—the B is the bridge.

call and response pattern A musical pattern common to much jazz and African music in which a "call," usually by a solo singer or instrumentalist, is followed by a "response" from one instrument, an ensemble, or the assembled participants in a ritual. In religious ceremonies the congregation may respond to the "call" of the preacher.

chamber music Music intended for small groups performing in intimate surroundings, as distinct from large groups performing in concert halls, theaters, and the like.

chance music Music based on chance or random relationships such as the throwing of dice.

Charleston A dance form that was extremely popular during the 1920s.

chord The simultaneous sounding of three or more tones.

chord changes A series of successive chords; also called *chord progression*.

chorus The main body or refrain of a song as distinct from the verse, which comes first. Very often an arrangement contains many choruses played by individual instrumentalists.

chromatic Refers to the scales or the alteration of scale tones by using half-steps.

collective improvisation A situation in which all members of a small group improvise simultaneously.

combo A small instrumental group consisting of three to eight players.

compact disc A disc smaller than vinyl records which holds digital information that describes the musical sounds.

concerto grosso A composition consisting of interplay between a large body of instruments (orchestra) and a small group of instrumentalists (combo).

Congo Square A large field in New Orleans where slaves gathered to sing and dance.

contrived Music that is planned beforehand.

Creole A person with Negro and French or Spanish ancestry.

crossover A style of music that appeals to more than one type of listener; usually refers to jazz/rock (*fusion*).

cross-rhythm Two or more rhythmic patterns played simultaneously.

diatonic Pertains to the precise arrangement of tones as found in the major and minor scales.

digital The use of numbers to describe a sound. The numbers can then be processed by computers or effects. The digital information is converted back to analog form for human hearing.

digital recording Computer method of recording sound through the use of numbers.

distortion The alteration of a sound; normally by over amplifying it to create a rougher sound.

Dorian mode The arrangement of tones found in the scale using only the white keys of the piano from D to D.

double-stop Two tones stopped by the fingers on a stringed instrument and sounded simultaneously.

double time When the tempo of the music becomes twice as fast.

drum machine An electronic device used to create drum patterns similar to those played by traditional set or trap drummers.

editing Cutting or reassembling a recorded tape. Editing was originally done by actually cutting the tape. It can now be done electronically as the final mixdown is made.

effects Electronic devices which alter electronic sounds e.g. reverberation, delays, distortion.

eleventh chord A chord consisting of six different tones, each separated by an interval of a third.

embouchure Disposition of the lips and tongue in playing wind instruments.

ensemble Usually a small group of performers as distinct from an orchestra or choir.

extended harmony Tones added to a chord.

field hollers A secret means of communication between slaves while they worked in the fields; sometimes called *field cries*.

fill-in Originally, a short interlude in a song (such as a blues song) played by an instrumentalist.

flatted fifth Lowering by a half step the fifth degree of the scale or chord.

flatted tone Used to lower the pitch one half step.

flügelhorn A type of brass instrument with valves, similar to a trumpet.

form Refers to the design of a composition, its repeated and contrasting parts.

free form A term used to describe free jazz's lack of traditional restrictions in form and structure.

free improvisation A descriptive term which stresses the complete improvisational nature of free jazz.

frontline Instrumentalists who are placed along the front of an ensemble.

fugue   A type of contrapuntal composition for a given number of parts. Each part is introduced individually, and successive parts are heard in imitation.

fusion   A style of music that appeals to more than one type of listener; usually refers to jazz/rock *(crossover).*

gospel song   A song whose lyrics recount passages from scripture.

guitorgan   A guitarlike instrument with an organ sound.

harmonics   The frequencies that collectively create a single tone; also used to refer to the higher chord tones in an extended chord.

harmonizer   An electronic device that creates a parallel melodic line to accompany the original melody.

harmony   Simultaneous sounding of two or more tones.

head voice   Technique of singing in the high range (not falsetto).

higher harmony   See *extended harmony.*

homophonic   A single melody, usually in the highest voice part, with harmony in the lower voices acting as an accompaniment.

horizontal thinking   Polyphonic texture; a simultaneous combination of melodies; the opposite of homophonic texture, which consists of a single melody with harmonic accompaniment.

hymn   A congregational song, whose words are not taken directly from the Bible, sung in praise of God.

iambic pentameter   A type of poetry consisting of an unaccented syllable followed by an accented one, with five of these combinations in each line of poetry.

improvise   To perform music that is made up (created) at the moment, not from memory or from written music; a manner of playing extemporaneously.

instrumentation   The different types of instruments making up an ensemble.

jam session   An informal gathering of musicians playing on their own time and improvising just for the "fun of it."

key   A classification given to a particular arrangement of tones in a scale. The first degree of the scale is the tonal center or key name, and the necessary flats or sharps for a particular key form the key signature.

liturgical   Pertaining to the rites and services of a religious service.

Mass   The principal service of the Roman Catholic Church. The part that does not vary is called the Ordinary, or Common, of the Mass and consists of the Kyrie, the Gloria, the Credo, the Sanctus with Benedictus, and the Agnus Dei.

master   The name of the final recorded product used to make records.

measure   See *bar of music.*

melisma   A melodic ornamentation; one syllable sung on more than one tone of a song.

melody   A succession of single tones varying in pitch and rhythm and having a recognizable musical shape.

meter   The division of beats into accented and unaccented groupings of two, three, or more.

middle register   The middle part of the complete range of the voice or instrument.

MIDI   Musical instrument digital interface. An established electronic standard used to carry musical information between synthesizers and computers.

mixolydian   The arrangement of tones found in the scale using only the white keys of the piano from G to G.

modal jazz   A jazz style that typically has slow moving harmonies and older modal scales. The chord relationships are generally not typical of the major-minor system.

monophonic   A single melody with neither an accompanying melody nor harmony.

mordent   A rapid movement from one tone to an upper or lower scale tone and back again to the principal tone.

multi-tracking   The ability to record several different sounds on separate parts (tracks) of the recording tape; see *overdub.*

new thing   An alternate name, used primarily by jazz players, for free jazz.

ninth chord   A chord consisting of five different tones, each separated by an interval of a third.

obligato   An accompanying or free melody played by a second instrument, less prominent and secondary to the main melody played by the lead instrument.

ostinato   A clear melodic and/or rhythmic figure that is persistently repeated.

overtone series   Tones that are related to the first (fundamental) tone sounded. A series of higher tones, or upper partials, which, when the first or fundamental is sounded, make up a complex musical tone.

pedal point   A tone sustained below while harmonies change.

pentatonic   A scale consisting of only five tones as represented by the five black keys of the piano.

phrase   A small unit of a melody.

pizzicato   A manner of playing stringed instruments by plucking rather than by bowing.

plagal cadence   A specific chord progression, namely, the IV chord resolving to the I chord; example, amen chords.

polymeters   Simultaneous use of several meters.

polymodal   The simultaneous sounding of several different modes.

polyphonic   The simultaneous sounding of two or more melodies of equal importance.

polytonal   The simultaneous sounding of tones in more than one key.

portamento   The movement from one tone to another higher or lower tone without any break in the sound.

quadrille   A square dance of five figures that was popular in the nineteenth century.

raga   A particular scale in Eastern music.

reggae   A Jamaican style of rhythm and blues.

reverberation   A series of rapid echoes that follow a sound.

rhythm section   The section of an instrumental ensemble that provides the most prominent rhythmic feel of the music, usually consisting of drums, piano, bass, and guitar.

riff   A short pattern of sounds repeated and played by a soloist or group.

rim shots   Produced by striking the edge or rim of the drum and drum head simultaneously.

rondo   A musical form in which one section of a composition recurs intermittently with contrasting sections coming between each repetition, for example, ABACADA.

root tone   The lowest note or tone of a chord when that chord is in its basic, or root, position.

rubato   A fluctuation in the tempo of the music for the purpose of giving music an additional element of expression.

salsa   A combination of jazz and Afro-Cuban rhythms.

sample   The individual number that describes the strength of a sound at any given moment. Samples can be taken of an analog sound up to approximately 40,000 times a second.

sampler   An electronic device tht analyzes a sound and converts that analog voltage into a ditial description that can be altered by a computer. The sampled sound can then be played back using a synthesizer keyboard.

scale   A precise progression of single tones upward or downward in steps. Chromatic scale: a twelve-tone scale with intervals of a half step. Diatonic scale: an eight-tone scale with a repetition of the eighth degree, pertaining to the major and minor scales. Pentatonic scale: consisting of five tones.

Schoenberg's twelve-tone system   A technique of composition in which all twelve half steps in an octave are treated as equal. A method used by Schoenberg in the form of a "tone row," in which all the twelve tones are placed in a particular order forming the basis of a musical composition. No tone is repeated within a row. The tone row becomes a "tonal reservoir" from which the composition is drawn.

sequencer   An electronic device that stores a musical series of notes to be played back later. Sequencers can be used to build up a performance by storing several musical sequences, one after another.

sharped tone   Raises the pitch one half step.

sideman   A player in the musical ensemble as differentiated from the leader.

soulsa   A combination of Latin jazz and "soul" music.

speakeasy   A nightclub in the 1920s.

spiritual   A name given to a type of religious folk song of the American Negro, usually of a solo-and-refrain design.

standard tunes   Familiar, well-established popular or jazz tunes. Copyright can be renewed for a certain number of years after the death of the composer.

stock arrangement   A published commercial arrangement, usually simplified and standardized.

Storyville   Red-light district in New Orleans which figured in the origin of jazz.

symmetrical   Exhibiting a balance of parts.

syncopation   To accent a normally weak beat or weak part of a beat.

tack piano   A piano with thumbtacks on the felts of the piano hammers to make it sound older and more authentic for playing ragtime and similar music.

tag   A short addition to the end of a musical composition.

tailgate trombone   A name deriving from the practice of early trombone players sitting on the tailgate of a wagon so that their slides could operate freely out the rear. The phrase became associated with the trombone part in a dixieland ensemble.

tango   A dance of Spanish-American origin commonly in 4/4 meter.

tape loop   A loop of magnetic recording tape which is used to repeat a sound. The speed of the tape determines how fast the repeats occur.

tempo   Refers to the speed of the underlying beat. The speed is determined by the number of beats counted over the span of sixty seconds.

theme and variation   A musical form in which the theme is introduced and successive repetitions of the theme, changed or altered in some manner, follow.

thirteenth chord   A chord consisting of seven different tones each separated by an interval of a third.

time signature   Sign at the beginning of a composition indicating the grouping of beats for each measure. The meter signature ¾ means that there are three beats in a measure and that a quarter note gets one beat.

Tin Pan Alley   Refers to the industry centered in New York that published popular music.

tonal clash   Tones played simultaneously that produce a discordant or clashing effect.

tonal sonorities   The overall effect of the juxtaposition of tonal sounds.

trading fours   Two solo instrumentalists alternating in playing four measures each.

twelve-bar strain   A composition or a part of a composition consisting of twelve meaures.

twelve tone system   A compositional system designed to avoid tonal centers thereby creating a balanced atonal music.

unison   Two or more instruments or voices sounding on the same pitches (tones) or an octave apart.

up-tempo   Fast tempo.

vamp   A transitional chord or rhythmic progression of indefinite duration used as a filler until the soloist is ready to start or continue on.

verse   The introductory section of a popular song as distinguished from the chorus. The latter consists commonly of thirty-two bars, while the verse may have an irregular number of bars and may be sung or played in a free tempo.

vertical thinking   Block chords that accompany a melodic part; opposite of horizontal thinking.

vibrato   Refers to the artificial wavering of a tone; rapidly recurring fluctuations of pitch. Most jazz uses vibrato for warmth and interpretation in imitation of the human voice.

vocoder   An electronic musical device that allows the player to choose the pitch of any syllable that he sings, and can blend two sounds at will.

walking bass   The bass part that was originally introduced in boogie-woogie in ostinato form. It concisely spells out the notes in the chords being used and is usually played in eighth notes.

well-tempered scale   Refers to the tuning system found on a keyboard.

Bibliography

Albertson, Chris. *Bessie.* New York: Stein & Day Publishers, 1972.

Allan, William Francis; Ware, Charles Pickard; and Garrison, Lucy McKim. *Slave Songs of the United States.* New York: Peter Smith, 1867.

Allen, Walter C. *Hendersonia: The Music of Fletcher Henderson and His Musicians, Jazz Monograph no. 4.* Highland Park, N.J.: Walter C. Allen, 1973.

Apel, Willi. *Harvard Dictionary of Music.* Cambridge, Mass.: Harvard University Press, 1955.

Armstrong, Louis. *Swing That Music.* New York: Longmans, Green & Co., 1936.

———. *Louis Armstrong: A Self Portrait.* New York: Eakins Press, 1971.

Baird, David. *From Score to Tape.* Boston: Berklee Press Pub., 1973.

Balliett, Whitney. *Dinosaurs in the Morning.* Philadelphia: J. B. Lippincott Co., 1962.

———. *The Sound of Surprise.* New York: E. P. Dutton & Co., 1959.

———. *American Musicians.* New York: Oxford University Press, 1986.

Bechet, Sidney. *Treat It Gentle: An Autobiography.* New York: Hill & Wang, 1960.

Berendt, Joachim. *The New Jazz Book.* Translated by Dan Morgenstern. New York: Hill & Wang, 1962.

———. *Jazz Book: From New Orleans to Rock and Free Jazz.* New York: Lawrence Hill & Co., 1974.

Bernstein, Leonard. *The Joy of Music.* New York: Simon & Schuster, 1959.

Berton, Ralph. *Remembering Bix: A Memoir of the Jazz Age.* New York: Harper & Row, 1974.

Blanco, Charles. *Sonny Rollins, The Journey of a Jazzman.* Boston: G. K. Hall, 1983.

Blesh, Rudi. *Classic Piano Rags.* New York: Dover Publications, 1973.

Blesh, Rudi, and Janis, Harriet. *They All Played Ragtime.* New York: Grove Press, 1959.

Bloom, Eric, ed. *Grove's Dictionary of Music and Musicians.* Nine vols. New York: St. Martin's Press, 1959.

Brask, Ole, and Morgenstern, Dan. *Jazz People.* New York: Harry N. Abrams, Inc., 1976.

Budds, Michael J. *Jazz in the Sixties.* Iowa City, Iowa: University of Iowa Press, 1978.

Buerkle, Jack V. and Barker, Danny. *Bourbon Street Black.* London: Oxford University Press, 1973.

Buszin, Walter E., ed. *Anniversary Collection of Bach Chorales.* Chicago: Hall McCreary, 1935.

Charters, Samuel B. *Jazz: New Orleans (1885–1963).* New York: Oak Publishers, 1964.

Charters, Samuel B., and Kunstadt, Leonard. *Jazz: A History of The New York Scene.* New York: Doubleday & Co., 1962.

Chilton, John. *Billie's Blues.* New York: Stein & Day Publishers, 1975.

———. *Who's Who in Jazz.* Philadelphia: Chilton, 1972.

Cole, Bill. *Miles Davis.* New York: William Morris and Co., 1976.

Collier, James Lincoln. *The Making of Jazz.* New York: Dell Publishing Co., Inc., 1978.

Coryell, Julie, and Friedman, Laura. *Jazz-Rock Fusion.* New York: Delta Books, 1979.

Dance, Stanley. *The World of Duke Ellington.* New York: Charles Scribner's Sons, 1970.

————. *The World of Swing.* New York: Charles Scribner's Sons, 1975.

Dankworth, Avril. *Jazz: An Introduction to Its Musical Basis.* London: Oxford University Press, 1968.

Davis, Nathan. *Writings in Jazz.* Dubuque, Iowa: Gorsuch Scarisbrick Publishers, 1978.

Dexter, Dave. *The Jazz Story.* Englewood Cliffs, N.J.: Prentice-Hall, 1964.

Dineen, Janice D. *The Performing Women,* 26910 Grand View Ave., Hayward, Calif. 94542.

Drake, Russell; Herder, Ronald; and Modugno, Anne D. *How to Make Electronic Music.* Pleasantville, New York: EAV Inc., 1975.

Ellington, Duke. *Music Is My Mistress.* New York: Doubleday & Co., 1973.

Ellington, Mercer, and Dance, Stanley. *Duke Ellington: An Intimate Memoir.* New York: Houghton Mifflin, 1975.

Feather, Leonard. *Inside Jazz.* New York: J. J. Robbins & Sons, 1949.

————. *The Book of Jazz.* New York: World Publishing Co., Meridian Books, 1959.

————. *The New Edition of the Encyclopedia of Jazz.* New York: Horizon Press, 1960.

————. *The Encyclopedia of Jazz in the Sixties.* New York: Horizon Press, 1966.

————. *From Satchmo to Miles.* New York: Stein & Day Publishers, 1974.

————. *The Encyclopedia of Jazz in the Seventies.* New York: Horizon Press, 1976.

————. *Pleasures of Jazz.* New York: Horizon Press, 1976.

Finkelstein, Sidney. *Jazz: A People's Music.* New York: Da Capo Press, 1975.

Flower, John. *Moonlight Serenade.* New Rochelle, N.Y.: Arlington House, 1972.

Francis, André. *Jazz.* Translated and revised by Martin Williams. New York: Grove Press, 1960.

Friend, David; Perlman, Alan R.; and Piggott, Thomas G. *Learning Music with Synthesizers.* Winona, Minn.: Hal Leonard Pub. Corp., 1974.

Gammond, Peter, ed. *Duke Ellington: His Life and Music.* New York: Roy Publishers, 1958.

————. *Scott Joplin and the Ragtime Era.* New York: St. Martin's Press, 1975.

George, Don. *Sweet Man: The Real Duke Ellington.* New York: G. P. Putnam's Sons, 1981.

Gillespie, Dizzy, and Fraser, Al. *To Be, or Not . . . to Bop.* Garden City, New York: Doubleday & Co., 1979.

Gitler, Ira. *Jazz Masters of the Forties.* New York: Macmillan Co., 1966.

Gleason, Ralph. *Celebrating the Duke.* New York: Dell Publishers, 1975.

Goffin, Robert. *Jazz: From the Congo to the Metropolitan.* New York: Da Capo Press, 1975.

Gold, Robert S. *A Jazz Lexicon.* New York: Knopf, 1964.

Goldberg, Joe. *Jazz Masters of the Fifties.* New York: Macmillan Co., 1965.

Gridley, Mark C. *Jazz Styles.* Englewood Cliffs, N.J.: Prentice-Hall, 1978.

Hadlock, Richard. *Jazz Masters of the Twenties.* New York: Macmillan Co., 1965.

Harris, Rex. *Jazz.* Baltimore, Md.: Penguin Books, 1956.

Harrison, Max. *Charlie Parker.* New York: A. S. Barnes & Co., 1960.

Hentoff, Nat. *Boston Boy.* New York: Alfred A. Knopf, 1986.

————. *Jazz Life.* New York: Da Capo Press, 1975.

————. *Jazz Is.* New York: Random House, 1976.

Hentoff, Nat, and McCarthy, Albert. *Jazz: New Perspectives on the History of Jazz.* New York: Da Capo Press, 1975.

————, eds. *Jazz.* New York: Holt, Rinehart & Winston, Inc., 1959.

Hodeir, André. *Jazz: Its Evolution and Essence.* Translated by David Noakes. New York: Grove Press, 1956.

————. *Toward Jazz.* New York: Grove Press, 1962.

Holiday, Billie, and Dufty, William. *The Lady Sings the Blues.* New York: Doubleday & Co., 1965.

James, Michael. *Dizzy Gillespie.* New York: A. S. Barnes & Co., 1959.

Jewell, Derek. *Duke: A Portrait of Duke Ellington.* New York: W. W. Norton & Co., 1977.

Jones, LeRoi. *Black Music.* New York: William Morrow & Co., 1965.

————. *Blues People.* New York: William Morrow & Co., 1963.

Jones, Max. *Salute to Satchmo.* London: Longacre Press, 1970.

Jones, Max, and Chilton, John. *Louis: The Louis Armstrong Story.* New York: Little, Brown & Co., 1971.

Jost, Ekkehard. *Free Jazz.* Wien, Austria: Universal Edition, 1975.

Kaufman, Frederick and Guckin, John P. *The African Roots of Jazz.* Sherman Oaks, California: Alfred Publishing Co., 1979.

Keepnews, Orrin, and Grauer, Bill, Jr. *A Pictorial History of Jazz.* New York: Crown Publishers, 1955.

Keil, Charles. *Urban Blues.* Chicago: University of Chicago Press, 1966.

Kennington, Donald, and Reed, Denny L. *The Literature of Jazz,* Second Edition. Chicago: American Library Association, 1980.

Kinkle, Roger D. *The Complete Encyclopedia of Popular Music and Jazz.* New Rochelle, N.Y.: Arlington House, 1974.

Lee, William F. *People in Jazz: Jazz Keyboard Improvisors of the 19th and 20th Centuries.* Hialeah, Florida: Columbia Pictures Publications, 1984.

Leonard, Neil. *Jazz and the White Americans.* Chicago: University of Chicago Press, 1962.

Lomax, Alan. *Mr. Jelly Roll.* New York: Grosset & Dunlap, Universal Library, 1950.

McCarthy, Albert. *Louis Armstrong.* New York: A. S. Barnes & Co., 1959.

————. *Big Band Jazz.* New York: G. P. Putnam's Sons, 1974.

Marquis, Donald. *In Search of Buddy Bolden: First Man of Jazz.* Baton Rouge, La.: Louisiana State University Press, 1979.

Martin, John H., and Fritz, William F. *Listening to Jazz.* Fresno, Calif.: University of California Press, 1969.

Meeker, David. *Jazz in the Movies: A Guide to Jazz Musicians, 1917–1977.* New Rochelle, N.Y.: Arlington House, 1978.

Megill, Donald D. and Demory, Richard S. *Introduction to Jazz History.* Englewood Cliffs, N.J.: Prentice-Hall. 1984.

Mehegan, John. *Jazz Improvisation.* New York: Watson-Guptill Publications, 1959.

Milhaud, Darius. *Notes Without Music.* New York: Alfred A. Knopf, 1953.

Miller, Hugh Milton. *History of Music.* New York: Barnes & Noble Books, 1957.

Muro, Don. *An Introduction to Electronic Music Synthesizers.* Melville, New York: Belwin-Mills Publishing Corp., 1975.

Nanry, Charles. *The Jazz Text.* New York: D. Van Nostrand, 1979.

Oliver, Paul. *Bessie Smith.* New York: A. S. Barnes & Co., 1961.

————. *The Meaning of the Blues.* New York: Macmillan Co., Collier Books, 1960.

————. *The Savannah Syncopators.* New York: Stein & Day Publishers, 1970.

Ostransky, Leroy. *The Anatomy of Jazz.* Seattle: University of Washington Press, 1960.

————. *Jazz City.* Englewood Cliffs, N.J.: Prentice-Hall, 1975.

————. *Understanding Jazz.* Englewood Cliffs, N.J.: Prentice-Hall, 1977.

Panassie, Hughes. *Louis Armstrong.* New York: Charles Scribner's Sons, 1971.

————. *The Real Jazz.* Translated by Anne Sorrelle Williams. New York: A. S. Barnes & Co., 1960.

Pleasants, Henry. *Serious Music and All that Jazz.* New York: Simon & Schuster, 1969.

————. *The Great American Popular Singers.* New York: Oxford University Press, 1959.

Reisner, Robert G. *The Jazz Titans.* New York: Doubleday & Co., 1960.

————. *Bird: The Legend of Charlie Parker.* New York: Citadel Press, 1962.

Roach, Hildred. *Black American Music: Past and Present.* Boston: Crescendo Publishing Co., 1973.

Roberts, John Storm. *Black Music of Two Worlds.* New York: William Morrow and Co., 1974.

Russell, Ross. *Jazz Styles in Kansas City and the Southwest.* Berkeley: University of California Press, 1971.

————. *Bird Lives: The High Life and Hard Times of Charlie (Yardbird) Parker.* New York: Charterhouse Books, 1973.

Russell, Tony. *Blacks, Whites and the Blues.* New York: Stein & Day Publishers, 1970.

Sales, Grover. *Jazz, America's Classical Music.* Englewood Cliffs, N.J.: Prentice-Hall.

Sanders, Ruby W. *Jazz Ambassador Louis Armstrong.* Chicago: Childrens Press, 1973.

Schafer, William J., et al. *The Art of Ragtime.* Baton Rouge, La.: Louisiana State University Press, 1973.

Schuller, Gunther. *Early Jazz: Its Roots and Musical Development.* London: Oxford University Press, 1968.

Scott, Allen. *Jazz Educated, Man.* Silver Springs, Md.: Institute of Modern Languages, 1973.

Shapiro, Nat, and Hentoff, Nat., eds. *The Jazz Makers.* New York: Grove Press, 1957.

Simpkins, C. O. *Coltrane: A Biography.* New York: Herndon House, 1975.

Simon, George T. *The Big Bands.* New York: Macmillan Co., 1967.

———. *Simon Says.* New Rochelle, N.Y.: Arlington House, 1971.

———. *Glenn Miller.* New York: Thomas Y. Crowell Co., 1974.

Skowronski, Jo Ann. *Women in America: A Bibliography,* Metucken, N.J., and London: Scarecrow Press, 1978.

Southern, Eileen. *Music of Black Americans.* New York: W. W. Norton & Co., 1971.

Standifer, James A., and Reeder, Barbara. *African and Afro-American Materials for Music Educators.* Washington, D.C.: Music Educators National Conference, 1972.

Stearns, Marshall. *The Story of Jazz.* London: Oxford University Press, 1958.

Stewart, Rex. *Jazz Masters of the '30s.* New York: Macmillan Co., 1972.

Stewart-Baxter, Derrick. *Ma Rainey.* New York: Stein & Day Publishers, 1970.

Strange, Allen. *Electronic Music: Systems, Techniques, and Controls.* Dubuque, Iowa: Wm. C. Brown Company Publishers, 1972.

Sudhalter, Richard M., and Evans, Philip R. *Bix: Man and Legend.* New York: Harper & Row, 1974.

Talmadge, William. *Afro-American Music.* Washington, D.C.: Music Educators National Conference, 1957.

Thomas, J. C. *Chasin' the Trane.* New York: Doubleday & Co., 1975.

Tirro, Frank. *Jazz: A History.* New York: W. W. Norton & Co., 1977.

Ulanov, Barry. *Duke Ellington.* New York: Farrar, Strauss & Young, 1946.

———. *Handbook of Jazz.* New York: Viking Press, 1959.

Ulrich, Homer. *Music: A Design for Listening.* 2d ed. New York: Harcourt, Brace, & World, 1962.

Walker, Leo. *The Wonderful Era of the Great Dance Bands.* New York: Doubleday & Co., 1972.

Williams, Martin T. *Jazz Masters of New Orleans.* New York: Macmillan Co., 1965.

———. *Jazz Masters in Transition (1957–69).* New York: Macmillan Co., 1970.

———. *The Jazz Tradition.* London: Oxford University Press, 1969.

———. *King Oliver.* New York: A. S. Barnes & Co., 1960.

Williams, Martin T., ed. *The Art of Jazz.* London: Oxford University Press, 1959.

Wilson, John S. *The Collector's Jazz: Modern.* Philadelphia: J. B. Lippincott Co., 1959.

———. *The Collector's Jazz: Tradition and Swing.* Philadelphia: J. B. Lippincott Co., 1958.

Index